THE SCOTTISH MOUNTAINEERING CLUB JOURNAL

| Vol. XXXVII | 1999 | No. 190 |

D'APRÈS VIRGINIA WOOLF

By Nigel Suess

1. Views of mountains

MRS RAMSAY smiled as, through the window, she saw the blue hills rising above the woods. She smiled at the memory of her visit more than 25 years earlier, before the eight children. On their first holiday together her new husband had led her high into those blue hills. He had hired a dog-cart and with young Mackenzie they had taken the rough road down the glen almost to the beach. She recalled it had been a calm, sun-drenched day at the start of the long summer vacation. In those days she wore fuller, heavier skirts and the walk over the moor had almost drained her strength. Once on the ridge a breeze had given her some respite, and at the summit Mackenzie had pointed out, yet higher, a towering pinnacle, and told her husband that it was unclimbed and perhaps would never be topped.

Mr Ramsay moved before her in front of the window. She knew well that he would not try to climb it now with Andrew and Jasper. She knew also that his ambition had been curtailed in other ways. His age made him physically weaker, but academically he had been overtaken by a new century's ideas. She did not mind for herself that she would not go up to those rocks again, but she knew that it had been their magnetic attraction that had made her husband bring the family to this house nearly every year.

She saw one of their guests, Lily, sitting on the lawn with her canvas set up to give her a perspective of sea, sky, earth, wood and rock. Lily judged that the attention to detail in the rockier parts would be an error, despite the late afternoon cross-lighting. Oh, yes the rocks are fine, but not what I want to emphasise. No, thought Lily, to give detail destroys the harmony of colour. The blues of sky, sea and hill and the greens of lawn, wood and moor could, she had confidence, be blended; but where to put the first brush-stroke? Such a symphony required no discordant note.

George Sawicki on the East Ridge of the Inaccessible Pinnacle, Sgurr Dearg. Photo: Noel Williams.

James, the Ramsay's youngest child, had intruded on her foreground. He wanted to be taken with Andrew and Jasper, and maybe Prue, up, up, up to the clouds. Why did father not want to take him to see this famous Inaccessible Pinnacle? Each breakfast he was told it would be too far, too windy, too wet, too rough. Father, he knew, had made the climb when younger, and mother too. Now the family was there again. He decided to talk to Andrew.

Andrew wanted to go but wanted to succeed. He knew that if he was to triumph now, in his last family excursion before going up to university, all omens would have to be favourable. A seven-year-old brother would ensure the expedition's failure. The writings of Whymper and even Sir Leslie Stephen's *The Playground of Europe* were well conned, and had encouraged Andrew in planning such a venture. Recently, father had given him Tyndall's historic notes, just issued in a popular edition, and a year earlier the late O. G. Jones's Lakeland exploits had been the stimulus to push beyond mere walking ascents. Now Andrew too was to embark on an exploration into the farthest margins of mountaineering. Father had contacted an academic of the same university, a chemist, who also visited the island regularly. The coincidence was greater in that he usually employed Mackenzie, his father's guide of many years earlier. Andrew's researches taught him that these were auspicious signs. The Classics showed that one must pay attention to entrails and certain prescribed signals from the Gods.

Andrew's attention was reclaimed by the hills; the early showers of the day had passed, the clouds had broken and the wind had veered into a cooler direction. He awaited the moment of decision at dinner. Mother intended it to be a grander dinner than any yet on this visit and Andrew keenly awaited one particular guest whom, he believed, would resolve the decision of the objective of the expedition.

Jasper moved out of the house and saw his younger brother eyeing the hills, anxiously, he thought. He too had been included in the sketched outlines of the expedition and had confidence in his physical capabilities. The Army ensured that its subalterns were fitter than students. He had climbed many hills, from the Misty Isle to the Cape. Jasper's hills were for strengthening the body or for giving a pony a good outing. The salvation of one's nervous energies, aye, and limbs, for warfare demanded the exclusion of military campaigns against tottering pinnacles. He told Andrew that he would have to go alone, alone of the family. The chemist and Mackenzie would suffice for his companions.

Jasper cast his eyes over the other guests who made up this assembly of family and friends, and asked himself again whether, perhaps, he should join the expedition. The choices apart were to take leisure in the garden with some novel, to discuss campaigns past with the poet of Empire, or to hire a horse from the town for a canter along the beach. Leave would be over in a few days and a long journey to Southampton would be followed by confinement on a vessel heading to West Africa. Perhaps a final fling at the hill would merit his time, but not gymnastics on pinnacles, inaccessible or otherwise. He broached the question with the poet of Empire. Jasper had heard that Carmichael had been favoured by the ruling class since his youthful epic saga on the campaigns after the Mutiny. He had lived in North India and had known early explorers of the Himalaya. Jasper also saw in him the signs of other Eastern acquisitions, and wondered if the hill station enthusers knew that they took their opium vicariously with his verse.

'Dear boy,' he pronounced, 'to advance beyond the plain yields a more pleasant view of our society.' Jasper was reminded by this epigram of the zoologist who, having devoted half his lifetime to the study of rats, expressed the view that the more he studied rats the less he cared for his own species.

Mrs Ramsay's attention was less loftily occupied. The boeuf en daube had been under near constant culinary attention for two days, in anticipation of the dinner which would be the pinnacle of the summer break. She had the usual help from cook, but if the meat emerged too sinewy or flavourless, the assembled academics, artists and even children would accuse the guide and not the guidebook. Escoffier proposed smaller portions of meat and of time, but a visit to Provence had suggested that a multiple of both quantities gave more flavour. The commitment had been made and she would stand by the consequences. Wine had been ordered from the hotel's cellars, table linen had been hired in the town, local crofters had been generously relieved of hard-won seasonal produce. Fruit, alas, could not be procured save for somewhat well-weathered raspberries. So the menu was to be soupe aux moules, sole sur chou-marin, boeuf en daube and raspberry, oatmeal, cream and whisky blended to a dessert defying French classification. For the younger children, she knew, some modifications were desirable.

The visitors for dinner distracted her. The chemistry professor was unmarried and would be called upon to hand Lily in to dinner. Carmichael could not be paired with any decent soul and so, as there was an imbalance, her eldest son would take care of him. Paul and Minta were now well paired. That left only her husband and herself of the adults and six of the seven children, 14 in all, far too many for the table. So, some of the children would need to sit...

Some hours passed and the boeuf en daube had been pronounced a credit to Mrs Ramsay's leadership of the culinary cohorts. Andrew saw an opportunity to distract the chemist, he thought not reluctantly, from the amiable but strictly horizontally inclined Lily. He asked directly if the Cuillin were on the agenda for the next day.

The long-limbed and quietly-spoken man did not reply immediately. He turned to look out of the window towards the West. Andrew's less-experienced eyes followed and noticed that, by now, the sky had cleared of all the cloud that had for nearly two weeks imposed a dull regime on the visiting mountaineers. He replied that he had spoken with Mackenzie that afternoon and they planned a specific objective which he had observed seven years earlier and had recorded on photographic plates.

Andrew's ignorance at first caused him to expect some new unclimbed summit, possibly the very last in Britain to stand untrodden by man. The scientist disabused him, recording that all of Scotland's summits had now been ascended, indeed one man alone had stood on every top. As for England, Wales and Ireland, the summits had long been fully explored. The challenge for the new generation lay in finding the most interesting geological features, some of which would, like the Inaccessible Pinnacle, require great skills in mountaineering to explore.

The next day he and Mackenzie would make an early start and take rope up into the Coire with a great boss of rock protruding like a wart on a toad as their planned destination. Other names have been given to such features but the scientist considered them somewhat coarse. If the two young gentlemen wished to walk up, their company would be most welcome. They could, if they chose, sit below to confirm that no engineering work on the rock would be undertaken. Andrew recalled that O. G. Jones had commented on such measures which the chemist had employed on one notorious occasion. Regrettably, it would not be possible on this occasion for Mackenzie to assist them on an ascent of the infamous pinnacle.

Later, as he lay in bed, Andrew counted himself fortunate to be a camp follower in this new venture of exploration, rather than to be the one-hundredth or whatever number to be dragged by rope (and pulley, so went the rumour) up the Pinnacle. Like all mountaineering objectives, it would remain for many years more.

2. Time passed

The house stood empty during four of the next 12 summers. Rain fell on the mountains, sun dried the rock, ice lingered in crevices. A few men who had been to the summit of the Inaccessible Pinnacle did not return again to the island, but lay instead in distant fields. Others who wished to make the ascent had been destroyed by shell, torpedo, mine or gas. Andrew was one, fallen in the Tyrol on an assignment with the Italian forces. Jasper was another, succumbing to foul disease in Mesopotamia.

Not only had the youth of a promising summer passed, but Mrs Ramsay was victim of a short and sudden illness. Carmichael's body could take no more abuse.

3. To the Inaccessible Pinnacle

James, now at university, entered the dimly-remembered holiday home of his childhood. Father, now in his 70s, had decided that this would be the last year that he would return to the island, and James did not care to plan his future beyond a year. He had seen the plans of his brothers, indeed of all of his family, shattered. Europe was at peace but not peaceful. So, recalling Andrew's ambitions, he knew that this might be his only chance to visit and perhaps to climb this Inaccessible Pinnacle. The family had a motor-car with driver, and next day were travelling to visit the hotel to renew a friendship. The vehicle followed the sinuous route along the fringes of sea-lochs, over heather moorland and through crofting townships depopulated by the Great War and the claims of Glasgow. James saw, always on his left-hand, the hills, both red and black. At last the road descended slightly to the head of a sea-loch notable, not for itself, but for the inn by the roadside and for the view of the executioner's axe blade poised over all onlookers beguiled by these mountains.

The chemist was in the hotel's lounge apparently intent on some research paper which had reached him from a distant laboratory. He welcomed his former colleague from the university and ordered tea to be brought. James felt that his appearance had not greatly changed in over 12 years. He must now be past his sixtieth year. Father had told James that the chemist had made advances in the sciences which would add greatly to the well-being of mankind in the peace which now prevailed. James had acquired not only Andrew's books on mountains and mountaineers, but also a strong interest in their contents. He judged that the chemist would be remembered among people such as himself for exploits on this island and on more distant ranges.

The chemist recalled their last meeting. He remembered that the strength imparted by Mrs Ramsay's boeuf en daube had helped him raise his earthly frame to a higher pitch, enabling the very first ascent of the Cioch. The afternoon conversation lingered on the relative merits of this route, standing in an ocean of pure rock, and the Pinnacle surrounded by unbounded airiness. Science and its methods are prosaic, but James saw in this man a concern for the symbolism of his mountain ascents. He learned that the relationship between climber and mountain should be experienced in many dimensions. The scientist had wanted to explore, to map, to photograph his subject. He also wished to experience through the relationship some mystical union with the rock. The oromaniacal blended with the analytical. James learned more. The mountains could deepen one's relationship with a companion. To some it appeared that the mountains were yet another arena for competitive challenge, to prove oneself superior to others through the ascent of yet steeper, holdless ground. The chemist thought that such conduct diminished the climber rather than the mountain.

Now that his age inhibited him from attempting those courses that had been within his powers before the Great War, he drew no less pleasure from the easier routes. His advice to the acolyte was to seek the path which brings one closer to union with the mountain.

Father asked after the health of the guide of his nuptial excursion. Forty years had not ended Mackenzie's preparedness to help others share his affection for these places, and it came about that the lead would be passed to James.

In the morning, Mackenzie was waiting at the junction where the road to the glen began. The car was to take them to the farm where the ascent would start. Unlike 1879, unlike 1906, there were others with similar ideas. James saw a car from Keswick parked there, and learned of other visitors staying at the cottage. He regretted that one could no longer enjoy these hills in isolation. Soon one might even encounter other rock-climbers on the same course. As they climbed, Mackenzie in heavy tweed commented on the lighter cloths which visitors from London and Manchester now preferred. He also noted the changing patterns of nailing boots.

His conversation was not continuous. He had learned to allow his clients to take this path steadily, to allow them time to learn the features of the Coire and also beyond the hills, if conditions allowed, the delicate line of the outer isles. The day was well advanced when James rested at the cairn below the Pinnacle. He could take only water on such occasions, though it was not through fear that his appetite had disappeared. He recalled the fast before Communion. As James moved the few yards to the rock he thought of it as a milestone in his father's marriage and, later, a beckoning lighthouse to dear brother Andrew. Now James was to confirm his self-belief and, perhaps, alter his life's course.

That day, the rock was welcoming to the hand that caressed it, and the guide was loving in his care.

ELEGY

The curve of the adze a smooth
crescent of chrome rainbow.
Its tonal edge, filed to sharpness
to cut another step, to resurrection
beyond the holds in whiteness.
A dimpled expanse rises in invitation.

Leave only rope trails on the route,
point, pick and spike marks,
a soft blueness in the rime.
The effort over, the rope moves slowly,
now ripples beyond the climb
drawn away to an unknown country.

Donald Orr.

SANDBAGGED BY A GHOST

By Mike Jacob

'Now up on Gimmer Crag as large as life,
There is a THING that climbs at dead of night,
The Spirit of a climber dead and gone,
Enough to give a bloke an awful fright.'

So goes a song, recited by a guitar-playing friend, climber and misfit, known to some as Grot, who died somewhere in the Cuillin a few years ago. Disillusioned with the conventional education system, he found a niche at the Loch Eil Centre, trying to impart what he called the three Cs – care, consideration and compassion.

CHORUS
'He leaves a bloodstain on every finger-hold,
As he climbs upon the cliff,
With 'is head tucked underneath 'is arm,
And his corpse is stiff.'

*   *   *   *   *

Well we, David and I, had seen no sign of the ghost as we climbed some of Gimmer's classics on a Philosopher's Stone of a day in early October. There was a balance between the warmth of the sun and a slightly cold east wind, and balance between the browns of dead bracken and the hues of green that define Lakeland in autumn. Balance was, therefore, our theme this day.

The song goes on, in humorously macabre vein, as the phantom
'a climber of the Old School it is clear.'
wreaks havoc, a shadowy form following climbers up the routes, unfastening their belays. Eventually, the Langdale cognoscenti have had enough of this terrorism and agree to exorcise the ghost. They shout and cheer as the Spirit fades away in the mist. The end, apparently, of the ghost but I think – I now know – that it merely moved on in the general direction of a more appropriate place . . . Pavey Ark.

Down in the Old Dungeon Ghyll we stayed off spirits and drank 'Black Sheep' and 'Cumberland Ale', good names and good beer. Round in Wasdale you can even get a pint of 'Scafell Pike'. The temptation was to stay and try them all, especially for David when the bar suddenly filled with nubile 20-year-old females. However, we had a date with a Cumberland Sausage and left.

By coincidence, back at the hut, the topic of songs cropped up again. I agreed to swop the words of Grot's ballad with those of a shanty that had filled the Tobermory night over a year before. As I had lain on my bunk after the last-night ceilidh of the 1997 Yacht Meet I had heard Robin Campbell's great rendition above deck. Head back, baying like a wolf to the moon, he must have caught sight of the massive wooden spars of the boat,

'Christ, Skipper, how many men does it take to hoist those?' he inquired.

'Three men,' came the reply, and a pause, 'but half-a-dozen of you SMC lot.'

* * * * *

The next day, October 4, 1998 (I give the date for good reason) wasn't so good. It had rained during the night and was no longer warm. The lower, roadside Langdale crags would have been a good choice but we were drawn to Pavey Ark. A certain lethargy or sense of anti-climax crept in as we approached the crag, totally different in appearance and atmosphere from Gimmer. Sure, you feed upon each other's lack of enthusiasm until you end up doing nothing, I recognised it from past experience. We dithered and David ate his lunch at 11 o'clock. I felt guilty, he had wanted to climb Kipling Groove the previous day but we hadn't got round to Gimmer's N.W. face. I had only met him a few weeks before, had never climbed with him before this trip and we didn't have the rapport of long friendship. It was grey and damp and the harder climbs looked unfriendly. We dithered. A voice said: 'What about Rake-End Chimney. It's only a Diff. Ideal for a day like this and we can climb it in walking boots and carry our sacks up. Always come back down and do something harder if we feel like it, or walk over the Pikes?'

Startled, I looked behind me – who had said that? But David, addressing me, said: 'Well, okay. Not my kind of climb. It's green. You can lead it.'

What did the guidebook have to say? – 'Two stars – an excellent climb – easy steps – walk up – finish easily.' Nae bother.

"Hey, look at this. First climbed by C. W. Barton – whoever he was – on October 1, 1898.'

One of Lakeland's first rock climbs and we were proposing to climb it 100 years' later, almost to the day.

1898? A time of Victorian slums and poverty, the rise of the trades union movement as the workers fought against exploitation; transport by horse and cart, and schooners plying the Solway. Only 22 years after Sitting Bull's victory at the Little Bighorn and 16 years before the outbreak of the First World War.

It seemed incomprehensible that in this era, from the 1880s until the early 1900s, was the origin of my present activity. Yet, in 1897, O. G. Jones climbed Kern Knotts Crack, still graded MVS. Techniques may have been primitive, with heavy, unreliable hemp rope and clumsy footwear but these pioneers were probably fitter and stronger than many of our pampered generation. Jones, for example, trained with weights and was a gymnast with abnormal finger-power. According to Bill Birkett, he once traversed round a railway engine using only the heads of the boiler rivets and could do one-arm pull-ups with someone held under the other arm.

In 1896, Jones led the two Abraham brothers up a new route on Scafell Pinnacle, which was the scene of a multiple fatality in 1903 when a second ascent was attempted.

The route, not surprisingly, developed a 'chop' reputation, and wasn't repeated until 1912 by George Sansom and Siegfried Herford, hotfoot from the Cuillin. They climbed in stockinged feet, realising that boots were too clumsy. This history is what gives the Lakeland crags their special appeal, despite the influx of the masses. Raeburn climbed here but that's another story.

*   *   *   *   *

No-one else climbing on Pavey Ark as we scrambled up grass and loose shale to the foot of the chimney. Many climbs are called, correctly or incorrectly, chimneys. This was a chimney. I left rockboots in my sack, along with lunch, pullover, gloves and suchlike. This turned out to be a terrible mistake, that is, ever contemplating wearing a sack in the first place, especially a modern one with all its sticky-out bits and flapping straps. The first few moves, clutching lumps of turf and mud, took me into the confines of the chimney. Shoulder-width – and steep. And certainly green and confined and brutal and it's all very well, if you've been there and done it, to say that there's Good Protection, but not where you need it and your most useful nuts are in your sack.

The left wall was smooth and slightly overhanging as I rubbed shoulders with it. At the back of the chimney were some loose-looking flakes. The right wall had one or two sloping holds, damp and polished, polished grey. You could bridge it if you were a 3ft. dwarf or prepared to be farther out, with no protection and vertically above your second. In the end, I 'rucksacked-and-footed' it, unable to look above me because the lid of the sack forced my head forward as effectively as a wrestler's arm-lock.

The trap sprang shut as I pulled up and over a chockstone that now formed the hearth of the chimney below two smooth walls that converged above me. I was wedged, shoulder to shoulder, between those unshifting tons, unable to bend forwards, unable to turn round because of my snail-like hump, barely able to move my head. If I stepped backwards I would fall off the top of the chockstone and out of the chimney. Ironically, I was perfectly secure, like a crag-fast sheep – but stuck like a pig.

I've no idea how long I remained in this ridiculous position. I heard a voice from below my heels, presumably someone on Jack's Rake.

'What the hell's that?'

'Rake-End Chimney,' replied David. 'It's a Diff.'

The latter comment was said with the hint of a sneer, and I was gratified to hear: 'That's no Diff. – looks like a VS to me.'

In front of me was the back of the chimney with a flared crack in it but out of reach. No matter which way I twisted and shoved, the sack just seemed to catch or jam on every slight bulge of greasy rock. There seemed little alternative to my idea of 'lung jams' but I wasn't prepared to try this high-risk manoeuvre without some protection. One hand managed to reach a karabiner that dangled from my harness, which I couldn't even see, and there – you beauty – was a Chouinard stopper No.7 on a long rope sling. Perfect. As I couldn't reach the crack I had to flick the nut into position.

Remarkably, this was accomplished at the second attempt but, just as I prepared to clip in, it seemed that an invisible hand pulled the karabiner from my grasp and it swung a tantalising few inches from my outstretched fingers. A gust of wind, no more than a breath, chuckled down the chimney. The ghost was extracting vengeance for its banishment from Gimmer, which is a friendly sort of a place. It is a crag of near-perfect design and position, quick-drying, clean and rough. Like Rannoch Wall or Sron na Ciche, it encourages precise movement, the world shut out while you solve the jigsaw and make the correct moves and time stands still. It is a place for dancing and I wished myself back there – the ghost, like all ghosts, was in my mind.

I sensed – oh! no! – dampness at arse level and an exploratory hand came back with sticky brown goo upon it. Gulp. But the sweet smell indicated squashed banana seeping out of the torn stitching in my battered sack. An earlier option, dismissed as being too difficult, now returned as being – well, the only remaining option. As if to reinforce my thoughts: 'Why don't you take your rucksack off?' Yawn.

So began a delicate striptease, dipping first one shoulder, then the other, fingering open the waist-belt, wriggling the hips, until the straitjacket hung around my legs. Like a fool, instead of booting the offensive object into space, being aware of how much money it had cost, I clipped it directly to my harness. This was actually mistake number three, for I should have used a long sling so that I could have hauled it up after me, as I was soon to discover. Now of normal human dimensions I was able to make proper use of the available – I hesitate to call them holds – rounded wrinkles, but as I progressed upwards there was a corresponding movement downwards as my waist-harness relocated to my ankles.

All this was accompanied by guffaws of ridicule and entertainment from below. Perhaps this lent strength to my cause because my normally feeble arms now managed, gorilla-like, to pull upwards and the rest of me trailed behind. I belayed to a large, loose boulder, sorted myself out, and tried to regain my composure. Never before had I felt so awkward or incompetent. Only once had I witnessed someone getting themselves into such an unbelievable position when, halfway up Labyrinth on Cir Mhor, Arran, my friend had ended up stretched horizontally across the rock and then tried to finish the pitch feet first.

David shouted at me and set off, his rope coming in at high speed before suddenly stopping, and staying stopped. I yawned, loudly, just as he, somewhat threateningly, called up: 'I hope you've got me.'

This request for slack rope met with cries of outrage, and, as he eventually reached my stance, I was pleased to note that he had replaced his trainers with sticky-rubber rock boots, a fat lot of good it was to do him though, as he now assumed command and said that he would lead the next pitch. A drastic amount of gear now emerged from his sack as he covered himself with metal bits and pieces, then demanded to see all my equipment, which I tipped in a pile. A disdainful toe poked around my precious slings and then selected one, in case an abseil was called for, then he disappeared into a cave under a big overhang. I was left to ponder.

*　　*　　*　　*　　*

I don't really believe all this stuff about ghosts but there's a story, recounted in one of Harry Griffin's books and told to him, I believe, by George Sansom himself. It concerns Sansom's great friend and climbing companion, Siegfried Herford. There's a photo of Herford not in a mountain setting but in military uniform because he enlisted with the 24th. Royal Fusiliers in 1915. It reminds me of thick, leather-bound albums, with tattered edges, which belonged to my mother. Therein were many similar images: sepia-brown, men in uniform, greatcoats with upturned collars and Army caps – relatives – all killed on the Western Front. They seemed like old men to my childish eyes but were only in their 20s and 30s. Herford was 24 when he joined up.

I imagine that he might have looked up at a single star, a point of light, as we see parallel lines of white crosses stretching to the horizon, converging in perspective to the same point. Was he then, after hours of bombardment, ordered up and out of a filthy trench, his hands grasping a Lee Enfield rifle? Did he strain every muscle, as when he lay-backed up the edge of the Great Flake on Scafell's Central Buttress, to gain a purchase in the mud, only to meet whistling lumps of lead which smacked through his neck? And, as his blood oozed away into the mud, were his thoughts of the walk by Hollowstones and the scree up, up to carefree days of adventure with his mate . . . Sansom . . .?

As Sansom tells it, he was walking down from Scafell on January 28, 1916, after a day in the hills on his own, when he spotted another, familiar, figure approaching him across the screes below Central Buttress and was amazed to encounter his old friend. They talked awhile but Siegfried was in a hurry to go . . . yes, you know the rest.

Herford was killed on January 28, 1916.

*   *   *   *   *

Two hours' later, or so it seemed, I could still see David's feet below the overhanging boulder as the rest of him tried to exit behind it. All his gear seemed to have had little impact, other than to have had the same effect upon him as my sack had had upon me, as I dutifully pointed out. His head appeared out of a black hole and gave me a silent stare. When my turn came I was, thankfully, hidden from his view as I made another complete balls-up of the pitch – sequences all wrong, position all wrong, everything all wrong, except one thing I did right. I didn't fall off. But I paid a high price in ripped clothing, scraped skin and bruises in strange places. The guide-book was correct about one thing – there was an easy walk at the top.

Now David is nearly 20 years' younger than me and an accomplished athlete and climber, and seemed rather quiet. We sat and shared my sandwiches and he gave me a wry smile as I pointed out that this kind of thing was all part of the Greater Mountaineering Experience and, well, not to put too fine a point on it, essentially Scottish. We agreed that we'd had enough for one day and, in unison, shouted: 'That's no Diff.'

We picked our separate ways round the outcrops of rock towards Harrison Stickle under a grey sky. It was almost as though he wasn't really there and a sudden thought came to me.

Grot's real name had been David.

TOWARDS COIRE LAGAN   JOHN MITCHELL

WELCOME TO THE CLUB

By David Hughes

I MUST tell you about this dream I had the other night. No, don't turn to the next page because, as you know, my dreams are *legendary*. You've not heard me talk about them before? Strange, I thought most people had. Anyway, the amazing thing is not just how weird my dreams are but how much I can remember about them the day afterwards. And the fantastic thing is that when I'm asleep I know I am dreaming. Weird or what? Like, as if I'm watching all these bizarre events unfolding and I can just switch off and wake up any time I want to.

Sometimes though, I get really scary nightmares. Not often; I think I can count them on one hand. I distinctly remember this nightmare I had at a campsite at Roybridge. Funnily enough it was just after I'd completed my 100th Munro. The tent was collapsing in from above. Something heavy was suffocating me, slowly but steadily squeezing the life out of me. I desperately tried to move but every muscle in my body felt as heavy as lead. I opened my mouth to cry out, but my voice sounded so weak and muted. I started to panic. This is just a dream, I thought; it's time to wake up. But try as I might I just couldn't escape, and I was beginning to think that I wasn't asleep. This was reality!

Then the next thing I remember was lying in my sleeping bag with the sun streaming in through the flysheet. It was daylight, I could breathe and I could move my limbs. A wave of relief passed through my body. Boy, that was one hell of a scary nightmare.

Anyway, going back to this dream I had the other night. You know that I've just finished the Munros, don't you? You don't? I thought you knew. I thought everybody knew. Tolmount at the head of Glen Callater, near Braemar. Yeah, that was my last one. Funny you should mention that because this was what the dream was about – my last Munro.

So there I was suddenly at this sort of compleaters' gathering where Munroists get together and swear in another person to their fold. That was me. And what I had to do, I had to get up on this stage to a sort of lectern with a microphone, a bit like a school prize night, and talk to this audience about my last Munro.

In fact, I'm sure it was the stage of my old secondary school, because there was a long line of us waiting to go on stage. Just like you were going on there to receive a prize of some sort. Except in this dream you didn't get anything but you had to talk to an audience about something. The bloke before me was on about driving along the M74 or something. And I thought, what a wally. Surely, if you're going to talk about your experiences of Munro-bagging you could think of better things to talk about than the journey up to the Highlands. I knew that I could do better than that, so I decided to talk about doing my last Munro. I don't know why I chose to do that; it just seemed sort of natural.

Anyway, when it was my turn to go on stage I was suddenly out in the open air with this absolutely massive audience. You just can't imagine how many people were there. All you could see were people, nothing else, just people. No matter how far they were away from me I could make out their faces. I just thought that the people there would be fellow 'compleaters', but I'm sure I recognised more famous climbers. You know, their faces were kind of familiar, but I couldn't put names to them.

Guests. That's what I worked out that they must be. Guests. That sounds about right. If something stranger than strange comes up in a dream I always find a reason for it, and the plot moves on. So that's what I concluded. Guests. Obvious really. But what about that girl I knew from junior school, what was she doing there, and why her? How strange!...I know, she probably did the Munros when she grew up. Obvious really.

Do you dream like that? I mean like have some sort of logical framework as if on a higher level your brain is trying to make sense of a series of unconnected past events. You don't? Well I said my dreams were legendary. The thing is that this one just got weirder. 'Ladies and gentlemen, unaccustomed as I am to public speaking,' I started. OK, so who's the wally now, I bet you're saying. But with so many people out there I suddenly felt very nervous and awkward.

'I've decided to tell you about my last Munro,' I continued, receiving in return encouraging smiles from millions of faces. 'It was a snowy Easter at Braemar. I just had Tom Buidhe and Tolmount to do to finish the Munros. The weather wasn't particularly good, but once I was there I had to finish them off. So the next day I set off to do a round of Glen Callater – Carn an Tuirc, Cairn of Claise, Tom Buidhe and finish on Tolmount.

'The day started slowly. I'd been staying at the Cairngorm Club hut at Inverey with my local mountaineering club, and everyone else was heading off back home because of work commitments. I decided to stay on for a couple of days – the perks of being a "rich sod", as some people in the club endearingly referred to me, and not having to work for a living.'

There was a faint ripple of laughter from my audience. I'd got their attention, they were listening. At least my story was going to be more exciting than driving along the M74. I began to grow in confidence as I continued.

'Anyway, there I was sat in my car at the foot of Glen Callater alongside the A93. Snow showers were rattling through at regular intervals, borne on by a strong northerly wind, a situation that had persisted throughout the Easter weekend. One minute your eyes were screwed up against the blinding sunshine reflecting off the white landscape, next minute black clouds unleashed more snow with the icy wind forever sending spindrift whistling across the mountain tops. I was pretending to read the map, check out the route sort of thing but my mind was in a quandary.'

'The dilemma of a solo walk in such dodgy conditions,' suggested someone from my audience. A female face, a concerned face, so familiar but who was it?

'Exactly!' I replied, pleased both with the fact that at least some of them were listening and that there was an empathy with my predicament; other mountaineers also faced similar indecisions and misgivings. I was beginning to feel a warmth and a camaraderie towards these people. After all we shared something in common, we'd all done the Munros.

'I was driven by the desire to finish the Munros,' I continued, 'but wanted very much to do it safely. You can guess what happened. The sun came out, the winter wonderland of pristine beauty beckoned and ambition won hands down. Boots and gaiters were donned, crampons and ice axe strapped to the rucksack and I was off, beating a way up the snow covered track to Lochcallater Lodge.'

Again the warning signals. I wasn't liking this dream. I mean, it wasn't a nightmare or anything as bad as that, but something was wrong and I couldn't put my finger on it. Something to do with the reality of the situation. Do you know what I mean? Like when you dream lots of past experiences and memories are interwoven into a bizarre set of events. But this was too real. OK, so me addressing an audience of millions of faces was strange, but my story of me doing my last Munro was exactly how it happened. Why was my dream just concentrating on one thing? There seemed to be no explanation so I just continued.

'The weather was kind at first. There was a heavy shower as I approached Loch Callater but it was quickly over and the world soon reappeared. Carn an Tuirc remained clear all the way to the top, but its broad north-easterly ridge lay open to the bitingly cold northerly wind. I reached the snow-choked summit cairn in good time and paused for a bite to eat. Then on to Cairn of Claise with easy walking on hard, compact snow. I felt elated, privileged to be there. What's more, the weather continued to be kind, and I seemed to be enjoying a window of good weather with no threat of showers in the immediate vicinity. However, the wind was just so cold, but I figured that if I kept moving then things would be all right. I was looking forward to the celebratory pint in the pub in a few hours, and inwardly laughed at myself for being so indecisive at the start of the walk.

'Tom Buidhe came and went with ease, and there to the north was it – Tolmount. My last Munro. Just a short descent to a frozen burn and then less than 100m of reascent to the summit. Half-an-hour away, if that, and yet it was the culmination of 20 years of roaming the Scottish Highlands in wind, rain, sun and snow. Thousands of miles of walking, thousands of feet of climbing.'

I paused to let the recounting of the elation at my impending triumph permeate my audience.

'But the day had a sting in its tail. Yes, you've guessed it, the good weather broke. Black clouds were gathering and had enveloped the Lochnagar plateau by the time I'd reached Tom Buidhe. So out came the compass. North-west down to the gap between the two peaks. Half-a-kilometre, that's 5 x 62 of my double paces. Then north up a broad ridge with just under one kilometre to the top. No problem.'

I wondered if my audience would understand this detail. I know you do, because you're a hill-walker like me. Perhaps not as good a navigator as me. OK, I know that sounds a bit cocky, but I know I'm pretty good at it. Sort of learnt by default really.

You see, when I started hill-walking I went on the hills in all sorts of weather – mainly bad weather I seem to recall. I remember this time when I'd just joined the mountaineering club and was on a meet in the Cairn-gorms. On one day we were on the plateau between Cairn Gorm and Ben Macdui in thick mist. At the time I was the least experienced of the party in terms of Scottish hills, but I seemed to be the only one who knew how to use a map, compass, pacings and timings. We got off the hill that day without much problem, but what surprised me was that the others regarded me as some sort of Mr Wonderful. On the other hand I was surprised at how inept they were at navigation.

But I digress. Getting a bit big-headed you might say. Anyway what I didn't tell the audience was how rusty I'd got at navigating. You see nowadays if it's poor weather I don't go out. Virtually all the hills I do now I have views from, and the compass stays in the bottom of the sack.

So this is how my dream and my story to the Munroist club continued.

'The descent to the dip between the peaks was fairly straightforward, but the snow and low cloud had already encased me. Fortunately, I was out of the main force of the wind, but even in this relative shelter the snow was still swirling about me. The rising ridge to Tolmount was only sensed at first but the compass bearing was right and I soon found myself plodding uphill, head down, hood up trying to shield my face and eyes against the increasing wind and the stinging spindrift.

'As the slope flattened out the spindrift became unbearable. The north-erly wind, funnelled by the narrow defile of Glen Callater, was being blocked at its southern end by the bulk of Tolmount. So it had no choice but to accelerate upwards and over the top. I was now feeling its full force. Unable to stand straight or look forward, I was staggering blind into the teeth of an almighty gale. I stumbled over a hidden boulder, the wind flipped me over and dumped me flat on the snow.

The cliffs of Creagan a' Choire Etchachan in full winter glory. Photo: Derek Pyper.
Brian Findlay on the first pitch of 'Djibangi' (V,4). Photo: Greg Strange.

'I was rapidly becoming exhausted. The wind shrieked over me while hailstones, snow and spindrift covered me in a ghostly translucent shroud. Part of my mind began to think rationally. How far was I away from the summit? I'd stopped counting paces as I started climbing, thinking that I couldn't possibly miss the summit. But this, this was a real white out. Visibility was nil. The only sense of direction was that of the wind. What should I do? I fought back a wave of panic by telling myself that these showers were short-lived. Only a few days before I'd been in a similar situation on the slopes of Carn na Drochaide. Then I'd just sat it out and 10 minutes later there'd been blue sky. So that's what I did here.'

This was no dream, this was a nightmare like the one I had in my tent at Roybridge. I couldn't move, but this time the elements were conspiring against me to keep me there on the snow. OK, time to wake up, I thought, but I couldn't and the nightmare continued.

'The storm didn't last 10 minutes,' I continued to tell my audience. 'I don't know how long it lasted but I seemed to be losing the will to get up and do anything. I felt unbelievably cold and tired. All I wanted to do was sleep, just wait for a couple of hours until it got dark so that I could fall into the oblivion of a really deep, long sleep at the end of an exhausting day. And the next day I'd wake up tired but peacefully happy that everything had returned to normal.'

My voice trailed away. The audience was still there. I was still dreaming. I realised that somehow I was stuck. Time had stopped. Suddenly, there was no future.

Almost there, but I would never reach the top of my last Munro. Was this the reality?

Not that I'd done the Munros, but that somehow I hadn't done them?

'I never got to the top, did I?' I inquired of my audience. 'I haven't finished the Munros. Why haven't I finished the Munros? What happened?'

I started to panic. I was frozen to the spot. Let this nightmare finish. LET ME WAKE UP NOW, PLEASE!

The audience was still there, now holding my hand. Millions and millions and millions of people holding my hand. The wave of panic subsided, the nightmare melted away, the dream vanished, but there was no waking up.

'Welcome to the club,' said the previous speaker. 'It no longer matters that you didn't complete the Munros, does it? Now you know why I was talking about the M74 – me, fatal car accident, you, hypothermia. As you see it's important that everyone talks about their final hours of life. Helps them to come to terms with death. Now let's listen to the next speaker.'

I smiled and took my place alongside my dead friends.

American climber Pete Takeda savouring the delights of Scottish mixed climbing on the first ascent of 'Never-Never Land' (VI,6), Observatory Buttress, Ben Nevis, during the International Meet. Photo: Simon Richardson.

FLASHBACK – A CAIRNGORM CHRONICLE

By Colin W. Whittit

IT IS JANUARY 1987. I was crammed into the back of Chris Forrest's ancient Datsun. Buried beneath a mountain of rucksacks and climbing gear, my face was pressed against the wet window as we ground and bumped in low gear over the ice-rutted roads of Braemar.

By the time I fell gratefully out of the back seat Chris was fixing his cross-country skis to his boots. He was quickly organised and disappeared into the darkness with an impressive, but ungainly, thrash of arms and legs. Chris wants to be an Alpine Guide and apparently needs more ski-mountaineering experience. Judging by the amount of effort required just to set off a great deal more!

Wilson and I shouldered our packs and set off towards Derry Lodge. The first part of the walk was uphill and Wilson suggested burning off Chris's ski efforts. We had not gone far before we saw Chris floundering upside down in deep powder snow at the side of the track, where he was trying desperately to get back to his feet. The more he struggled the deeper his heavy rucksack seemed to press him into the snow. I went to help him but Wilson caught my arm: 'Leave him, he needs the practice.'

I shrugged and glanced once more at the struggling tangle of arms and legs below us. Chris seemed to be completely unaware of our presence as we watched his heroic struggle from above. I turned around and once more strode out after Wilson. I was keen for conversation and tried, yet again, to match his pace. When I caught up however, he was stoic and silent. Besides, it is hard to speak and gasp simultaneously for air.

Ten minutes or so passed before a snow-covered figure clattered up behind us. 'I fell,' gasped Chris. 'Had to take my rucksack off to stand up.' He passed us with a grand flourish of his ski sticks. 'Great conditions for skiing.' Then he was gone. Skating away into the blackness of the Glen Derry path at lung-bursting speed.

Wilson, setting his own pace, soon passed far ahead of me and I was left to the miserable drudgery of the long, flat walk in to the Hutchison Hut, anxious that I might miss the turn-off, more anxious that I would miss the bridge over the burn and even more certain that I would have an epic finding the hut in the dark.

My doubts were ill founded. The tracks left by Wilson's footsteps were easy to follow and once off the estate road, the route to the hut was well marked by large holes in the snow where Chris had fallen over.

Being last to reach the hut does have some advantages, and I arrived to a warm welcome of broad grins, hot drinks and the inevitable peanut butter sandwich which is the principle constituent of Wilson's diet. That night the temperature inside the hut plummeted and was one of the coldest I had experienced. I woke up shivering several times during the night and once even found my hair stuck – frozen solid to the wall of the hut.

We rose early the next morning and prepared to set off as dawn crept quietly into the freezing coire bowl. We had a major objective in mind and we knew that we were not the only climbers in the hut that morning with the same plan in mind. Djibangi, it was rumoured, was in climbable winter condition.

Despite the cliffs being so close to the hut I was breathing heavily by the time we reached the red slabs, and a little rock outcrop which Wilson floated over to reach the base of the route was much harder to climb than it looked. Chris and I bypassed this obstacle with a short zig-zag traverse left then right to bring us to the base of the cliff.

Standing at the bottom of the wall, the lower slabs were sheathed with thin ice, spilling over from the ice trap of the Red Chimney. The big corner of Djibangi soared above us, a thin strip of snow or névé clinging to the slab and wall junction, inviting us upwards to the airy overlap high above.

Wilson set off immediately, traversing way out left to the edge of the slab overlooking Red Chimney. He climbed as beautifully as ever but I was confused as to why he was heading away from the main corner. I was unfamiliar with the summer line and imagined some horrible thin ice forcing us out into no-man's land in the centre of the big slab.

The climbing, after a steep pull onto the slab, was wonderful. Delicate foot placements and gentle stabs with the picks allowed steady progress to be made, not dissimilar to the best summer padding. The situation, the ice and the climbing were absorbing as I searched the surface of the slab for subtle thickenings or tell-tale ripples where footholds could be found. This type of winter climbing was so different from the other routes I had climbed that it was with a little regret that I found myself approaching the first stance and belay.

The next pitch promised more variations on this icy theme, and Chris padded neatly and confidently into a belay niche in the main corner. It was now my turn to lead, and I could not believe my luck as I craned my neck backwards to see the corner soar away above me. The névé trapped in the open book of the corner was perfect, and just wide enough to accommodate my cramponed boots side by side.

Each step upwards was unique; a little dab with the axe here, a hook for the hammer in the crack in the right wall there, two solid thuds into thicker snow ice, axe picks an inch apart. Step, kick. Step, kick. Reach up high and lean outwards to place a runner on the right wall. I moved on. Moved up. Only 10ft below the roof now. The névé started to narrow alarmingly and I was forced to stand with one foot above the other to maintain contact with the wall. I panicked as I imagined the consequences of the ice above me becoming too thin or narrow to climb. Another perfect runner placement boosted my confidence and any self-doubt vanished.

I was now under the small roof which constitutes the summer crux and my calves were beginning to strain. An *in situ* nut, jammed at the overlap, made arranging the protection easy and I now felt relaxed and in control. I saw the normal belay platform above me on my right and I decided to pass it by; stepping out onto the ledge from the security of the corner looked horrendously difficult. Later, on our descent from the crag, I was mightily impressed to see Greg Strange swing delicately out of the corner onto that stance.

Leaning out slightly, I peered anxiously above the overlap. The thin strip of snow ice continued up the corner to easier ground. With a swing of my wrists the axes thudded into the névé. I stepped up. Pulled. Feet up. Points in and it was all over. As I heaved over the lip of the overhang Wilson called to me: 'Come on Colin! It's only 4b in the summer.' I looked down between my feet to see his huge beaming grin and whooped with delight, baying loudly to the mist sheathing the crags.

I climbed on and was able, just as the rope drag was becoming troublesome, to manufacture a good belay on some granite ribs poking out of the snow on the left. Both Chris and Wilson cruised up the corner, noisily enthusiastic as they reached the stance. We all talked at the same time. No-one listening to what the others were saying, each of us desperate to relate our own personal experience of the corner pitch we had just climbed.

Above us the route had become a steep snow bay ending in a *cul de sac* which Chris led into. Wilson told him that the route broke out onto the buttress on the right. When Chris was gone Wilson smiled and informed me that: 'Chris is a great climber but he hasn't got much experience on the buttresses yet.'

Sure enough, Chris took ages to climb this pitch. When I followed him, I too found it tricky. Pulling up onto the edge was committing and exposed. Teetering up the final, typically Cairngorm rib, with its rounded grooves, turf filled cracks and well-spaced protection was a sustained and surprisingly delicate finish to the route.

The plateau was gained by surmounting a small cornice and Chris confessed that the upper buttress was: 'Bloody hard.'

I smiled to myself, amazed at Wilson's dark sense of humour and wondered how many times I too had been the victim of his ploys without even being aware of it. I found myself wondering just what he said to

Chris as I set off to lead the corner pitch earlier. My sense of self-satisfaction at Chris's expense was short-lived however, when, one hour later, he effortlessly climbed through the complex overhanging icicles at the crux of Red Chimney. I had a really hard time following this pitch and the memory of that lead remains with me as one of the most competent performances I have seen on steep ice.

The next day conditions were perfect when we climbed Carmine Groove to claim an unexpected second ascent. Afterwards, Wilson and Chris romped off to solo some Grade IV ice. I didn't join them because, I said, I was knackered The real reason, however, was that I was so pumped with adrenaline that I didn't really trust my judgment any more. I had not slept well the night before, and the number of big-name climbers on the crag had me psyched out.

As I boiled water back at the hut, I watched party after party grind up the lower snow slope, drawn by the powerful magnet of Djibangi. Some intrepid individuals climbed it direct, some just inspected it and moved on, others found it hard and gripping. Testing their skills to the full. There is one thing, however, on which all agree: Djibangi in winter is an outstanding route.

Two months passed, and it was March of the same year before Wilson, Chris and I climbed together again. This time we were based at Glenmore Lodge, guests of Jas Hepburn.

Since our last climb on the Etchachan cliffs Wilson and I had climbed Cumming-Crofton route in a fast time, and I even managed to avoid the unscripted bungee jump down Slochd Wall which I had performed the year before on an ascent of Mitre Ridge. Wilson apparently arrested my fall by jumping down the East Wall side of the terminal ridge and is still scrounging free drinks on the strength of this war story.

The day was mild when we set out from the Coire Cas car park and I was, to say the least, surprised that after 45 minutes of walking, we were still all together and the pace steady, even comfortable, to follow. Chris was on foot this time. I supposed that the conditions were 'not so great for skiing' today.

As we contoured the rim of Coire an Lochan, passing the foot of the Vent, my avalanche phobia gradually began to subside as the snowpack stayed attached to the great slab. I had seen too many photographs of the fracture line on this area of snow to feel comfortable here, while any time beyond February starts me worrying about the annual spring thaw which triggers this huge snowfield to tumble into the coire bowl below.

Despite the mild weather when we set off, it was very cold in the shadows of the coire and we decided to solo some of the easier routes to warm up. We quickly thudded our way up Oesophagus and descended via the Couloir. This turned out to be the start of another Moir ploy since the bottom of the gully brought us neatly to the start of Fallout Corner which was still waiting for a second ascent. I wanted to have a go at Savage Slit but Wilson had already climbed it and Chris, uncharacteristically, said nothing. Fallout Corner it was.

I lead the first pitch to below the roof. The climbing was very awkward and much more strenuous than it looked. The rock jutted out in big blocks split by wide, fist-sized cracks – but nothing that you could really get a hold of.

Most of the climbing involved jamming and steep mantelshelf moves in clumsy, mittened hands. The pitch was similar to the overhanging wall on Scorpion, but much more sustained. It was with relief that I heaved myself, one hour later, into the comparative sanctuary of the little cave below the overhang. Arms pumped, lungs heaving and sweat dripping from my chin onto the snow at my feet. Wilson and Chris were less than impressed by my effort and announced that they were 'almost hypothermic'. Wilson fixed the rope to the belay at the stance below and both of them quickly disappeared to 'heat themselves up'.

I was furious; I had worked really hard to get to this point and felt like I had been abandoned. When they returned 20 minutes' later I was shivering with cold and in a foul mood. Wilson is a superb climber and consequently he seconded my pitch in about five minutes flat. 'Solid Grade V that pitch,' he told me. I grunted an acknowledgement and we changed the gear over quickly. He set out onto the overhang. His feet seemed to be level with my head for a very long time and his efforts were punctuated with much grunting, the rattle of gear, but very little actual movement. Suddenly, there was a heave and Wilson moved jerkily upwards, crampons scratching noisily on the bare rock.

I looked out from my eyrie under the roof. He had his right arm locked off, the pick of his hammer twisted in a tiny slot and his left hand grabbing above the roof of the overhang. His teeth gritted in determination as he found the hold he needed and with a sinew-stretching heave, disappeared from view. 'That's hard,' he called down to me and I heard him gasp as he banged in a peg.

That the moves were hard was obvious, and my enthusiasm to climb any farther faded fast as the icy fingers of cold which were creeping steadily into my body caused me to shiver uncontrollably. I belayed Chris up to the little cave and he too climbed the first pitch of the route depressingly quickly. I used this chance to play the hypothermic excuse and persuaded him to lower me back to the coire floor to allow me to heat up. I had, of course, no intention of returning up to the cave and happily soloed the Vent and wandered back down the Couloir to the foot of the route. Chris was now above the overhang and a red rope snaked down the buttress to the well stomped platform that I was standing on. I generously announced that Wilson and Chris should complete the route themselves as a 'faster' rope of two. My mouth dropped open when Wilson called down in a matter of fact tone: 'You'll have to come up. We left your gear below the overlap!'

I was incredulous. They must have sensed my indecision and deliberately left my gear in place obliging me to climb on.

I was so angry that the first pitch passed in a blur of sweat and misdirected aggression. The roof however was indeed 'hard'. My crampon points somehow balanced on rounded edges and my axe pick hooked into the tiny slot in the wall above my head

I pulled hard. I pulled again, harder, and moved upwards, but found myself off balance. My left hand slapped and groped speculatively above the roof but couldn't find the hold I so desperately needed. I was tiring quickly and knew that it was now or never. I wrapped my arm around Wilson's ankle, regained my balance, climbed up his leg and collapsed half on, half off the ledge.

The ledge we were standing on was about 2ft long and 2ft wide. We were attached by a complicated network of ropes and slings to one, less than inspiring, peg. Chris was looking very unhappy as he shivered in the corner, head hanging against the wall, one foot on the ledge and the other bridging out onto the right wall. Changing the gear over was complicated and time consuming and it was some time before Chris started up the main corner. The corner itself was plated with snow and he made only about 8ft of progress before he returned to the ledge, knackered. Wilson looked to me. 'Do you want to have a go?'

'I shook my head. 'Down it is then.'

The abseil from the dodgy peg was worrying, but uneventful, and it was only when we turned at last to the Lodge and Chris collapsed that I realised how ill he had been. Chris had apparently been in bed for several days with flu but did not want to miss the chance of climbing Fallout Corner. I was humbled by his endurance and impressed with his remarkable commitment to climb a route of this difficulty when he was clearly so unfit to do so.

Later, with Chris rested and partially recovered, we passed the evening in the warm hospitality of Planet Lodge. I drank far too much beer; listened in awe to the modestly-related tales of The Guru, Andy Nisbet; discussed secret plans and vaulting ambitions with Andy Cunningham and later, I'm told, recommended some 'good Grade 3s to Dave Cuthbertson!'

RISK AND MOUNTAINEERING

By R. T. Richardson

*The following three articles expound, in one way or another, on the complex series of choices and decisions which mountaineers undergo on each and every outing, consciously or not. The title article by R. T. Richardson, attempts to set the scene, while Messrs Anderson and Peden provide real life descriptions of resulting situations. A fourth article in this issue, Join the Club, may also be profitably read in conjunction with the aforementioned three. (**Hon. Ed.**)*

To QUOTE W. Inglis Clark in 1899 [1].

'The mountaineer is essentially a searcher after the beautiful. It is true that this is not his only object in ascending summits or visiting mountain districts. Readers of Mr Maylard's interesting papers [2,3] on *Climbing considered in its Physiological Aspects,* will remember that he has there shown how complex and beneficial are the results of mountaineering on our muscular and nervous systems. In the belief of some, these purely physical results are the only aim of those who scale precipitous cliff or narrow arête *en route* for the summit. With others, the climber is credited with a mad ambition to imperil his life, while heart and nervous system are strained to the utmost by the excitement of imminent danger.

'...the rock climber finds in his pursuit such a fascinating exercise of balance and concentration and of judgment in considering probabilities and possibilities that while he in no wise undervalues the scenic importance of his climb, he may count his time well spent...'

It is the question of how we exercise this judgment and the complexity of the mental processes, conscious and unconscious, which underpin it that I would like to discuss. We may go on the hills to enjoy the beauty of the scenery or to delight in the exercise but when we say we are going climbing or mountaineering we imply that possibility of physical harm and uncertainty of outcome which is the real attraction. Considered risk and the application of physical skill and strength in situations which satisfy our love of the vertical is what attracts us.

There is probably no other *sport* which has such an extensive literature as mountaineering, and certainly no other body of literature devoted to a physical activity (including sex) which takes itself so seriously and has such intellectual pretensions. Mountaineering literature covers a wide range of approaches to its subject – lyrical description of scenery, topographical description, physical description of mountains and routes, gear worship, hero worship, ego-stroking, polemic, humour, horror stories etc. What is rarely presented is any serious examination of the nature and scale of the risks involved in mountaineering and the way that mountaineers judge them. The possibility of hazard is often mentioned, but the conscious judgment of risk is rarely discussed in the generality of mountain literature.

There are, of course, some notable and classic exceptions. Three of these may be found in anthologies, *The Games Climber's Play* [4] and *Mirror in the Cliffs* [5]. Lito Tejada-Flores's essay on climbing as a game hierarchy is well known, as are his often-quoted remarks on the necessity of maintaining a degree of uncertainty as to the eventual outcome in order to achieve satisfaction in climbing. Harold Drasdo's essay on *Margins of Safety* is a marvellous exploration of the psychology of mountaineering but I disagree in some respects with the concept of margin of SAFETY. Mike Thomson's elegant essay on *The Aesthetics of Risk* – reprinted in *Mirror in the Cliffs* – takes a generalised, if interesting, approach to risk in mountaineering which demonstrates a knowledge of the theoretical aspects of risk perception as well as risk management of financial investments. (His classification of risk-takers into Buddhists and Hindus has a certain apt humour in climbing circles.) But, for an activity which undoubtedly involves the possibility of hazard, climbing literature takes very little explicit recognition of the nature of the risks and the approach of mountaineers to them.

Risk in all its aspects is now considered a respectable area of study and there is a considerable literature of academic study of risk. The most useful and accessible text is probably John Adams's book *Risk* [6] and I acknowledge a debt to it for many of the ideas in this article. Risk is a universal human activity and the literature on it is well worth studying.

There is, however, a problem in reading the literature of risk and trying to apply its concepts and models to mountaineering. The usual definition of risk is based on the combination of a statistical probability of an event occurring and the *detriment* that would accompany that event. It is the statistical concept of probability as a frequency that is the problem. When applied to a large number of repeated similar actions (e.g. incidence of lung cancer in cigarette smokers) this may be valid, but a mountaineer does not think in terms of 'if I repeat this pitch 10 times, how many times will I fall off?' Rather, mountaineers think in terms of what Harold Drasdo called 'margin of safety'. I would rephrase that as 'margin of success'. This probably applies to much of human behaviour, with the individual being concerned with one particular event, or course of action, at a time and the risk theorist being concerned with the cumulative statistics of that activity as performed a large number of times.

When we climb, or drive a car, or cross the street, or have that extra whisky, we consciously or unconsciously make a risk assessment. These are self-imposed or voluntary risks and either we accept the perceived risk of a particular action, and then carry it out, or we reject the risk and avoid the action. There is another class of risk which we are subject to – for example the risk of contracting spongiform encephalopathy from eating beef or of being killed in an air crash, or of a large asteroid hitting the Earth. These are involuntary risks which are largely imposed on us and are outwith our direct control – unless we avoid eating beef or refuse to travel by plane etc. But we cannot take personal action to avoid asteroids hitting the Earth. They have done so in the past – and there is no reason to think they will not do so again.

There is a dramatic difference in attitudes to voluntary and involuntary risk. If we attempt to explore the levels of involuntary risk that the public regards as acceptable we enter a very overgrown bramble patch. Much depends on the nature of the perceived hazard, but there are very strong sociological factors as well. What is apparent, however, is that it is the perception of the risk rather than the *real* risk that drives public response. There are currently some classic examples of this, e.g. human infection arising from BSE in cattle, disposal of nuclear waste. The perception of the hazards associated with these is such that rationality is not on stage.

The acceptable/unacceptable boundaries are often expressed by means of a graph of scale of hazard (penalty) versus risk (probability). But this can only give a general description of the average person's response. It is interesting to briefly consider the level of imposed risk which individuals are willing to accept. Obviously, this will vary widely but, in general, surveys have shown that for an imposed event resulting in the death of one individual a probability of greater than once in 10,000 years is considered unacceptable. For events resulting in multiple deaths the "unacceptable" frequency falls sharply. It is also apparent that there is a greater fear of some hazards than of others and that fear (rational or irrational) has a strong influence on governmental legislative response.

Consider the ban on the sale of beef 'on the bone' instituted in 1998 and since rescinded. The Government solemnly said that there was a risk of one in 60 million that eating beef on the bone could lead to spongiform encephalopathy. Most statisticians would suspect that the level of confidence on a frequency of this magnitude to be rather low and that, consequently, the stated frequency has very little meaning. At the same time there are a multitude of other human activities with fatal consequences and much higher probabilities that do not attract government bans (it is estimated that, on average, 10 people a year die in the UK from allergy to peanuts). It is the nature of the detrimental event that lies behind this ban. The general horror of dementia and death resulting from prior infection drove this extreme and dubious legislation, while other much more probable routes to unpleasant death are ignored. It also appears that if people are asked about probabilities that they consider "safe" and "dangerous" for involuntary risks, there is no sharp dividing line; rather, there is a large "gray area" between the acceptable and the unacceptable.

When we look at voluntary risk, the whole scale of acceptable and unacceptable probability changes and the variation between individuals becomes very much more marked. People will cheerfully accept comparatively high levels of risk when crossing the road or driving cars. Some will accept probabilities at Russian Roulette levels or (with some climbers) evens or worse. Why? Because they think they are in control of the situation. In technical terms, they think they are managing the risk because they believe they have a measure of control over the outcome. This is sometimes referred to as optimistic bias. People usually go into these situations because they perceive a benefit from the proposed action but rarely carry out more than the most superficial risk analysis. See the average driving style.

Many people are attracted to activities which depend, in some part at least, for their attraction on an element of risk of physical harm or death. Such people will seek to operate on their own perceptions of the boundary between the safe and the unsafe. Each individual is mapping out an area on the perceived risk/hazard surface within which they find satisfaction. They will derive much of their satisfaction from having successfully managed self-imposed risks. This is the territory explored in Drasdo's essay. When they consider these voluntary risks though, they don't knowingly operate on a probability versus penalty graph. The climber doesn't consciously think: 'If I do this move 100 times I estimate that I will fail on 10 of these occasions.' Instead, to my mind, we replace probability with something which you might call *margin*. Drasdo calls it *safety margin* but I think this is too restrictive a description, I would rather call it *success margin*. This is a conscious estimate of the extent to which attempting a particular route or undertaking a particular move will take us to our physical and technical limits and I would claim that most people taking part in risk sports think in the same way.

Mountaineering is certainly a risk sport but one of the things which distinguishes it from the likes of motor racing or downhill ski racing is the fact that climbing requires a whole sequence of *probabilities and possibilities* to be considered at a relatively slow pace. It is this process of deliberate and conscious judgment of both the practicality and the possible penalties of the next move (or sequence of moves) which gives climbing its intellectual superiority over those sports which merely require one quick commitment or which depend on a continuous flow of adrenaline-fuelled reactive judgments taken in haste. The climber has (usually) the time to consider the consequences of his or her actions.

Many people find that the satisfaction in climbing comes from pushing their boundaries into that area where they are uncertain that they will avoid harm on the next move (or sequence of moves) but still retain their *optimistic bias*. A guarantee of success would reduce the climb to a gymnastic exercise or a tour of mountain scenery – pleasant enough but lacking the bite of the authentic climbing experience. But, we each have our own concept of where these boundaries lie. Or, to put it another way, of how much we are willing to reduce our margin.

The factors that underlie this can be illustrated by a model known as the *risk thermostat*.

The individual consciously or unconsciously adjusts their thermostat in the light of their own personality, i.e. the propensity to take risks. (Adams's book discusses the various types of risk-taking personality – hierarchists,

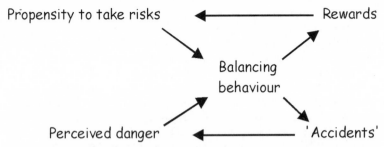

individualists, fatalists and egalitarians. See also Drasdo's essay.) This, and their perception of the danger of a particular situation, results in balancing behaviour which may range from placing a runner to avoiding a route altogether. (*Balancing behaviour* is an apt concept in our context.) The perception of danger will be based on a number of factors – weather, rock or snow conditions, risk of rockfall, constitution of the party etc. which are, to a great extent, dependent on experience. Too much *balancing behaviour* may reduce the *rewards*.

The adjustment of the risk thermostat can be illustrated by the connection between the so-called advances in safety engineering in motor cars and the way in which people drive. Most people will exploit better brakes, seat belts etc. by driving faster. They adjust their behaviour to operate in a constant risk envelope. The application to climbing is obvious. To quote Drasdo: 'Whenever a significant step forward is made in equipment or technique, the average climber makes a compensation. He (sic!) does not want to widen his safety margin indefinitely; he wants to hold it to a satisfactorily narrow measure... His safety margin has to seem as marginal as ever.'

It is interesting to speculate on the *rewards* sector of the risk thermostat in the mountaineering context. I would suggest that these are complex and highly variable from individual to individual. There is (I hope) an aesthetic component by which we derive satisfaction from our encounter with the mountain or crag environment through appreciation of the perceived beauty and grandeur of our surroundings. Many of us, I suspect, derive satisfaction from the sculptural elegance of even short routes. There may be sociological components – a desire to be part of a community of people whom we admire and to have standing within that community.

On a more basic level, there may be physiological rewards. The stress situation results in the release of chemicals in the body. The most familiar chemical response is adrenaline. This is the *fight or flight* chemical which is released from a gland near the liver and speeds up the release of glucose in the muscles, thus leading to increased rate of muscle fibre twitching. Most of us are familiar with the tingling sensation that accompanies adrenaline release – *the adrenaline rush*. But sensation lies in the brain and here things become much more complex. The following is a very simplified description of some aspects of brain chemistry. Sensation is the result of the transmission of electrical impulses (firing) of nerve cells and this firing is brought about by the release of chemicals. Much current research on addiction is concerned with these chemical mechanisms, although some of them (e.g. the effect of ethanol) have been understood for a long time. Other endogenous (i.e. released within the brain) chemicals are associated with pleasure sensations. It is now widely accepted that intense physical exercise or experience of *risk* situations can result in the release in the brain of chemicals classed as endorphins. Endorphins are endogenous chemicals which affect particular neurological sites (the opioid receptors) in the brain and are responsible for the 'high' that may be experienced after a successfully completed route. (The opioid receptors are so-called because morphine and related chemicals bind to them.) Unlike adrenaline, which gives a relatively short-term *rush,* endorphin release effects are long-lasting.

It is widely recognised that physical exercise can be addictive (long distance runners are notorious for this) and this addiction is linked to the production of endorphins in the brain. It may be that mountaineering, which exposes its practitioners to prolonged stress/exercise experiences, can also lead to endorphin addiction. More worryingly, a high level of endorphin activity is associated with compulsive-obsessive disorders.

If we recognise risk, it is only to be expected that we will either avoid the risk or attempt to manage it in some way. The management of risk is now recognised as a subject of study and there is a huge literature on this subject. However, *Risk Management* means different things in different spheres of activity – financial risk management, engineering risk management, environmental risk management, to name but three.

Risk management in climbing and mountaineering takes a variety of forms. The acquisition of information from guidebooks and from consultation with other climbers. Assessment of the weather and of the snow or rock conditions. The choice of climbing partners. Assessment of one's own physical condition and climbing form. The choice of equipment – and so on. But rarely is this combined into a conscious risk-management strategy. We feel like attempting the route or we don't feel like attempting the route.

Changes in equipment have probably brought about the biggest *advances* in climbing standards over the last 50 years. At least, for the average climber – perhaps the standards at the top have changed less than we think.

Today the average climber uses specialised footwear, usually two ropes if they are Scots, a harness, a variety of expensive devices for running belays, and possibly wears a helmet. The capital cost of all of this is formidable. The object of all this technology and expense is mainly to reduce the hazard in the event of falling off. This reduction of hazard allows the climber to accept a higher probability of falling off and still stay within their individual *envelope* of risk, i.e. to indulge in risk compensation. Although they may climb at higher *standards* than the pioneers of earlier days, the overall risk is not greater and is probably significantly less. *The leader does not fall* is not universally applicable nowadays.

Climbers have embraced risk compensation in a big way. We have used the engineering embodied in camming devices, wedging devices, light-weight ropes, sticky boots etc. to push out climbing standards. As far as the risk management of ascent goes we seem to have been fairly successful. There are very few fatalities recorded in the *Accident Reports* which arise from falls during a climb. Where mountaineering deaths do occur they are usually associated with the descent – principally from avalanche or from slips. This can be taken as a warning that when the risk is perceived to be less immediate and dramatic, the risk management becomes less con-scious. This is obviously bound up with our perception of, and psychologi-cal approach to, risk, which varies from individual to individual.

What about sports climbing? Here it appears at first glance that the hazard has been eliminated and that the acceptable failure probability is very high. The point is to overcome technical and physical difficulties so that *failure* results in damage to self-esteem rather than to the body. The risk envelope has changed not only in terms of probability and extent of penalty – the penalty itself has changed. A risk activity has become a gymnastic sport. This is not entirely true; there are physical risks associated with falling off overhanging walls on to bolt runners, while tendonitis is common, but broken limbs and death are not usually in the scenario (unless a bolt fails).

In solo climbing the increase in hazard has to be offset by a drastic reduction in the probability of failure or an acceptance of much higher potential penalties. This is a contentious area but one in which the aesthetic values of climbing and the psychology of the climber become very important.

Should climbers study Risk Management as a discipline? Probably not worthwhile. One doesn't want to construct fault trees for a climb (we all do it instinctively) but the fault tree methodology might be worth while for an expedition. (A fault tree is a diagram which examines the connections between possible events which could lead to a catastrophic overall result and estimates the resulting probability.) I think it is worthwhile though, to think consciously in terms of hazard and probability (or margin, if you prefer) and to be more aware of the way in which we can minimise these without taking the point out of climbing. Or to put it another way – to take our own individual risk envelope into more interesting territory.

To risk is to live (if you get your risk management right).

1. S.M.C.J. 1898, v., pp121-125.
2. S.M.C.J. 1897, iv., pp267-275.
3. S.M.C.J. 1898, v., pp17-23.
4. The Games Climbers Play. Wilson, Ken (Ed.) Diadem Press (1978) ISBN 0-906371-01-5.
5. Mirror in the Cliffs. Perrin, Jim. (Ed.) Diadem Press (1983) ISBN 0-906371-95-3
6. Risk. Adams, John. UCL Press (1995) ISBN 1-85728-068-7

THE LEDGE

By Douglas Anderson

THE Twin Otter skimmed in over a cluster of icebergs grounded in shallows at the river mouth.

We seemed to be heading straight in. The landing place was an area of flattish gravel marked only with two torn pieces of fluorescent pink material. But no, the plane banked left pulling round the head of the river valley. We four sat gripping the arm rests at the very back. In front of us our food and equipment was piled in a random heap. Looking forward, past the shoulders of the crew, through the front windshield, a rock wall slipped by. The plane banked more steeply and beyond the wing tip I watched the icebergs then gravel come round again. More steeply still the plane turned until I thought the pile of equipment was sure to break loose. I contemplated the havoc created should centrifugal force for a moment lose its grip and send our 80kg outboard motor careering round the cabin. A deadly cargo of 400 litres of petrol in plastic bags lay wobbling about like jellies at a kids' party. I had visions of the engine flattening the fuel bags and sending a wave of four star sweeping through the plane. But such are only the imaginings of a family man who is afraid of flying. I needn't have worried, the nose dipped and with only a slight bump, we were soon rolling to a halt on the gravel bar.

Trying to play down my relief I unclipped and scrambled forward. I had something new to worry about and that was how to get a ton of gear hundreds of yards to the sea. I had no illusions about who would soon become the primary pack animal and I wanted to cut the length of the relays to a minimum.

With a generosity of spirit typical of those who navigate the northern skies, our crew unhesitatingly agreed to drive round the tundra in search of a good drop off spot. In the distance was the outline of a river leading in the direction of the sea, and soon we were bumping off towards it. As we drew nearer I began to have misgivings. On stepping down it was immediately obvious that the river was very shallow, and definitely not up to the job of floating our impedimenta to the sea. If we put in here, we would face an impossibly arduous drag through miles of braided shallows to reach water deep enough to float. I was embarrassed because the crew still had to fly on to Station Nord, and asking them to continue taxiing around this delta was not going to shorten their day. Without prompting, however, they suggested we try another direction. Guilty, but relieved, I clambered back on board and we set off again, bouncing heavily over increasingly rough ground. For what seemed a long time we trundled on until unexpectedly lurching to a stop. Had we arrived? No. The pilot shoved the throttles forward, the engine revs increased alarmingly, but the plane did not budge.

I looked anxious. 'Don't worry…Sand,' said the pilot, giving the throttles another shove. The plane strained and rattled, and then heaved itself forward, bouncing dramatically into the air before crashing down again. 'No problem' said the pilot. Onwards we bounced, until even he thought things had gone far enough. We had made it to within a quarter of a mile of the water's edge.

We tumbled out and hurriedly unloaded. In five minutes all our gear was spread on the ground and we stood shaking hands. The pilot looked at us, me, my wife, the two children and referring I think, to our plans to circumnavigate Milne Land and boat down to the Liverpool coast, expostulated: 'Kind of crazy'…(he paused as if considering the sanity of our undertaking)… 'But good'…I was relieved, I didn't want to be condemned by this maniac for being reckless. A minute later the Twin Otter was trundling over the gravel again and suddenly it was airborne. Turning on a wing tip it was back, and we all ducked as it swooped so low we felt we would be scalped. We stood staring after it until it merged into the clouds.

We looked around and tried to take stock. 'Wow!' We were certainly alone, just the four of us, standing alone on this Arctic river delta with our gear. I began to worry again about the size of the pile, the remaining distance to the sea, and the other objective dangers that would threaten tomorrow's outcome. By 10pm camp was pitched and we were in the tent cooking tea. It had been a long day, but tomorrow looked like being harder. It started to rain but I for one was too knackered to care.

I woke early and lay thinking about the effort needed to move the gear. What stressed me was the need to make a depot at the water's edge, not usually problematic, but on this occasion it meant putting progressively more and more of our indispensable supplies into harm's way. The sand spit on which I planned to build the depot was threatened by the icebergs we had flown over the previous day. I was acutely aware that, should any of them decide it was time to roll over, a tidal wave would sweep my carefully built pile into the sea before some family smart arse could say: 'I knew that was going to happen.'

This proved not to be just idle paranoia on my part for, about two weeks' later, this did happen to another expedition in exactly this spot.

At 6am I got up, I couldn't stand the anticipation any longer. I knew the day was going to be a killer but this year I had an innovation, a secret weapon, and I was keen to see if it was going to work. The device consisted of the lid from our small crate, the boat hook, the ice chisel, and two launch wheels from the boat all tied together into a rude conveyance by two metal ties. It may sound a bit Heath Robinson but it actually performed brilliantly as a hand cart, even when loaded with 100kg of fuel. In particular, its balloon tyres prevented it sinking into the 600 yards of mud that separated me from the sand spit. Nonetheless, it took 12 hours of stoically plodding back and forth across tundra, mud and tidal pools until all the items were moved from the drop off point to the sand spit. Meanwhile, Andrea sorted the loads and the children did what children do at the sea side.

It rained gently on and off most of the day, but I can't say I really noticed. By the time I got to load 16 I wouldn't have noticed a blizzard. This was just as well since the weather was deteriorating and we still had to get under way. By 7pm all goods and chattels were embarked and we put to sea with our six-foot, No. 2 inflatable, overloaded with fuel, in tow. This second innovation was not successful in the choppy waters, and had to be abandoned, its contents brought on board after only half a mile. The incident, though trivial, stressed our patience. We pressed on as the weather continued to deteriorate, constantly casting about for anywhere that might afford a campsite and shelter for the boat. Eventually, about midnight, we found a well-protected bay by which time everyone had had enough.

Day two was spent recovering. After that we began to explore the region in a more relaxed fashion. Leaving a depot of half our food and fuel, we set off to circumnavigate Milne Land. This large island is roughly triangular in shape, measuring about 40 miles on each side. Off the north-east corner lie the Bear Islands, a string of small islands inhabited by birds and seals and perhaps polar bears, although they eluded us. We explored these isles until the weather improved and then set off into Island Fjord.

Island Fjord brings new meaning to the word spectacular. Both shores are iron-bound for 40 miles with cliffs of mountainous proportions rising up to 5000ft on the southern shore, and 7000ft to the north. The only breaks in this vertical rockscape are created by unscaleable glaciers plunging from the icy plateaux above.

That evening we enjoyed a clear sky and mirror calm water for which we were very grateful, as fierce katabatic winds can blast down from the inland ice and, funnelled by the cliffs, build heavy seas over the fjord's 40-mile reach. The evening sun was low, making the water sparkle as we planed over its glassy surface weaving easily between well-spaced 'flows'. The huge scale of the great precipices was difficult to grasp. Immense sheets of rock facing seawards and tower after rocky tower marching inland. The snail's pace at which we seemed to crawl along their base belied the fact that we were bettering 15 knots over the water. There was more unclimbed rock here than you could shake a stick at.

For 20 miles we hugged the southern shore without seeing a single landing spot. Then we tried the northern side to see if we might fare better there. Finally, after another 10 miles, we rounded a slabby buttress to discover a tiny bay. The bay was bounded on the west by a grassy promontory. A 200ft scramble up scree brought us to a fine, elevated camping spot with commanding views up and down the fjord. The broad summit gave us plenty of space to spread out. Leif lit a small tundra fire and we sat round preparing our meal and watched the colours of the water, ice and rock change in the evening sun. In the Arctic calm the silence of the wilderness brought peace.

It was a fine night and around midnight we turned in without bothering to put up the tent. Around 5am I awoke feeling distinctly chilly. A blanket of fog hung over us, soaking the surface of the ground and our sleeping bags. I pulled the wet fabric around my head, shut my eyes and hoped it would not rain. Thankfully it didn't, and around 8am a pale sun burned its way through; by the time everybody was ready to rise all was dry.

Without a full Yosemite rock rack the scope for land-based exploration was limited. However, behind the camp an easy looking gully split the lowest rock buttress and seemed to lead to an extensive terrace at about 1000ft I thought a short excursion to the terrace would be good for the constitution and provide some worthwhile views. Orea, regarding those who enjoy unnecessary exercise as terminally afflicted, declined my invitation to explore the gully. Leif was enthusiastic at first but retreated as soon as the ground got steeper.

Andrea and I pressed on however. In retrospect, youth showed the better judgment. All that can be said about my own was that, despite 25 years' mountaineering in distant lands, I seemed to have learned very little about the deceptiveness of easy gullies. Inevitably we kept climbing upwards, unroped for we had none, thinking each minor obstacle would be the last. It wasn't long before we had accumulated enough of these obstacles for the exposure to be no longer minor.

At some indeterminate point the adrenaline began to flow freely, the ground got steeper and looser, and the ledge simultaneously more desirable and more inaccessible. Only a little higher and I got myself into a real nervous sweat, trying to bridge an open corner that proved increasingly difficult. I had to down-climb and bypass it on a pile of shifting blocks. We were by now totally committed and only a further half an hour of careful movement and high concentration got us to the top without causing a major avalanche or other disaster.

Hauling out onto the terrace, Andrea and I immediately agreed that it had been one of life's least pleasant experiences, and one we were not going to repeat under any circumstances. I remembered a number of grassy rakes that cut down across the buttress and I was pretty sure that one would provide a saner descent. If not, the glacier which passed the end of the terrace certainly would. In any event nothing was going to persuade us to try down-climbing the gully.

For half an hour we explored the terrace and took in the magnificent views. We could see Orea and Leif 1000ft below sitting on the ground sheet playing cards. Our boat looked tiny lying at anchor in the little bay. The scenery and isolation of the place was inspiring, but we had already been away longer than I had expected and I would be more comfortable when we had found a safe way down to *terra firma*.

The first choice was to check out the possibility of a descent onto the glacier since this seemed likely to be the quickest route. A closer inspection soon dispersed that theory. It would be quite unattainable without an abseil, and it was so crevassed that it represented a very suspect method of salvation.

I remained confident about the grassy rakes but the trick would be to identify a viable one from above.

After a couple of false trails I found what looked likely to be a major line running down across the cliff. The angle was a bit steeper than I had hoped for, but I set off down with a determined air. Andrea followed without comment. After about 200ft. the rake petered out. The slabs above and below were now steeper still. However, I managed to down-climb a small rock step to reach another, narrower rake. Andrea followed without enthusiasm. It began to rain.

This new rake fizzled out pretty quickly, merging into the cliff face. Moving out onto the face I found myself hand traversing unroped across a huge expanse of rock. I was 500ft off the deck and the holds seemed to be getting smaller and wetter. I paused and looked down at the camp but the kids had disappeared under the ground sheet out of the rain. This level of fear hadn't been in the morning's game plan, and it was again getting out of hand. One slip and the team would have to appoint a new skipper from their midst to navigate back to Constable Point. Barely in control I struggled back to the ledge where Andrea stood with a stressed look on her face. Without discussion we retreated back up the rakes, both concentrating intensely to avoid slipping on the now wet grass. Half an hour later we were back on the terrace having used up almost as much adrenaline as in the gully.

There was nothing for it now but to return to that hellish place. We both knew it, so we didn't waste any time wringing our hands over the matter. Moving close together to reduce the momentum of rocks we might disturb onto the other, we entered the gully again in defiance of our so recent promise. Never again, that eternal but unspoken thought, as we moved slowly down, taking incredible care with each step, every muscle taut, silently cursing any rock that shifted. Going down was more difficult than climbing up but we were psyched up to succeed. The prospect of the kids having to fend for themselves in this lonely Arctic fjord 100 miles from anywhere added all the incentive we needed to ensure no mistakes.

An hour later we exited the gully, relief exuding from every pore. Back at camp we rightly got an earful of abuse from the kids for being away so long. We apologised profusely, but felt too embarrassed and guilty to explain the reasons. They firmly believed we were just having fun.

DECISIONS, DECISIONS

By John Peden

'THERE'S A lot of snow coming down here,' said Anthony. 'Aye, and going back up again!' I replied as another blast funnelled up the gully. 'I hope this stuff is well stuck down,' he said, 'Hmm,' I replied, my eye slightly off the ball. I was tired you see. Five months of inactivity, at least in terms of going up hills, had taken its toll and I was content now to plod up in his footsteps.

Wednesday had been a super day, all blue skies and autumn richness. Cruachan, my shining hope, was resplendent in early November snow as I gazed out of the office window. It had been a fairly relentless spell, balancing the demands of a new business and new family. Funnily enough, Mandy and I had just been talking about it the previous day. 'You should give Anthony a ring,' she said, 'See if he fancies a day on the hill.' Why not, I thought, as I realised I had no inescapable commitments for the morrow. 'Why not,' said Anthony 30 seconds later. 'Aonach Mor's supposed to give good early-season sport.' However, it transpired that the Nevis Range had, with impeccable timing, closed the gondola in order to send essential bits back to Austria for repair. So we decided to see what Glencoe had to offer. The forecast that evening was for a wee depression to whip through on the strengthening airflow, bringing some overnight rain falling as snow higher up, and clearing back to showers by lunchtime.

Thursday dawned cold, wet and blustery. Just as I was about to set off Anthony phoned from the north. 'Er, running a bit late here, and there's two inches of slush on the road, so it will be nearer 10 before I get there. 'OK,' I replied. 'I'll meet you in Nevisport and we'll see what the day's doing.'

It was still raining as we sipped our coffee and chatted, having not seen each other for months. Then blue sky appeared and we felt a stirring. There followed a sedate procession behind a straggling RV all the way to Ballachulish, which ensured that it was 11.30 before we stood at Achnambeithach, gazing hillward. The rising cloud base revealed a new snowline just clipping the top of Aonach Dubh and no particular evidence of ice higher up. This together with an arrangement to take children to the fireworks display in Oban that evening, convinced us it was not a day for ropes and gear. 'An ideal day for a quick burn up the hill,' said Anthony. 'OK, but let's take both tools just in case we find a wee patch of ice to play on.' (It did not occur to either of us to take helmets as a logical sequitur to this decision.) Thus equipped we set off up the path to Coire nam Beith, with Bidean in mind. 'And maybe Stob Coire nan Lochan if we're going well.' I added, ever the optimist.

Well, of course, I wasn't going at all well, despite setting the early pace, and by the time we got above the waterfall I could appreciate the full horror of my unfitness. Still, it was good to be on the hill again. I dug in and trailed after Anthony, now ploughing a furrow through the new snow towards the upper corrie.

By now the day was much fresher, with squally showers of hail driving through on the north-westerly wind. I breasted the rise below Diamond Buttress to find Anthony parked in the uncertain lee of a smallish boulder. I collapsed thankfully in the snow beside him, badly in need of some fuel, and took out my pieces. After the usual exchange of unpleasantries the conversation drifted inevitably towards the Plan. The buttresses had a respectable covering, and indeed there had been some ice low on Stob Corrie nan Beith. Already there was not too much of the day remaining, The shortest route to the top was of course Central Gully, for the squat shape of Collie's Pinnacle sat directly above us. But which side to choose? The normally banked-out right branch (or should that be root?) showed a fair amount of bare and rather steep rock, promising some interest. However, the slightly nearer left side could be inspected at closer quarters and abandoned without loss of height should it look too awkward. Three or four large chockstones filled the middle section, but there appeared to be a line of snowy ramps zig-zagging through them.

Closer inspection did not discourage us, so I led up the short snow slope to a comfy wee cave below the first obstacle, there to don our crampons. It did not occur to me to test this snow for lurking menace, but Anthony later confirmed that he had dug a pit and had been reassured by finding new snow lying directly on the scree.

I started up the left-hand side of the chockstone while Anthony tackled the other; as there was little to choose between them for difficulty. I was pleasantly surprised to find good ice for the critical first few moves and was up in no time, suddenly feeling good.

Anthony was still working away while I moved up the 30ft or so to the foot of the next pair of blocks, wedged side by side. The snow was now deeper but, in retrospect, had a hint of bite at depth. Now that I could see it close to, the snowy ramp up the right-hand inclined block looked uninviting; steep unconsolidated snow on an apparently smooth rock substrata. However, the more broken rock of Collie's Pinnacle to our right seemed to offer sufficient purchase to get us up the bulge, beyond which the gully opened up to join the right-hand branch.

A squall had crept up behind us and there was soft hail flying around. For other reasons too I was disinclined to hang around. I was increasingly aware of the pressure of time and I was also still a bit cold from our lunch stop despite having a fleece and shell jacket on over my new Buffalo shirt, on its first Scottish winter hill trial! I barged unscientifically up the cruddy old snow below the inclined block to gain a small rock platform against the pinnacle, without consciously registering the snow's age.

Anthony was moving up the middle snowfield as I started to attack the final bulge. It was only two or three moves but much more awkward than I had expected. An out-of-balance hook on the right, a high, sloping rock hold for the left crampon; nothing of substance for the left foot on the lip of the chockstone; thrutch up, right tool now at hip level, tiny crampon hold below it; then a sort of left knee – right shoulder jam until both tools could be scrabbled into some sort of placements above the boulder to allow a step up, with some satisfaction, on to an unmistakably (in hindsight) two-layer snow pack.

From his position 10ft below Anthony announced that he didn't much fancy it. I couldn't blame him, and quickly scrolled through the alternatives. They were surprisingly many despite our lack of a rope, but most were uninviting. 'Go for it Anthony,' I said encouragingly, 'it's only a couple of moves and there are good placements.' I justified this embellishment of the truth on the grounds that a positive attitude is important on such occasions. Anthony was persuaded and set about it with renewed energy. He didn't like the initial out-of-balance hook and spent some time looking for my good placements in the groove itself. I kept up a running commentary while he devised an alternative sequence, and I was mighty relieved when he landed beside me in a flurry of oaths and snow.

It was now past two in the afternoon. We had to be back at the road by 5pm so we needed to get a move on. Still, with the difficulties seemingly over and only three or four hundred feet of interesting scenery to negotiate before reaching the summit of Bidean, there did not appear to be a problem. Anthony moved up and round the corner into the main gully, then broke trail for 50ft or so to the foot of some iced-up slabby rocks. The weather was now making things unpleasant as I forged on up the rocks to the snow above, where Anthony took over again.

It was here that the opening exchange took place. What prompted Anthony to question the snow's adhesion at that moment I do not know. On reflection I was by then already thinking at a low level of consciousness about getting over to the edge of the gully. It didn't matter – two steps farther on the surface layer of windslab triggered.

Perhaps there was some sub-sonic precursor, or maybe it was the same cerebral tape-slippage that is said to cause déjà-vu, but I seemed to be aware of the movement long before the cracks appeared. I could see the crown wall just above Anthony, who was now in rapid motion trying to get above it. In the short space between him and me the slab was breaking up into blocks which were piling down on top of me. Already off balance, I cast right and left for the nearest safety and made an ineffectual lunge to try to lodge a pick into something solid. Then I was tumbling.

There wasn't a lot of snow travelling with me when I reached to the top of the rocks. It all happened very quickly I'm sure, but such is the speed of the CPU (brain) on turbo that there was time for an amazing amount of conscious thought. Firstly, I was keen to avoid the vagus response to snow hitting the back of the throat. This can cause layngo spasm and eventual suffocation, so I was trying hard to tuck my head inside my jacket. Then as I approached the rocks I thought: 'Sod it, I haven't got a helmet on.' I took slight comfort from having a woolly bunnet under my Buffalo hood which together might provide some padding, but made a conscious decision to protect my head with my arms. In retrospect this was perhaps rash as I still had two sharp tools in my hands. It also conflicted with the requirements of my next conscious thought, remembering that you are supposed to flap around to try and stay on top of the snow.

To my surprise there was no feeling of terror, just the same gentle resignation to the inevitable, whatever that should turn out to be. I have felt this before, at a moment of acceptance that I no longer had any influence over the trajectory of my car: 'Oh well, here we go. I wonder how this is going to turn out.' I have no memory of my foot being wrenched sideways, shattering and dislocating the ankle, only of being buffeted in the face by icy snow as I bounced down the rocks. Presumably, my crampon lodged in a crack, momentarily immobilising my foot while my body continued to rotate.

At this point I must have lost my presence of mind, for I am ashamed to report that I made no conscious effort to brake once I reached the snow below the rocks. But the Reaper was evidently away on other business that day, for somehow I did stop, in an upright position level with the top of the left branch.

My first thought after the pleasant realisation that I was capable of such (ergo sum) was to move rapidly sideways to get out of the way of anything else coming down. Three or four paces were sufficient to alert me to the fact that all was not well. My right foot seemed curiously floppy and a glance down confirmed that it was pointing east instead of north. I swore emphatically and decided against further movement until I could appraise the situation. The next thought was: 'Oh God, what's happened to Anthony?' I felt sure he was still above me but feared he might have been less lucky than I and be lying unconscious, or worse, out of sight at the foot of the rocks. This worried me a lot for I knew I would have trouble reaching help alone. In particular, I did not know the height or steepness of the rocks which lay between me and the corrie. My fears grew as time passed with no sign of Anthony. I had just begun to consult the pages of *Touching the Void* for inspiration when I saw him moving carefully down towards me and a great wave of emotion washed over me.

The analgesic power of adrenaline is remarkable, but at this point I started to become aware of pain for the first time.

Anthony reached me and took in the news. There was little need for discussion about what needed to be done and he helped me move to a little wind scoop below a projecting rock just above us on the right. The pain of movement was excruciating, but once settled on my little ledge things improved. After arranging a goodie bag and headtorch within reach I sat on my rucksack while Anthony wrapped his space blanket round my legs. That nipped a bit. Then I was reasonably comfortable with my feet dangling over the side.

I persuaded a reluctant Anthony to take a photograph of me sitting on my ledge making what I thought was a fair approximation to a grin. He was understandably anxious to get down to the glen fairly smartly as it was now after 3.30pm. My final injunction to him was to be sure to tell Mandy to take the kids to the firework display, then he disappeared off down the gully. It was disheartening to see him reappear a while later having failed to find a satisfactory route down the lower rocks, but I felt happier than ever that I had stopped where I did. A brief inspection of our ascent route convinced Anthony that he did not fancy that prospect either, then he set off once more, this time up the gully towards the summit of Bidean.

From then on life had an episodic quality as I strove to close down all parts of my brain which were either unnecessary or positively unhelpful towards the business of survival. I was impressed by the effectiveness of mind games in this process, but glad there was no-one around to hear the one hundreth awful rendition of *The Balaena,* and the other songs of my limited repertoire. To my surprise time seemed to pass quite quickly, punctuated by highs and lows. The frequent heavy hail showers blasting into the gully were unpleasant but there was a gibbous moon shining through the cloud so it was never especially dark. During a brief clearing I saw Anthony's headtorch as he turned the corner at the foot of Coire nam Beith and knew that no ill had befallen him on the hill.

Remarkably soon afterwards, I caught a glimpse of two headtorches racing each other upwards and took comfort from their acknowledgement of my signal letting them know I had seen them. Hearing the helicopter down in the corrie and seeing its floodlights dimly through the mist were a big boost. Hearing it heading back down to the glen was corresponding disappointment. Noises off, at the foot of the gully: Hooray! Then it all went quiet: Boo! Voices again, in the left branch this time, then torches flashing. 'Over here boys, good to see you!'

Soon strong substances were coursing through me and I started taking an interest in the proceedings again. Fortuitously, the cloud lifted at this point and moonlight flooded over the flank of Stob Coire nam Beith facing us. The team recalled the helicopter, a Navy Sea King from Prestwick, and moved me down the gully on their stretcher to a point above the rocks where the helicopter could get close enough to pull me out.

I am so glad I was in a fit enough state to fully appreciate the drama and excitement of a helicopter evacuation from high on a Scottish mountain late on a winter night. The sight and feel of the huge black machine hovering motionless in the gusting wind just above the hoary walls of the gully; the winchman spinning down through the floodlit snow blowing around in the downdraught; the incessant noise and the heady smell of burned fuel. All this combined to make it a breathtaking and sensuous spectacle. And there was me with a walk-on part too! Thank you to all concerned for a superbly executed rescue.

Incidentally the Buffalo shirt passed its test. The staff at the Belford Hospital were surprised to find that I wasn't even slightly hypothermic, even after eight hours of sitting around.

While reflecting on these events I am astonished by the large number of minor circumstances and concomitant decisions, in the preceding 24 hours alone, which had a bearing on the way in which things developed. Also I find it difficult even now to separate out fully those elements of luck and judgment, both good and bad, which influenced the final outcome.

During my subsequent incarcerations in hospital I have been surprised and a little dismayed by the automatic assumption of many of my visitors from outwith our community that this incident naturally marks the end of my climbing career. This unsavoury proposition is invariably presented with a veneer of kindly solicitude but is clearly prompted by feelings varying between incomprehension of why an apparently intelligent adult should willingly seek out danger, and disapproval of such irresponsibility to his family. Of course, neither my family nor my climbing visitors have ventured any such absurd thoughts.

I have, though, been brought face to face fairly sharply with the reality of what we all court, whether consciously or not.

At first sight it may seem illogical, in evolutionary terms at least, that we choose an activity which invokes mortal peril for purposes of recreation. This lifestyle of ours is far more irrational, however. For as we all know, and as others manifestly cannot comprehend, exposure to risk in spiritually uplifting surroundings, and the achievement of a satisfactory outcome in its presence, have a life-enhancing quality that transcends the potential for unpleasant consequences should things go wrong. A risk-free existence is no more desirable than it is attainable. Perhaps those who would push society in this direction are after all doing our species an evolutionary disservice.

The last word must go to my surgeon at the Raigmore Hospital, who has reconstructed a number of climbers in his time: 'I know you guys – mountaineering is non-negotiable.'

ON SEEING THE CUILLIN FROM THE CAIRNGORMS – AGAIN

By Grant Hutchison and Jonathan de Ferranti

CAN ANY part of the Cuillin Ridge be seen from the Cairngorm massif? This is a question that has surely fuelled many a late-night discussion, as well as several spontaneous arguments around various Cairngorm cairns. There is no doubt that the Cuillin are potentially visible from the Cairngorms – from Ben Macdui to Sgurr Alasdair is a distance of 155km; the sea-level horizon, seen from the summit of Ben Macdui, is around 140km away; therefore all but the lowest few metres of the Cuillin ridge are above Macdui's horizon. *Quod erat demonstrandum,* were it not for the nearer summits that stick up inconveniently in the foreground. The Cairngorm massif is high enough to offer a view over the Monadh Liath but, farther away, the peaks around Glen Shiel clutter the Skye-ward view. Glen Shiel itself, fortuitously aligned with the line of sight, provides the only potential window in that barrier.

So the opening question can be restated as: What, if anything, can be glimpsed through the Glen Shiel gap?

In 1956, in this journal, Guy Barlow described his efforts to answer that question [1]. The main topic of his article was the view from Cairn Toul. (He had previously established that no part of the Cuillin was visible from Macdui, and had therefore moved a little southwards in an attempt to open up the visual notch formed by Glen Shiel.) Here is how he approached the problem. First of all, he plotted the line of sight between Cairn Toul and Sgurr na Banachdich on an inch-to-the-mile map, using spherical trigonometry to calculate the latitude and longitude at several positions along the great circle arc connecting the two peaks. Then, he sketched profiles of the glen at various points along this line of sight, ranging westwards from Sgurr an Fhuarail to The Saddle. The profiles were constructed for a restricted range of altitudes (2000ft to 3000ft), because the curve of the glen serves to obscure the lower slopes, making them irrelevant to the line of sight. He also prepared a profile of the Cuillin, using maps and photographs.

With these profiles in hand, he now had to superimpose them so as to reproduce the actual view seen from Cairn Toul. This needed an adjustment of relative heights to simulate the effects of Earth curvature and atmospheric refraction. For refraction, Barlow referred to a 1935 article by James A. Parker [2], who cited the 13th edition of W. J. Macquorn Rankine's *Manual of Civil Engineering,* published in 1880. In essence, the argument concerning refraction goes like this. Light rays travel along slightly curved paths within the atmosphere. This curvature makes the rays follow, to some extent, the curvature of the Earth. Because of this, we can effectively see a little beyond the simple, geometrical horizon – it is as if the Earth's surface curved slightly less than it actually does. Macquorn Rankine calculated that the effect of refraction was to reduce the apparent curvature of the Earth's surface by a sixth – equivalent to increasing its diameter by 20%.

Barlow used the above reasoning, together with a slightly inaccurate figure for the radius of the Earth, to arrive at an apparent Earth radius of 4748 miles (7641km). From this, he calculated how the Earth's surface would appear to curve between Cairn Toul and Sgurr na Banachdich. In effect, he treated sea level as if it bulged upwards along the line of sight, forming an arc that reached a maximum *height* of 1265ft (386m) at a point midway between the two peaks (Fig. 1). He then calculated the vertical displacement necessary to make the bases of his Glen Shiel profiles lie along this sea-level arc, so that they were aligned in a way that simulated the curvature of the Earth.

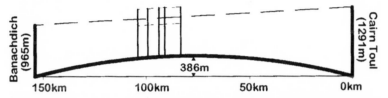

Fig. 1. Barlow's construction of the line of sight between Cairn Toul and Sgurr na Banachdich (vertical scale greatly exaggerated). His five profiles of Glen Shiel were taken in the positions marked by the five vertical lines. The 2000ft and 3000ft contours are shown as dashed lines connecting the profiles.

A quick look at Fig. 1 suggests a possible source of error in Barlow's calculations: the vertical direction at Cairn Toul is shown as being parallel to the vertical at Sgurr na Banachdich. In reality, both verticals point towards the centre of the Earth, and so they diverge slightly from each other. The Cuillin Ridge, in fact, leans slightly away from Cairn Toul, and this has an effect on its apparent height. But the exaggeration of vertical scale in Fig. 1 makes the problem appear much worse than it actually is. The angle between local verticals in Skye and the Cairngorms is 1.4°, and the resulting error in apparent heights is less than one part in 3000 – comparable to the error introduced by using heights rounded to the nearest foot, and therefore negligible in this context. Barlow built a wood and paper model based on Figure 1, but felt that errors would inevitably arise – the thing could not be guaranteed to maintain the precise shape intended for it. So he did some perspective calculations and produced a pen-and-ink drawing of all his profiles superimposed on a single sheet of paper. This turned out to agree perfectly with the view generated by his model.

His profiles are shown in Fig. 2 (reproduced from the original article). They have been combined without correction for Earth curvature or perspective – this is the view that would be seen on a flat Earth, by an observer at an infinite distance (and presumably possessed of infinitely acute eyesight). In Figure 3 (also from the original article), the profiles have been adjusted for perspective, and have been displaced vertically to reproduce Earth curvature and atmospheric refraction.

Barlow wrote: 'All that can be seen of the Cuillin is the north summit of Sgurr a'Ghreadaidh, with a narrow shaving of its northern ridge extending down to the Eag Dubh…' He goes on: 'If we now move northward to Ben Macdui the Glen Shiel gap, contracting and rising, shifts southwards along the Cuillin. On the left in Fig. 3 is shown the gap as it appears from Ben Macdui. The lowest point is now 3220ft, hence the Cuillin is hidden.' Moving in the other direction, he speculates: '…if we go a little south of

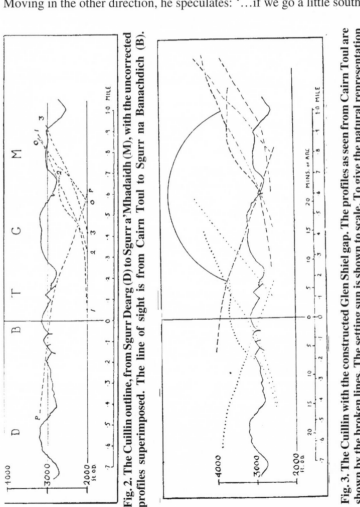

Fig. 2. The Cuillin outline, from Sgurr Dearg (D) to Sgurr a'Mhadaidh (M), with the uncorrected profiles superimposed. The line of sight is from Cairn Toul to Sgurr na Banachdich (B).

Fig. 3. The Cuillin with the constructed Glen Shiel gap. The profiles as seen from Cairn Toul are shown by the broken lines. The setting sun is shown to scale. To give the natural representation this diagram would need to be viewed at a distance of 21ft.

the Cairn Toul cairn, 150yds perhaps, we should get a glimpse of the south-west peak of Sgurr a'Mhadaidh.'

A 40-year-old glimpse of the Cuillin, afforded by nothing more than pen, paper, ruler and trigonometrical tables.

But a lot has changed since Barlow's day. We have pocket calculators to perform our trigonometry, and personal computers to produce our graphics. The Ordnance Survey provides algorithms that allow direct conversion between spherical and grid co-ordinates [3], so that great circles have become rather easier to plot on OS maps. And maps themselves have entered the digital domain. For $50, the US Geological Survey will send you five CD-ROMs containing land-surface elevation data for the whole Earth, at one-kilometre resolution [4]. The USGS also provides Digital Elevation Mapping at 30m horizontal resolution for the whole of the US, and similar products are available for many other countries [5]. In the UK, the Ordnance Survey produces a large variety of computer mapping products, including digital elevation maps and vectorised contour models [6]. These data are more for rent than for sale – you'll pay an initial purchase price, and then an additional yearly retainer.

So we can perform Barlow's calculations without ever having to lift a pencil, unfold a map, or pick up a ruler. In fact, the general problem of reconstructing the view from any point in the UK can now be addressed. One of us (JdeF) uses computer technology to do just this – creating 360° colour-coded panoramas which are commercially distributed under the name Viewfinder [7]. For this article, a Viewfinder panorama from Cairn Toul was generated, and compared with Barlow's original work. The starting point for any Viewfinder panorama is a set of vectorised contour data based on the Ordnance Survey 1:50000 map series. The contour interval is 10m, and data points are spaced at 50m horizontal intervals. This gives the computer a three-dimensional model of the landscape surrounding the chosen viewpoint, but the terrain is flat – there is no allowance for Earth curvature. To introduce curvature to the model, the computer program performs a manoeuvre analogous to Barlow's – it displaces the terrain downwards by an amount proportional to the square of the distance from the viewpoint. This doesn't generate the precise spherical surface that Barlow used for his calculations – it produces a parabolic shape that very closely approximates a sphere over the relevant distances. At 150km, the difference between the parabolic and true spherical surfaces is of the order of a metre – considerably less than the contour interval used. (This technique of choosing an acceptable approximation will crop up again. Remember that Barlow was examining a single line of sight, and therefore had a small number of calculations to perform, which he was able to do very accurately; in contrast, the Viewfinder model is performing millions of calculations across the whole field of view. So, even with the benefit of computer speeds, rapid calculation is essential.) The specific case of

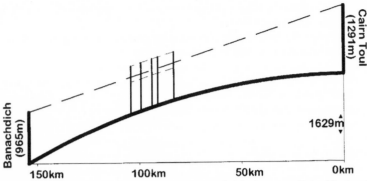

Fig. 4. The Viewfinder construction of the line of sight between Cairn Toul and Sgurr na Banachdich, for comparison with Figure 1. The position of Barlow's profiles is again indicated.

Barlow's line of sight is shown in Fig. 4. Geometrically, it is very similar to Fig. 1, although the small errors in depicting the local vertical are once again emphasised because of the exaggerated vertical scale.

After suitably arranging the terrain, the Viewfinder program sends out imaginary lines of sight across the curved computer landscape, extending each line until it either strikes the Earth's surface or disappears off into the void. Each piece of terrain is then colour-coded according to its distance from the viewpoint. By repeating this process over and over, an image of the surrounding landscape is assembled. Again, an acceptable approximation must be used to speed calculation. Spherical trigonometry is complicated, and the Ordnance Survey's algorithm to convert grid co-ordinates to latitude and longitude is tedious, even when performed only once. The plotting of a true great circle for every possible line of sight would be extremely time-consuming. Instead, the line of sight is assumed to be a straight line on the OS grid. This deviates a little from the great circle but, for the line from Cairn Toul to Sgurr a'Ghreadaidh, the maximum error is around 35m – less than the horizontal resolution of the computer dataset. So some inaccuracies may occur if a long line of sight crosses very steep ground at its midpoint, but otherwise the error is negligible. This line-of-sight method (called *ray tracing* in the technical jargon) embeds within it all the perspective calculations that Barlow had to carry out separately. The final product is a true perspective view. One final difference between the Barlow and Viewfinder calculations should be mentioned. Barlow increased the apparent radius of the Earth by a factor of 20% to allow for the effects of atmospheric refraction. Viewfinder simulates refraction in the same way, but with the Earth's radius increased by only 14%. The effects of refraction are therefore less potent in the Viewfinder world. This choice was made on the basis of field observation, and comes close to the refraction allowance Parker cites for alpine conditions, based on a paper by

Alfredo Galassini in 1895 [8]. It is clear that refraction conditions will vary from season to season, day to day, and even hour to hour. There is no single *correct* value. Depending on personal bias, some folk will claim that the Viewfinder value is unduly pessimistic, while others will accuse Barlow of wishful thinking when he settled on the higher figure. For the purposes of this paper however, we've used a Viewfinder image based on Barlow's figures – the image reproduced here uses Barlow's more optimistic refraction values, favouring Cuillin visibility.

A *flat earth* view is presented in Fig. 5, to give the relationship of the various mountains. This differs from Barlow's Fig. 2 in that perspective effects have been preserved – the high vantage point of Cairn Toul therefore allows us to glimpse the Cuillin Ridge beyond the summit of The Saddle. Notice, too, at this point, that the summit of Bla Bheinn is almost perfectly aligned with Sgurr a'Ghreadaidh.

In Fig. 6, we present the Viewfinder version of Barlow's calculations. Only Bla Bheinn can be glimpsed through the Glen Shiel gap – the curvature of the Earth has taken Sgurr a'Ghreadaidh out of sight behind it. In retrospect, it seems clear that Bla Bheinn should present a significant

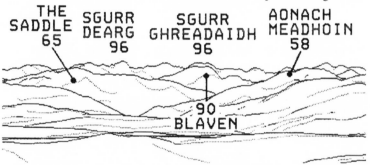

Fig. 5. Viewfinder 'flat earth' view. The 280° bearing (OS grid) is marked. Other numbers indicate the distance in miles to the mountain indicated.

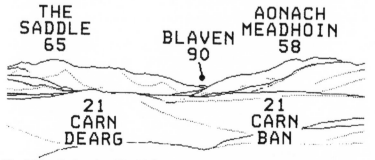

Fig. 6. Viewfinder view. The 280° bearing (OS grid) is marked. Other numbers indicate the distance in miles to the mountain indicated.

problem. From Cairn Toul, the summits of Bla Bheinn and Sgurr a'Ghreadaidh lie on bearings that differ by less than two minutes of arc. The southern summits of the two mountains are separated by a similarly tiny angle. Using Barlow's original construction, it can also be shown that Bla Bheinn, viewed from Cairn Toul, will appear half-a-minute of arc higher than Sgurr a'Ghreadaidh. For refraction to lift Ghreadaidh into view would need an effect equivalent to increasing the Earth's radius by 50% – requiring atmospheric conditions of near-Venusian density! How could Barlow have forgotten about Bla Bheinn? In fact, he didn't. He mentioned it twice, on page 21 of his article. He wrote: 'The true line of sight passes over the south ridge of Blaven,' and, 'Blaven also gives no interference.' His omission arose from the sheer laboriousness of his calculations. He could reasonably deal with only one line of sight, and his paper starts with the assumption that Sgurr na Banachdich is the most likely candidate for visibility from Cairn Toul. So he constructed his great circle between Banachdich and Cairn Toul – and that line of sight does indeed pass over the south ridge of Bla Bheinn, as can be seen in Fig. 5. But Banachdich turns out to be obscured by the slopes of The Saddle, and it became evident to Barlow, once he had made his construction, that Sgurr a'Ghreadaidh was the summit that did align with the Glen Shiel gap. By this time he was presumably rather weary of the whole undertaking, and didn't go back to specifically examine the new line of sight between Cairn Toul and Sgurr a'Ghreadaidh. In contrast, Viewfinder, with its ability to check each line of sight individually, has no difficulty in picking up the Bla Bheinn problem.

So even under conditions of near-perfect visibility and favourable refraction, only a Cuillin outlier is visible from Cairn Toul. Will the arguments now stop? Of course not – so long as there are optimists, and other summits, the Cuillin will always be there, just on the thin edge of perception.

References and notes:

1 On the possibility of seeing the Cuillin from the Cairngorms. Guy Barlow. Scottish Mountaineering Club Journal Vol. 26, No. 147, May 1956, pp 16-24.

2 Curvature and visibility. James A Parker. Scottish Mountaineering Club Journal Vol. 20, No. 119, April 1935, pp 317-324.

3 The ellipsoid and the transverse Mercator projection. Ordnance Survey. Geodetic Information Paper No. 1, 2/1996 (Version 2).

4 USGS. Eros Data Center, Customer Relations, Sioux Falls, SD 57198, US.

5 In the UK: WoolleySoft Ltd. Cluanach, Auchtubhmor, Balquhidder, Lochearnhead FK19 8NZ. In the US: Omni Resources. 1004 South Mebane Street, PO Box 2096, Burlington, NC 27216-2096, US.

6 Contact: Customer Sales, Ordnance Survey, Romsey Road, Southampton SO16 4GU.

7 Jonathan de Ferranti, Lochmill Farm, Newburgh, Fife KY14 6EX.

8 Metodo por lo studio degli orizzonti. Alfredo Galassini.
Bollettino del Club Alpino Italiano Vol. 28, 1895, p 283.

SCOTTISH HILL-NAMES
The Outer Mongolian Connection
By Peter Drummond

WHEN in 1997 the Honorary Editor received the author's article, *Scottish hill-names - the English Connection,* following on the preceding years' *Irish* and *Scandinavian Connections,* he wrote that he looked forward to receiving further in the series including, in the millennium, the Outer Mongolian Connection. He was, I believe, jesting. But...

...the Mongolian (Inner and Outer) words for mountain appear from atlases to be *uul* for a high peak and *nuruu* for a mountain range. (Peoples to the south tend to use *shan,* peoples to the north and west *khrebet). Nuruu* is probably a cousin of the Russian word *nagorye* (the Nagorye Sangilen range crosses the Russian-Mongolian border). And there is an echo of *uul* in the Russian *uval* for hill, and it is probably the root of the Urals range, named when Genghis Khan swept past them into Europe proper. But Mr Khan and his hordes never reached Scotland, and there is no apparent connection to that word. However, *khrebet,* which is used in areas astride the modern Mongolian border (e.g. – Daurskiy Khrebet, less than 200 miles from Ulan Bator), has its ancestral fingerprints on mountains across a wide area, in *khrebet, hreben, greben, grzbiet, grebano, grepon, kreben, kribenn, cryb and crib* – respectively in the languages of Russian, Slovak, Austrian German, Polish, Italian, Swiss French, Breton, Cornish and Welsh. The scene of Victorian Alpinist A. F. Mummery's 1881 triumph on Le Grepon, and the celebrated Welsh ridge of Crib Goch, can easily be picked out from this list. But what about Scotland?

Easier to climb, closer to home, but prophets without much honour in Scotland are the several Crib Laws and Crib Heads in the Lammermuirs and southern Border hills, clearly related through the former Brittonic language to those in Wales. (Crib can also mean a coping stone in Scots). In the Highlands, the Scottish – and Irish – Gaelic word *cnap* for a hill is pronounced in some dialects as crap (krahp, to be polite), and the Gaels' pronunciation of p is very close to standard English sound b: in speech and hearing then, there would appear to be a link to the Welsh and Cornish end of the branch, *cryb* and *crib.* Then there are the Gaelic hill-name elements *gnob and groban,* meaning hillock (sometimes pointed) of which there are several examples west of the Great Glen. A link, then, from the Cairngorms' Cnap a'Chleirich, Speyside's Cruban Mor, and the Fannaichs' Graham called Groban, back to the dry heart of Asia?

It has long been accepted in comparative linguistics that the many tongues of Europe speak with the accent, so to speak, of a common Indo-European heritage – a set of shared root-words from which branch a basic range of concepts [1]. Number-words for example show similarities across a wide range of languages, Indian, Middle Eastern, central Asian and

---

[1] *Cambridge Encyclopaedia of Language,* David Crystal, 1997. p 298 et seq.

European: and important features like rivers and mountains would be similar foundation-words for any people. There is no mystery about the processes at work: as tribes moved across the continent, as migrants or marauders, refugees or conquerors, they took with them a vocabulary which changed when brought within the hearsight of other languages: Scotland's own distinct wordstore – both for hills, and many other things and concepts – has been created from pre-Celtic, Norse, Gaelic and English influences [2], and the same process was at work (and still is) in Europe.

So Europe's common heritage includes hill-names. However, what can unite peoples can also divide them, as I found out in mountain Europe a few years ago...

...Pyrenean mountain huts on the French side are very civilised. No self-catering, because your overnight fee includes the evening meal. It is cooked just as you would expect the French to cook. It is served to tables of eight in tureens, so one person plays mummy and serves the group: in this set-up, conversations with strangers flow easily, swirling past language barriers.

One such evening in July 1991 in the Refuge Baysellance saw further lubrication of international discourse courtesy of the house wine, Cuvee de Refuge (a fine Medoc). I raised the question of what our mountain of tomorrow, the Vignemale, meant, and opened the floodgates of toponymic discourse with a *savant des montagnes* sitting opposite. A fellow mountain-name enthusiast to be quizzed on the local mountains and name-elements – ideal company at a dinner table! So I thought, but I was dimly aware as we talked of the emptying of the benches beside us: Ian, my companion on the tops, shook his head wearily and went outside to watch the Spanish girl scouts splashing under a tap in the evening sunshine (can't imagine why); my interlocutor's son followed suit with much Gallic rolling of eyes, heard-it-all-before ennui. 'The Vignemale...pah' exclaimed my new friend *(en francais, bien sur)* '...typical of the Parisian surveyors, they didn't understand the local patois...'

Shades of the 19th century OS Surveyors in Gaeldom,' I nearly responded, but he was already laying into them: '...they did not understand that *"vigne"* was really *"bigne"* because the letters b, m and v are often transposed here.'

Shades of Gaelic,' I thought, 'where b and m often aspirate to sound v.'

'*Bigne* means simply a mountain, like *pigne in* the old patois, or *pena in* Spain,' he continued.

'*Bigne* – nearly an anagram of bingo,' my synapses crackled. '– and *mal* is bad, so could bigne-mal be the equivalent of our Ben Nevis, a little bit of Gaelic evil that is forever Pyrenean?'

Monsieur had already confirmed this before I had managed to download

---

[2] SMCJs 1996, 1997, 1998, articles by Peter Drummond on the Norse, Irish and English connections respectively.

this thought. 'Ah, ces experts soi-disants parisiens,' he snorted, squeezing the last word through his nasal tubes.

I had scarcely noticed the family of four from the French capital – silent now, tight-lipped, leaving the table as we moved onto other local name-elements – for I was a gold miner coming across a lucky seam. Terms like *hourquette, malh,* and *soum* were explained as little fork, rocky top, rounded summit. Our discussion echoed round the now empty hut. How to lose friends and understand toponymy.

Next day we successfully climbed the *evil mountain* without mishap, traversing the main glacier where, later that month, two Spanish climbers perished in a crevasse (and were reclaimed exactly four years' later by friends returning to commemorate the anniversary [3]. We had followed a Spaniard's tracks across the glacier, one whom we'd met in the hut that morning: he was called Jesus...there into a crevasse went we but for the grace of God... Ben Nevis indeed.

Six years later, again in the Pyrenees, I spent a morning in the library of Bagneres de Luchon pouring over a turn-of-the-century volume [4], on local place-names, and was able to confirm the wisdom of the Baysellance oracle – in the author's childhood, for instance, local shepherds called our mountain the Bigna-Mala or Pigna-Mala; elsewhere in Europe, other local peasants had their *mont maudit* or beinn nibheis And what about Pic de Campbieil, a ten thousander *(trois mille, si vous le voulez err metres)*...could it have Scottish connections, perhaps to a celebrated SMC President (and occasional book reviewer)? After all, Lugless Willie Lithgow was one of the first explorers of the area. Romantic thought yes, but accurate no – the leather volume revealed that it is old French for peak of the old field *(champ vieux).*

Other generic terms for Pyrenean peaks have Gaelic echoes – the Spanish *pena* with *pen* (Welsh and Brittoruc, as in Scotland's Pennygant, Penvalla, and probably the Pentland Hills, and *ceann:* :when Brittonic words appeared in Gaelic they underwent a phonic shift from p to q (written as c) so that, for instance, pen became ceann [5]. The Aragonese word for mountain *mallo* or *malh* relates to *meall* or *maol, the* Catalan *turo* with *torr,* and others besides. Concepts as well as words are mirrored – the Pic des Quatres Termes, a meeting point of four properties, is one more than Carn nan Tri-tighearnan near Inverness: while Pico Royo and Pico Blanco are colour-cousins of the many Carn Deargs and Geal Charns. But there are also strong connections between the terms used for hills in Scotland and high ground elsewhere in Europe, not just in the Pyrenees. Today we equate Celtic cultures with the Atlantic fringes, but the Celtic peoples, in fact, had their origins in central Europe and on the northern fringe of the Alpine region, spreading west into France [6]. We can reasonably expect

3 *The Scotsman,* 26 July 1995.
4 *Les Deformations des Noms de Lieux,* Emile Belloc 1907.
5 For example, see G. Price *The Encyclopaedia of the Languages of Europe* 1998, p.84.
6 *The Celts,* Nora Chadwick, Penguin, 1991.

European connections between Gaelic and other languages' generic elements for hill and mountain names.

1	Gaelic (Sc.)	torr(an)	maol, meall	braigh	monadh
2	Gaelic (Ir.)	tor	maol		
3	Basque				mendi
4	Breton	tour	moal		monid, minez
5	Catalan	turo	malh		
6	Cornish	tor		bre	meneth
7	English	tor	mell		mountain
8	Finnish	tunturi			
9	French	turge, turon	mall, mail	brec, bric	montagne
10	German	turm, turon			
11	Icelandic		muli		
12	Italian	tauro, toro			monte
13	Albanian		mal		
14	Macedonian	taur		vrah, vrh	
15	Polish	turnia			
16	Romanian		mal		munte
17	Russian	tau			
18	Scots	tore		brae	mounth, mount

therefore to find roots for Scottish mountain-names into the Alps, and beyond.

In the above table, I have indicated just a few of the apparent connections between four examples of Gaelic hill-words with others in Europe, from my database of around 700 European words for hill, mountain, summit or similar eminences. (Or as Dr. Johnson would have said, 'considerable protuberances': not a word used by the Glen Shiel Gaels nor their European cousins: but then, he was a city sybarite with no eye or idiom for the hills.) If I were an academic I should probably have entitled this article *Towards an Understanding of...* that cautious hedge against accusations of speculation and worse. I have no doubt that there *is* a connection between many of Europe's hill-name elements. It needs more research time than my day job presently allows, but it is perhaps better to get the view from a few, onto the connections, than to rush to be a compleater. The Hon. Editor will, however be relieved to hear that you can't see the High Atlas from the Pyrenees, and that *The Timbuctu Connection* is not one he will have to proof-read in 2000.

I would like to acknowledge the helpful comments on a first draft of this article by Professor W. F. H. Nicolaisen, Aberdeen University, author of the landmark work *Scottish Place-Names*, 1976.

ONE AUTUMN DAY

By I. H. M. Smart

QUITE unexpectedly I ran into my old friend Quintus Horatius Flaccus. It was one of these sunny mornings you get at the back-end when the air is clear and sharp and the floors of the glens are dusted with the gold leaf on autumnal birch trees and everything else is silver with frost. I had just crossed the Coupall by the stepping stones and was passing in front of Jacksonville on my way to the Buachaille when he emerged from that fabled howff. He left with a cheery: *'Valete, sodales'* [1] to those inside. He was followed by equally civil wishes from the inmates. I could make out:

'I in pace, O Horatio.' [2].

'Bene ambula et redambula.' [3].

'Deos obsecro, ut te nobis conservent et valere nunc et semper patiuntur.' [4].

'Πολυς ταραγμος εν τη τοις θειοις ενι

κ'αν τοις βροτειοις' [5]

Then from someone improvising Julius Caesar's celebrated introductory line,

'Heh, Horace – In Scotia hiemes longae sunt!' [6].

The voices carried quite clearly in the still air. It was all a great credit to the old system of schooling in Scotland.

'I didn't know you were a member of the Creag Dhu,' I said as we saluted each other.

'I've just been made an Honorary Member for my poem on Soracte and some of my more earthy songs which were judged true to reality.'

He spoke English with a pleasant Scots accent with good pure vowels. He did indeed have a slight Glasgow intonation which was not surprising considering the company he had been keeping.

'They are a good lot,' he said nodding towards Jacksonville, 'Remind me of the Thracians in my time. We had a good party last night. I introduced them to the delights of undiluted Falernian wine and we sang songs together in the pentatonic scale. Got a bit racy by the end but we Romans can handle that. The Falernian wine seems to have got the better of them; they're a bit hung-over this morning.'

Quintus Horatius Flaccus, let me remind you, is/was a sturdy man of middle height with a young face and prematurely silvering hair. He was dressed in a sort of hippy kilt, acceptable enough by today's standards.

'So how are things up there in the Elysian Fields,' I inquired companionably. I always feel relaxed in his company.

'I am not going to waste a day like this going into the metaphysics of Paradise with someone who isn't dead yet and therefore has not the conceptual vocabulary to talk about it. Let's just enjoy the here and now.

I can tell you, however, that although Elysium is a very fine place it's not as good as Scotland on a day like this.'

I have always suspected this. It was nice to have my intuition confirmed by someone who really knew for sure.

We climbed to the foot of the Curved Ridge talking about the qualities of different landscapes. I was fascinated by his descriptions of Athens and some amusing stories about Catullus.

At the bottom of Rannoch Wall he said he would really like to do Agag's Groove and the Crowberry Ridge.

'They all say they are classics.'

'They?' I queried.

'Yes, Bill, Hamish, Alec, Tom, George, all the members of your Club I meet up there in Elysium.'

I was understandably silent for a while sorting this one out. I could see him watching me from the corner of his eye. We reached the foot of Agag's.

'I'll lead,' he said gently. 'If I fall off it won't matter since I'm dead already.'

This seemed logical in a surreal sort of way.

He made a good job of it, moving lightly from hold to hold, belaying skilfully. Whoever had taught him the basics had done it well. I did suspect him of cheating once or twice or at least relying on special attributes for he appeared to levitate up the crux.

'I shouldn't like to have done this when I was alive,' he said, 'It would have been more terrifying than at Phillipi. It's surprising how bold and reckless the living can be.'

We crossed over and came down the Curved Ridge. Then we did the Crowberry Ridge in similar style, stopping frequently to admire the view. On the crux he even paused for a few minutes, holding on with one finger and the toe of his sandal while he turned to explain about the seige techniques of his day. They often used pitons and chocks as aids to get up citadel walls, he informed me. When I expressed surprise he said pitons were not new even in his day. Alexander the Great used them. He had heard of spikes being used in Homeric times, probably made of bronze then.

Wooden wedges were used before history began, he opined. After all, a wooden wedge was a trivial thing to make compared to a wooden horse. He recommended to me a smith named Hephaestos, the head of an old-established firm that had a name for making good state-of-the-art pitons.

On the summit we tarried, admiring the view over the vastness of Rannoch Moor.

'They were right,' he said, 'Your range of blues are better than anything we ever had in Italy or Greece; even the Elysian Fields couldn't do better than this.'

We walked back over the moor and reached the Kingshouse as dusk was falling. Maybe half-a-dozen people were sitting around in the lounge. The barman was someone I had never seen before – a genial soul with a beard who wore a colourful robe of superior make with a geometric design in gold round the hem. He looked like a well-to-do hippie left over from the swinging Sixties. Surprisingly, he seemed to know Horace; they greeted each other warmly and chatted away in a strange tongue I eventually recognised as Greek. Some really charming loose-girdled barmaids polished glasses in the background. Things had certainly changed here since my last visit. I assumed the old Kingie had been taken over by some Hellenic entrepreneur, probably the inevitable Rio Stakis.

Horace seemed to confirm my guess when he introduced me to what I thought he said was his 'old friend Rio'.

'Pleased to meet you, Rio', I said.

'No, no my name is Dio – not Rio. Dio – short for Dionysus.'

I did a double-take. They both laughed.

Dio spoke English with a pleasant Hebridean accent. When I remarked on it, he said it was because he came from the Greek equivalent of the Hebrides.

'I come from the fair isle of Chios. It is a sort of Aegean version of Islay except we produce good wine there instead of good whisky. Try some of this. It is the Chian equivalent of Lagavuillin.'

The girls brought us each a silver tassie half-filled with the sea-dark wine. Horace paid with a gold coin he produced from a leather purse. Without pausing in his conversation Dio picked it up, flicked it in the air, caught it then tossed it towards the till some feet away. The drawer opened to receive it and then closed. Quite a trick. Horace gave him a look. 'Don't overdo it,' he muttered.

Horace started topping up the glasses with water.

I tried to stop him. 'Hey, what are you doing?'

'Oh sorry I forgot. Here you drink wine undiluted. I don't advise it. That's why the Dhu were so hung over this morning. Still this is the famed Chian wine. We'll have the next glass undiluted.'

They chatted away amiably about arcane matters I couldn't quite follow. Then I got them on to talking about the mysteries of such well-known mountains as Olympus, Helicon and Parnassus. They told me a lot but first made it clear that it was privileged information and was only to be passed on to people responsible enough to receive it. I tried to keep my end up in the conversation by proposing that the clashing rocks encountered by both Odysseus and the Argonauts were icebergs. [7]

I mentioned that I had some experience of sailing among such things myself. They could easily be interpreted as icy mountains not fixed to the seabed. Phoenician sailors who had been beyond the Pillars of Hercules, I continued, must have picked up the story from the locals and taken it back to the Mediterranean where they became rocks as no-one knew about ice. There was a silence. It was broken by Dio shaking his head sadly and saying: 'Odysseus was an awful liar and Jason was not much better.' By implication I was included among that august company. I felt flattered. This was the first time I had ever been bracketed with larger than life heroes unless, of course, you include my associations with members of our Club, notably with such people as Slesser, Peden and Hay.

'I started to order another round but Hora (I was now using the familiar diminutive form of address) [8] said: 'Tonight is on me. I owe you such a debt of gratitude.'

'You owe *me* a debt of gratitude. Come on. How? Why? It's the other way round surely.'

'I'll maybe explain later,' he said, then turned to the others in the lounge and invited everyone to come over and join him in a glass of Chian wine.

I may say that the conversation in the rest of the room had stopped long ago; the others were watching us from their tables with wide eyes and dropped jaws as they registered wonder, even frank dismay. This was understandable. The crowd I was with were arrestingly picturesque.

And so we all ended up leaning on the bar – us patrons on one side and Dio and his strangely sophisticated barmaids on the other. The wine loosened tongues and the party got a glow on. The barmaids radiated charm. Our personalities and conversational ability expanded and the ambient world seemed brighter. I became involved in a conversation with one of the barmaids. It became fairly deep. She possessed disquieting intellectual and artistic insights. She was quite a lass.

Horace rather fancied one of the girls on our mortal side of the bar. She acted a bit snooty but otherwise was a fair stunner. I was sure I had seen a picture of her on the cover of a climbing glossy, looking lythe and sinuous in a grass-green lycra suit with swirls of yellow accentuating her curves. Horace was fascinated and started to chat her up. After a time she seemed to become more compliant and I recognised his Ode III, xxvi coming out. [9] Fortunately, he declaimed it all in Latin. I was very glad of the absence of Classics from the modern school curriculum otherwise her boyfriend, a formidable looking character from somewhere up in the Grade VIIIs, might have taken offence. Even so he started to close his fist as if he sensed something – particularly at the last couple of lines when Horace put his hands together in the praying position and looked towards the heavens. He really was enjoying himself – Horace that is – not the boyfriend.

All this was interrupted by the phone ringing. Dio answered.

'Yes, I'll tell him.' He turned to Horace,

'That's MacAenas on the phone. He'll pick you up outside right away.'

Horace's face fell. He turned to the crowd saying: 'I must go now. Valete sodales,' then to me: 'Come, see me off.'

We left to the farewells and expressions of regret from the others. At the door I turned to wave goodbye to the mysterious barmaid.

'See you later', she said. She was a disturbing girl, probably had other sides to her character, probably good with the scissors.

'Much later, I hope,' I heard myself saying. She gave an entrancing smile as if to say: 'Don't worry, it may not be all that bad.'

Outside, some kind of vehicle was waiting. Harness clinked in the darkness. It was difficult to make out anything in the shadows.

Horace turned and said: 'Once again can I say how grateful I am to you.'

'Oh come off it. How do you get that idea?'

'If it were not for you, I really would be dead. You and people like you are my monument more enduring than bronze. [10]. If people like you didn't exist neither would I. I would have to spend all my time in Elysium – which is okay but, all things considered, it is not as richly rewarding as being alive and in Scotland. You can't understand yet how good it is to have a day off with congenial living company. The poor souls in Elysium who aren't remembered by you mortals never get a day off. That's why I'm grateful to you, my friend.' He laid his hand on my shoulder and said: 'Before I go I would like to give you this blessing: 'May Providence bestow on you good health, a sound mind, relish for life and an old age that still maintains a stylish grip on the lyric metres. [11]. Or in your case, since you have no sense of rhythm and don't really understand what a lyric metre is, let's say: 'a stylish grip on the handholds of life.'

He embraced me, mounted up beside the driver and the vehicle, whatever it was, passed towards the bridge. A fairly large coin was tossed to a shadowy figure lurking in a gloomy booth I had not noticed before. [12]. The conveyance passed over. As it faded into the darkness the sound of hooves and wheels merged with the noise of the river. I can assure you it was no spooky phantom carriage that bore him away for it left distinct wheel marks in the gravel.

I hope I see him again. I would like to ask him more about the climbing gear Hephaestos used to make; it would be interesting to know if we have re-invented the wheel.

References and notes:

1. 'Farewell comrades.'
2. 'Go in Peace.'
3. 'Fare well and haste ye back.'
4. 'I implore the Gods to preserve you for us and to keep you in health now and always.'
5. ' There is as much confusion in the world of Gods as there is in ours.' This quotation from Euripides was not a bad effort at nine o'clock in the morning from a man with a hang-over.
6. 'In Scotland the winters are long.' The first line of 'Caesar in Britain and Belgium' begins: *'In Gallia hiemes longae sunt'*. This used to be the standard book that every school child had to translate in days of yore when Latin was considered a normal part of the curriculum. Many students never seemed to get much beyond this initial sentence. The speaker was well aware of this. The line was, of course, delivered on this occasion in appropriately flat-toned, dead-pan Glaswegian.

7. It is not impossible that Odysseus reached the Hebrides and even further north into iceberg country during his ten years of haphazard, if not frankly incompetent, navigation. The classical accounts of the narrow, turbulent, rock-infested straights of Scylla and Charybdis, for example, correspond exactly to the description in the Clyde Cruising Club Pilot of the tide race through the *Bealach a' choin glais* – the Narrows of the Grey Dog between Lunga and Scarba. Scylla was of course a dog-headed monster.

8. There is no reference in classical literature to Hora being used as a diminutive for Horatius. I think I heard Dio using it and followed suit. It is declined like *nauta,* a sailor - one of the few masculine nouns of the first declension. The feminine noun 'hora' means an 'hour'. I tried to make a pun of this by coming out with the well-known motto still found on present-day sundials *Horas non numero nisi serenas* – 'I do not count the hours/Horaces unless they are serene.' He looked pained and said, 'You're two thousand years too late with that one. Besides, if I were you I wouldn't experiment with that word with these girls around; you could use it wrongly and offend them; that could be dangerous.'

9. In this delightful ode Horace addresses the Goddess Venus asking her not to involve him and his old bones in yet another affair of the heart - except maybe . . . well, perhaps . . . maybe, just this one more last time. The poem ends something like this:
'Here is my last request, Goddess ruler of the blest . . . whose sublime whip bends proud girls' knees – one last little flick for snooty Chloe, please.'

10. He was referring here to his Ode III, xxx. The one that begins, 'I have made a monument more enduring than bronze...' It continues... 'because of my poems, ...*non omnis moriar...* not all [of me] may die...'

11. He was paraphrasing here from his Ode I, xxxi.

12. The Styx has evidently been bridged and the ferry discontinued. Charon, once a skilled boatman, has been degraded to a booth attendant. The tolls have, of course, been increased; the size of the tossed coin was much bigger than the original obolus of classical times. Evidently even Pluto, originally a grim, unpitying deity, a severe punisher of wrong-doers (whose psychological function in the Classical World was to serve as a metaphor for incorruptible standards) has responded to the mood of our times and in order to receive attention (the food of the Gods) has become a role model for the grasping and vulgar, but see Note 5 .

Towards the ridge, Coire a Ghreadaidh   Jim mitchell

THE CLASSIC SCOTTISH ICE ROUTES
A cautionary tale

By Charlie Orr

STRANGE isn't it how things pop into your head at the most inappropriate times? There I was standing by the graveside of a friend I hadn't seen in 10 years, it was freezing, and a boss of ice had formed from a burst hosepipe. I watched as a rather cold-looking robin tried to take a drink from the last trickles of water still free of the ice and as the minister was incanting his ashes to ashes bit, I'm thinking that if it's like this in Edinburgh, how superb conditions would be on the Ben. Worse than that, as his wife and mother, quietly weeping, are supporting each other in the bitter cold, I'm thinking of an old boss of mine excusing his late and drunken arrival home from a funeral such as this, in the week between Christmas and New Year, by telling his wife that the ground was hard!

I hadn't seen Michael since University days. We had done a bit of climbing together but we lost touch when I went to work in London. Michael loved the hills but he was never really that great a climber, his nerves always got the better of him and my geographical change, coupled with the fact that we had different targets as far as climbing was concerned, all contributed to our losing touch. Even when I moved back to Edinburgh I didn't make a point of tracking him down, it had been so long, nearly 30 years.

Michael had always harboured an ambition to climb Crowberry Gully on the Buachaille in winter, but had accepted that it was a bit out of his league, contenting himself with straight-forward ascents of some of the more accessible Munros when under snow, an increasingly short commodity these days. He had once even done the long walk in from Tyndrum with his eye on that test piece of the pioneers, the Central Gully of Ben Lui, but by the time he reached Cononish Farm he had talked himself out of it, the looming steepness of its north face assuming Eiger-like proportions in his overworked imagination.

Don't get me wrong, Michael was no armchair mountaineer, although, like all of us, he had done his fair share of that. As a teenager in the early Seventies he had read and re-read Murray's *Mountaineering in Scotland,* to the extent that he felt almost like the fourth man on the rope, somewhere between MacAlpine and McKenzie I imagine. He eventually acquired his own copy, realising that he had paid enough in library fines to have bought two. Even now, 30 years on, it lies, well thumbed, atop the pile of magazines in the bog in his Edinburgh flat, although it has to be said that its pre-eminent position nowadays seemed due not so much to its being regularly read as to its prodigious weight, which kept the numerous computer magazines and occasional copy of *Penthouse,* which made up the rest of the pile, in order.

No, Michael had done his bit, rock climbing as a student at Edinburgh University starting on the wall at Meadowbank in the days when a climbing wall consisted of a vertical wall with a few strategically-placed bricks sticking out of it. He didn't kid himself that he was a tiger, far from it, V. Diff was about his limit, and even then he preferred to avoid the business end of the rope. He had even made a guided ascent of the 'Voie Normale' on Mont Blanc, having some vague idea that it would qualify him, in his own eyes, as a real mountaineer. Two hundred quid it had cost him but it still wasn't enough.

It was against this background that the Crowberry Gully on the Buachaille in Glen Coe had assumed an almost mystic significance in his mind, a touchstone, a benchmark if you like, of his abilities as a mountaineer. To say that this was an obsession with Michael would probably be to overstate the case but there were little signs. For instance, how many people have a cat called Crowberry? I also found out from his wife that he even used Crowberry as a password on his computer at work.

Weather – fine, visibility – good, snow – firm, freezing level – 500ft., fitness level – excellent. Christmas morning 2001 and here he was with his new-found partner, Wullie Gates, roping up at the foot of the first pitch. It was amazing, they had left the car at Lagangarbh an hour ago and walked up the path just as he had done so often in days gone by, and now, standing at the bottom of the climb that had occupied so much of his thoughts over the years, he could actually feel the butterflies in the pit of his stomach.

Having made the decision to climb the route, Michael had also decided to lead it, and as he selected two of the new drop-pick SMT™axes, Wullie stood quietly below him roped to an ice screw and a rock peg. Michael made one or two practice stabs with his axes, he had still not quite got the hang of it properly, even although he had spent a good part of the morning practising, and it was with some trepidation that he committed to pulling up on his axes and placing the front points of his Footfangs – no, it was Stubai step-in crampons he had selected, on to a bulge of ice at waist level. 'Climbing' he shouted to Wullie, thinking as he did so that it was as well there was nobody around to hear him.

It was when he didn't turn up for dinner at his mum's as arranged on Boxing Day that the alarm bells started ringing and, being on call that day, I was first on the scene and found the body. He was still wearing the helmet, and at the post-mortem the police surgeon said that he had suffered a series of epileptic fits known medically as *status epilepticus,* the single bruise in the centre of his forehead being caused when he fell forward out of his chair and struck his head on the coffee table. As soon as I saw the CD case lying on the table, *The Classic Scottish Ice Routes on interactive CD – Vol.1,* I knew it would be Crowberry Gully – it just had to be. I had a quick look at the replay, wondering if he had been avalanched, or had simply fallen off, but no, he had climbed it in good style, led the whole thing, so I suppose that was some consolation. It must have been the excitement of getting up it that triggered the fits, or some fault in the VR helmet.

(The Scottish Mountaineering Club, designers of the software, have strenuously denied any liability, citing the warning regarding use by persons suffering from epilepsy included with the packaging of the disc.)

I've no doubt that the ready availability of this new technology will please many in the conservation lobby, as it will relieve pressure on the popular winter venues such as Glen Coe and the Ben, while the 'Angry of Morningside Brigade' who annually rail against the irresponsibility of those who climb in winter in the pages of *The Scotsman* will like it too. But, while accepting the inevitable, there are those who, no matter how good the virtual reality technology is, or how stunning the graphics are, will still take pleasure in actually physically going to the hills, and although a committed convert myself, I feel that we in the mountaineering fraternity should accept the situation as it stands and rely on natural wastage to take care of what is fast becoming the anachronistic pastime of a few dyed-in-the-wool traditionalists.

For those of you who might need persuading, may I suggest *The Nevis Winter Classics.* This is millennium compatible and requires a minimum of 128Mb of RAM and a third generation Pentium processor for maximum effect. 'Point Five' with a dual-shock controller is, I assure you, out of this world!

AXE ADVICE

Clad and armed for frost,
ice warrior, gully raider, snow clown.
I know the skarts and scrapings,
the thrutchings and flailings
that blunt my good edge down.

I impact in a runnel,
hook into cold hope.
Will the ice screw just driven
take the weight of your whim,
test the strength of your rope?

You cannot resist an ice fall
and I too return home scarred,
gripped with effort and boldness.
But I will keep my blue coldness,
and the arctic odour of my adze.

Donald Orr.

A CREDIT TAE US A'

By Robin Shaw

The Ben:

IT WAS February and conditions were great. As George and I trudged up to the flanks of Tower Ridge we saw only one other party on the hill. So you can tell immediately it was in those halcyon days before you could drive from London for a weekend's ice climbing. The previous day we had done a new route to the left of the Italian Climb, and in fear and trembling at the end of a long, unprotected steep runout, I had lost my axe while attempting to lasso a spike of rock. It winged into space propelled by the loop of my rope and 100ft below drew curses from George as it whizzed past. I skittered to a ledge once I'd found the slater's pick in my sack.

Today, we were looking below the climb for the axe. While we hunted the slope we heard and saw climbers on Carn Dearg, and having given up the fruitless search, we went across for a look.

'Join the fun,' a voice shouted. It was Robin with whom I'd climbed quite a bit. We'd met first at an outrageous party and ended the evening in drunken building climbing and explanations to the cops. He was at Edinburgh University, I was at Glasgow, but despite this we got on well.

When we joined Smith at the top of the ramp leading on to the middle of the buttress, he was sitting on a platform with his characteristic grin. He held a rope that inched back and forth as, up above, Dougal Haston was trying to make progress on the corner of Route 2. Dougal returned puffing and we sat around swapping stories and looking at other lines near the one we'd finished the day before.

I was never as comfortable with Dougal as I was with Robin; sometimes in his company, Robin seemed to put on a mantle of toughness that was absent when he was alone. Today however, Dougal was uncharacteristically generous, and suggested I have a go at the route. Probably he had assessed rightly that I wouldn't succeed and after about half an hour during which I failed to reach his high point, I retreated, thankful to be off the steep, verglassed rock. Then Robin tried with no success.

Dougal set off again and this time, once he'd found a safe runner just below the break-out onto the slab, to our astonishment he started to take off his boots. Sure enough, his socks would hold better on the glazed rocks, but we all thought this to be a bit over the tae top. Naturally, we didn't say so; just exchanged glances and chatted away about other possible routes on Tower Ridge where Robin had seen us the previous day. Shouts and curses told us all was not well.

'I've dropped a bloody boot,' screamed Dougal and minutes later, lowered on the runner, he was hirpling around beside us on the ledge while we stifled grins. On the way down to the hut Robin mimicked Dougal's lopsided gait and broke frequently into cackling laughter with which Dougal joined once we'd found the missing boot below the buttress.

Ardgour: Pissing with rain. Lying in a tent below the cliffs of Garbh Bheinn talking philosophy with Robin. Just as well we're philosophical. Water everywhere and the marsh moving below us like one of these American motel beds you put a quarter in to relieve the aches of the day. We're close together, not through some dubious wish to be tactile but due to the drips running down the thin canvas. And there is one feature that would have brought tears to a stoic's eyes. 'You bring the tent and the stove and I'll get the food. We can divvy up after.' And I had trusted him, not even asking what delicacies he had in his pack before we left the road. So here we were with about five teabags, a few Knorr Swiss cubes and a packet of biscuits that I'd had festering in my sack for ages. But, somehow, I could never bring myself to be angry at Robin. It was just the way he was and I should have known. It was my fault, I tried to tell myself.

So, in the morning, with the rain having slowed to a mean drizzle, we squelched our stiff damp underfed bodies to the foot of the Leac Mhor which was living up to Robin's name for it, the Great Leak. No guidebook of course, no idea of where the route went. Well, I ask you, would Mozart carry a guide to the composition of symphonies in his pocket? Up we went, and God knows where, over slimy unprotected slabs and vicious little overhangs. Irrepressible Smith held it all together. With anyone else I would have suggested – No! – insisted, on getting the hell down to the nearest warm pub. The only bit I remember in detail was when we were brought to a stop below a shiny bulge with a holdless slab to its left. Robin managed to fix a sling on a rare spike and swung about 20ft across the dripping slab to lodge in a crack. I surfed over screaming on a tight rope, did a slippy slidy on the next pitch claiming intent and then we were up.

Despite the prospect of a couple of biscuits each for dinner and another day of wet desperation, Robin wanted to stay. But it was my tent and I wasn't playing so we ended up steaming and drinking at the Corran Ferry, a pub which only the preceding deprivations made tolerable. To his credit, after a pint or three, Robin did not hold it against me that I had aborted the great Garbh Bheinn expedition.

Glen Coe:

We're on our way up the long platform running under the North Face of Aonach Dubh. Little clouds of midges lazily gnaw at our calves. It had been a great week, hazy summer days of warm rock and great routes.

Above us, at the far end of the cliff lay unknown rock at the edge of Pleasant Terrace. A great corner blocked by a large overhang beckoned and we were confident. Robin was ahead as we ambled up the ramp under his magnificent line, Yo-Yo. The ramp steepened to a scramble on broken, hold-strewn ledges, easy but exposed. Ahead of me Robin stopped, looking upwards. I waited, lighting a cigarette and looked upwards with him at the possible route in the big corner. He moved up a bit, then down again. Then a few moves up and back to his ledge. Then up again, then down. What was going on?

'Let's get the rope out,' he said. 'Pass me the end and get a belay.'

This must be hard, I thought, nervously stubbing out my fag and uncoiling the rope. Tied on he waltzed upwards without a pause and when I joined him at the top of the simple scramble he was laughing and shaking his head.

'Some chance we have with the real thing,' he said. It was probably the first and last time that Smith had ever roped up for a Moderate!

Two hours' later we still hadn't managed to solve the problem of getting into the corner. A bit like Hangman's on the Buachaille, only the moves to the crack were steeper, and 40ft of wall climbing made a formidable barrier. A rotten rib had to be passed and neither Robin nor I could summon the bottle. As the shadows purpled on the Aonach Eagach, we gave up. We made our way up Pleasant Terrace and soloed the top pitches of Shadboldt's Chimney in the gloaming, tired and happy.

A couple of weeks later I returned with Jimmy and managed to get over the rotten rib and into the corner, whooping in triumph. With increasing confidence and excitement I led out a long pitch up the steep corner. Then at the obvious belay, to my horror I found a sling. Someone had beat us to it and had obviously abseiled off. I looked up in dismay. The next pitch must be even harder. I brought Jimmy up and set off. The climbing was hard but much easier than the preceding pitch. What had happened? Was it the next pitch which seemed to be straight-forward and led to a large ledge? On the ledge, without having had much difficulty, I found another sling. As I looked up it began to dawn on me. Above, a grass curtain reared for about 100ft, dripping and unpleasant. The climb was over and the best way off was by abseil.

When I got home a letter was waiting. Robin had done the climb – the Stook – the previous weekend. I hadn't been available and he apologised for leaving me out. Rather than climb the grassy choss above the corner he'd abseiled. The climb had been enjoyable; perhaps we could give it another go together, he suggested. And there was another good line he'd sussed out. But it was not to be. We only climbed together once more before his death.

Some of my friends found Robin a difficult character; if some of their stories are accurate, he could be insensitive and boorish. For my part, I found him kind, thoughtful, unpompous and modest, and I consider it a privilege to have shared some great times with him.

Paul Allen and Wilson Moir on 'Sandpiper' (HVS 5b), Seana Mheallan, Torridon, Photo: Niall Ritchie.
(Left): Rab Anderson on 'Reaching the Limit' (6c), Sunnyside, Glen Ogle. Photo: Christine Anderson.
Rab Anderson and Dave Cuthbertson on the first ascent of 'Star Wars' (E3 6a), Ardnamurchan. Photo: Christine Anderson.

NEW CLIMBS SECTION

OUTER ISLES

LEWIS, Griomaval, Tealasdale Slabs:

Comes the Breanish – 275m HVS**. R. and C. Anderson. 16th July, 1998.
Start right of Lochlan at the right side of the small overlaps, at the same point as The Scroll – the cairn mentioned in the guidebook was dismantled to stand on to keep the feet dry. A fine direct line.
1. 55m 4c. Step right and climb straight up to the left-trending weakness of The Scroll, then continue straight up on to a quartzy protuberance. Climb a thin crack past a small, narrow wedged block to reach a white slab (Lochlan and The Scroll belay over to the left) and continue straight up passing a block on its right side to belay higher up beneath an overlap at the top of a short, right-facing corner (good wires in a horizontal in the overlap). A superb and generally well protected pitch on perfect rock.
2. 55m 5a. This pitch goes up the middle of the main seepage area and although it can be climbed fairly direct when wet, it would be much better if dry. Step left and pull onto the white, quartzy slab above the overlap, then climb straight to the left end of an overlap with a pointed bit in its middle. Climb the bulge on the left, just left of a thin crack (possibly easier farther right if dry) and continue to a short, overlapped corner. Climb this, or if wet step right and move over a small overlap, onto a smooth white slab. A few thin moves gain a small quartz overlap (gear). Step left, back into the top of the corner, then follow slabs, holds and quartzy seams to a small grass ledge. Gain a grassy, horizontal break and move right to a short, left-facing corner.
3. 55m 4b. Step up right, then go up and follow thin cracks in a quartzy line trending up right, passing over a crackline to reach a more obvious crackline. Climb the crack for a short way to a small ledge just short of the grassy rake of Golden Gully.
4. 55m 5a. Move right along the ledge a little, then climb up and slightly right heading for a twin quartzy crackline in the left side of the headwall. Make tricky moves up the cracks and continue to reach a ledge occupied by some blocks.
5. 55m. Move right, then climb easily to a wide crack and up to the summit cairn.

HARRIS, Sron Ulladale:

The Beautiful South – 75m E7. D. Turnbull, J. Arran. 22nd May, 1998.
Start up a left-trending open groove to the right of Crackhead.
1. 25m 5b. Climb into the groove and continue to a good stance in an alcove beneath a narrow roof beneath blank rock.
2. 20m 6b. Move up right to a flake and hidden PR (very poor). Make bold moves up to the bulge (PR), then move immediately left to a 120° overhanging wall. Climb this with difficulty to easier ground leading to corners above.
3. 30m 5c. Move up and rightwards up blank corners, then back left to join the easy exit ramp.
Note: Climbed ground up in one day; pitch 2 was worked. The Scoop and Stone were also repeated.

LEWIS SEA CLIFFS, Aird Griamanish (Sheet 13, MR 994 213):

D. Collier and J. Hartley note short crags rising straight off the beach near Aird Griamanish with variable rock quality, some of which could give hard routes given

Autumn colours of Cul Mor from Stac Pollaidh. Photo: David Ritchie.

(Left): Stob Coire Sgreamhach, Glen Coe. Photo: Donald Bennet.

Sgurr an Fhidhleir and Ben More Coigach from Stac Pollaidh. Photo: David Ritchie.

time to dry out. One-and-a-half hours' approach walk. One route climbed, Obskua,12m Severe 4a, 28th May 1997, which ascends a thin quartz flake to the left of an overhanging arête.

The Hooded Wall (SMCJ 1998):
Black Edged – 30m VS 4c*. R. and C. Anderson. 11th July, 1998.
A short crack left of Paint it Black leads onto the arête of the fin which is followed to a finish up left.

Pitch Black – 30m E2 6a. R. and C. Anderson. 11th July, 1998.
The flared, left-leaning groove behind the abseil leads awkwardly to Black is Black, up which a finish is made.

Islivig Geo (NB 982 275):
This Geo, due west of Islivig and just north of a cairn on the skyline, is a narrow inlet 150m long and 25m high. Easily reached by walking down into it, the initial section of the Geo is non-tidal. Unfortunately, despite the south-facing wall being sunny, sheltered and appearing to be one continuous wall of good looking rock, it is loose and disappointing, hence the reason why only one route was climbed, another was backed off. For those less discerning and not so worried by looseness there are a number of lines to go at. There are, however, much bigger and more dangerous loose cliffs to climb on, so a trip here is probably not worthwhile.

Disappointment Arête – 25m HVS 4c. R. and C. Anderson. 14th July, 1998.
The first section of wall ends at an arête where the wall steps back and continues out to the end of the geo. Climb the arête on its right side.

Aurora Geo:
Wonder Wall - 30m E4 6a**. D. Etherington (unsec.). May, 1998.
Start from the left-hand end of the ledge at the foot of Newton's Law. Go directly up to a sloping ledge and move right to the right-hand end of an overhang. Make moves up a thin crack to a small quartz band, move back left for 3m and make difficult moves up a thin crack trending rightwards. Strenuous. Pre-placed gear used and graded for that.

The Cioch Wall:
A. N. Other – 20m VS 4c. A. Cunningham, L. Hughes. 10th May, 1998.
Climb the crackline to the right of Anonymous.

Rubh'an Taroin (North Bay):
Less Awkward than the Principle – 30m E3 6a. D. Etherington, G. Reid. May, 1998.
Start in the next bay to the right of Twelve Years On. Climb out of the left-hand side of the bay through a steep roof crack. Follow the crack up and leftwards to the arête just to the right of Twelve Years On. Move up and right into a V-groove, followed directly to the top with great interest.
Note: The route would seem to be the same as Achevalier (SMCJ 1998, p562) but with a different start.

Mungarstadh Area, Geodh an't Slaucain:
Follow the track that leads from the road to Mungarstadh sands, cross the beach and go up the slope on the opposite side. The next bay is Geodh an't Slaucain. On the left side of the geo (facing out) is an obvious fin of rock at MR 0055 3095 which givesthe following.

Morning Star – 25m VS 4b**. K. Archer, A. Norton. 6th August, 1998.
Access is from the north corner of the geo at very low tide in calm conditions or, much more likely, by abseil down the line of the route (back ropes needed). From the undercut base of the fin, pull around the seaward face and climb it just right of the arête. Gain the arête above a niche and follow it.

Rabbit Wall Area (MR 0040 3105 to 0045 3110):

From the Morning Star area follow the edge of Geodh an't Slaucain northwards. In front is a small rise with two small peaks. Go over this and drop down to a level grassy ridge which runs out to sea. This is Rudha Geodh an't Slaucain, with a small stack, Stacca Chais, at the seaward end. Map and photo-diagram provided. At the seaward end, abseil down a corner on the north side. From the abseil (facing in), scramble left to the base of a cracked slab leading to a corner and overhang:

Mercy Killing – 22m E1 5b**. A. Norton, K. Archer. 8th August, 1998.
Follow the cracked slab to the corner (wet) and up this to the overhang. Traverse right and pull up into a worrying-looking crack to finish.

If it's Loose Leveret – 20m V. Diff. A. Norton, K. Archer. 7th August, 1998.
The corner of the slab gives a cautious escape route. Follow the corner, then on to a rib and up easy but loose ground.

Fab's The Word – 20m VS 4c. K. Archer, C. Archer. 12th August, 1998.
Left again 10m is a slabby corner with an overhung cracked rib. Climb up to the rib, then turn it on the right. Follow a groove to small ledges, make an awkward pull on to the upper slab which leads to the top.

Loose Luke – 20m V. Diff. A. Norton, L. Norton. 12th August, 1998.
Follow a slabby blunt arête 3m left again, then step left to finish up the headwall.

Scramble left again and the next two routes can be seen on the impressive series of overhung slabs that form a small geo. Access is by abseil down the arête of the left wall, which gives the line of:

A Poodle Called Maurice – 22m Severe**. K. Archer, A. Norton. 10th August, 1998.
Climb the blocky arête on its right side into a corner that leads to a slab. Follow this, then up the left wall to finish.

The Ecclesall Road – 50m E2***. A. Norton, K. Archer (alt.). 14th August, 1998.
The classic of the crag. Start from a small pedestal 5m up from the start of Poodle.
1. 25m 5a. Descend a ramp on the left wall towards the left corner. Gain this, then follow the back of the second slab to a corner below an overhung groove.
2. 25m 5b. Make difficult moves to gain the arête of the right wall and traverse round the arête into a niche. Traverse rightwards along a break (mediocre protection) to where the break meets easier ground.

NORTH UIST, Leac na Hoe Point (MR 980 725):

Summertime Grooves - 20m Severe 4a*. R. Carter, C. Ravey. 20th April, 1998.
Start 3m right of Spark, climb the wall to a ledge, then continue straight up into a thin crack recess to an overhang which is surmounted at the right-hand side. Continue straight up to the top.

Two Step – 20m VS 4c. C. Ravey, R. Carter. 20th April, 1998.
Start 4m right of Summertime Grooves. Climb the wall to a flake, continue up the

wall to a box groove, then make a difficult move up to a curved crack which is followed to the top.

Weary Teary – 20m V. Diff. R. Crater, C. Ravey. 22nd April, 1998.
Start 6m right of Two Step. Climb a crack to a sloping ledge at 6m. Climb left and up on big holds to the base of a left-slanting crack which is followed to the top on loose holds.

Dolphin Wall – 20m HVS 5a*. R. Carter, C. Ravey. 23rd April, 1998.
Start 1m right of the rounded arête. Climb the broken crackline up to a small ledge (strenuous). Finish straight up.

NOTE: Jex's Midnight Runners was felt to be H. Severe 4b as opposed to VS 4c.

Loch Thacleit (Map Ref 948 710):
Maceo's Cat Scratch – 12m Severe 4a. R. Carter. 14th January, 1998.
Start 3m right of an obvious gully with a chockstone. Climb the right-hand crack (crux), then ascend on good holds past heather at 8m and continue up on dirty holds.

SOUTH UIST, Beinn Mhor, Hellisdale Buttress:
Curley Wurly Cuckoo – 40m E1 5a. C. Ravey, E. Stewart. 12th May, 1998.
The middle of the buttress which is situated to the left of the farthest right gully. Start left of centre of the buttress and follow holds rising rightwards to a steeper section. Surmount this on small but good holds (crux) on to the slab above. Climb to a break at the bottom of a steep wall and follow this leftwards to below a groove with hollow flakes. Move up the groove and flakes to finish on broken ground.

PABBAY, Banded Geo:
Fools Rush Out - 30m E1 5b*. P. Thorburn, R. Campbell. 27th May, 1998.
The flake cracks in the wall left of Chocaholic. A ramp left of the belay would give a good second pitch. From a ledge 12m up, follow the right-slanting cracks across the brown wall to a thin break. Climb the thin flake above and left, then traverse right under a roof to belay. Finish by Chocaholic (E2 5b).

Left of Endolphin Rush is a crackline; left again is a large very steep brown wall with a low roof slanting up left. Abseil from a belay below two blocks on the path (60m) to a ledge on the left, or traverse in (low tide). The route overhangs 11m in 45m.

Ship of Fools – 45m E5 6b***. P. Thorburn, R. Campbell. 28th May, 1998.
From the easy ramp, climb boldly up biotite to gain the roof 4m left of its lowest point. Gain the flake above the lip with difficulty, move up left to cross the bulge by some flakes, then continue straight up until the rock becomes compact (calcite). Move up right, then back left through a bulge, then move up right again and pull through a bulge to a flake. Step right past a detached flake into the black niche. Step right and climb straight up to belay on a slab. Scramble to the top.

Poop Deck:
Thursday's Setting Sunrise – 30m E5 6a**. P. Thorburn, R. Campbell. 28th May, 1998.
The central crackline left of Bogus Asylum Seekers. Make one move up the right-hand crack, then traverse left to a niche (alternatively, step into the boulder in the pool and up the crack). Make difficult and committing moves to a jug, then climb

the crack direct to a break (Friend#4). A flange on the left gains the lip, pull up right, then take parallel cracks on the left to the top.

One Last Look – 25m E4 6a/b**. P. Thorburn, R. Campbell. 29th May, 1998.
At the left end of the wall is a shallow recess with a large pegmatite vein on the right wall. Climb to a man-size spike, follow cracks up the recess, then hand traverse right through the roof. Make hard moves into a scoop to gain a hole on the right, step left and go direct to the top.

Pink Wall:
Raiders of the Last Auk – 80m E3***. P. Thorburn, R. Campbell. 26th May, 1998.
Climbs the central groove and crackline. Abseil down the line (as for Tomorrow People) and lasso the cracked block (bird free).
1. 20m 5c. From the block, climb the tricky wall on the left to gain a hanging right-facing groove. Climb it and the cracks above on the right to belay on the left end of a narrow ledge.
2. 20m 5b. Climb the steepening groove above, then make a long traverse left to a vertical crack, climbed to a ledge.
3. 40m 5a. From the right end of the ledge, follow In Profundum Lacu to the top.

In Profundum Lacu – 80m E4***. R. Campbell, P. Thorburn. 26th May, 1998.
The next line to the right.
1. 20m 6a. Step right off the block to gain cracks and follow them into a hanging V-groove (crux). Climb up and left to a long narrow ledge. Take a hanging belay off the right end (no belays above).
2. 20m 5c. Make awkward moves up a crack on the right, then gain a left-facing flake. Traverse left and gain a pegmatite flake above the bulge. Continue up left to gain and climb a bottomless groove.
3. 40m 5a. Climb a crack on the right and continue to a steep blocky left-facing groove. Climb this and straight up to the top.

The most distinctive feature of the right-hand side of the wall is a large left-facing hanging corner. The next route gains and follows this.
A Cormorant's Out of the Question, Then? – 85m E5***. R. Campbell, P. Thorburn. 25th May, 1998.
Start below and right of a series of strange flakes under the corner.
1. 20m 5c. Gain and climb the flakes, then follow the diminishing flake line on the right to a break. Traverse left, gain the easy corner and belay half way up.
2. 25m 6b. From the top of the corner (Friend#4), traverse left to a crack in the roof. Go up this and make hard moves to pegmatite flakes. From a vertical flake, undercut left to gain a diagonal line of jugs. Follow these to belay in a break.
3. 40m 5b. Step left, then climb a steepening to make an awkward pull left on to a shelf. Continue up a groove to another shelf. Traverse left below a steep wall with a loose flake, then step left around a lichenous arête. Go straight up to the top.

The Ancient Mariners – 85m E5***. P. Thorburn, R. Campbell. 25th May, 1998.
This route climbs the cracks right of the hanging corner. Start in the same place.
1. 40m 6a. Climb the flakes and make a hard pull right before the break. Climb the cracks above until a flared crack is encountered. Climb the groove to the right, then traverse left to gain the pegmatite flakes. Follow these past a pair of spikes to the break. Traverse right and belay under a groove with a short wide crack.

2. 45m 5a. Climb the groove to a ledge, then continue in the same line joining The Guga to finish.

Big Block Sloc:
Let Sleeping Storks Lie – 25m E5 6a**. P. Thorburn, R. Campbell. 27th May, 1998.
Enjoyable bold climbing up the left arête of the wedge. The crux is protected by microwires, but the route is low in the grade. Belay as for Lifeline and follow its initial crack as it curves round to the arête. Climb the right wall of the arête, then step round to a good hold on the left side, under the overlap. Gain a small groove above (crux), then follow it to the break. Climb the right side to the ledge, then finish up the left side of the arête.

MINGULAY, Guarsey Beag:
Haunt of Seals – 50m E1 5b***. L. Thomas, M. Turner, G. Latter (on-sight). 1st June, 1998.
Scramble down and left from the left end of the long ledge at the base of most of the routes to belay on a small ledge. Step left off the belay. Climb the wall directly to a niche below the distinctive thin crack in the middle of the wall (right of the right-slanting corner of Oh No, Norman's Due Back Tomorrow! Climb the crack (good small wires) to a slanting break, and follow this rightwards, then directly up the wall to a big break. Finish up the black wall just left of a corner.

Hill You Hoe – 50m E4 6a**. G. Latter, M. Turner, L. Thomas (on-sight). 1st June, 1998.
Start beneath the right-facing groove on the right side of the pillar of Ossian Boulevard. Climb the groove, pulling slightly leftwards to large sloping holds on the ledge (crux). Pull right and up the crack to the long ledge on Ossian Boulevard. Move slightly leftwards on good flat holds on the wall above, then finish directly.

Save Our Soles – 60m E6**. M. Turner, L. Thomas, G. Latter (on-sight). 1st June, 1998.
Good climbing up the right side of the wall taken by Lost Souls. Start on ledges on the far right.
1. 40m 5c. Step down right into a groove and follow the groove and cracks directly to the prominent quartz niche with a crack in the back. Pull out right and head up to a small flake, then straight up on perfect juggy rock to a good ledge beneath the roof.
2. 20m 6b. Move easily up right to a break near the right end of the roof. Reach out to a good flat hold half way out (Rock #3 in a horizontal slot), then make hard moves to reach and pull over the lip. Easily to finish.

Three routes on the south-facing wall of a geo immediately north of Guarsey Beag (photo-diagram provided). The geo faces west, and is between Baigh Shleiteadh (to the east) and Guarsaigh Mor and Beag (to the west). MR Sheet 31, 553 844 (the head of the geo, where one can scramble in to Wurst is at 554 845).
Wurst – 20m Diff. K. Hannavy, R. McCaffrey. 27th April, 1998.
Near the head of the geo and approached by scrambling in from it. Start at a ledge just left of an obvious damp stepped corner. Go straight up the wall to the left of the corner for about 10m to a ledge. Move to the left end of the ledge and straight up the wall above.

The Schnook – 20m V. Diff. K. Hannavy, R. McCaffrey. 27th April, 1998.
In the centre of the wall is an obvious corner. Follow the sigmoidal crack in the next corner right of the obvious one (approached by abseil).

Easuspeasuslemonsqueezuz – 20m Diff. K. Hannavy, R. McCaffrey. 27th April, 1998.
A left to right slanting crack in the wall to the left of the obvious corner. Approached by same abseil.

Dun Mingulay (MR 534 820):

Les Voyageurs – 120m E3***. M. Turner, G. Latter, L. Thomas (on-sight). 2nd June, 1998.
A fine direct line up the cliff just right of the arch at the north end. Start beneath easy open grooves 10m right of the end of the ledges.
1. 15m 4b. Trend up leftwards to a large ledge at the base of a flake crack.
2. 30m 5b. Follow the flake crack to its top to belay on small foot-ledges.
3. 35m 5c. Climb the wall, moving rightwards to a groove. Climb the groove to a small corner under a roof. Traverse right to break through the roofs on huge holds. Follow the big crack back left to belay.
4. 40m 5b. Step left and round some huge flakes to pull out right at 10m onto the wall at prominent spiky flakes. Continue up the wall to beneath a slim smooth groove. Traverse left 5m and climb the wall above on good holds, easing towards the top.
Note: K. Howett and H. Harris climbed a similar line the previous week, although the last pitch was different, called The Hurried Path.

Perfect Monsters – 150m E7***. M. Turner, G. Latter, L. Thomas (1 PA; on sight). 4th and 5th June, 1998.
An outrageously exposed route following a diagonal line rightwards through the impressive roofed arch at the north end of the cliff, topping out above the apex. Abseil as for Children of the Tempest.
1. 50m 5c. Follow a line of shallow grooves and cracks to undercut right at a diagonal line of smaller roofs, 6m beneath the main roof system. Belay on flat spike and nuts in the left-most of two grooves, directly beneath the big roof.
2. 20m 6b. Move up to the main roof. Undercut right to a jammed block jug, then launch over the roof to a good jug over the lip (the finger points the way!), then step out right to a cramped peg and nut belay on the wall, on the lip of the large horizontal roof. A spectacular pitch.
3. 20m 6b. The awesome overhanging slanting roof/corner. Undercut, bridge or whatever seems right to good nut belay at a small foot-ledge where it becomes a vertical corner. Gear good – Friends up to 3 and couple of PR's. (1 rest point taken near the end of this pitch).
4. 15m 6a. Climb the short black corner to the roof, then undercut this rightwards to pull round into a slim cracked groove. Climb this, pulling leftwards over the bulge on good holds. Step left and up to belay (Friend #2+, #3 and hex #8) under the roof above.
5. 45m 6a. Another truly awesome pitch – sustained and pumpy. Traverse right along the obvious juggy handrail for 8m, then pull up through the roof to gain a good knee-bar rest on a horizontal spike. Psyche up and launch straight up on perfect monsters jugs to finish up an immaculate vertical wall on good holds.

Sula – 100m E2***. M. Turner, G. Latter, L. Thomas (on-sight). 3rd June, 1998.
A wonderful direct route up the centre of the cliff, at a surprisingly reasonable grade for the ground covered. Start 10m left of The Silkie, at a shallow square-cut groove directly below a triangular roof at 15m.
1. 30m 5b. Climb the right side of the groove then head up towards a flaky crack at 15m (5m right of triangular roof). Move into a shallow groove (spike) and climb to the break. Traverse right a few metres past a bomber hidden runner (Rock #8) to a good nut belay over the roof at the apex of a triangular roof.
2. 40m 5b. Climb straight up past good flakes to a delicate section which leads to a small overlap (good wires). Continue straight up, moving slightly right before surmounting a nose of rock below the steep section. Climb the huge flakes in a wild position to pull onto a vertical wall with big holds (8m left of the quartz groove of The Silkie). Pull up the wall to a yellow ledge and belay.
3. 30m 5a. Climb the steep juggy wall to the top.

Seal Song Geo:
The extensive geo just north of the headland of Rubha Liath.

North Wall (MR NL 551 815):
A good, fairly extensive south-facing wall set back from easy-angled tidal ledges. Descent: Scramble down an easy grassy rake, then a short rock step (easier descents further west) to a large flat shelf with a prominent large block perched immediately above the top of the crag. Abseil down to good ledges at the base.

Fergus Sings the Blues – 35m E4 6a**. G. Latter, F. Murray (on-sight). 3rd June, 1998.
Excellent sustained climbing breaking through the roof on the right side of the crag. Start at the base of the corner. Move up and leftwards along a good flake handrail. Climb the wall above past some good horizontal slots to the roof. Pull out right to two good undercut flakes, then make a long reach to a good break (Friends #2+, #3). Pull up the wall above on jugs, then left and follow slabby twin cracks. Finish quite boldly up the steady impending wall above.

Delayed Reaction – 30m E1 5c**. L. Thomas, M. Turner, G. Latter (on sight). 3rd June, 1998.
The prominent hanging crack on the right side of the wall, gained via the lower corner. Climb the corner on good holds to a huge platform on the right. Traverse left on good holds to gain the crack. Follow the crack, the crux being saved for the final moves to gain good holds just short of the top.

Arnamul Promontary:
Mingulay Magic – 75m E1***. M. Davies, G. E. Little (alt.). 27th May, 1998.
Start below a break in bulging rock about 15m right of the crack up the right side of the pillar (taken by Lament to the Abyss).
1. 45m 5a. Climb up through the break and then directly up to a large ledge below roofs.
2. 30m 5b. Climb the big corner to below the main roof, then move right to an exposed edge. Climb straight up to finish. A brilliant pitch.

The Green Eyed Dragon Slayers – 80m E2*. G. E. Little, M. Davies (alt.). 28th May, 1998.
An obvious fault defines the left side of the pillar with a distinctive wide slot

through the roof about 25m up. This is the line of the route. The route name derives from two eye-like holes full of stagnant green slime at its base.
1. 35m 5c. Gain and climb the fault with strenuous moves through a bulge and surprisingly less demanding climbing through the slot to a good ledge just left of a guillimot colony.
2. 25m 5b. Ascend the green corner above for a few metres until a swing out right gives access to a hanging rib. Climb this in an exposed situation to reach a wide ledge.
3. 20m 4c .Climb straight up to finish.

The Fulmar Monty – 75m E3 *. M. Davies, G. E. Little (alt.). 28th May, 1998.
Start about 25m right of the cracks up the right side of the pillar taken by Lament to the Abyss.
1. 45m 5c. Climb up to and through a left-facing groove with stepped roofs to a small ledge. Move up and right, then back left, then straight up to a good ledge.
2. 30m 4c. Take a direct line up the slightly vegetated wall on good holds.

The Black Dyke Affair – 70m HVS*. G. E. Little, M. Davies (alt.). 28th May, 1998.
This obvious left-trending diagonal fault lies well to the left of the pillar where the access ledge begins to fade.
1. 45m 5a. Climb the fault with interest until a section of black dyke gives awkward moves and access on to a wide sloping ledge on the right.
2. 25m 4b. The flared chimney above holds some dubious blocks, so step across to the left side and ascend a steep wall on good jugs to finish.

BERNERAY, Barra Head, Giants Pipes (MR 557 794):
This striking cliff, composed of a series of huge ribs and corners, lies on the west side of Barra Head and faces due south. Access is by abseil (90m) and is dependent upon calm seas.
Barra Head Games – 105m E3***. G. E. Little, K. Howett (alt.). 31st May, 1997.
A route of immense character, virtually bird free and comparable in quality to Prophesy of Drowning on Pabbay. Start on a sea-washed ledge at the foot of the westernmost and most distinctive of the main corner systems. This is gained by abseiling from a large square block, well back from the cliff edge, then swinging in to gain the ledge.
1. 20m 5b. Enter and boldly climb the off-width slot (left and parallel to a deep chimney) to reach a ledge. Make difficult moves into a V-recess. Move out on to the right edge of the recess (effectively into the chimney), then traverse left across a slabby wall under a roof, moving up to take a belay at a ledge on the edge.
2. 40m 5c. Pull up into a hanging groove, step right into a short corner, then right again to gain a projecting ledge (crux). Move up and left back into the main corner. Climb it over a series of bulges to enter a red open-book corner and belay on a ledge a few metres below its capping ledge. A brilliant pitch!
3. 45m 5b. Continue up the corner to the roof, then traverse right on to an exposed edge. Reach left and climb a hanging groove holding an hourglass-shaped plaque. Step left and climb a left-trending diagonal crack. Step left again on to an arête, then back right through a bulge to continue by the line of least resistance to the top, finishing at the point of the abseil.

The Great Auk – 90m E1***. G. E. Little, M. Davies (alt.). 24th May, 1998.
This amazing line takes the central and largest corner system at a remarkably

friendly grade. Abseil from the big square block well back from the edge taking a line between the two main corner systems to belay in a roof-capped slot a safe distance above the sea.
1. 40m 5b. Ascend the slot, then move out on to the left edge to reach the base of an immaculate slim corner. Climb it to its capping roof, then pull out right and step right to a big flat-topped flake – excellent.
2. 50m 5a. Climb straight up, then move left into the base of the main corner. Climb this, crossing a bulge, to the capping roofs. Bypass the roof by ascending the strenuous right wall, then continue to the top.

Eye of the Eagle – 95m E3***. G. E. Little, M. Davies (alt.). 25th May, 1998.
This excellent route lies to the left of the central corner system taken by The Great Auk, tackling the left wall of its main corner. Abseil from the big square block to end up at the base of the guano-splashed pillar immediately left of the roof-capped slot taken by The Great Auk.
1. 20m 4c. Ascend the crackline on the left edge of the pillar (overlooking the deep recess taken by Barra Head Games) to reach a good stance above.
2. 35m 5c. Climb a short corner to a slim vertical rib between the two cracklines. Climb the rib to its capping roof. Pull right, then strenuously back left to follow the continuation rib and wall above to belay on a small ledge next to a large shaky flake – a sustained pitch.
3. 40m 6a. Move up, then step left on to fragile-looking flakes. From their top, make thin moves to a break (crux), then continue over a series of bulges to the top.

Creag na Beiste:
Atlantic Affront – 175m E3*. G. E. Little, M. Davies (alt.). 26th May, 1998.
The vast south-facing wall on the north side of Sloc na Beiste is, with the exception of a great shield of slabby grey rock, heavily colonised by birds. This route climbs the grey shield and the upper two tiers by a largely bird-free line. Abseil from a flat flake (thread) down to the main terrace (passing the upper terrace) – about 80m. Abseil down the grey shield to obvious ledges some 25m above the sea – about 75m.
1. 25m 4c. Climb a left-trending line to the top of a semi-detached pillar.
2. 40m 5c. Mantelshelf from the top of the pillar, then traverse right for 5m to the base of thin vertical cracks. Climb these with increasing difficulty until a horizontal traverse left leads to a distinctive (side-on) W-shaped flake. Ascend this and the thin slabby wall above until possible to traverse up and left to ledges by the corner-crack (forming the right side of a huge semi-detached pillar – the most obvious feature on the whole face).
3. 25m 5a. Ascend the groove to the right of the corner, step back into the corner and climb it to exit on to the main terrace to the left of a guillemot colony.
4. 40m 5c. Pull up directly at a nose, then step right to avoid a bulge. Move left above the bulge and then climb trending generally leftwards up a series of steep walls to gain the upper terrace.
5. 45m 4c. Follow the obvious diagonal fault up right to an exciting exit over big wedged blocks. Finish up easy ground.

RUM, Trallval, Longship Crag:
Neptune's Disco – 30m E1 5b. L. Johnston, A. Brooks, M. Collins. 2nd May, 1998.
Go awkwardly up the right-hand side of the detached arête to the right of Breenge on to the pedestal, then up the arête starting at the left (quite necky).

The Ancients of Mumu – 30m VS 5a. M. Collins, L. Johnston, A. Brooks. 2nd May, 1998.
Follow a crackline and groove system up the rounded arête to the left of the V-groove of Breenge. Sustained and well protected.

MULL, BALMEANACH:
Red Drupelets – 22m E3 5c*. C. Moody, C. Black. 2nd July, 1998.
Start at the same place as Yellow Snail, follow the fault up left past the right end of the overhang then step left above it. Continue straight up over another bulge just left of some big pockets. Climb slightly left to the top.

SCOOR:
Hot Tin Roof – 15m E1 5b. C. Moody, L. Gordon-Canning. 23rd May, 1998.
On the wall opposite Bluebell Blues is a steep flake which finishes below a ledge. Climb the flake then gain the ledge, move left and climb the arête.

ARDTUN, Creag Eilean an Duilisg:
Gong Bird – 15m E2 5c/6a*. C. Moody, A. Soloist 27th June, 1998.
The finger crack left of Eye Of Toad (SMCJ 1997). Step left at the top on to heather, then an easy finish.

Parakeet Of The Baskervilles – 20m E1 5b. C. Moody, B. Taylor. 6th September, 1998.
Right of the 5m pillar (right of Jonathan Livingston Dodo) are short fallen pillars. Start on top of these. Climb the corner crack which bends right and avoids a vertical wall. Move right again and climb past some loose blocks.

Waterfall Wall:
Roadrunner – 20m E2/3 5c*. C. Moody, A. Soloist. 27th June, 1998.
Gain the top of the block left of Sheryl Crow. Above is a blank corner; climb the crack left of it which soon gets thin. Move left for protection, step back right, climb up then step left above the gear (it might be possible to continue straight up from the first gear). Continue up the fault line slightly leftwards and where the angle eases (at a right-facing corner crack), step right and climb easily to the top.

The Green Hill:
Free The Torosay Five – 10m E1 5b*. C. Moody, M. Burgess.
Twin cracks right of Splash. Might be HVS as the top was wet.

IONA, Phort Bhan, Tolkein Crag:
Unnamed – 20m VS 4b. C. Moody, M. Burgess. 15th August, 1998.
Climb the two big boulders at the right end of the crag, then the centre of the red slab.

Goirtean Beag (MR 263 246):
Walking north past the left side of Tolkien Crag a long rocky hillock is ahead. Walk down the corridor left of it and squeeze past the boulder. The slab is just right. About five minutes from Tolkien.
Close To The Edge – 20m VS 4b. C. Moody, M. Burgess. 15th August, 1998.
Start on the boulder at the left side of the slab. Pull out right past a bulge, then move left and climb up left of a line of thrift to a steeper finish.

Fragile – 20m VS 4b. C. Moody, M. Burgess. 15th August, 1998.
Start at the right side of the slab. Follow the crack up left easily and finish up a wide crack/flake.

Unnamed – 12m Severe.
The shallow chimney right of the slab.

CREAG LIATH (MR 472 392):

This is a small dolerite crag on the north side of Loch Na Keal. It lies close to the shore in the trees and faces south. The smell of rotting carcasses might prevent climbing in spring. Drive towards Ulva Ferry from the head of Loch Na Keal and stop just after the high point on the road when the crag is directly below.
Sloeworm – 18m E1 5b**. C. Moody, B. Taylor, C. Black 4th September, 1998.
An obvious line. Climb a finger crack past the overhangs then climb the wider crack past the rowan.

LAGG, ISLE OF JURA:

A 10-minute walk in an easterly direction over Cnoc na Moine from the road between Gatehouse and Lagg leads to some huge overlapping slabs which sweep majestically into the sea (MR 594 775). The southern edge of one of these forms a long 10m-high sandstone wall which offers some excellent short climbs. Routes were climbed on 12th December, 1996 and 15th-16th April, 1997 by M. Shaw, M. Bagness, M. Boyle, D. Ritchie, R. Rozga and C. Rozga.

Camus Wall:

Routes described from left to right are:
Snakes and Adders – V. Diff. The slab on the left.
No Smoke Without Fire – V. Diff. The chimney right of the slab.
McLever the Robber – Severe. The crack up the middle of the central wall.
Orange Skyline – H. Severe. The right side of the wall.
Coastal Capers – V. Diff. The left edge of the undercut wall.
Hot Spot Spider – HVS 5a. Start just right of Coastal Capers, climb up and traverse right, then finish up a fault in an overlap.
Holy Terrors – HVS 5a. The prominent crack through the overhang.
Shenanigan – V. Diff. The left-slanting crack.
Shilly Shally – V. Diff. The crack to the top.

Above and left of Camus Wall is an east-facing square-shaped wall with some routes. Left to right:
Devil's Dwarf – VS 4c. Climb the crack, traverse right and continue up.
Stapull Crom –VS 4c. The tiwn cracks.
Black Fairy – HVS 5a. The right-slanting groove. Hand traverse to the edge and up.
Black Fairy Variations:
1. HVS 5a. From the same starting point, continue straight up the layback crack and break out right avoiding Devil's Dwarf.
2. HVS 5a. Gain the start of the hand traverse, but continue straight up the crack.

SKYE

SGURR NA H-UAMHA:
West Gully – III. M. Shaw. 11th February, 1999.
Good climbing following the summer line.

Cuill Climb – 250m II/III. M. Shaw. 22nd February, 1999.
This takes the curving snow chute on the NE flank and begins with an icefall which lies 30m right of a short overhanging wall that runs up the buttress edge. High on the route the snow chute straightens and eventually meets the upper slabs. At this point move out left and up grooves to finish directly on the summit.

SGURR NAN GILLEAN, Third Pinnacle:
Feusaig de'n t-Sneachd – 80m III. R. Bervie, M. E. Moran. 13th March, 1999.
Climbs the ramp line running left across the face of the Third Pinnacle, starting 100m up 3/4 Gully. Finish up a short buttress to the crest of the ridge. Needs a good banking of snow.

AM BASTEIR, North Face:
The following two routes explore the left to right slanting ledge systems on the North Face. They were climbed when the face was thickly hoared but with consolidated snow on the ledges. Although with only short harder sections, both routes offered fine situations with good belays but poor protection in places. There appear to be some discrepancies with the current guidebook. The diagram of Am Basteir suggests that Am Basteir Chimney takes the obvious chimney on the steepest section of the face. However the summer route The Squeeze Box (*SMCJ* 1998) follows this same chimney. Am Basteir Chimney and North Face Route must start much further left on less steep ground, and therefore White Spirit may be a winter ascent of much of North Face Route.
Note: Agreed by A. Nisbet, who initially thought The Squeeze Box looked impressive for a V. Diff, but later came to the same conclusion.
The Deadline – 195m III,4. D. Ritchie, M. Shaw. 8th March, 1999.
1. 30m .Start just left of the lowest rocks. Climb a short ice pitch, then snow.
2. 50m. Move right and up easy ground to a large ledge system rising from the left.
3. 45m. Move right, climb a corner and right-slanting chimney (crux) to gain the upper ledge system, not obvious from below, and an alcove.
4. 50m. Climb the ramp past a pinnacle.
5. 20m. Continue up the ramp to finish at the notch on the east ridge of Am Basteir.

White Spirit – 260m IV,5. D. Ritchie, M. Shaw. 9th March, 1999.
Start some 50m right of The Deadline at a chimney immediately left of a steep black wall.
1. 40m. Climb the chimney and shallow gully above.
2. 40m. Climb easier ground and a snow slope to below a steep chimney.
3. 50m. Traverse hard right following the obvious ledge system for 40m. Climb a corner to gain a higher ledge system.
4. 50m. Follow this fault rightwards over broken ground and ledges to a chimney (The Squeeze Box).
5. 40m. Climb the chimney and fault above to finish just short of the summit.

COIR' A' GHRUNNDA:
Rapid Progress – 40m HVS 5a**. M. Lates, C. Scott. July, 1998.
An obvious crackline 15m to the right of Cuckoo Groove (Guide, p163). Constantly interesting climbing with a steep move to finish. Finish up the 5m continuation above.

SGURR NA STRI:
Lost Chord – 180m V. Diff. J. Gillespie, A. Currie. June, 1998.
The climb takes the line of least resistance above the Bad Step. Climb from the middle of the traverse on the Bad Step in four pitches.

MARSCO:
Allt Fiaclan Dearg – 150m IV,3. S. Helmore, R. Williams. 24th February, 1999.
MR 503 254. The route is a waterfall cut into a 10m-wide dyke on the west flank of Marsco and requires a low freezing level for several days to form. The upper half is visible from the Sligachan hotel. The difficulties begin at an altitude of 375m, with a steep 25m pitch out of the small gorge. After two more pitches, scramble up the frozen stream bed to the upper west slopes of Marsco.

CLACH GLAS, West Face:
Penelope – 70m V,6. D. Ritchie, M. Shaw. 6th December, 1998.
By the summer route. Although short, this route offered fine climbing, a superb outlook and a fine finish directly at the summit of Clach Glas.

Arch Gully – 190m IV,5. D. Ritchie, M. Shaw. 10th March, 1999.
By the summer route in 4 pitches. The overhanging start was avoided on the left with some thin mixed climbing. The second pitch was climbed round the huge chockstone. The top two pitches under the arch were banked out and straightforward. Better conditions would ease the initial difficulties.

Bealach Buttresses:
The Cailliach – 130m IV,4. D. Ritchie, M. Shaw. 16th January, 1999.
Climbs the left-hand of the two parallel faults on the east-facing buttress south of the Clach Glas – Sgurr nan Each col, left of Slighe a' Bhodaich (*SMCJ* 1998, p590). Avoid the initial rocks by starting up Slighe a' Bhodaich until below its initial steepening, then follow an obvious ledge left to gain the left-hand fault line. Follow this over highly-vegetated ground to easier climbing and a finish on the main ridge of Clach Glas.

ELGOL, Schoolhouse Buttress:
No Excuses – 6m VS 5a. N. Hockley, A. Eakins. 20th March, 1998.
At the right-hand end of the crag (nearest the school) is a large niche under an obvious nose.
The thin vertical crack 2m left is reached by reachy moves (harder for the short) and followed to the top.

Maggoty Mutton – 20m E1 5b. C. Pasteur, A. Hume, A. Matthewson, J.May. September,1998.
Climb overhanging wafers as for Wafer Wall, then move right on a ledge to the prow. Ascend this via an overhanging crack to gain a final tapering corner.

STRATHAIRD, Suidhe Biorach:
Hovis – 30m E6. D. Turnbull, J. Arran (flashed on-sight, ground up). 24th May, 1998.
Start beneath the roof 10m right of Mothers Pride
1. 15m 5b. Weave up through overhanging breaks and ledges to belay under the roof just right of the only line of weakness.
2. 15m 6b. Move left and gain the lip using small flakes. A very difficult heel hooking/mantel manoeuvre gains a precarious standing position on the lip where bold moves lead first left then right up the blank wall.

NOTE: M. Lates and J. M. Norman climbed the fault through the right-hand end of the overhangs to the right of Mother's Pride on 17th May, 1996. It was called Cameron's Climb, E2 5c, and precedes one or both of the routes in *SMCJ* 1998, p 590.

NEIST, The Upper Crag, Financial Sector:
The following routes lie between A Fist Full of Dollarite and Wall Street.
Gampy's Wallet – 30m E2 5c**. E. Ash, T. Bridgeland. 23rd May, 1998.
Start at the large corner left of Wall Street. Climb the corner to below the large roof. Move left on good holds to gain the base of a prominent groove. Climb this to a rest, then launch over the capping bulge (the finish may share some ground with Wall Street).

The following two climbs are on the seaward face of the buttress with the leaning pinnacle on its left. Start from a belay on top of the pinnacle.
Piggy Bank – 25m E3 5c***. T. Bridgeland, E. Ash. 23rd May, 1998.
A brilliant route taking the groove in the right side of the face. From the belay, step down and pull round the arête onto the face. Move up to two good pockets then continue boldly rightwards to the base of a curving ramp. Follow this, then move up and right to gain the groove, which provides a fine upper half.

Gammy's Purse – 25m E2 5c**. E. Ash, T. Bridgeland. 23rd May, 1998.
Takes the crack and groove in the left side of the face. Follow Piggy Bank to the pockets. Move out left above the belay to gain the crack. Climb this then move right to the bottom of the groove, which is followed to the top.

Cumhann Geodha:
Between Bay 4 and Conductor Cove is a long narrow geo, with an extensive series of groove lines on the south-west facing wall. Descent is by abseil from a block well back from the edge, down the wall just left (looking in) of Quite Fatigued. The following three routes are all situated above the large ledge at the left (north-west) end.
The Old Warden – 15m HVS 5a*. G. Latter, J. Rabey. 4th April, 1998.
The left-facing corner crack at the left side of the pillar. After some ledges, step right and finish up a hand crack in the arête.

Quite Fatigued – 15m HVS 5b*. G. Latter, J. Rabey, D. Rabey, L.Gordon-Canning. 8th April, 1998.
The groove on the right side of the pillar, easing in its upper half.

Before the Deluge – 15m H. Severe 4b*. G. Latter, J. Rabey, D. Rabey, L.Gordon-Canning. 8th April, 1998.
The left-hand of two narrow chimney-cracks.

The Lower Crag, Poverty Point (*SMCJ* 1998):
Chugger's Elbow – 20m Severe. C. Moody. 15th November, 1998.
The wall left of Broken Wing (*SMCJ* 1998). Broken Wing is the crack at the right
end of the wall (V. Diff). Superlager For Breakfast (*SMCJ* 1998) is probably HVS
5a.

The Lower Crag, Destitution Point:
The next prominent headland a few hundred metres north of Poverty Point (*SMCJ*
1998, p 592). The following routes are found on the south face which contains a
steep corner with a slabby right wall. A steep prow sits to the left of the corner.
Cogless – 20m VS 4c. S. Kennedy, M. MacLeod. 15th November, 1998.
Makes for the hanging groove in the upper section of the south end of the prow. Start
from wide ledges and climb a crack just left of the right edge. Step right below a
bulge and enter the groove which is followed to the top.

Man of Straw – 20m VS 4c. S. Kennedy, M. MacLeod, C. Moody. 14th November,
1998.
Climbs the clean slab on the back wall to the right of the corner. Abseil to ledges
close to the corner. Climb cracks in the lower section then move right to the edge
of the slab. Continue up the edge, then step right below the short headwall into a
corner to finish.

The following are left to others for their precise location:
Half-a-mile to the north of Supercharger beneath upper cliffs by the sea. Start at a
wave-cut platform 80yd right of a sea arch.
One Way Bottle – 30m E5 6b. C. Wentworth, A. Scott. May, 1996.
Climb an arête past thin cracks right then back left to a ledge on the arête (peg).
Climb the arête to the top.

Bavaria – 30m E4 6a. A. Scott, C. Wentworth. May, 1996.
Start just right of the sea arch. Climb a slabby arête up and left. Pull through a small
bulge to finish straight up the wall above."

STAFFIN BUTTRESSES:
These routes are at the right end of the buttresses, just south of Staffin Slip Buttress.
The best approach is from above. Go up the grassy slope south of Staffin Slip
Buttress and abseil in or scramble down just north of the routes.
What Did The Greeks Ever Do For Us? – 20m HVS 5a*. C. Moody, L. Gordon-
Canning. 9th May, 1998.
At the right-hand side is a pillar with an overhang high up. Climb the crack on the
left.

Hippy Complex – 25m E2 5b*. C. Moody, L. Gordon-Canning. 10th May, 1998.
Farther left are two corner cracks either side of a rectangular roof. Climb the twin
grooves right of the corners. There are a couple of suspect flakes low down.

Wild Garlic – 25m E2/3 5c**. C. Moody, L. Gordon-Canning. 10th May, 1998.
The corner past the right side of the roof.

Melon Crack – E1 5b. M. Lates, W. Gordon-Canning. July 98.
A crack farther left with a wide section high up.

Licking Nettles – 30m E3 5c***. C. Moody, L. Gordon-Canning, M. McLeod. 12th June, 1998.
Left of Melon Crack are two chimneys. Climb the hand crack left of these.

The following route is about 400m south of the above (diagram provided) and is the cleanest-looking line hereabouts:
Total Recoil – 45m E2 5b**. M. Lates, R. Pepe. October, 1998.
Approach by abseiling from a thin but solid fence post some 20m back from the clifftop. The line has an obvious right to left dogleg at 20m (belay taken here).

STAFFIN SLIP:

Sunear – 20m HVS 5a*. C. Moody, L. Gordon-Canning, M. McLeod. 12th June, 1998.
Left of East Chimney Crack, walk up the hill to reach a crack with a shallow gully on the left and a black streak to the right. Climb the right side of the flake and continue up the crack; near the top move left on to a rib. Easy for the grade.

COIRE LALLADALE:

An icefall climbed on the cliffs north of The Storr (unsure of relation to summer routes):
Finished at Last – 120m V,6. M. Lates and partner (pitch 1) on 25th December, 1996; M. Lates, M. Francis (pitches 2 and 3) on 9th January, 1997.
Climbs the leftmost steep icefall.
1. Start at the right-hand side of a huge slab of ice. Rise leftwards to the centre to finish up the curtain of ice which is necessary to turn the overhang. Escape left was used here.
2. Huge up turned cups of ice remained of the old ice. These were climbed awkwardly for 12m after which mixed climbing took the corner on the left.
3. Follow slabs of ice for 12m to below vertical ice. This was too thin and skirted on the left-hand side.

GLEN LORGASDAL SEA STACKS:

About 3km north-west of Idrigill Pont lie two 35m sea stacks in a bay where the Lorgasdal river falls 80m down vertical basalt cliffs (MR 221 381). Approach from Orbost taking the good path to Idrigill Point and MacLeod's Maidens. Continue north-west along the coast to reach the Glen Lorgasdal waterfall (about three hours). The stacks were reached by an 80m abseil from a large boulder 50m north of the waterfall. From the boulder beach, the South Stack was reached by a 25m swim. This was followed by a 100m swim to the North Stack. A long approach, difficult access, compulsory swim and suspect rock all add up to a challenging sea-stack experience.
South Stack – 35m HVS 4a. S. Richardson, G. Muhlemann. 26th September, 1998.
Climb a left-facing corner in the centre of the seaward face to reach steep grass. Scramble up this to reach the south edge of the stack, step left and climb a short wall to the rock blade summit. Very loose in its upper section.

North Stack – 35m E1 4c. G. Muhlemann, S. Richardson. 26th September, 1998.
1. 25m. Climb a corner on the left side of the seaward face for 10m then move up and left across the vertical left wall on huge holds to reach the north arête of the stack. Continue up this to reach an easing below the summit tower.
2. 10m. Cracks on the seaward face (loose) lead to the summit ridge. Climb this gingerly to the summit block.

Mark Garthwaite soloing 'The Conger' (E2 5c), Connor Cove, Swanage. Photo: Garthwaite Collection.
(Left): Neil Stevenson on the first ascent of 'Ishmael' (E3 5c), Skerray sea cliffs. Photo: Roger Webb.
Robin McAllister on the first ascent of 'Moon Safari' (E3 5c), Creagh Ghlas, Strathconnon. Photo: Andrew Fraser.

NORTHERN HIGHLANDS
SOUTH AND WEST (VOLUME ONE)

SGURR AN LOCHAIN:
Enchanted Falls – 150m III. N. Taylor. 22nd December, 1996.
The stream cascading from the NE Coire of Sgurr an Lochain passes through an enchanting ravine (to join the Allt a' Choire Reith). For much of its length it is enclosed by slabby walls and is inescapable. Needs a good freeze.

THE SADDLE:
Forcan Double Direct – 450m and 4.8km III. Kintail MRT party. March 1990.
The purest variation on a much-loved classic. Start from the nose of the ridge. Hug the line of the main ridge, picking your line so that you can always see over the top of the ridge. Resist the published descent route by the leg-breaking dyke. Descend by reversing the route along the ridge. For maximum atmosphere, do under moonlight.

BEINN FHADA, Sgurr a' Choire Ghairbh:
Guide's Rib – 100m IV,6. G. Ettle, J. Lyall, R. Milne. 27th December, 1996.
Based on the summer line, this gives an exciting outing. The steepest section is ascended on the right; the final section is taken on the left.

GLEN ELCHAIG, Cragaig (MR 992 273):
Several gneiss crags on a south-facing hill. Stop at the car park and walk or cycle four miles to the cliffs; driving farther will jeopardise future access. Next to the track is a steep wall, Arabian Wall. Higher up slightly right is The Cioch, higher and right again are The Tongues. Left of these is the main wall which faces down the glen catching the afternoon sun. Other routes have been climbed.

Arabian Wall:
The left wall has a long overhang; the crack at the left end is 8m Severe.
Unnamed – 18m HVS 5a*. C. Moody, R. Lupton, L. Gordon-Canning, W. Gordon-Canning. 18th April, 1998.
Climb the left arête of the main wall, keeping on the left side. Near the top move farther away from the arête. Sticking to the arête would probably be E2.

Fritillary – 25m E3 6a*. C. Moody, L. Gordon-Canning. 18th June, 1998.
In the upper central part of the main wall is a prominent crack containing a tree. Start below this, just left of a black streak. Climb a thin crack to a break (Fr#4), then continue up slightly left to gain and climb a better crack. Finish up the prominent crack past the tree.

The Cioch:
Pine Processionary – 25m Severe. C. Moody, L. Gordon-Canning. 15th April, 1998.
The fault line at the left side of the crag which is shaped like an inverted S.

Drinking With The Priest – 25m E1 5b. W. Gordon-Canning, L. Gordon-Canning. 17th April, 1998.
Right of Pine Processionary is a detached looking flake/block. Gain the flake then climb up the left side of it, the top section of the climb being easy.

Middle Tongue:

This is broken into three slabs. Routes on The Tongues usually involve padding with very little protection, therefore soloing is a good idea. First ascentionists unknown.

St. Andrew's Slab – 40m V. Diff*.

The left slab has a cross low down formed by a vein and a crack. Climb straight up through this.

Shining – 50m Severe/VS*.

Up and left from the last route is shining slab with a crack running up left. The base of the slab forms a wall. Climb cracks to gain the slab at a moss streak, step left and follow the crack up left.

Boomerang – 30m Diff.

The slab round right of St. Andrew's slab. Move up slightly rightwards then continue up slightly leftwards.

Right Tongue:

Blanco – 100m Moderate.

Follow the slab slightly leftwards to the top, there is a grass ledge at a third height.

DUNCRAIG (CREAG AN DUISILG), Western Cliff:

No Stars No Moon No Nothing – 150m E4. I. Dring, J. Codling (alt., on sight). 23rd May, 1998.

Features the fine hanging corner at the right-hand side of the crag. More direct variations look possible, particularly a more direct finish up a fine groove line starting at the base of the grassy ramp but which would require some cleaning effort. Start at a flake-crack at the lowest point in the buttress.

1. 20m 5b. Climb the flake-crack to a ledge (peg runner). Step left and go up a steep wall to below a roof.

2. 25m 5a. Traverse right under the roof passing a peg runner, step down and then go diagonally right up a fault to the base of the corner. Traverse 6m left to a ledge and two-peg belay.

3. 35m 6a. Step back into the corner and go up this passing a peg to a small niche (peg). The overlap above is the crux. Exit up the left wall to a grassy alcove.

4. 45m 4c. Step up left to gain a grassy ramp. Go up this to a short vertical crack down and left of a large flake.

5. 25m 5a. Go up the flake (Friend#4) to its end. Hand traverse left and mantelshelf on to a ledge. Continue to the left arête and go up this (peg) to grassy bays.

GLAS BHEINN:

Right-Hand Gully – 150m III. R. Webb, N. Wilson. March, 1999.

The gully bounding the right end of the crag.

SGORR RUADH:

Raeburn's Buttress – 130m to shoulder V,6. D. McGimpsey, A. Nisbet. 14th January, 1999.

A line close to the crest right of Narrow Gully. Start at the foot of the crest at the base of the right wall of Narrow Gully.

1. 25m. Climb the steep crest, thin moves but several peg runners, particularly blades, to a big ledge. Move 5m right to a ramp which cuts through the steep wall above.

2. 20m. Climb the ramp to a bigger boulder-strewn ledge.

3. 85m. Climb a series of grooves, close to or just right of the crest, then easy ground to the shoulder

Raeburn's Buttress, Variation – 160m to shoulder V,6. R. McAllister, A. Nisbet. 16th April, 1998.

A different line until the easy ground near the shoulder. Start at the same place.

1. 20m. Traverse horizontally right along a narrow ledge.

2. 25m. Find a left-slanting flakey line leading to a bigger ledge.

3. 25m. Traverse right and climb two short steep walls to a big terrace.

4. 45m. Climb easier ground just right of the crest.

5. 45m. Climb the crest to the shoulder.

MEALL NAN CEAPAIREAN, North Face:

Stressful Buttress – 180m IV,5. A. Nisbet (backroped). 6th November, 1998.

The steep central section of the face forms a nose between a big bowl on the left and steep broken ground on the right. A ramp leads up right from the bowl to the crest of the nose at about half height. The nose is also cut horizontally and near its base by parallel ledges close together. Climb a short gully to reach the left end of the upper ledge. Find a way through the steep turfy ground above to reach the ramp and follow it until just short of the crest. A fairly direct line keeping left of the crest was taken, involving some short difficult walls, to finish at the top of the crest.

MEALL GORM:

Shamrock Gully – 300m III. U. Mulcahy, S. McMurrow, A. Nisbet. 10th February, 1999.

The well-defined gully which starts near the base of Global Warming but angles rightwards up the large eastern buttress. Climb the gully for two pitches, then make an easy traverse right to reach the base of the long well defined section. Below the Spiral Terrace there is a short vertical pitch avoided using the rib on the right, otherwise the gully is followed.

Trident Gully, Central Branch III (1999) – S. McMurrow, M. E. Moran. 9th February, 1999

From the fork, climb the central branch, which contains several short steps and one 15m barrier near the top, climbed by a chimney.

NOTE: Trident Gully, Right Branch was climbed by a more direct variation at III by M. E. Moran, D. Otteson and L. Wells on 10th February, 1999, moving right from a cave along a shelf, then up a corner to easier ground. The precise line of the original ascent, by A. C. Cain and G. Wallace in 1982 is unknown, as the description was lost in the Moratorium.

SGURR A' CHAORACHAIN, South Face:

Skullsplitter – 130m IV,6. R. G. Webb, N. Wilson. February, 1999.

Climbs the chimney line between Sword of Gideon and Anduril.

BEINN BHAN, Coire na Feola:

D. Morrison, R. Simpson and A. Fisher note an ascent of the obvious gully leading to the central col on the A' Chioch ridge, easy Grade II with one tricky step which would bank out with more snow. The gully is pictured in *Scottish Winter Climbs* between pages 70 and 71.

Coire Toll a' Bhein, Breach Buttress:
GBH – 250m III. A. Nisbet, C. Preece, O. Preece. 4th March, 1999.
The ridge left of Breach of the Peace was followed direct from its base. Avoiding a steep pitch at mid height by a chimney on the left and passing the top tower on the right would reduce the grade to II.

Main Buttress:
The Bill – 200m II. A. Nisbet. 27th February, 1999.
The gully on the right of the ridge with the pinnacle, starting some way up Main Gully. A steep section in the middle was avoided by a ramp on the left leading to an easy finish. To make a different finish to Indecent Exposure, the pinnacle was gained and the ridge above followed (Grade II), but the finishes should be exchanged.

LIATHACH, Coire Dubh Beag:
The Torture Chamber – 160m III,4. B. Davison, D. Wilkinson. 14th March, 1999.
Between Access Gully and Thumbscrew is a large snow field above the first sandstone tier. This route takes three short ice falls through the left side of the snowfield and just right of Access Gully. Go part way up Access Gully until below the icefall on the right. A short lower icefall on the left-hand side of the lower tier leads to the left side of the snowfield (20m), then easy ground to a rock buttress on the left side of the snowfield (70m). A second fall goes through this and leads (50m) to a third icefall directly above and going through the final rock tier (20m).

Brainless Fall – 140m VI,6. V. Chelton, D. McGimpsey, A. Nisbet. 12th March, 1999.
Climbs some steep ice which occasionally forms on the wall right of Headless Gully. Climb ice leftwards to reach a ledge below the ice which forms on the wall just right of overhangs which run across from Headless (10m). Climb an icefall on the wall which is just below vertical (25m). Move 5m left and climb thicker vertical ice which soon eases (30m). Go up a short wall and easier ground to the final tier (50m). Climb the tier by a groove on the left to easy ground.

Coire Dubh Mor:
The Bender – 120m IV,4. B. Davison, A. Nisbet. 6th March, 1999.
Climbs the leftmost icefall on the main face, virtually on the corner where the face bends round on to the gully wall of Way Up. Quite short but useful as a second route, being accessible from the col by descending Way Up and traversing from 50m below the base of Over Sixties Icefall. Start below the icefall and climb easily to an iced corner which leads to the main icefall. Climb the icefall to a ledge at its top. Move left to slabby mixed ground leading to a big terrace. Finish easily by a choice of lines.

Test Department – A free ascent at VI,6 by B. Davison, A. Nisbet, S. Anderson, M. E.Moran on 6th March, 1999 after the lower icicle formed.

Brainstorm – 50m VI,6. B. Davison, D. McGimpsey, A. Nisbet, S. Ohly, D. Wilkinson. 13th March, 1999.
The direct start to Brain Drain, a thin steep icefall some 10m right of the chimney start and 6m right of The Stem.

Meall Dearg, North Face:
Gully Obscura – 200m III. A. Bull, M. Kinsey, A. Nisbet. 10th March, 1999.
The leftmost gully on the face starting at the same point as the two diagonal shelves but going straight up to join Terminal Buttress on the crest leading up to Meall Dearg. The steepest pitch was climbed by the leftmost chimney close against the left wall, returning right to the main line immediately above.

BEINN EIGHE, Coire Mhic Fhearchair, Far East Wall:
Far East Gully – 70m III,5. R. McAllister, A. Nisbet. 19th April, 1998.
The gully at the right end of Far East Wall, between it and the small buttress with Karaoke Wall. Includes a chimney section with an awkward move over a chockstone.

Eastern Ramparts:
The Unknown Warrior – 130m VII,7. B. Davison, A. Nisbet. 10th January, 1999.
A winter line starting up The Unknown Soldier, continuing up Forgotten Warrior and finishing up Samurai. An independent finish up Forgotten Warrior looks worth a try for a party with daylight to spare. The summer lines were not followed precisely, so a full description is given. Start at a break 15m left of the cave which is about 15m up on the first pitch of Samurai (and 10m left of Samurai winter).
1. 45m. Climb about 10m to a ledge below a large triangular shape of rougher rock. Go right and back left to a V-shape formed by a right to left ramp between the triangle and a smaller triangle to its right. Go slightly rightwards up a crackline in smooth rock to a good ledge level with a pinnacle on the right. The pinnacle seems to be a dead end so pull out left on an undercut flake-crack (well seen from the cliff base) and climb a thin crack in a small smooth ramp (crux) to the Upper Girdle. Alternatively, find the start and follow your nose.
2. 10m. Traverse right along the Girdle past a section where the ledge disappears and belay in a niche immediately after the ledge reappears (Forgotten Warrior belay).
3. 40m. Climb Forgotten Warrior pitches 2 and 3, but apart from the start, keep to the fault line. At the top, move out right under a chockstone to belay as for Samurai.
4. 35m. Finish up Samurai (the final gully on ice on this occasion).

Gashtrognome – 210m VI,7. R. McAllister, A. Nisbet. 12th April, 1998.
Takes the line of least resistance up the concave scoop formed just left of East Buttress to a spectacular escape on to the buttress.
1. 25m. Climb The Gash to beyond its through route.
2. 35m Go up a shallow gully to a terrace and walk 10m right until below a pale corner (probably icy).
3. 20m. Climb the corner and its left arête to a ledge up left.
4. 35m .Step back down and traverse right above the corner along a ledge. Where the ledge ends, climb a left-facing corner, then take a left-curving line to below a big roof.
5. 20m. Continue left across a pale slab and up a groove to a ledge (probably on Gnome Wall).
6. 30m. Go left again until just right of the Gargoyle. Pull right on to a sensational jutting ledge (the diving board). Continue right, still sensational, to easier ground.
7. 45m. Go up the easing angle and a final short wall (on East Buttress).
Scramble to the top.

Central Buttress:
Central Corner – VII,8. A. Mullin, S. Paget. 21st January, 1999.
By the summer route. Partly iced.

Hamilton's Route – VI,6. D. McGimpsey, A. Nisbet. 17th November, 1998.
A similar standard to Piggott's, perhaps a little more sustained but without the very awkward crux. The quartzite start was gained easily via West-Central Gully. Start up a vegetated groove right of the summer start and only about 20m from West-Central Gully. Follow this into a corner on the right which leads to the end of the traverse on the summer route. Follow the summer route thereafter, including the final tower.

Sgurr nan Fhir Duibhe, North-West Face:
The Dark Ridge – 130m IV,6. B. Davison, A. Nisbet. 27th March, 1999.
The steep-fronted right-hand ridge at the right end of the cliff. Start easily up its left-hand side until a chimney leads back right to the crest below a steep wall (50m). Climb the short wall (crux), then traverse left to a corner and round its bounding wall to a groove (20m). Climb the groove, then the right-hand of two faults to gain the crest. Follow the crest to the top (60m).

Double Gully Left – 120m III. A. Nisbet. 5th January, 1999.
The well defined gully just right of The Dark Ridge has two ice pitches. The right version is mentioned in SMCJ 1997 (Grade I).

Black Gully – 130m II. B. Davison, A. Nisbet. 27th March, 1999.
The gully left of The Dark Ridge has several small steps and one larger one, passed on the right.

Carla's Gully – 80m II. A. Nisbet. 5th January, 1999.
Parallel gullies lead to gaps in the Black Carls section of the Beinn Eighe ridge. This is the right and more obvious gully. At the top is a short pitch and a through route emerging on the col.

Rubble without a Cause – 90m IV,4. R. McAllister, A. Nisbet. 5th January, 1999.
The buttress between the two gullies. Start near the base of Carla's Gully and climb a tricky groove (might be Grade III with loose blocks well frozen) leading to an easy finish passing right of an upper tower.

Bodach Gully – 80m II. A. Nisbet. 5th January, 1999.
The left but less defined gully has a harder pitch.

RUADH STAC BEAG:
Ruadh Ridge Beag – 100m III. A. Nisbet. 6th February, 1999.
` Near the left end of the cliffs SE of the summit of Ruadh Stac Beag is a well defined ridge right of a gully (well seen from the Black Carls section of the Beinn Eighe ridge). Climb the crest with two steep but very helpful sections.

BAOSBHEINN, North-East Face:
Direct Route – 300m III,4. R. G. Webb, N. Wilson. January, 1999.
Directly below the summit is a large triangular face. The route takes a line directly to the apex of the face, more clearly defined in the upper third.

BEINN ALLIGIN:
For the Chop – 100m III,4. B. Davison, A. Nisbet. 9th January, 1999.
Climbs the ramp system overlooking the Eag Dubh on the left. Start just inside the
Eag Dubh, climb a short wall and traverse left round the corner to a groove which
leads to a ledge with a large block (25m). Stand on the block to gain and follow the
ramp proper (50m). Finish up the upper of two ramps (the lower would be easier)
to the summit of 'The Hatchet' (25m).

Wailing Wall – 110m VII,7. D. McGimpsey, A. Nisbet. 21st January, 1999.
A very steep fault line to the right of Wall of the Outcry. Climbed in icy conditions,
useful to solidify the mossy vegetation. The technical crux is well protected. Start
as for Wall of the Outcry.
1. 45m. Climb the initial left-slanting grooves of Outcry (about 20m), but then go
straight up to the ledge system of its traverse. Traverse right under some huge
blocks (now under the main fault line) and climb just on their right to belay on top.
2. 10m. Step right into the fault line and follow it to a ledge under an overhanging
smooth section.
3. 35m. Traverse a ledge right for 6m to a crack. Use this to gain a prominent grass
ledge above and left. Pull out left on to a flake (technical crux) and continue left,
hopefully on ice, into the fault line. This ascent pulled out on to its left arête and
went 5m up left for runners, returning down to the fault. Climb the fault to a ledge
(no runners found here). Traverse 15m right, climb the short wall above and return
part way left.
4. 30m. Traverse easily right, climb a short wall and easy ground to the top.

SEANA MHEALLAN, Western Sector (*SMCJ* 1995, p 650):
The first routes are on a prow with three grooves (cairn below) which offers a
preliminary change of aspect 50m before the main change and the rest of the routes.
Incognito – 15m E1 5b*. J. Lyall, A. Nisbet. 2nd July, 1998.
Right of the three grooves, on a small west-facing wall, is a fine snaking crackline,
started direct (crux).

Correction to previous information: The routes all lie on the SW-facing wall in the
following order (left to right):
*Moaning Minnie, Fleeced, Unmasked, Flakey, Nasal Abuse, Mechanical Sheep,
Skate* (same route as *The Brotherhood*), *Polythene Bag, Clingfilm* (same route as
Big Cigar).

The Age of Confusion – 20m E3 5c**. C. Moody, L. Gordon-Canning. 17th June,
1998.
The rib between Nasal Abuse and Mechanical Sheep. Start left of the rib. Move up
right to a horizontal break (Camalot#4). Reach up then right to a crack. Follow the
crack, step left before the final overhang and climb the rib.

Bedrock Buttress:
Off With Her Head – 15m VS 4b*. L. Gordon-Canning, C. Moody. 12th May, 1998.
On the quartzy slab just left of the main part of the buttress with the route Bedrock.
At the right side of the slab is a vertical grassy crack. Start left of this. Climb straight
up to a shallow right-facing corner and finish up this.

The Black Queen – 15m Severe. A. Nisbet, G. Nisbet. 22nd June, 1998.
Climb the slab just right of the grassy crack to finish up a steep juggy crack in the headwall. Good protection for the final move (crux).

Bedrock (1994)

Wriggle – 10m VS 4c. L. Gordon-Canning, C. Moody. 12th May, 1998.
Wriggle right on to a shelf to gain the start of Archangel. Step left and climb the arête, slabby then cracked.

Archangel (1994)

Porpoise Scandal – 10m E1 5b. L. Gordon-Canning, C. Moody. 12th May, 1998.
Right of Archangel is a short right-facing corner with a dead tree just right again. Climb the corner, step left on to its arête, then back right to climb the crack. Hard for short folk.

Turned Turtle – 10m E1 5c. J. Lyall, A. Nisbet. 2nd July, 1998.
The roof crack and easier continuation right of the dead tree and in the centre of the roof system.

Bleached Whale – 10m E2 5b/c*. L. Gordon-Canning, C. Moody. 12th May, 1998.
A good looking line. Go up a short block, gain an overhanging hand crack and its continuation.

Dolphin Friendly – 10m E1 5b*. L. Gordon-Canning, C. Moody. 12th May, 1998.
The big right-facing corner next right.

The Knob – 10m HVS 5b*. J. Lyall, A. Nisbet. 2nd July, 1998.
Right of the big corner is a short corner leading to a roof. Move left round the roof and up cracks to finish up the arête.

Flintstone Buttress:
This is 150m farther on and slightly higher, above a flat area.

Wilma – 12m HVS 5a. J. Lyall, A. Nisbet. 2nd July, 1998.
The right-hand of two ramps (the left is capped by a roof) and the groove above.

Pebble – 12m H. Severe. J. Lyall, A. Nisbet. 2nd July, 1998.
The slabby wall to the right. Start 6m right and climb up to an alcove, then out left and up to the top.

DIABAIG, The Little Big Wall:
Calcite Corner – 30m HVS 5a*. G. Latter, A. Siddons (on-sight). 12th October, 1998.
Steep well-protected climbing, taking the prominent right-trending corner at the left end of the wall. Follow the corner, stepping out right near the top to finish on the heather and tree-covered terrace. (An ancient rusty peg was discovered about at about one third height – previously ascended in the dark ages?). The fine corner of The Dedo up on the left provides a logical and very worthwhile finish.

Feelin' Groovy – 25m E3 5c*. G. Latter (on-sight). 29th June, 1998.
Spectacular well protected climbing up the prominent right-slanting overhanging groove bounding the right side of the wall. Scramble up easy slabs to belay on a small ledge. Climb the groove, with hard moves to pull round onto the slab. Follow a left-trending line up the slab to belay on a small rowan.

Pointless Eliminates – 20m E2 5c. G. Latter, A. Siddons (on-sight). 12th October, 1998.
Above the path on the approach to the Main Cliff (approximately 100m left of Dead Mouse Crack) is a prominent chockstoned gully with a large holly immediately above the initial barring chockstone. This route climbs the centre of the slab forming the left side of the gully – quite bold, and a bit of an eliminate, with much easier (VS?) ground just to the left. Descent was made from a sling on a small spike at the top, though other descents looked possible by traversing either left or right from the top.

DIABAIG, Hidden Crag (MR 788 586):
The crag is situated on the south side of the peninsula across the bay from Diabaig. Its beautiful location with an outlook across Loch Torridon to Applecross and Skye is ideal for those midge-infested days when an exposed venue is sought. It catches the sun for most of the day. The best climbs follow well-protected cracklines on excellent rock. The climbing is strenuous.
Access: Follow the Diabaig-Inveralligin path past the Main Wall and continue, dropping to the shore until a flat boggy area between the mainland and the peninsula is reached. Pass the derelict croft at its far end, heading for a bay, and contour rightwards up the hillside passing a fenced enclosure. One hour.

White Wall:
At the low right end is a bulging wall split by three obvious lines.
Epsilon – 8m H. Severe. A. Brockington, J. Fisher. 5th September, 1998. The first crack.
Delta – 8m E1 5b*. J. Fisher, A. Brockington. 5th September, 1998. The second crack, sustained.
Gamma – 10m V. Diff*. A. Brockington, J. Fisher. 5th September, 1998. A right-trending ramp.

Rolling Wall:
The crag's showpiece, a fine formation of smooth bulges split by impressive cracklines.
Beside the Point – 15m VS 4c. J. Fisher, A. Brockington. 5th September, 1998. The crackline left of a vegetated ramp.

The Ice Bulge – 15m E1 5b**. J. Fisher, A. Brockington. 5th September, 1998. Climb direct to an obvious quartz bulge, put your crampons on and —.

The Low Girdle – 30m E1 5b. F. Bennet, J. Fisher. 3rd October, 1998.
Start beneath the impressive unclimbed crack right of Brave New World. Climb up to the start of the crack. Make thin moves left until easier climbing concludes the traverse.

Brave New World – 25m E3 6a (One rest)***. J. Fisher, A. Brockington. 5th September, 1998.
An angelic climb up the impressive cracks in the centre of the rolling wall. Climb the initial crack for a few metres until a delicate traverse leads left to above the first bulge. Follow the crack on good finger jams to a hard finish (crux). Repeated and considered E2 5c.

The Sea, The Sea – 25m E2 5b***. J. Fisher, A. Brockington. 5th September, 1998.
Another gem up cracks left again. Start 2m right of the thin starting cracks, traverse boldly in beneath the first bulge and continue up the crack to below the final bulge through which the cracks peter out. Step up and left to finish in an exposed position up the left edge of the Rolling Wall.

Rolling Home – 40m E2 5c**. J. Fisher, F. Bennet. 3rd October, 1998.
Start 2m right of Feelies crack. Climb cracks up the blunt arête to a junction with The Sea, The Sea. Step delicately on to 'The Roll' and traverse beneath it, exiting at the far right crack (crux).

The Feelies – 30m VS 4c. A. Brockington, J. Fisher. 5th September, 1998.
An interesting route up the crack at the left end of the wall, finishing up a steep spike-choked corner.

Submission – 30m HVS 5a*. S. Grey, A. Reid, J. Reid. 3rd October, 1998.
Start left of The Feelies. Climb a diagonal crack for 2m, going up and right to a flake. Climb the arête left of Feelies corner.

Boatman's Call – 30m E1 5b*. S. Grey, A. Reid, J. Reid. 3rd October, 1998.
Start left of a hawthorn bush. Surmount two overlaps rightwards. Cross Submission and The Feelies to finish up the slightly mossy corner right of The Feelies.

The Orange Wall:
Two small buttresses lie 30m left of the Rolling Wall; each is split by cracks.
Ewar Woowar – 8m H. Severe 4b. J. Fisher. 5th September, 1998.
Cracks up the right side of the right buttress.

Alice's Overhang – 8m VS 5a*. J. Fisher (unsec.). 5th September, 1998.
A slab and bulge up the left-hand buttress.

Beached Boat Buttress (MR 789 592):
Facing Diabaig, near the end of the peninsula, is a slender buttress above a gully. This climb starts in the gully, then climbs the slender buttress via a corner and rib.
Beached Boat Buttress – 60m HVS*. J. Fisher, A. Brockington. 5th September, 1998.
1. 20m 4c. Start down and left of a thin crack. Climb the arête.
2. 40m 5a .Scramble down and left for 20m. Climb the corner past a holly, then up the rounded rib.

Crofter's Crag (MR 795 587):
Situated opposite the ruined croft, facing north, is an area of steep broken crags.
The Applecross Jam – 20m E3 5c***. A. Coull, A. Sharpe, J. Fisher, F. Bennet. 3rd October, 1998.

The clean central wall is split by a compelling crack. A steep start leads to a ledge and rest. Climb the final overhanging wall on spaced holds and jams to a strenuous finish. Note: an abseil sling found at the top of the wall; new sling and krab left to avoid an awkward descent.

8-Ace – 20m VS 5a. S. Grey, A. eid, J. Reid. 3rd October, 1998.
The left arête of the clean wall follows a curving ramp.

Approaching the peninsula, just beyond a birch woodland, is a fine wall of orange rock.
Red Crescent – 15m E1 5b**. S. Grey, A. Reid, J. Reid. 3rd October, 1998.
Climbs the smaller wall left of the main wall. A steep ramp leads to a crescent. Go diagonally up and left along a break to a pod. Go directly to the top.

Ugly Crag (MR 800 588):
Up the hillside 100m from the birch wood is a west-facing crag of steep juggy rock.
Ugly Wall – 20m E1 5b**. F. Bennet, J. Fisher. 4th October, 1998.
Start just right of the highest part of the crag and 5m left of an orange corner. Climb up and left on big holds to a large flake below a roof. Pull over directly and make an awkward exit leftwards. An exciting outing.

Ugly Mug – 55m E2***. J. Fisher, F. Bennet. 4th October, 1998.
A wild route, steeped in exposure and character. Takes a rising traverse line from bottom left to top right. Start at a pile of blocks beneath a big block in an open corner.
1. 25m 5c. Climb up and rightwards, then pull steeply over a bulge to a good ledge. Traverse strenuously rightwards on good holds to a precarious exit on to a hanging slab. Belay at its right end.
2. 30m 5c .Drop down and continue traversing rightwards on huge holds in a spectacular position to the flake on Ugly Wall (good runners). Step up and right to a good slot (Friend #2), then make a hard move rightwards to another good flake. Pull directly over the bulge above. Exit leftwards.

Pretty Crag:
Opposite Ugly Crag and visible from Diabaig is a slab of immaculate white gneiss.
Pretty Crack – 8m VS 4c*. J. Fisher. 4th October, 1998.
The left-hand crack.

Pretty Scoop – 8m VS 4b. J. Fisher. 4th October, 1998.
The left-hand scoop. Unprotected.

White House Crag (MR 801 577):
Access: Follow the Diabaig-Inveralligin path past two lochans and down to a bay with a white house. Approaching from Wester Alligin is a similar distance and time. The crag is directly behind the path. One hour.
The crag is a 50m dome of gneiss with a steep juggy band at 20m and a terrace at 35m. On the terrace is a lone tree from which an abseil is possible, omitting the much easier second pitches. The most obvious feature is a short, shallow but well defined central groove in a slabby lower section (taken by the original route Rendezvous). Left to right:
Bare Faced Cheek – 45m E1 5b. R. Brown, J. R. Mackenzie, G. Cullen. 16th May, 1998.
A steep brown slab lies to the left of the grassy groove of Rock Stripper. Climb the

central plinth to a horizontal, then take the bulge above to a foothold. Continue up the central cracks in the slab, a good pitch (25m). Continue up right of a dirty corner-crack, following the best line, rather scrappy (20m).

Rock Stripper – 50m VS 4c. R. Brown, J. R. Mackenzie. 8th May, 1998.
Start left of the short central groove and right of a grassy groove. Climb the slabby wall to a chokestone in a bulge which is climbed to step right and up directly to twin overhangs. Surmount the lower (crux) and traverse left beneath the upper to enter a groove which is climbed up and right to the terrace (40m). Continue straight up to finish (10m). Quite bold in places.

Indecent Exposure – 50m HVS 5a*. R. Brown, J. R. Mackenzie, G. Cullen, A. Nisbet. 16th May, 1998.
Either start as for Rock Stripper or to the left of its grassy groove and climb blocky rock to surmount the chokestone. Continue up a steep slab with a small aspen to the overhangs on the right. Move right on huge jugs to a small triangular niche on the nose (exposed). Climb the crux wall directly above to the terrace (35m). Finish up the top tier (15m). Well positioned climbing with a short crux.

Rendezvous – 50m HVS 5a*. M. Welch, M. Arkley. October, 1993 (see *SMCJ* 1994).
The original route on the crag taking a central line (and approached by canoe from Applecross). Scramble up easy rocks to a short wall beneath the central groove. Climb a wall and thin crack to enter the groove which is climbed to overhangs. Step right and surmount the overhang, then another and continue up on holds that keep appearing to the terrace (35m). Climb the wall left of the tree and a slab to the top (15m).

The Full Monty – 50m E1 5b**. J. R. Mackenzie, R. Brown. 8th May, 1998.
A better companion to Rendezvous, more exposed and sustained. To the right of the central groove is a thin red crack. Climb the slabs directly up to it, then climb the crack to the overhang. Move right and pull over this to climb the wall to a horizontal crack. Move left, surmount the bulge and climb the exposed wall directly, making a step left near the top to the tree (35m). Climb the wall to the right of the tree and slab above to the top (15m).

Promiscuous Groove – 30m HVS 5b. G Cullen, A. Nisbet, J. R. Mackenzie, R. Brown. 16th May, 1998.
To the right of The Full Monty is a red wall. Start left of a juniper bush and climb the slab to the wall. This provides awkward climbing to a better wall above which leads to a blocky groove of suspect rock.

Above White House Crag is a slab.
Walking on Crystals – 40m Moderate to V. Diff. R. Brown, J. R. Mackenzie. 8th May, 1998.
The slab is easiest on the left but more entertaining up the red crystalline gneiss to the right.

Quartz Inspector's Slab – 10m V. Diff to Severe. J. R. Mackenzie, R. Brown. 8th May, 1998.
At the top of the slab is a 10m slab of faultless white gneiss to the left. Various lines climbed.

GAIRLOCH CRAGS, Meall Lochan a' Chlerich, Creag nan Cadhag (MR 864 722):
Central Corner – 25m Mild VS. A. Brooks, T. Doe 3rd January, 1989.
The big central corner of this overhanging lichenous crag. The corner chimney-crack was climbed until it became too narrow and the route finished up the left wall.

The Trail of the Lonesome Pine Marten – 25m HVS. A. Brooks, T. Doe, D. Jones 18th June, 1989
Start a few metres left of Central Corner, below a boulder on a ledge. Go straight up with increasing difficulty to finish by the obvious overhanging jamming crack.
Note: The same party also climbed a version of Bald Eagle/Open Secret and The Lum pitch1/Questionable Crack pitch 2.

Stone Valley Crags, Viking Crag:
Between Rum Doodle Arête and Red Wall Crag lies this small crag marked by large fallen blocks and short walls. Good rock. Descents right or left.

Helga's First Time – 35m Severe*. D. S. B. Wright, A. K. R. Parker. 14th June, 1998.
There is an obvious broken groove with twin cracks above. Climb the pleasant rough slab on the left of the groove to a boulder-spike. Step left on to a wall, then by interesting moves right to a spike, finishing directly up the rib.

Uphellya – 30m VS 4c*. G. Ettle, D. S. B. Wright. 18th June, 1998.
Take the obvious broken groove, step left, then up right to climb the twin cracks (harder if the dubious block at the top of the cracks is not used). Follow a crack on excellent rock to finish just right of the crest.

Little Valhalla – 12m VS 4c*. G. Ettle, D. S. B. Wright. 18th June, 1998.
A few metres right of Uphellya, is a very obvious groove. This gives delightful, well-protected climbing. Much better than it looks.

Norse Face Route – 12m E2 5c*. G. Ettle (unsec.). 18th June, 1998.
Starting up Little Valhalla, a pedestal on the right is gained. A shimmy up the arête and mantleshelf gains a pocket with a vital Friend 3+ runner. An extended wire into a slot on the right protects hard moves right to a crack. Further hard moves up lead to a right-trending fault-line and easier finish. The overall grade increases if the extended runner cannot be placed.

Red Wall Crag:
Burnt Offering – 25m E2 5b*. G. Ettle, D. S. B. Wright. 2nd June, 1998.
Bold as Brass is followed to below the flange, when a wall on the right is climbed to a groove with tiny tree below an overlap. This is passed on the right, with a deviation right which avoids the hardest direct moves.

Flaming Crack – 30m VS 5a. G. Ettle, D. S. B.Wright. 2nd June, 1998.
The crack of Flaming June is followed throughout. Will improve with time.

Schiltrom – 25m E1 5b*. G. Ettle, D. S. B. Wright. 18th June, 1998.
Starting at a small spike in the heather ramp right of Lucky Strike, make a hard move left to gain the bottom of a rightward-trending flake-line. This leads to a semi-detached spike just left of Strike Two, from where a move leftwards gains an overlap which is overcome with difficulty. Climb the clean slab above, with a delicate move left to finish.

Flowerdale Wall:

Scraggy Slab – 30m HVS 4c. G. Ettle, D. S. B. Wright, K. Grindrod. 3rd May, 1998.
Below and left of Flowerdale Wall, a series of smaller outcrops leads leftwards.
This disappointing route takes the biggest slab, about 200m left of Flowerdale
Wall, on dubious rock with poor protection.

Fruity Crag (See *SMCJ* 1998, MR 794 714):

Passion Fruit – 10m E4 6a**. G. Robertson (unsec.). 21st March, 1998.
Climbs directly up the front face of the pillar right of Lemon, at the left end of the
crag. Excellent fingery climbing, but bold. (top-roped prior to leading).

Banana – 10m V. Diff. A. Crofton, T. Rankin. 21st March, 1998.
The chimney right of Passion Fruit.

Kiwi – 10m VS 5a*. I. Fischer, G. Robertson. 21st March, 1998.
The fine crack right of Banana.

Starfruit – 10m VS 5b. A. Crofton. 21st March, 1998.
The wall right of Kiwi, with a hard start.

Pineapple – 12m Moderate.
A useful descent route. Follows the obvious left-trending fault right of Starfruit.

Paw-paw – 10m E2 5c**. T. Rankin, D. Laing. 21st March, 1998.
A great fingery little route taking the obvious left-facing shallow corner in the
smooth wall right of Pineapple. Microwires useful.

Vegie Crag:

From the foot of Fruity Crag, walk left (facing the crag) and head diagonally left
up the hillside heading for the col between two hills. The crag is on the left side of
the pleasant grassy col. The crag is very sheltered and faces east. The rock is clean
and sound although the base is quite boggy. Ten minutes from Fruity Crag.
Neep – 10m H. Severe. A. Crofton, D. Laing. 21st March, 1998.
The left-hand line of weakness out of a steep bay. Start at the left end of the highest
part of the cliff. Continue up short slabs to the top.

Swede – 10m VS 5b. A. Crofton, D. Laing, T. Rankin. 21st March, 1998.
Climbs the centre of the steep bay. Start below the left-facing corner in the upper
part of the crag. Climb the bouldery start to join and finish up the corner. A good
wee route.

Sweet Potato – 15m Severe. T. Rankin, D. Laing, A. Crofton. 21st March, 1998.
The obvious left-slanting crack gives the best route here. Start up the short corner
to the left.

Turnip – 10m H. Severe. T. Rankin. 21st March, 1998.
Climb the steep crack 4m right of Sweet Potato. Continue up the slab to finish up
the right edge of the upper wall.

Rubha Mor (Sheet 19; MR 876 978):

A couple of promontories on this section of coast offer short routes on clean sound
Torridonian sandstone. Approach via the single track road west of Mellon Udrigle,
followed by a boggy 1km walk round the coast. The first promontory at MR 879
978 has a long NW-facing easy-angled wall accessed by scrambling down a long

ramp line. Where this fades out, a left-facing slabby groove (12m, V. Diff) has been climbed. Some distance right of this is a short red slab directly below two large cairns. There are two pleasant lines; on the left side is Severe and the right side is VS 4b. The next promontory to the west (MR 876 978) offers better but limited climbing on its NW tip where a steep wall rises above a rock platform (part tidal).

Heather's a Blether – 10m HVS 5a. D. McGimpsey, J. Lines, R. McAllister. September, 1998.
Juggy climbing up a slim corner 5m left of a left-leaning black corner. Finish out right on steep layaways.

Chrome Melons – 10m VS 5a. D. McGimpsey. September, 1998.
The left-leaning black corner. If wet at the top, move out left and climb a short stepped corner (4c).

Moving round to the left, a more broken wall faces the open sea. At its far left there is an overhanging wall.
Melons in a Muddle – 10m E1 5b. J. Lines, D. McGimpsey, R. McAllister. September, 1998.
Climb a short corner to gain a right-trending break. Go along this, then up and left to a finish on the left arête.

Aztec Tower (Sheet 19; MR 815 784):
There are now nine routes on this 20m crag, Diff to HVS. The crag lies 2km north of Gairloch and is seen as a reddish tower to the west of the road. Details in the next guide.

An Groban:
Growbag Grooves – 60m E1 5b*. A. Nisbet, G. Nisbet. 29th April, 1998.
Start as for Hatman but climb rightwards up an inset slab to where it meets Straker. Step left and climb shallow grooves up the crest of the buttress (35m). Scramble to the top.

CREAG MHOR THOLLAIDH, Lower Tollie Crag:
Sarah'n'Dipity and the Forgotten Pill – 55m E3**. S. Hill, D. S. Shephard. 4th June, 1998
An excellent climb in an impressive situation, taking the fine shallow groove in the centre of the wall, between The Trip and Decadent Days. Climbed on sight with no pre-inspection or cleaning.
1. 15m 4c. As for The Trip to the large oak.
2. 25m 5c. Continue 6m up until it is possible to step right past a perched block. Move up and right to gain good holds at base of a shallow groove. Follow this over a slight bulge to a junction with Catastasis; follow this diagonally left to a niche and old peg belay.
3. 15m 4a. Pull out of the top of the niche into a slanting crack. Follow this to finish easily.

GRUINARD, Carn Goraig (Sheet 19, MR 995 860):
This is a three-tiered west-facing gneiss crag overlooking the River Gruinard not far from its source at Loch na Sealga. Access is straight-forward being about 6km from the main road following a well maintained estate track until opposite Carn Goraig; about 1hr. 15min. walk or 45min. by mountain bike. Ford the river

(difficult when in spate) and cross the boggy flats to the crag. The crag is solid clean rough gneiss, generally slabby climbing with a steeper two-tiered lower section. The climbs usually follow cracklines with good protection. Some of the routes are on the top tier only with access to the heather terrace being on the right. Descent possible left or right. Routes described right to left starting with two routes on the right side of the top tier.

The Fatwah – 30m HVS 5b**. A. Cunningham, F. Fotheringham. 7th October 1998.
The fine crack rising out of the obvious red groove. Follow the crack in the same line after the easing.

Dispossessed – 30m E1 5c**. F. Fotheringham, A. Cunningham. 7th October, 1998.
Start at The Fatwah and move left into a scooped line of cracks, small ledges and hidden holds to gain the easing by a small protruding spike. Climb in the same line via cracks and blocks to finish.

Ramadan – 65m E1**. A. Cunningham, F. Fotheringham. July, 1995.
1. 10m 4a. Climb cracks on the right side of the lower tier to a belay by a large overhung recess (or walk round!).
2. 25m 5b. Climb a steep widening crack out of the right side of the recess and up to belay below a wide blocky Y-crack in the upper slabs.
3. 30m 4c. Move up and rightwards via the crack and pull left through the bulge to follow the continuing left-hand crack.

Wailing Wall – 70m E1**. F. Fotheringham, A. Taylor. 11th March, 1987.
1. 20m 4b. Start at the foot of the lowest rocks near the right of the first tier. Climb a slab and gain a recessed scoop and exit via a crack on the right on to a stance on the terrace.
2. 25m 5b. Climb steeply to gain a shelf. Follow a left-trending fault and climb a rounded bulge and up to a heather terrace. Belay below the obvious twin cracklines, the closer right-hand two of three parallel cracks.
3. 25m 5a. Climb the left-hand crack initially until it steepens and step right to gain the right crack at the bulge. Climb this and follow the crack over the top bulge.

Call of the Muwazzin – 25m E2 5b/c**. A. Cunningham, F. Fotheringham. 7th October, 1998.
A good pitch on the top tier, following the crack immediately left of the twin cracks of Wailing Wall - the left-hand of the three parallel cracks. Where the crack peters out at the half height bulge, move right into the left-hand crack of Wailing Wall (where that route moves right) and move immediately back left into the original line after the bulge.

The Highland Cragsman – 90m E3**. J. R. Mackenzie, D. S. B. Wright 7th October, 1998.
1. 20m 5c. Start to the right of the undulating scoops of Wailing Wall and climb to an arrow-shaped slot. Climb the crack above and step left then back right up a pair of thin cracks to the ledge.
2. 35m 5c. Start just left of the smooth scoop and reach an undercut flange; go strenuously up this to a foot-traverse right across a small shelf. Climb up just left of the blind exit crack to hand traverse right below it to a heather patch below a steep

crack. Climb the crack and continue up the slab and heather to belay at the base of the central deep scoop left of Call of the Muwazzin.

3. 35m 5b. Climb the rib left of and join Call of the Muwazzin for a farther 10m or so to a point where it is possible to do a thin traverse left to join another hidden crack above a grassy crack and scoop below. Continue up this crack on good holds until possible to step left to reach a prominent flange which is climbed to a rounded ledge and exit up the short top wall. Some excellent sustained climbing on the lower two pitches with a more relaxed final pitch in a delightful situation.

Whoopers – 90m E3/4 6a**. G. Latter, A. Siddons. 13th October, 1998.
In the centre of the lower tier is a smooth-looking scoop, split by some very thin cracks.

1.15m 6a. Climb the easy lower slab, then by a good crack which soon fades. Continue up the scoop, with a hard move to gain a thin horizontal break. Step up right and pull over the final bulge, using a good jug in the crack on the right.

2. 20m 5c. Directly above is another, smoother scoop. Climb the steep flake crack on the left arête, then traverse right and up to the base of a fine hanging crack. Layback into the crack and pull over onto the slab above.

3. 10m. Scramble up to belay.

4. 35m? Climb the thin left-slanting crack above, then by a thin crack in the crest of a vague blunt rib, over a tricky bulge. Finish more easily up a wider mossy crack.

Return to Mecca/Alba – 100m E2**. Top pitch (Return to Mecca) – F. Fotheringham, A. Taylor. 6th September 1998. Pitch 1 (Alba) – J. R. Mackenzie, D. S. B. Wright. 29th September, 1998.

1. 35m 5a. On the left of the lower tier is a continuous steep rib bottomed by reddish slabs. Climb the slab direct to the rib which is climbed centrally to exit via a rightwards slanting crack; a well sustained pitch.

2. 20m. Scramble up broken ground to below a bowl-shaped scoop on the left side of the top tier.

3. 25m 5c. Climb the crack on the left of the bowl to a wall. Traverse left across a bulge to a thin crack which is climbed strenuously, crux, to a slab which is climbed up right to a wall. Move back left to a rightward-facing ramp which is taken in a good position to the top. A good pitch; constantly varied and interesting.

Olden Glory – 95m VS**. D. S. B. Wright, R. Brown. 2nd October, 1998.

1. 35m 4b. To the left of the steeper rib of Alba's lower pitch is a lesser one which is climbed direct on good to slabs.

2. 15m. Continue up pleasant slabs to a prominent short groove above.

3. 35m 4c. Climb the awkward groove via cracks to a small tree. Move up left round a shallow rib to a flanged crack which is climbed to a topmost bulge. Hand traverse below the bulge to a break and exit up this to the top, a fine pitch taking the easiest line up the top tier. A good climb that deserves to become popular.

Car Park Area:
Molly's Ridge – 15m Diff. J. and P. Richards, J. and K. Bolger, C. and S. Steer. 23rd June, 1996.
The blunt ridge above the V. Diff. Slab.

Mutt's Crack – 8m Severe. J. and P. Richards, J. and K. Bolger, C. and S. Steer. 23rd June, 1996.
The thin crack on the far right of the ridge's flank.

Members of the same party climbed other short routes nearby. Flake Buttress lies right of and slightly below V. Diff. Slab and has a large flake at its right end. There are three 6m routes; the crack on the front of the flake (5a); the flake-chimney forming its left side (V. Diff.), and scoops and slabs on the left (V. Diff.).

Gruinard Crag:
Ueejit – 18m E4 6a* N. Morrison, J. Reed. August, 1997
Climb the right side of the reddish wall with three diagonal cracks between Halcyon Days and Utopia up a line of small flakes leading from a small ledge at the right end of the middle crack to the topmost crack (runners) and a hard move above it. Sustained and thin.

Coupe du Monde – 25m E4 5c*. G. Ettle, D. S. B. Wright. 16th June, 1998.
Between Red John and Overlord is a groove and steep wall. The route climbs these, moving slightly right up steep flakes to a difficult finish in a small groove. Low in the grade.

NOTE: How the West was Won was climbed with a direct finish above the shattered flakes by P. Thorburn and J. Lowther, same grade, on 16th August, 1998.

Quail – 30m Diff. D. S. B. Wright, G. Ettle. 16th June, 1998.
The obvious short fissure at the right end of the crag is climbed to a heather ledge, followed by a fine groove round the corner.

Inverianvie Crag, The Bayview Wall:
The Pleasure Beach – 15m Severe*. G. Ettle, D. S. B. Wright. 21st May, 1998.
Start just to the left of Gneiss and Easy. Climb via flakes and cracks to a ledge. Avoid the vegetated groove above by climbing the cracked wall on the right.

Double Matured – 15m VS 4c. A. Nisbet, G. Nisbet. 18th October, 1997.
The heathery crack, starting up the wall immediately to its left and moving into the crack above the tree. Not unpleasant, with bridging past the heather.

Decommissioned Arms – 20m E1 5b. A. Cunningham. 31st August, 1998.
A route up the middle of the slim buttress to the left of Chokestone Gully. Start by climbing a thin undercut crack and move up a left diagonal crack until a swing right leads to ledges. Easier up the middle of the buttress to finish.
Note: A less direct version with a vegetated start to the left was climbed by A. and G. Nisbet on 10th May, 1998 (Severe).

Inverianvie Crag, Optic Wall:
The long wall right of the huge wedged block is composed of less good rock.
The Parting Glass – 20m HVS 5a. G. Ettle, D. S. B .Wright. 21st May, 1998.
From the lowest point, a rightwards-trending line is taken to breach the obvious roof by a crack. On the first ascent, a lens fell from the second's spectacles.

The Dundee Dram – 25m VS 4c. A. Nisbet, G. Nisbet. 10th May, 1998.
Climb the right edge of the wall up a cleaned crack, moving right to keep near the edge and up to a heathery finish.

Gruinard Jetty Buttress:
Running on Empty – 40m E2 5c. J. R. Mackenzie, R. Brown. 26th April, 1998.
Climbs the blank wall to the right of North-West Arête. Start to the right of the fence

post and climb the bouldery wall direct to beneath the widest point of the overhang above, vital runners. Pull over this to arrive beneath a shallow black scoop, marginal RPs only. Move up, then step left to a rounded edge and gain easier ground common to NW Arête. Despite being an eliminate, it offers good tenuous climbing that is serious above the overhang.

Prizefighter – 25m E3 5c**. J. R. Mackenzie, R. Brown (alt.). 26th April, 1998.
Climbs the arête bounding Charlie's Corner on the left, then the overhanging crack immediately to the right of the Direct Finish to that route.
1. 10m 5a. Climb the elegant but poorly protected arête direct to a ledge.
2. 15m 5c. Move up right and gain the overhanging shallow corner-crack right of the ivy-choked direct finish and climb this increasingly strenuously, well protected, to a fighting finish up the overhanging crack above.

CARN DEARG AN DROMA (MR 971 944):
This slabby gneiss crag faces south and lies north of the A832. It is well seen from the layby near Miotag but most easily approached from the layby at MR 981 934 in 20 minutes. Several routes were climbed in the easier grades by J. Richards and S. Steer on 29th August, 1996, the best being:
Game Boy – 25m Severe.
Start at the steep wall right of Tetrus. Climb this direct, then take a crack in the wall above to join a flake-crack leading rightwards up the top slab.

Tetrus Rocket – 25m Severe.
Climb the obvious corner and deep groove line, moving right at the top of the groove to finish.

Little Faith - 30m V. Diff.
Climb the pleasant rounded slabby arête above a right-slanting turf break.

Shrapnel Crack – 30m V. Diff.
Climb the right-slanting crack left of Little Faith.

CREAG BEINN NAM BAN (*SMCJ* 1998), Fluted Buttress:
Right of Creag Beinn nam Ban is a gully containing Hang Dog Pinnacle. Right again is another parallel gully at the top left of which is a 20m buttress. This can be seen from the road just south of the layby and is characterised by left-slanting cracks and grooves. The rock on this buttress is a little more brittle than elsewhere.
Put a Sock in it! – V. Diff.*. N. J. Smith. 3rd May, 1998.
The leftmost crack on the front (SW) face of the buttress with a right handrail.

Beaufort Scale – V. Diff. T. A. Murray, C. A. Watt. 4th May, 1998.
Immediately right of the last route is a slight recession with two shallow chimneys. This is the left chimney.

Force Six Chimney – V. Diff. N. J. Smith, J. R. Mackenzie. 4th May, 1998.
The right chimney is rather loose.

Class Struggle – HVS 5a*. J. R. Mackenzie, N. J. Smith. 4th May, 1998.
Right of Force Six Chimney is a steep jam crack in a shallow left-facing corner. Climb the crack direct exiting right.

Absentee Landlord – V. Diff. N. J. Smith. 5th June, 1998.
The left-slanting groove immediately right of Class Struggle is clearly seen from
the road and identifiable at close quarters by a rockfall scar low down.

Prole's Crack – M. Severe. N. J. Smith, J. R. Mackenzie. 4th May, 1998.
At the right end of the face is an undercut crack with a small square-cut overhang
at half height. Gain crack from the left and turn the overhanging block on its right.

Fin Buttress:
Left of Fluted Buttress is a small slabby buttress. Left again is a buttress with a
prominent fin of rock separating two grooves. The left-hand groove has a small tree
low on its right.
Social Climber – VS 4b. J. R. Mackenzie, N. J. Smith. 4th May, 1998.
The right-hand groove. Start just right of the lowest point and pull up a short
bubbled wall leftwards to a slab. Move up to a groove and so to the top.

Lords a Leaping – VS 4c*. N. J. Smith, J. R. Mackenzie. 4th May, 1998.
The left-hand groove. Start at a slab left of the lowest point and climb the groove
which is more awkward than it might appear.

High above Creag Beinn nam Ban and at much the same altitude as the last two
buttresses is a low-angled pink slab. It looks impressive in profile from the top of
Fin Buttress but is rather broken with only its right end being clean and continuous.
It can be reached by continuing up the gully from Hound Dog Pinnacle until the slab
is on the left.
Solo Slab – 50m Moderate. N. J. Smith. 5th June, 1998.
Climb the slab on excellent rock.

Badrallach Crag (Sheet 19; MR 104 914):
At the NW end of Beinn nam Ban two tiers of crags overlook Badrallach. The lower
tier is vegetated but the upper tier contains a small slabby crag which can be
identified by a small cave at its foot. The rock is excellent rough sandstone. The
crag, which catches the afternoon and evening sun, is quick drying and offers a
number of low grade routes in a fine setting. Park at a large layby 300m south of
the Allt na h-Airbhe hairpin bend at point 236 on Sheet 19. Avoid the lower tier by
striking up to the north ridge on the left, then returning rightwards to the crag – 15
minutes. Routes are described from right to left.
Windy Ridge – 70m Easy. N. J. Smith. 5th July, 1997.
A pleasant scramble up the blocky ridge which bounds the crag on its right. Start
at the lowest rocks right of the cave. Climb to a heather and bearberry ledge at about
50m. Another shorter band of rock is climbed easily. From the top the summit is
but an easy stroll.

The following routes are 35m to 45m and terminate on the ledge. Descend by
reversing Windy Ledge.
Garden Party – V. Diff. T. A. Murray, C. J. Watt, N. J. Smith. 1st May, 1998.
The botanically interesting groove right of the cave. Low in the grade.

Lapsang Suchong – Severe. N. J. Smith, C. J. Watt, T. A. Murray. 1st May, 1998.
Start at the right side of the cave. Climb a slab to the roof of the cave and make a
long step right on to an arête. Move up to easier ground, then climb a corner which
leads to the ledge.

Laird's Loss – HVS 5a*. C. J. Watt, N. J. Smith, T. A. Murray. 1st May, 1998.
Climb direct to the awkward hanging groove above the centre of the cave. A deep
crack in the slab above leads more easily to the ledge.

Pillar of Society – VS 4b . N. J. Smith, T. A. Murray, C. J. Watt. 2nd May, 1998.
The left wall of the cave is formed by a giant pillar. Climb the wall on mega jugs
to the top of the pillar. A crack now leads up the slab trending left. Protection is
spaced.

Poacher's Prize – VS 4b**. N. J. Smith, T. A. Murray, C. J. Watt. 2nd May, 1998.
Left of the cave is a wide crack where the pillar joins the slab. Left again is a
prominent crack which runs the full height of the slab. Start steeply below the crack
and follow it to the top. Protection is spaced.

Hunter's Moon – HVS 4c**. N. J. Smith, C. J. Watt, T. A. Murray. 2nd May, 1998.
At the foot of the slab and left of Poacher's Prize is a large boulder. From the top
of this a crack starts up the slab but runs out. Climb the crack, then continue boldly
in the same line to a slight steepening which is climbed on improving holds to the
ledge.

BEINN LAIR, North-East Face:
Y Gully, Left Fork – 250m III. P. F. Macdonald, C. G. M.Slesser. 11th April, 1998.
First ascent in thin conditions, when a large chockstone in the fork section provided
the main obstacle; the grading assumes more of a build-up around this. Fine rock
scenery.

Angel Buttress, Ordinary Route by Wrangham's variation – IV. R. F. Allen, R.
Richardson. 11th April 1998.
The summer line was followed. The main challenges were a series of chockstone
pitches in the chimneys, one of which offers a through route for the most slender
of leaders! Recommended.

AN TEALLACH, A'Ghlas Thuill:
Unnamed – 300m II. A. Cunningham, F. Fotheringham, D. Williamson. January,
1997.
Climbs the buttress between North Gully and Hayfork Gully. Start at the toe of the
buttress and climb easily to a steep band at half height. Take a line leading out right
to overlook North Gully, then follow a shallow gully/ramp which is formed
between the crest of the buttress and North Gully to finish near the top of the latter.

Toll an Lochain:
Lucky Strike – 200m II. V. Chelton, R. McAllister, D. McGimpsey, S. Mearns. 24th
February, 1999.
Climbs a ramp bounding the right side of Gobhlach Buttress and leading to a short
gully. Gain the ramp from midway up the easy gully (Central Gully).

Corrag Bhuidhe South Buttres, Original Route – 350m II. V. Chelton, R. McAllister,
D. McGimpsey, S. Mearns. 24th February, 1999.
Climbs the east face overlooking Loch Toll an Lochain, probably following the

Glover and Ling original climb on this buttress. Start up a shallow gully just right of the barrier wall at the base (which drops into the lochan). Climb this and trend easily left towards a very steep wall with a ramp and obvious icefall. Make a long traverse left until it is possible to climb up mixed ground to a snowfield below the main rock barrier on the face. Traverse back right to the crest until turfy steps lead up to a left-trending ramp-cum-gully breaching the barrier wall. At its top, climb up left into a small basin. A short turfy groove on the left (crux) leads to easier ground. Either climb straight up to the final crest or up and left across snow to the top.

Corrag Bhuidhe, South Buttress Direct – 350m IV,4. D. McGimpsey, A. Nisbet. 26th February, 1999.
Start up the gully as for the original route and trend easily left to the steep wall and icefall. Start up the icefall but soon go up a prominent diagonal line leftwards with a through route to reach a terrace. Gain the next terrace below another steep tier. Climb a turfy groove just left of the crest, breaking out left at half height and returning right above. Follow the crest to the top.

Corrag Bhuidhe, South Buttress by the Mental Chimney – 350m V,6. D. McGimpsey, A. Mullin, A. Nisbet. 28th December, 1998.
Start as for the Direct Route but continue to gain the base of a gully which is formed right of the buttress crest. A pitch with three difficult steps in the gully bed leads to two further pitches where the difficulties are passed using the rib on the right. The crest is gained soon above and followed easily to the summit. Very icy conditions might drop the grade to IV,5.

Corrag Bhuidhe Buttress – 400m VI,6. D. McGimpsey, A. Nisbet. 24th January, 1999.
This is the buttress which bounds the main face of Corrag Bhuidhe on the left, left of Lady's Gully. Gain the triangular snowfield from its bottom left. Continue in the same line up a ramp which cuts up rightwards into the buttress (100m). Climb a steep step to gain an upper continuation and follow this to steeper ground. Go up a short way, then traverse sensationally left along a ledge (50m). Continue the traverse until a line back right allows an upper ledge (about 25m higher) to be reached and followed right (50m). Find a way through steep slabby ground to reach a large ledge (40m). Traverse right along the ledge to gain and follow the easier crest of the buttress which is left of Lady's Gully (160m).

Cnocturne – 450m VI,6. N. Johnson, D. McGimpsey. 10th January, 1999.
The long curving arête left of Lords Gully and joining 1978 Face Route near its top. Climbed in poor conditions of heavy snow, the route described could become a grade easier with ice on the lower pitches. A more logical but less direct start would be the short gully on the left leading to the right of the triangular snowfield; with a better build-up, this would make the route IV,4. Start at the right side of the lowest rocks, and below a large right-facing corner-ramp which leads into Lords Gully. Go up to icy ground and climb to a ledge below a steep wall (40m). Traverse left for 15m, then climb up and left on small tufts and compact rock into a scoop below a left-facing groove (serious). Gain a ledge on the left and climb up, then back right to a ledge directly above the groove (45m). Go up the steep wall above, then move left to gain the continuation groove. Climb this (technical crux), then up to the right end of the triangular snowfield (40m). Two pitches of easier turfy climbing lead up

and right to the snow arête. From its top, a 40m traverse left on to 1978 Face Route was made to join and finish up this route. (It looks possible, and easier, to climb direct from the start of the traverse to join 1978 Face Route higher up.

The corrie face of Sgurr Fiona gives some long ice climbs in good conditions. The face is crossed by two big ramp systems which rise to the right. The higher and larger ramp starts near the base of Lord's Gully with the most obvious and regularly forming icefall above this ramp and right of centre (Fiona Verticale – *SMCJ* 1995). The distinctive features of the ice lines lie above this ramp although they have lower continuations to the base of the face.

Fifi's Chimney – 350m V,6. D. McGimpsey, A. Nisbet. 23rd February, 1999.
The leftmost of the ice lines on the face, following a chimney which leads into a left-slanting snow ramp which finishes halfway up the crest leading from Lord Berkley's Seat up to Sgurr Fiona. Some great moves; pity the best section is short. Start just right of Lord's Gully and climb low-angled ice to the upper ramp and the base of the icy chimney. A steep back and foot pitch (30m) and a pitch with three awkward bulges, the last being climbed by mixed moves on the right (30m) leads to the easier upper section.

Lady in Waiting – 350m IV,5. D. McGimpsey, A. Nisbet. 23rd February, 1999.
Climbs ice which forms in a right-facing corner above the upper ramp. The lower continuation has one steep section. The corner has a considerable bulge low down which was traversed from the recess on the left (good runners) to less steep ice on its right. Continuous ice leads to a final kink right on thinner ice which gains easier upper slopes and a finish close to or just right of Sgurr Fiona.

Fiona Diretissima – 400m VI,6. B. Davison, D. McGimpsey. 7th March, 1999.
In good conditions a steep icefall forms over the wall below the upper ramp and icefall of Fiona Verticale. This route links this icefall with the Fiona Verticale one above to provide a long natural but escapable line to finish right of the summit of Sgurr Fiona. Start directly below the lower icefall. Climb easy iced slabs and snow for two pitches to reach the ice (the lower free-standing column was very fragile and avoided by steep snow on the right). Belay in an excellent ice cave behind the start of the ice proper. A very steep start up an icicle led to easier climbing up and right across the icefall to finish up a steepening icy corner. Easy ground follows to a short wall 50m below Fiona Verticale. This was climbed by a wide 10m pillar (avoidable). Climb the main icefall direct to its top. To finish, a steep narrow icy chimney directly above the icefall led to mixed ground and the top (Fiona Verticale finishes farther left?).

Lost Gully – 200m IV,4. D. McGimpsey, A. Nisbet. 19th January, 1999.
Below the lower ramp which crosses Sgurr Fiona is a steep wall which bounds the cliffs on the right. This gully, well hidden from most angles, cuts through the ramp. Climb the gully, steep and poorly protected for 20m but graded for good ice, to reach the ramp. Follow the ramp rightwards on less steep ice to a short crest which leads to the slopes of Sgurr Fiona.

The Spectre – 160m II. D. McGimpsey, A. Nisbet. 19th January, 1999.
Start further up the steep wall from Lost Gully, immediately left of a big arête at its top right corner. Climb a big ramp through the steep wall, then trend rightwards on mixed ground to finish up the sharp arête.

NORTHERN HIGHLANDS
NORTH AND EAST (VOLUME TWO)

THE CROMARTY FIRTH, North Sutor Cliffs (Sheet 21, MR 813 686):
Despite this being one of the driest areas of Scotland, the rock cannot be described as an adequate lure. It is a smooth and brittle unidentified metamorphic rock with the worst properties of both granite and sandstone. Varying from brick red to yellow, it is an artist's dream, but climbingwise, only some of it is solid and reliance on any single hold is risky. Protection is only as good as the rock though it can look quite convincing at times. High-angled grass above the crags encouraged the pioneers to carry a short ice axe, which proved useful.

Approach from Nigg Ferry and take the farm road east to a layby before the hill. The beach, then a rocky scramble (at high tide) leads to grassy cliffs. The route below takes a line up the next section of more continuous crag, marked by a bright, yellow arête and a right-facing chimney above a shallow cave. This cave bottoms a cleaner overhanging section of cliff that looks clean but did not entice.

Shake, Rattle and Roll – 60m HVS 4b and Grade II. J. R. Mackenzie, R. Weld. 19th August, 1998.

The cave provides two options to gain the right-facing chimney above, either straight up below it or harder, better and solid, climb the undercut left-slanting ramp that leads into it. Climb the chimney to a shallow cave and assortment of belays (20m 4b). Now traverse left across the bright yellow arête and into another shallow scoop. The rock above is quite steep and very loose, crux, and leads on to the grass field which was front-pointed up to an easing (belay on a broom brush and axe pick) – 40m 4a.

STRATHCONON, Slab Crag (MR 358 362):
The crag is south-facing and of granulitic schist. The climbs are 10m long, by A. Mullin in June, 1998, involve friction and are quite bold, with small wires useful. **Approach:** As for Hidden Crag but continue through the woods. Once out of the woods, turn left and follow the heathery hillside for 1+ km. Allow one hour. The climbs are described right to left. The main feature is a corner-line.

Slab Crack – VS 5a.
Start at the obvious crackline 2m from the right end of the slab. Climb the crack leftwards, step into the obvious niche and follow the crack above to the top.

Slab Corner – VS 4c.
Climb the obvious corner, using the arête at intervals.

Howling Arête – Severe.
The arête forming the left side of Slab Corner. Big holds but no protection.

Polythene Pam – HVS 5b.
Start 5m left of the arête at the foot of a small overlap. Take the prominent right-slanting crackline.

Dandgee Crack – Severe.
The right-slanting crack left of Polythene Pam. Easier than it looks.

CREAG GHLAS, East Buttress:
Charge of the White Brigade – 165m IV,6. J. R. Mackenzie, R. Biggar. 28th February, 1999.
Possibly the route most often in condition on the crag. It takes the right-hand face of the East Buttress, following a line up the steepest part just to the right of a shallow chimney/gully. Approach by the easy gully that lies below this section of face and start at an easing right of a crag containing a broken chimney, approx. half way along the face. Climb up to slabs and belay to the right (50m). Continue up the slabs which are more difficult than they look and aim for a corner to the right of the chimney/gully. Climb a thin subsidiary corner which contains a couple of small trees (60m). Escape up to the right via the short but hard crux wall. Continue straight up and exit over another corner to some flakes on the right below a wall (30m). Climb the flakes and finish above (25m).

West Face:
The slab to the left of Victory Crack has three good lines. Left to right these are:
Super Discount – 16m E3 6a. D. McGimpsey, R. McAllister, A. Fraser. 19th September, 1998.
The twin crackline on the left. The left-hand and lower crack is climbed to an awkward transfer to the upper right-hand crack. Climb this with interest to crux moves near the top.

Julian's Line (unnamed) – 20m E3 6a. J. Lines, R. McAllister, D. McGimpsey. September, 1998.
Climbs the slab and hanging crack to the right (4m left of Tales of the Old Days). Climb the bold slab to gain the crack (assortment of dubious gear). Climb the crack, mainly on its right side.

Tales of the Old Days – 30m E5 6b. R. McAllister, D. McGimpsey, M. Harrison. September, 1998.
Start to the right of a slabby recess left of Victory Crack. Climb the thin slab to gain the right edge of a crescent-shaped crack and follow this to a good pocket at half height (first good gear). Continue up and right to an awkward mantelshelf move. A long stretch (6a) or dyno (6b) gains the top break (poor cams). Follow this leftwards to a short finishing crack. Very bold on the lower half.

Chameleon – 60m E2 5c**. J. R. Mackenzie, R. Brown. 31st August, 1998.
Left of the heather corner that lies left of the Salamander slab is another steep slab with a shallow right-trending curved overlap. The route takes shallow cracks running straight through this feature. There is an optional first pitch (which was soloed) that avoids heather.
1. 15m 4c. Start below the overlapped slab to the right and climb two short slabs to move left to a short crack below the overlap.
2. 45m 5c. Climb boldly up to and through the overlap (small Friends) with more unprotected and delicate climbing to the base of the thin crack. Climb this (crux) which is well protected by wires to a wobbly flake and small ledge. Move up rightwards through an overlap and make a delicate step up right to the edge which is followed more easily to the heather ledge. An excellent sustained pitch.
Either scramble off leftwards along the exposed ledge or continue in another two pitches as for Spoils of War.

Salamander Pitch 4 Variation (Legoland) – 20m E3 5c. D. McGimpsey, R. McAllister. August, 1998.
Instead of traversing the slab into the left-facing corner, continue up the blind crack directly above the belay. Poorly protected and tenuous.

The Victory Crack Crag:
Peak Freans' Trotskyite Selection – 20m HVS 5b. R. McAllister. 24th August, 1998.
The narrow clean slab immediately below and right of Victory Crack.

Note: *Victory Crack* worth ***. *Spoils of War* Grade E2 5b.

The Lower Tier:
To the left and below the main crag and beneath the Victory Crack wall is a subsidiary slabby wall seamed by cracks and with a square recess near its right-hand end (described in *SMCJ* 1995). While short, the rock and climbing is good and the routes are a stocking filler to bigger things. Routes described left to right. Left of centre are three parallel cracks, the leftmost of which is Centipede Crack.

Spider in a Dark Dark Room – 20m E1 5b. A. Fraser, R. McAllister, D. McGimpsey. 20th September, 1998.
The thin central crack, sheer fun.

Anonymous Chimney – 20m VS 4c. D. McGimpsey, A. Fraser, R. McAllister. 20th September, 1998.
The wider right-hand crack, a bit awkward and dirty in places.

Glazed and Confused – 20m E1 5b. A. Fraser, R. McAllister, D. McGimpsey. 20th September, 1998.
The wall to the right of Anonymous Chimney, being the wide central wall of the crag, climbed in the middle. Move easily up the lower part of the wall and over the central bulge to reach a hairline crack through the upper wall. Fine moves up this lead to a nubbin, good ledge and the top.

Moon Safari – 25m E3 5c. R. McAllister, D. McGimpsey, A. Fraser. 20th September, 1998.
An excellent route up the largest buttress, at the right end of the crag. The improbable lower section is climbed left of centre, holds appearing when least expected. Move slightly rightwards to the upper section. This is climbed right of centre, moving across left at the top and gives technical and intricate climbing.

Ra-Ra Rabbit – 10m VS 5a. R. McAllister, D. McGimpsey (solo). 20th September, 1998.
The small buttress to the right of Moon Safari, with a ledge at two thirds height. Good moves but unprotected.

Explosive Joseph – 10m E1 5b. R. McAllister. 20th September, 1998.
The small rightmost buttress on the crag, to the right of an obvious black water streak.

SGURR NA MUICE, North-East Face:

The Boar – 155m VI,6**. J. R. Mackenzie, D. Broadhead (alt.). 10th January, 1999.
Though rarely in condition, this challenging line is worth waiting for. Take the
right-hand approach gully to the iced slab. Climb the slab to the base of the big
central groove to the left of The Wolf.
1. 50m. Climb the groove which is steep, sustained and has overlaps. A thin ice
runnel is essential as there is no turf apart from a central boss. Exit steeply to ice,
then snow, and follow to below a prominent narrow ice runnel that forms on the
right wall of a shallow groove; this is the natural continuation of the groove below.
2. 25m. Climb the bulging ice which can be rather thin in places, to a steep exit up
right which leads to a secure recess.
3. 30m. Move up left over a turfy bulge and then over snowy or iced slabs to a wide
groove on the left.
4. 50m. Move into the wider groove and climb this over pleasant steepenings to
easy ground a short distance below the summit cairn.

SGURR NA FEARSTAIG, East Face:

Snowdrop – 155m IV,4. C. Grindrod, J. R. Mackenzie. 9th March, 1999.
Between Red Campion and the corner of Sorcerer's Apprentice is a steep area of
crag that has two shallow gullies with a thin streak between them high up. This
climb takes the main right-hand gully, much of which is hidden from below. Start
below these features and climb steepening snow and ice to a point where it is
possible to move right over a rib to join the rightmost gully. Climb this, moving left
to a prominent saddle belay (60m). Continue towards the thin streak, then enter the
hidden gully to the right via a good ice pitch. Go up the gully (45m). Climb a thin
mixed groove to the right which ends below the girdling snow band. Climb steep
snow to a potentially problematical cornice.

SGURR NA LAPAICH (AFFRIC):

Birthday Blast – 140m III. C. Jones, A. MacDonald. 19th February, 1999.
From Loch Lapaich (MR 157 246), walk up to the shield of rock guarding the lower
part of the left side of the corrie.
1. 30m. Follow the central groove in the middle of the wall (slightly contrived – a
snow gully left of the rock wall could be climbed).
2. 60m. Go up easier broken ground to the foot of the upper face.
3. 50m. Take a rising traverse left into a gully and follow the left branch into a wide
and well protected exit chimney. The right fork is an alternative finish.

AM FAOCHAGACH, Creag Clachach:

N. Kempe notes that he climbed the frozen stream at MR 328 813 in 1996 at Grade
II/III.

FANNICHS, Sgurr nan Clach Geala:

Bungalow Buttress (No.1 Buttress) – 100m III,4. A. Nisbet. 6th December, 1998.
Start from a small bay roughly central on the front face of the buttress. Climb a left-
slanting turfy line of weakness (parallel to Alpha Gully), steeper than it looks, to
finish left of the summit of the buttress. The summit, which is close to the top of
Alpha Gully, is easily gained.

Canary Wharf – 140m V,5. D. McGimpsey, A. Nisbet; A. Clarke, R. McAllister (variation). 18th November, 1998.
Climbs the right-hand face (front face) of Sellers Buttress, with two variations. Start below the left end of the face and slant easily up right to below a turfy line. Climb the turfy line until about 10m below the shoulder. Go diagonally right to a projecting block and swing round it to a traverse ledge which soon leads to the central corner in the upper part of the face. Climb the corner and the wall on its left to easier ground leading to the top of the buttress.
Variation: Stand on the projecting block in order to step left into the left-hand corner. Climb this and the arête above to the top of the buttress.

Sellers Tower – 160m V,6. R. McAllister, D. McGimpsey, A. Nisbet. 22nd December, 1998.
The right side of the front face of Sellers Buttress gives a fine improbable route, generally well protected. Start as for Canary Wharf but continue trending right, then curving upwards to a belay under steep ground and almost overlooking the start of Epsilon Gully (80m). Move left on to the arête of a right-facing corner and pull up to prominent turf. Traverse left along a narrow turf ledge past another corner and go up to a pedestal below the main roof system (20m). Pull through the roof (small at this point) and move left into the base of a left-facing corner, half of a pair of big corners about 5m apart and facing each other, the best indicator of the line from below. Climb this right corner, then a crack between the corners and finish up the left corner to reach easier ground. Move right and go up to a ledge below the top of the buttress (50m). Reach the easy final crest. (10m).

BEINN DEARG, Gleann na Sguaib:
Beano Buttress – 150m III,4. I. Rea, A. Cunningham, A. George. February, 1995.
At the start of WhatawaytospendEaster there is a narrow snow gully on the right. Climb the crest of the buttress between the two gullies. (Missing out the crux start to Beano Buttress by climbing Just Dandy for a pitch and cutting back left across turfy ledges onto the crest, reduces the grade to II/III – A. Cunningham, B. Gordon on 11th January, 1999.)

Just Dandy – 180m II. A. Cunningham, F. Curtler. February, 1998.
Climb a narrow snow gully on the right of the start of WhatawaytospendEaster for 70m and take an icy ramp and awkward step on the left wall on to easier ground. Follow round below Beano Buttress to the top.

Garvachy Road – 180m II. A. Cunningham, J. MacRea. 20th February, 1999.
Left of WhatawaytospendEaster, climb into a snowy depression leading into an icy steepening below bulging rock. Move up to an overhang and turn it on the left leading to easier snow slopes to finish.

Sidewinder – 230m V,5*. G. Robertson, P. Robertson. 22nd February, 1999.
A good icy line in the crest right of Fenian Gully. Start just left of the lowest rocks.
1. 40m. Move right on to the crest, then trend left past an awkward crack and up steepening turfy grooves to a perch overlooking the gully.
2. 30m. Go horizontally left to gain and climb a little hanging groove, then move up and make an exposed traverse back right to regain the crest.

3. 50m. Climb the iced corner on the right to gain a large snowfield, then move easily left to a groove in the crest.
4. 40m. Climb the icy groove in a fine position to a good ledge.
5. 80m. Pull strenuously out right and continue more easily to the top.

The West Buttress:
Note: P. Robertson climbed the prominent icefall direct start to Gastronomes Gully at IV,4 in December, 1998 and the small buttress right of Inverlael Gully via an icy groove (Inverlael Buttress, Grade II, 21st February, 1999).

Coire Ghranda:
Cold War – 145m VI,6*. T. Rankin, P. Robertson. 6th March, 1999.
A fine and varied route between Ice Bomb and Body Freeze. Protection is sparse. Start at a prominent right-trending groove midway between the previous two routes.
1. 40m. Climb the groove for 25m to a bulging wall. Traverse steeply up and left across this, then left again into a V-chimney, on top of which sits a fine spike belay.
2. 45m. Go directly up turfy walls before moving left to gain and follow an icy fault to a good ledge.
3. 30m. On the right is a thinly iced groove. Follow this to an overhang, then traverse a large flake rightwards to easier ground. Continue up and right to below a short groove.
4. 30m. Climb the groove, then take the easiest line through bulging ice walls to the top.

BEINN GOBHLACH, North Face:
No Option – 250m II. A. Cunningham, F. Curtler. 1st March, 1999.
Approaching from the west and about halfway along is a widening gully breaching the buttress. Climb into the narrows over a few icy steps and take the main left fork leading easily to the top.

ULLAPOOL, Creag nam Broc:
Jug O' Doon – 15m E2 5b**. G. Robertson, T. Rankin. 4th May, 1998.
The obvious hanging groove between Primitive Dance and One Arm Bandit. Start by a small birch tree and take the left side of an arête before stepping blindly round to gain the groove. Finish up One Arm Bandit (which would appear to be a sandbag at HVS?).

Head to Head, Direct – E2 5c**. T. Rankin, G. Robertson. 4th May, 1998.
The fault followed throughout.

SEANA BHRAIGH, Luchd Coire, Central Massif:
To the right of The Posts and Press-on Gully, the Central Massif is broken and easy-angled with no large areas of exposed rock. Moving farther right the Massif steepens and develops into two distinct tiers with a big raking terrace at about two-thirds height. Below the terrace there are three obvious left-facing corners, the rightmost being the steepest and narrowest. These corners are set on a series of slabs which form the largest continuous area of exposed rock on the massif. Icefalls form down each corner. To the right of the corners a blunt turfy ridge rises to meet a broad

depression which develops into a shallow gully above the terrace. This is presumably the line of Flowerpot Buttress.

Saxifrage – 210m IV,4. M. Bass, J. Clamp, S. Yearsley. 18th April, 1998.
This route takes the rightmost of the three icy corners described above. Scramble up easy ground to belay below the bottom right of the corner.
1. 45m. Climb left to enter the bottom of the corner. Continue upwards on improving ice over a steep bulge.
2. 30m. Climb up the corner for 15m, steeply at first. Traverse leftwards for 3m to enter the central icefall. Climb this for a short distance, then up easily to the mixed rib on the right.
3. 50m. Climb easily up the buttress to gain the terrace. With better ice conditions it may be possible to continue up and left on the icefall to the terrace.
4. 45m. From the terrace climb the buttress to the left of the broad shallow gully (this gully is probably the upper half of Flowerpot Buttress). Enjoyable with short steep walls.
5. 40m. Finish up the short blocky crest to easy ground and the plateau.

RHUE SEA CLIFFS, The First Prow:
The Freaks Come Out – 12m E2 5b*. L. Hughes. 23rd May, 1998.
The wall between Food for Thought and The Bee's Knees. Move out left onto the wall from a dark overhanging corner and up into a crackline. The crack peters out at half height and climb directly up the steep headwall to finish.

ARDMAIR, Evening Wall (see *SMCJ* 1995):
Tick Collector – 20m E3 6a**. G. Latter (on-sight). 1st July, 1998.
Well protected climbing up the stepped grooves on the overhanging wall at the right end of the crag. Climb up to the main groove and pull round awkwardly (crux) to a good ledge. Hand traverse this right to a jug, then pull over to a short hand crack in the final slab.

CAMUS MOR SEA CLIFFS:
Bounty Hunter – 70m HVS*. J. R. Mackenzie, R. Brown. 24th September, 1998.
To the right of Freebooter's lower pitch is a roofed concave red wall of unsound rock that ends at an overhanging flake crack near the gully at the start of Keelhaul.
1. 20m 5a. Gain the flake crack via a ramp and strenuously up this on good holds to a tricky landing on a terrace.
2. 20m. Climb one of several lines to a terrace and cross this to below a short steep wall.
3. 10m 4a. Climb to a shelf on the left of a crack and continue up the wall to below the final steep wall.
4. 20m 4c. Near the right end of this wall and left of the overhung scooped slab are some flanges. Climb these and continue up right of a crack on excellent rock directly to the top. A superb pitch, much easier than it looks.

Broadside – 50m HVS*. J. R. Mackenzie, R. Brown. 24th September, 1998.
This entertaining and quite serious route takes the vertical left wall of the gully. Scramble up the short chimney to the right of Keelhaul's start to a thorn bush below the entrance to the gully.
1. 20m 5a. Climb the wall by big holds to a horizontal crack, then traverse left to

an overhung niche containing a huge block. Pull over the block and roof via a superb bollard, then traverse the jam crack leftwards to a nose; pull up this and continue up a slab to below the honeycombed corner and overhang.

2. 30m 5b. Move up the wall and make a tricky right traverse to an exposed nose, round this and move right to below a short niche. Climb into this (wobbly) and continue up slabs and bulges to exit up a loose funnel. Some lichen and loose rock high on this pitch which will soon clean with use.

Aspen Bay Crag (MR NC 079 026):

A steep west-facing wall in a fine little sheltered bay, directly below the coastal footpath from Culnacraig to Blughasary. The main wall is above a grass platform about 15m above the beach, running down rightwards to a more broken area of rock rising directly above the beach.

Approach: Park at the end of the single track road at Culnacraig. Walk down the road on the right, which leads past a couple of cottages, then continues parallel to the coast, to the crag which lies a couple of hundred metres west of Geodha Mor – 45 minutes.

Descent: Down the open gully leading to the base.

Aspen – 20m E2 5c**. G. Latter. 29th September, 1998.

In the centre of the main wall are twin cracks up the initial wall. Climb these to some pocketed rock beneath a roof. Step right into The Fluttering, then move back left and follow the slightly left-slanting crack past some small pockets. Finish quite boldly past a thin crack.

The Fluttering – 20m E2 6a*. G. Latter. 29th September, 1998.

The prominent crackline 5m left of the unappealing chimney on the right side of the wall. Step up right into the initial wide crack, and follow this and a direct line above, with a short difficult section past a thin finger crack. Finish directly in the same line. Slow to dry.

Antler – 20m HVS 5a. G. Latter, C. Prowse (on sight). 29th September, 1998.

Start down on the beach, at a steep undercut groove 3m right of the arête. Climb crumbly pocketed rock, then move up right and follow the groove. Pull out right at the top into a recess, then pull over some blocks to gain the top.

STAC POLLAIDH, West Buttress (No.1):

Jack the Ripper, The Fred West Finish – 30m E3 6a. G. Robertson, T. Rankin. August, 1998.

Climbs the obvious crack system in the headwall to the left of the grooves, taking the hand crack obvious from below the route. A fine pitch.

No. 2 Buttress:

Cat on a Hot Tin Roof – 60m E3. A. Crofton, G. Robertson. August, 1998.

1. 40m 5c. Climb the thin cracks left of Vlad the Impaler's first pitch until they join that route after 15m, then continue up Vlad to the platform.

2. 20m 5c. Left of Vlad's second pitch is a prominent hanging finger crack. Climb this to a step left at the obvious foothold. Move up using the left arête before stepping back right and pulling through the bulge (crux) to the easier crack above. Sustained and well protected.

No.3 Buttress:
Consider the Lillies – 25m E2 5c*. G. Latter, A. Siddons. 15th October, 1998.
The crack and corner on the slender fin about 40m right of the base of Summer Isles Arête. Gain the leftmost of the twin crack-lines from ledges on the left. Follow it, stepping right into the more prominent crack which leads to a ledge. Finish up a short fierce layback crack in the corner round on the right.

CUL BEAG:
Time in the Fall – 105m HVS. G. Robertson. 29th September, 1998.
Lies well to the right (south) of the Y-shaped gully, just before the cliffs break up. From the south the line is obvious as a clean nose forming the right side of a flat-topped tower. Start at the lowest point of the nose.
1. 30m . Climb direct to where the nose steepens abruptly at a projecting block.
2. 30m 5a. Climb up cracks just left of the nose, steeply at first, to reach some big flakes which lead to a fine broad perch on the crest.
3. 20m 5a. Climb a vertical cracked wall, then an easier groove, and continue to the summit of the tower.
4. 25m 4c. Traverse horizontally right for about 5m, then climb delicate cracks up the right side of the slab in a fine position.

The Red Wall:
Pebbledash – 20m E3 5c**. G. Latter, C. Murray. 1st July, 1998.
Bold climbing up the centre of the slab. Start just left of the wide crack at the base. Climb the wall just left of the crack to the ledge, then move right and place friends in a good horizontal. Climb the wall above the left end of the ledge by good edges to a good break on the slab (RPs in horizontal slots on left). Continue more easily directly up the easy-angled slab above.

REIFF: Pinnacle Area:
Immaculate Walk – 15m E3 5c**. A. Cunningham, L. Hughes. 26th March, 1999.
A link pitch. Climb the crux of Immaculate Deception and hand traverse right on the lower horizontal break to finish up the final crack of A Walk Across The Rooftops.

Worm On Viagra – 10m E4 5c***. L. Hughes, A. Cunningham. 26th March, 1999.
Climb Channering Worm to the break, move left and finish steeply via the thin right diagonal crack.

A Song In The Air – 10m E1 5b*. A. Cunningham, L. Hughes, P. Holmes. 26th March, 1999.
An eliminate but good climbing nonetheless. Start up the direct start to Hy Brasil and climb straight up the wall between it and Westering Home, touching neither of course!

NOTE: Reiff Case (*SMCJ* 1998, p621) has been climbed before by N. Morrison and not recorded because it was soloed as a boulder problem. Considered about 6a/b.

Brace Yoursel' Becky – 8m E2 6a*. L. Hughes, A. Cunningham. 26th March, 1999.
Very steep climbing up the middle of the leaning headwall to the left of Diagonal Crack. Climb via two short breaks and a long reach.

Rave On – 8m V. Diff. P. Holmes. 26th March, 1999.
Round left of Chimney Corner on the front face, climb a short steep right-diagonal crack.

John Dunne – 8m Moderate. P. Holmes. 26th March, 1999.

Paddy O' Leary – 10m V. Diff. P. Holmes. 21st March, 1999.
Start left of John Dunne and climb the slabby front face to a large ledge. Finish up a short steep corner.

Old Rockers Never Die – 10m HVS 5b*. A. Cunningham, P. Holmes. 21st March, 1999.
Start just right of Rockette's Climb (on the steep wall round left of Paddy O' Leary) and lurch up the wall to the large ledge. Climb the steep crack in the edge above.

NOTE: Rockette's Climb was thought to be worth HVS 5a.

Black Rocks:
Legover – 20m E2 5b*. R. Baines, G. McShane. June 1998.
Start up Auld Nick and at about 4m break out onto the leaning pillar on the left. Climb a crack to the big break (rest) and launch up the final headwall direct.

Minch Walls:
The first climb is on the broken black rock just past the bouldering wall at the right end of Minch Walls:
Livi's – 10m Diff. L. Kerr and partner. 12th August, 1998.
The straight in crack starting from the base of a left-trending ramp.

Lynx – 8m HVS 5a. A. Cunningham, R. Baines, P. Peacock, J. Cunningham. 1st April, 1998.
Climb the crack in the arête right of Scavenger.

In Yer Face – 10m E1 5b*. A. Cunningham, R. Baines. 1st April, 1998.
The slab between Judicial Hanging and Dunskiing. With a high runner in Dunskiing, make an awkward step right onto the black slab and up to a horizontal break. Easier to finish.

The Anteater – 15m E1 5c/6a**. L. Hughes, F. Fotheringham. May, 1998.
After the crux starting moves of Green Ants, move up to and part way rightwards along the next break. Climb a short crack to the next break and swing right onto the arête (5b). Go up the right side of this to finish.

Stone Pig Cliffs:
Pigs Don't Fly – 12m E1/2 5c. L. Hughes, A. Cunningham. 5th May, 1998.
Climb the steep narrow barrel-shaped buttress to the right of Swine Dyke via horizontal breaks. Finish to the right.

The following routes are on the leaning south-facing wall of the huge tidal bay. Access to the base of the wall may be made at low tide from either side. At other states of tide – abseil in. Left to right:

Miss Moneypenny – 15m E5 6a***. L. Hughes, A. Cunningham. 14th June, 1998.
A central line up the wall. Climb the initial wall to the right of a deep off-width to a break. Pull over a roof moving left and back right into the line. Climb a very steep crackline to the top.

If You See Kay – 20m E3 5c**. A. Cunningham, L. Hughes. 14th June, 1998.
Start centrally and climb the initial wall to a large ledge. Pull through the middle of the roof via twin right diagonal cracks and move right into a right-curving line. Go steeply up this to finish.

Manumission – 15m E4 6a/b***. L. Hughes, A. Cunningham.18th June, 1998.
Takes a direct line to the right of If You See Kay. Start up a right-diagonal crack above a small pool to the large ledge. Climb the roof above at the widest point and up into the crackline and shallow right-facing corner to finish.

Sonique – 15m E4 5c***. L. Hughes, A. Cunningham. 5th May, 1998.
Near the right side of the wall and before the jaws of the deep slot is a vague crackline with twin cracks at one third height. Climb to the left of the cracks via horizontal breaks to a small overlap. Move right into the line at a small niche and finish by long reaches on flat holds.

Mechanics Geo – Blairbuie:
This is a steep narrow SW-facing geo directly under the road at the Blairbuie junction, the top of which is visible from the road before the junction. Access is best from the north (Reiff end). Left to right:
The first two routes lie at the shorter left-hand end to the left of an obvious broken groove. There are two main short steep cracks:
Exhaust Pipe – 10m E1 5c*. L. Hughes, A. Cunningham. 18th June, 1998.
Climb direct up the rock between the two cracks including the top bulge.

Shifting Spanner – 10m HVS 5a*. A. Cunningham, L. Hughes. 18th June, 1998.
Climb the right-hand crackline just to the right of Exhaust Pipe.

Rear Differential – 15m E2 5c*. A. Cunningham, L. Hughes. 18th June, 1998.
Start off the first huge block encountered on the traverse under the main part of the crag. Climb a steep crack to a horizontal break and make some awkward moves leftwards into the right-facing corner. Finish up this.

Rubha Coigeach:
Milk Tray – 15m HVS 5a. G. Latter, C. Prowse. 30th September, 1998.
Good climbing up the left side of the black wall taken by Black Magic, with the crux the first 4m to gain a good horizontal break.

Slab Inlet, North Side:
Penguin – 12m VS 5a. G. Latter (solo). 30th September, 1998.
The stepped groove round the arête right of The Ali-Shuffle, with the crux pulling through an often wet roof near the top.

Polar Bear – 22m HVS 5a**. G. Latter, C. Prowse. 30th September, 1998.
A fine line taking the prominent diagonal crack line up the wall right of The Ali-Shuffle. Start at the right end of the ledge at the base of The Ali-Shuffle. Follow the diagonal crack line (the lower of two) to its end, then step left and climb the wall above.

Stone Pig Cliff:

Save ma Bacon – 12m E2 5b. T. Rankin, G. Robertson. 29th August, 1998.
Climbs the steep cracked wall right of Swine Dyke to finish up the short corner above. Good climbing but escapable out right on the strenuous lower wall. Possibly climbed before.

QUINAG, Bucket Buttress:

Note: A route recorded as Brendan Voyage (45m V,6. F. Bennet, B. Reid. 28th February, 1998) turns out to be a variation on Kane Mutiny, climbing a corner and capping roof left of Kane's 'right-facing corner' as the only difference.

Fell for Lorna – 40m V,6. M. Cooper, F. Bennet. 13th March, 1998.
The thin groove line immediately left of Bounty Hunter via a hanging corner at half height.

Barrel Buttress:

Direct Route – 60m VI,8. R. G. Webb, N. Wilson. December, 1998.
Climb the main corner direct throughout.

THE POINT OF STOER:

Playaway – 60m E2*. P. Donnithorne, E. Alsford (alt.). 20th June, 1998.
The overhanging wall between the two obvious corners seen from the Old Man. Start as for the left-hand corner (the right corner is Great Corner, VS?).
1. 15m 5b. A leaning corner leads up and left to a ledge.
2. 20m 5b. Go up the wall, then left to a small corner. Go up to a roof, then traverse left to a ledge.
3. 25m 5b. Step left, then go up to a short crack and finish up leftwards.

Breakaway – 60m E3. E. Alsford, P. Donnithorne. 21st June, 1998.
The route is in a slabby cove 30m south of the Old Man. Abseil to ledges just above the sea.
1. 30m 5b. Take the most obvious leftward-diagonal crack to a ledge, then traverse right and up a short groove to more ledges.
2. 30m 5b. The shattered groove above leads 'with interest' to the final short crack. Some poor rock.

CREAG AN FHITHICH (near Kinlochbervie; *SMCJ* 1997, p 331):

Ruby Wall – 40m E3 5c/6a***. M. Charlton, A. Cater. May 1997.
Climb the wavy wall left of centre using a vertical line of pockets to a ledge. Go up and rightwards to an overhung slab. Break through the roof at its highest point, move up and pull left to a good side pull on the ledge. Move right and up into an overhung niche. Traverse left via a good crack around the top of a block in a spectacular position. Pull up and left to a steep heathery finish on poor holds.

SHEIGRA, First Geo:

Dying Direct – 25m E4 5c/6a**. L. Hughes, A. Cunningham, A. Cain. 4th June, 1998.
Start between Dying In Vein and Blind Faith. Climb a right-trending crack to the pedestal of Blind Faith (hard). Follow a direct line to a small niche left of the base of the pink groove on Blind Faith Direct. Climb the steep crack above and finish through the roof as for Dying In Vein.

AM BUACHAILLE, Coastal Cliff:

Massage Man – 90m E3. M. E. Moran (on sight), C. Jalon, D. Laddiman. 23rd June, 1997.

Some 60m north of the stack, the coastal cliff forms a slim buttress. This route takes the obvious left-leaning groove line just left of its crest. A good line, exposed and inescapable with variable rock. The buttress is easily located by the foul overhanging gully which bounds it on the left.

1. 50m 5a. From the toe of the buttress, trend up right into the groove which is climbed to a tiny stance (assorted belays in the groove above).
2. 20m 5b. Bridge the overhanging groove above with a leftward deviation at a roof and continue to a block ledge.
3. 20m 5b. Go up the corner above the stance until a step left can be made into a deeper corner. Climb this over a bulge to the top.

CAITHNESS SEA CLIFFS, Latheronwheel, Big Flat Wall Area:

Illuminations – 18m E2 5c**. S. Clark, R. Macaulay. 30th June, 1998.
The wall between Gle Mha and Macallan's Choice (see *SMCJ* 1994).

Cask Strength – 18m E1 5b**. S. Clark, R. Macaulay. 26th August, 1998.
Two cracks start very steeply in the shallow cave in the right half of the Big Flat Wall. This route takes the left crack and continues direct. (The right crack is the unclimbed direct start to Macallan's Choice).

Stack Area:

The Lama - 12m E4 6a**. S. Clark. 16th June, 1998.
A direct route up the north face of the stack, superseding Flight from Sadness. Start just left of centre.

ORKNEY, Yesnaby, The Arch Wall:

Nuckelavee – 20m E4 6a**. G. Latter (on-sight). 22nd June, 1998.
A good line giving spectacular climbing through the centre of the arching roof. Start directly beneath the centre of the wall. Climb an easy flake to a ledge at 3m, then up the wall with a long reach to a good undercut under the roof. Reach straight over for a good hold in the horizontal break, span left and finish on good holds.

HOY, Rora Head:

The Rocks and the Water – 60m E1**. G. Latter, K. Martin (on-sight). 18th June, 1998.
About 80m west of the waterfall is a buttress with a prominent wide crack (facing east) in its middle third. Start on a huge flat boulder just right of a rectangular block overhang at 2m.

1. 20m 5a. Climb the rib right of the overhang, then step left on to a ledge. Move up 3m, then follow an obvious traverse line left, then up by an obvious weakness. Move right over ledges (past fulmars!) to belay at base of the crack.
2. 30m 5b. Climb the crack and the fist-wide flake to pull out right at the top. Continue over ledges, trending rightwards to belay in a corner beneath the final red wall.
3. 10m 5a. Finish up the corner, or easier slightly farther right.

CAIRNGORMS

LOCHNAGAR: Southern sector:
Once Upon a Time in the East – 75m V,5. B. S. Findlay, R. Ross, G. S. Strange. 24th January, 1999.
The slabby groove on the left side of the well-defined buttress immediately left of The Red Spout. Climbed on partly consolidated snow and bits of ice.

Windfall – 100m III. S. Richardson, C. Cartwright. 3rd January, 1999.
The right edge of the buttress between the Red Spout and The Cathedral (which contains Perserverance Rib near its left side), is cut by a slanting gully line.
1. 30m. Climb the gully to a good stance on the right.
2. 40m. Continue up the gully to a short snow slope, cross this and climb two successive short chimneys to a platform.
3. 10m. Steep snow leads to the cornice.

The Cathedral:
Magic Pillar – 80m IV,5. C. Cartwright, S. Richardson. 15th November, 1998.
The well defined pillar between Cathedral Chimney and No Worries Groove. Delightful climbing and considerably easier than it looks – a little gem! Start by climbing easy mixed ground to the base of the pillar.
1. 20m. Follow the crack in the crest to a niche.
2. 40m. Step round the roof to the right and continue up crack-chimney to its top.
3. 20m. Finish easily up the final gully of Cathedral Chimney.

Spellbound – 120m VI,8. S. Richardson, C. Cartwright. 15th November, 1998.
The rib separating the grooves of Sepulchre and Judas Priest forms a fine tapering arête defended near its base by a large roof.
1. 20m. Start directly beneath the roof and climb a short wall to a niche. Continue up the steep left-slanting corner and pull over the left end of the roof. Belay on the ledge above.
2. 40m. Continue up the arête, following the crack-line which splits the crest.
3 and 4. 60m. Finish as for Judas Priest by moving right a long the terrace and up through a narrowing to reach the exit gully of Cathedral Chimney.

Central Buttress:
Incision – 100m V,5. S. Richardson, C. Cartwright. 3rd January, 1999.
The crack and groove line between Centrist and Sciolist.
1. 40m. Start at the foot of Shallow Gully and trend left up sloping shelves to the foot of a steep wall. Step left to enter the crack and follow it to a stance in a niche level with the roof of Centrist.
2. 20m. Continue up to a narrow groove left of the prominent square-cut corner of Scioilist.
3. 40m. Climb the groove and continue up easier ground to finish as for Centrist on the crest of Central Buttress.

Magical Mystery Tour – 120m V,6. S. Richardson, C. Cartwright. 31st January, 1999.
This varied mixed climb takes the natural line of weakness parallel to Shallow Gully before finishing up the front face of the square-topped tower to the right of White Wizard.

1. 50m. Climb Centrist for 10m to join the right-slanting fault. Climb this past a short chimney crossing Incision and Sciolist to reach a broad depression.

2. 30m. Continue up and right past an overlap to a ledge at the left side of the square-topped tower below the final groove of White Wizard.

3. 40m. Move up and right to below the centre of the front face of the tower. Pull over the overhang above and move up to the headwall. Climb this via a right-facing crack in the centre to reach the crest of Central Buttress. An excellent pitch.

Shadow Buttress A:
Interim – 50m IV,4. M. Bass, S. Yearsley. 22nd January, 1999.
This short climb takes the buttress between Bell's Route and Vortex. Start 5m right of Vortex. Climb the lower section of the buttress, and continue up the narrow hanging gully 7m right of the groove line of Vortex. Abseil descent from the balcony on Spiral Terrace, or continue to the plateau by Vortex or Shadow Buttress A Original Route.

The Stack:
Redemption – 125m VIII,7. S. Richardson, C. Cartwright. 10th January, 1999.
The overhanging fault-line on the front face of The Stack overlooking the Black Spout. Poorly protected, sustained and strenuous. The first pitch requires ice or a good build up which compromises protection high up. Start at the foot of The White Spout below a smooth inset slab.

1. 40m. Climb mixed ground to foot of slab. Climb the left-slanting corner bonding the right side of the slab to reach the second stance of Torquing Corpse.

2. 15m. Climb Torquing Corpse pitch 3 to a cave stance.

3. 20m. Exit left from the cave and move up to the fault-line which leads to a good ledge and block belay of The Undertaker.

4. 20m. Continue up the fault over two bulges to the headwall.

5. 30m. Traverse left below the headwall (bold), step down to enter the exit gully, and follow this to the top.

West Buttress:
Note: T. Rankin and G. Robertson repeated Quasimodo on 10th February, 1999 with a different line at the crux, following the thin turfy central crack (7) gained from the left. On the last pitch they climbed the final 5a crack of Dod's Diversion (7) – overall VII,7.

Prince of Darkness – 70m VI,7. S. Richardson, C. Cartwright. 20th December, 1998.
An imposing tower rises from the upper reaches of West Gully to the right of The Gargoyle. This superb mixed climb takes the steep front face of the tower. Very sustained. Start at the foot of the tower in West Gully.

1. 25m. Climb a turf ramp up and left for 5m to a ledge. Move right along a flake to reach a niche, climb the wall above to reach a second niche, then step right around the arête to reach a hanging groove. Climb this to a good stance below the prominent right-facing corner which runs up the right side of the tower.

2. 25m. The corner leads to a good platform. A superb pitch.

3. 20m. Steep cracks lead through the headwall to the top of the tower. Another excellent pitch in an exposed situation.

Life for Lust – 270m V,6. G. Scott, P. Evans. February, 1999.
Takes the line of steep grooves and chimneys to the right of West Rib. Difficulties

are short but steep with just adequate protection. Start at the same point as West Rib.
1. 35m. Either follow a line of right, then left-trending ramps to belay under the black triangular wall of West Rib or follow the first pitch of West Rib up the short icefall (taken on a first attempt).
2. 25m. Climb the steep groove to the right of the wall (crux), then continue up the turfy groove to a chimney on the left.
3. 30m. Continue up the groove line until stopped by a steep wall. Climb this on the left by a short chimney and continue straight up to a ledge under a steep wall.
4. 40m. Traverse left along a thin ledge into the centre of the wall to gain a groove. Climb this steeply, then continue straight up to reach easier ground below a wall with three chimney lines – possible belay. Climb the rightmost chimney, interesting moves to get established, then continue up.
5. 40m. Traverse slightly left to reach a flakey chimney line; climb this and then head straight up following easier ground.
6. 40m. Follow short walls and ramps trending slightly left to the crest of the buttress overlooking West Gully.
7. 60m. Descend the gully on the right and traverse under the next buttress to gain a step groove line with an interesting step at the top. Continue easily to the plateau.
Note: West Rib Direct would be the best finish. An independent finish could also have been made up the final buttress.

The Stuic, North-West Face:
Solid Air – 70m IV,4. B. S. Findlay, R. Ross, G. S. Strange. 20th December, 1998.
The first feature right of the crest of Stuic Buttress is a shallow left-facing corner. This route climbs the next fault right, which is a straight slot. Start below and slightly right of the slot and climb a shallow groove. Easier ground then leads right into a recess with a prominent corner on the right. Climb a steep fault with a hanging block left of the corner to a ledge (35m). Traverse left and climb the slot, exiting left at the top on to the crest.

Daybreak Corners – 80m III. S. Richardson. 28th December, 1997.
About 50m right of the crest of The Stuic, below the apex of the face, is a depression. Climb the series of right-facing corners on the right side of the depression.

The Slot, Left-Hand – 70m III,4. S Richardson. 28th December, 1997.
About 40m right of New Boot Groove is a short, but prominent, two-tier buttress split by a deep chimney. This route takes the groove system just to its left.

Stegasaurus Rib – 50m II. S. Richardson. 28th December, 1997.
The right side of the North-West Face is defined by a wide gully – a convenient descent. This route takes the low-angled spiky rib to its left.

Feadaige Buttress – 80m III. S. Richardson. 28th December, 1997.
Approximately 500m west of The Stuic, below the col between the The Stuic and point 1006m, is a small buttress (MR 223 852). Climb the chimney-line cutting through the crest to the top.

CREAG AN DUBH LOCH, False Gully Wall:
Note: There have been criticisms that the route An Spearag (*SMCJ* 1998, p637) finishes in the middle of a wall (presumably by abseiling off) when there is a logical second pitch. If so, the criticism would seem to be justified.

Central Gully Wall:
Note: Vertigo Wall. Regraded VII,7 after the opinion of two recent ascents.

GLEN CLOVA, Winter Corrie:
Central Gully, Right-Hand Variation – 120m II. R. Kerr, S. Turner. 7th March, 1999.
Where Central Gully begins to bend left, there is a obvious snow slope going up to the right. Follow this slope diagonally upwards towards rocks. On the right side of these rocks is a small narrow gully (to the right of a large boulder) leading to a hollow over looking Easy Gully. Move back out left to finish up the turf ridge separating Easy Gully from Central Gully.
Note: Seems likely to have been done before; claims/comments requested.

Juangorge:
Mikado – 110m IV,5. S. Richardson, C. Cartwright. 21st February, 1999.
On the right side of the crag is an amphitheatre bounded by a triangular buttress on the right. This route follows vegetated grooves up the left side of the buttress. Start below a prominent left-facing chimney crack which cuts through the middle of the lower tier.
1. 40m. Climb the chimney-crack and continue through trees to reach the central groove line which cuts through the second tier.
2. 20m. A steep entry leads into the groove. Follow this to a steep corner-crack.
3. 20m. Avoid the corner-crack by climbing the groove on the left, and make a difficult traverse right at the top to gain a steep ramp.
4. 30m. Climb the ramp past a tree, and continue on the left side of the buttress to the top.

BEINN A' BHUIRD, Coire na Ciche:
Jammy Sods – 120m IV,6. J. Currie, C. Fogwill. 20th October, 1998.
The barrel-fronted slabs left of Twisting Gully are bounded on the left by a curving corner/groove, the line of the route.
1. 22m. Climb the chimney-fault below the groove to a booming flake.
2. 28m. Ascend the groove with a step left to a rest on the arête at 8m. Continue up the groove-line with a step right to easy ground. Move up to a point overlooking (about 20m above and right) the detached block of Slugain Buttress.
3,4. 70m. Easily to the top.

Coire an Dubh Lochain:
One Foot in the Groove – 60m II. C. Cartwright, S. Richardson. 8th November, 1998.
The gully to the right of the tower taken by Birthday Route. Easy snow leads up to an enclosed chimney which leads up and left to exit between the tower and the plateau. An early-season route that comes into condition quickly and is probably impossible later with a large cornice.

Wrinkled Rib – 50m II. S. Richardson, C. Cartwright. 8th November, 1998.
The rib defining the right side of Birthday Cleft is cut by a shallow groove on its right side. Climb this to a col behind the rib, and make steep exit through the cornice to the plateau.

Dividing Buttress:
Dividend Route – 180m IV,6. A. Crofton, G. Robertson. 6th December, 1998.
Takes the obvious, slightly right-trending fault in the centre of Dividing Buttress, left of Sentinel Route. Start at the lowest rocks.
1. 25m. Climb up to a prominent overhung recess in the lower section (may partly bank out).
2. 45m. Climb back down a few metres, then go left up a turfy groove before breaking right through an awkward slot in the overlap (crux). Continue up increasingly easy ground to the base of an obvious groove/fault.
3. 30m. Follow the fault to a cul-de-sac.
4. 80m. Climb out steeply, then follow a rib with interest to easier rocks.

Garbh Choire:
Bewitched – 200m V,4. D. McGimpsey, A. Nisbet. 7th January, 1999.
Effectively a direct version of Mandarin Buttress climbing close to Witch Doctor. Gain the left edge of the triangular slab and pull out left through a wedge in its left bounding wall. Move rightwards into the chimney above the top of the triangle. Climb the chimney and subsequent long groove to the halfway terrace of Mandarin Buttress. Finish up Mandarin.
Climbed in unusually snowy conditions, very poorly protected, and graded as such. Normally, it might be safer but more technical.

CARN A' MHAIM, Luibeg Slabs:
Curio – 90m HVS. G. S. Strange, R. Ross. 3rd August, 1997.
On the low-angled slabs north of Silver Chimney. Towards the left side is a prominent pink water streak. Start just left of this and climb easy slabs to a ledge (55m). Continue up grey slabs, move right and cross an overlap at a short bulging corner (crux). More slabs to finish (35m).

COIRE SPUTAN DEARG:
Aurora Variation: By stepping right from the belay at the top of pitch 1, J. Currie and A. Liversage on 18th October, 1998 followed a line of tufts into the 'grassy depression' of the summer line, then followed it over the 'blocky rock' to easy ground. No change in grade.

Cherub's Buttress via the Depression Direct – 120m II. D. McGimpsey, A. Nisbet. 25th November, 1998.
Climb the depression between the legs of Cherub's Buttress, taking the right-hand of two upper options, to join the normal route at the amphitheatre.

Precocious Gully – 70m III. D. McGimpsey, A. Nisbet, J. Preston. 30th October, 1998.
The gully right of Flake Buttress, taking the steeper left branch with a chimney section. Mostly on ice despite the early season.

Arachnophobe – 70m III,4. D. McGimpsey, A. Nisbet, J. Preston. 30th October, 1998.
Climb 'the low-angled corner' at the left end of Spider Buttress with a tricky start which should bank up. The corner leads into the right branch of Precocious Gully and an easy finish up right.

Boris – 70m IV,6. D. McGimpsey, A. Nisbet. 25th November, 1998.
Start with the 'scrambling' pitch of The Chebec (10m). Traverse right round the arête of Flying Saucers and move up to a ledge which leads to the S-shaped crack of The Fly, climbed to flakes (25m). Climb a flake-crack up left, avoid a bulge on the left and go up a short deep chimney (25m). A final bulge leads to easy ground. The finish is a less direct version of The Fly.

CAIRN TOUL, Corrie of the Chokestone Gully:
The Navigator – 100m III. B. Davison, A. Nisbet. 26th March, 1999.
A parallel fault to The Waster, between it and Sasquatch.

The Explorer – 80m III. B. Davison, A. Nisbet. 26th March, 1999.
Right of and almost overlooking The Wanderer is a ramp leading to a narrow chimney. Climb these and continue in the same line slightly leftwards to finish up an arête on the right.

The Environmentalist – 70m III,4. B. Davison, A. Nisbet. 26th March, 1999.
A big corner next right and near the right end of the cliff (there is another big but shorter corner which is the last feature at the right end of the cliff). Much of the climbing was on ice, and easier than it looked. Climb the corner until an overhang forces moves left on turf. Return to the corner and follow it to a platform. Climb the wall on the right, then trend back left to finish up the arête as for The Explorer.

BRAERIACH, Garbh Coire Mor:
Cavalier Edge – 120m V,6. C. Cartwright, S. Richardson. 13th December, 1998.
An interesting mixed climb up the right edge of Crown Buttress overlooking Great Gully. Start 30m up Great Gully where a break in the left wall leads left to the arête.
1. 20m. Cross the break (easy snow or a blank rock slab depending on conditions) to reach the crest. Move up this to a stance.
2. 40m. Continue up the crest to a good stance overlooking Great Gully below the steep upper headwall.
3. 30m. Climb easy snow up the chimney-groove of Crown Buttress Original Route for 10m, then break out right on to the impending gully wall. Follow a steep crack system to reach the prominent right to left groove which cuts through the headwall. Pull over a bulge into the base of the groove and belay in a slot on the right.
4. 20m. Continue up the groove past a chokestone to a ledge. Climb the steep wall on the right and continuation corner to the top of the headwall.
5. 10m. Finish easily along a horizontal ridge to the cornice.

Hawkeye – 120m IV,5. S. Richardson, C. Cartwright. 29th November, 1998.
The right-facing corner between the Hot Lips buttress and Pinnacles Couloir. Start 5m right of the Hot Lips buttress below a narrow chimney.
1. 45m. Climb the chimney for 15m and continue up the groove above to steep snow slopes. Move up to the foot of the corner.
2. 45m. Climb the corner to its top. Move right and belay in the col at the top of Pinnacles Couloir.
3. 30m. Continue up Pinnacles Buttress to the plateau.

Coire Bhrochain:
Hobo – 100m IV,4. A. Crofton, G. Robertson. 27th February, 1999.
Start a short way right of North-West Chimney's first pitch at a prominent icefall.

1. 40m. Climb the icefall direct and step left at the top bulge.

2. 50m. Climb a 5m wall to snow slopes and move up left across these to a good spike.

3. 10m. A short pitch gains the top.

Braeriach Pinnacle:

South Face Original Line – 150m II. A. Nisbet. 20th April, 1998.

Start from the Slab Terrace where snow leads up right on to the face (same place as Left Face – *SMCJ* 1998). Make a slightly rising traverse right, then a short traverse right around a nose to reach a snowy trough leading diagonally right to the crest. Climb blocky ground right of the crest to the right end of the headwall. Go up left under the headwall and up a shallow gully to the top.

Note: Central Buttress Gully was used as a descent, no cornice and seemed a fine route, despite its demotion to a mention in the current guide.

CARN ETCHACHAN, Upper Cliff:

Time Traveller – A. Powell and A. Benson made a free winter ascent at an unchanged grade on 24th January, 1998.

Guillotine Direct Finish – A. Mullin, A. Nisbet and S. Paget made a free ascent at VI,8 (perhaps just VII,8) on 31st January, 1999. A more direct line was taken, climbing out of the Guillotine chimney by a wide crack (crux) which led straight into the main line, which was freed with the help of a little ice. The previous line via the groove on the left would be less technical but a little more serious.

NOTE: G. Ettle and M. Garthwaite repeated Nom-de-Plume with the direct finish (as for Snakebite, winter?) and thought VI,6. Also Winter Palace, thinking V,6.

Main Cliff:

Roy Castle – 85m VI,7. G. Ettle, R. Milne, A. Perkins. January, 1999.

A direct line between Winter Palace and Bastille. Start from the diagonal shelf, just left of Route Major's alternative start at a very steep wall.

1. 25m. Balance up a narrow leftwards ramp to spectacular moves up the wall above.

2. 30m. Follow easy ground up left, then right to belay beside Bastille/Kremlin.

3. 30m. Descend leftwards and climb the rib left of Bastille.

SHELTER STONE CRAG:

Threadbare – 150m VII,8. A. Mullin, A. Nisbet. 16th April, 1999.

A line up the right side of Raeburn's Buttress, based on Threadbare (on which it eliminates about eight points of aid). Well protected. Pitches 2-6 are mostly common to the summer line. Start up Sticil Face.

1. 40m. Go to the left end of the Low Ledge, then leftwards up steep turf to under a short overhanging wall. This is joining Threadbare which comes up a big slabby ramp to the same point (the first half of this ramp was used by Consolation Groove winter).

2. 10m. Climb the central of three cracks (crux) to pull out right on to a turf ledge. Originally aided.

3. 10m. Start up a steep corner (originally aided), then reach left and mantelshelf on to a turf ledge. Go left (out of the main line) to a groove.

4. 10m Climb the groove to a small bay. Traverse right using a prominent sod of turf to regain the main groove line.

5. 30m. Climb the main groove to where it goes smooth. Move on to its left edge and pull into a smaller groove which soon becomes the main line. Belay at a chokestone 5m below steep walls.

6. 10m. Climb a small groove with crack up the left wall to ledges (now close to Consolation Groove).

7. 20m. Work up leftwards on awkward blocky ground until just left of the long overhang.

8. 20m. Pull through a bulge into a small ramp which leads to the shoulder. There are now a number of options but this ascent traversed left and abseiled into Castlegates Gully.

NOTE: N. Gregory and K. Pyke climbed a thin ice streak just left of the start of Citadel (as a start to Sticil Face). On the day, 50m VI,5, but it is known to form much thicker, close to banking out, in peak conditions.

Bad Karma – 255m IX,8. S. Paget, A. Mullin. 30th October, 1998.
Climb the winter start of The Needle to the terrace. Start up the slanting crack of Postern and after the difficult bulge go left to a large bay (35m). Above is a slabby wall with two right-facing corners. Start below the right-hand corner at a small overhanging wall. Climb this to gain the corner and after the corner, exit left to ledges. Continue rightwards to 'the crack for thin fingers'. Climb this (as a short pitch and using two rest points) and continue to join and follow the winter Needle to the top (no aid).
Note: The grade is for a one-day ascent taking 17 hours of continuous climbing.

HELL'S LUM CRAG, LOW SLAB:
Firestarter – 35m E4 6a. J. Lines, R. McAllister. 30th August, 1998.
Climb a thin crack in the slab left of Hell's Gate (*SMCJ* 1997, p345) to a ledge to where a white streak comes down. Move left and right up the slab (or harder direct above a short corner) to a capping bulge. Pull through the bulge via tiny holds.

HELL'S LUM CRAG:
The Exorcist – 120m VII,8. A. Mullin, S. Paget. 19th October, 1998.
1. 25m. Started right of the summer start at an obvious thin crack going up a steep slab. Climb the crack for 5m and move right to a corner. Climb the corner and trend up leftwards to gain a short corner leading into the recess of the summer route. Following the summer route is an easier alternative start.
2. 35m. Climb the summer route through the roof, then traverse immediately right (serious) to gain obvious ledges. Go straight up to belay below an obvious chimney.
3. 30m. Climb the chimney and move up and left on ledges to a large bay.
4. 30m. Trend up and leftwards on easy ground to the top.
Note: The route was climbed with two adzes because of wide cracks and a rest taken on pitch 2. Also the roof was yo-yoed from a second rest point (ie. two falls without hands rest).

Devilicious – 20m E5 6a. J. Lines (on sight solo). 5th September, 1998.
Climb the concave slab right of the first pitch of Clean Sweep. Start just right of a pink streak. Climb through a first overlap into the centre of the scoop. Climb direct through the upper overlap and continue nervously to a good hold.

Unnamed – E4 6b. J. Lines, R. McAllister. 30th August, 1998.
Desperate padding up the slab left of Two Little Devils (*SMCJ* 1996, p92),

protected by a side runner at the top of the Y-fork in its crackline. Climb the blank slab to a ledge, then the bold rib above to easier ground. Take the single crack through the headwall.

STAG ROCKS:
Get Rid of the Free Radicals – 140m IV,5. R. McAllister, V. Chelton. February, 1999.
Climbs the groove line immediately right of Afterthought Arête. Start 15m up and left of Afterthought Arête.
1. 50m. Climb an icy corner for 12m and move right to a spike on the arête. Swing round and climb a short right-facing corner to a ledge. Climb easier ground up and right to belay.
2. 30m. Climb a turfy groove on the left past a thread runner to the top of a large amphitheatre.
3. 60m. Awkward moves gain ice in the back of a hanging groove on the right. Follow the natural line above with interest to blocks on the left.

COIRE AN T-SNEACHDA, Mess Of Pottage:
Note: A. Clarke and R. McAllister added a VI,6 Direct Start to The Firefighter, independent of Droidless.

Frozen Assets – 55m IV,6. B. P. Kellet, J. Lyall. 9th February, 1999.
A line up the right side of the squat buttress to the left of the upper part of Hidden Chimney. Climb smooth right-facing corner from the toe, then step left around an awkward bulge and follow the groove, corner and crack to ledges. Easier to the top.

Aladdin's Buttress:
Deep Blue – Vll,8. A. Huber, A. Mullin. 10th March, 1999.
This is the direct finish to White Magic ie. close to the summer line, providing a fitting climax to the lower pitch, being more sustained and technically difficult. Instead of the traverse right, gain the diagonal crack line directly above the lower crack, Climb it diagonally rightwards before returning leftwards and a difficult exit on to a slab and the top. Climbed in a long pitch, but could easily be split.

Fiacaill Buttress:
The Great Escape – 75m E1 5c. G. Ettle, P. Thorburn. 23rd June, 1998.
This fine line heads for and ascends the hanging diedre above and left of Stirling Bomber. Start just left of the start to Houdini.
1. 45m. Ascend a shallow groove to a crack-split roof, then pull over to move right into Houdini. Climb cracks right of the corner until possible to traverse the exposed rib on the right to gain a slab at the bottom of the diedre.
2. 30m. Climb the diedre direct to finish on the midway ledge.
Winter: VII,8. B. Davison, G. Ettle, A. Huber. 8th March, 1999.
A winter ascent of the summer line, climbed in four pitches. Many falls taken and yo-yo tactics used. Double set of Friends helpful (including large ones).

COIRE AN LOCHAIN, No.1 Buttress:
The Rebel Alliance – 30m VII,8. A. Mullin, K. Thaw. 9th March, 1999.
This route climbs the obvious overhanging fault line in the centre of the small buttress immediately down and left of No.1 Buttress. The *in-situ* peg runner is the last piece of protection until the belay is reached making the route bold and serious (one rest on pitch 1).

1. 15m. Climb rightwards by ledges until a traverse can be made back left to reach the base of a stepped corner. Climb up to reach a sloping foot ledge and the in-situ peg at foot level. Move up and then across right on to the overhung wall to gain the obvious break and climb through it (thin) to reach a large block.

2. 15m. Climb straight up the fault to reach the base of a block overhang which provides a good finish on to easy ground.

NOTE: A. Mullin and S. Paget made an ascent of the summer line of Daddy Longlegs on 6th December, 1998. The 'two consecutive vertical cracks' were climbed as two separate pitches with two rest points on each. The first pitch (common to Big Daddy) was freed and considered easier then either of the crack pitches. G. Ettle and A. Huber later repeated Big Daddy free and thought VII,7. G. Ettle and M. Garthwaite also repeated Citadel and thought VII,7. As usual, there would seem to be different opinions regarding increasing standards – Ettle and Garthwaite who would down-grade existing routes while A. Mullin and S. Richardson would add extra grades.

No.3 Buttress:
Ewen Me – 55m IV,5. G. Ettle, J. Lyall. 13th March, 1993.
Another direct/variation start to Ewen Buttress. Start at the lowest rocks and work up slabs to a vague slanting groove which runs parallel to the direct start.. Climb this and steep rock to the crest, then join the normal route.
Note: A. Fyffe notes another start, which has been climbed before, from the base of The Migrant, going up turf leftwards to join the normal direct start (the latter is technical 6 in most conditions). This start is perhaps slightly easier.

No.4 Buttress:
Note: Torquing Heads continues to see failures and is VII,7 at least.

CREAG AN LETH-CHOIN:
Collie's Route – 75m IV,5. H. Burrows-Smith, J. Lyall. 25th February, 1997.
Start up the steep fault right of Irish Wolfhound, but after 10m, traverse right across giant flakes and blocks to a belay on the edge. Climb the buttress up left, then straight up to a hard corner/chimney with a tricky exit.

NORTH EAST OUTCROPS

Whisky Cliff (p 28):
On the Rocks – 20m E3 6a. W. Moir, G. Elrick. 3rd June, 1998.
Start as for Islander to reach the ledge. From the left end of the ledge, move out left to climb the obvious crackline.

Long Slough (p 33):
Lofty's Lunge – 10m E5 6c**. G. Lennox (unsec.). 12th September, 1998.
Climb up to the flake of Bob's Overhang from the right. Climb the crack above to good holds on the lip. Pull up on to the short slab above.

The Inlets of the Red Rocks (p 38):
Indecent Exposure – 20m E4 6a. T. Rankin, C. Adam. May, 1998.
Just left of Vibrator is an obvious undercut arête. Climb Vibrator until established in the crack. Place a high Friend, then traverse left to the arête. Climb the arête on its right side (RP2 in thin crack) to finish by pulling out right to the top of Vibrator. Good climbing in a wild position.

Humpback Gulch (p 41):

Glintin Eye and Bulgin Pocket – 15m E3 5c. T. Rankin, G. Robertson. July, 1998.
Climb the crack of Nooky Wall to the break (loose jugs). Move up left into
Boundary Corners. Now move up and right across the wall heading for the lower
of two horizontal breaks. Follow the line of holds back left into the centre of the wall
and finish straight up. Good sustained face climbing; pre-practised.

Herbivorous – 10m E2 5c. T. Rankin, J. Ormond. August, 1998.
Start at the corner forming the left side of the arching roof. Climb the corner to pull
out left and climb the steep rib until possible to step right above the roof. Move right
and climb a flake to the top.

Divine Perception – 10m E4 6b. T. Rankin, W. Moir. August, 1998.
Start as for Herbivorous but climb the slab right of the corner to below the roof.
Power over the roof using small holds on the lip. Finish up the wall left of the
Herbivorous flake.

Misconception – 8m E2 5c. T. Rankin, J. Ormond. August, 1998.
Climb through the roof at the obvious down-pointing spike right of Golden Shot.
Finish up a short groove.

Mr Potato Head – 28m E2 5b. J. Currie, T. Rankin. 23rd October, 1998.
An exciting right to left girdle of the gulch. Start by descending into Bernie, then
traverse left across the lip of the roof into Central Crack. Move left into the niche.
Continue in the same line into Boundary Corners (loose rock) and finish up this.

Bruin Cove (p 71):

Seabird Pie – 10m Diff. C. Adam. 3rd May, 1998.
Climb the first obvious line, a slabby corner and a variety of finishes.

Hareness (p 74):

Hareness Prow – 10m E3 6a. T. Rankin, M. Reed. September, 1998.
Halfway between the quarry and the sea wall of Bottom Boys is a short steep prow.
Approach south from the base of the lower quarry. Climb the prow by the line of
a crack to pull out right on to a slab to finish. A great wee route (on sight).

Jenga Groove – 8m VS 4c. T. Rankin. 6th October, 1998.
A good little problem up the groove in the pillar on the right side of the upper quarry.
Well protected. Probably climbed before.

Hareness, South Park Bay:

This is the small non-tidal bay on the north side of the headland. From the left
shoulder of the upper quarry, descend easy rocks to the north to gain a rock platform
just above the high tide mark. Walk round westwards to the bottom of the routes.
Belays are hard to find at the top of some routes.
Gritstone Mantel – 10m HVS 5b. T. Rankin (shunted, then soloed). 5th October,
1998.
At the left side of the bay is an obvious wet gully; the route climbs its right edge.
Climb to a ledge on the right. Move up and left to stand on a ledge on the arête
(demonstrating the name). Continue up the interesting arête to finish. The rock on
the right gully wall is suspect but can be avoided.

Chef – 6m Diff. T. Rankin. 6th October, 1998.
Climb the chimney slot on the left side of the yellow lichen slab on the right side
of the bay.

Mr Hankie – 6m V. Diff. T. Rankin. 6th October, 1998.
The pleasant crack in the slab right of Chef.

Weight Gain 2000 – 6m E1 5c. T. Rankin (shunted, then soloed). 6th October, 1998.
Climbs the right side of the wall using the thin crack and right edge. Gaining a
horizontal break is the crux.

Oh My God – 8m E1 5a. T. Rankin. 6th October, 1998.
The best route here. Right of the slab is a shallow red groove set in the right edge
of the buttress. Climb the deceptively steep groove to a hard pull out left to finish.
Good rock but poorly protected.

They Killed Kenny – 8m VS 4b. T. Rankin. 6th October, 1998.
Climbs the steep fault line just right of the previous route to a grassy finish.

Unnamed – 10m VS 4c. T. Rankin. 6th October, 1998.
Right again is an obvious V-groove above half height. Climb into the groove either
direct or from the groove on the right. Climb the left edge of the groove in a good
position to pull out left to a sloping finish.

Clashrodney, Bareside Point, Central Buttress (p 82):
Sphincter Cannon – 10m E3 5c. T. Rankin, J. Currie. 23rd October, 1998.
A serious little problem up the left end of the Stone Roses wall. Make steep
bouldery moves up and left to reach the obvious spike (crux). Pull out left to finish
easily. Some poor rock.

The Second Coming – 10m E3 5c. T. Rankin, J. Currie. 23rd October, 1998.
A direct finish to Stone Roses with equally good climbing. Climb the scooped wall
left of Stone Roses to join it where it moves right. Move up and left to a good flat
hold (crux, poorly protected). Continue over the bulge to finish up the recess as for
Stone Roses.

Clashrodney (p 84):
Sunlover's Traverse – 30m E1 5b. W. Moir. 19th April, 1998.
A left-to-right traverse of the south-facing wall running landward from Look
Sharp. Scramble down the grassy ridge just south of the crag to reach a secluded
boulder beach. Make a low level traverse of the wall, keeping below the small black
overhangs until forced to climb a right-facing corner (two thirds across) to reach
the big horizontal break. Follow this round to the ledges at Look Sharp. It is also
possible to move higher after the initial traverse to follow the big horizontal
(junction of red and black rock) all the way but this gives an inferior route.

Earnsheugh (p 87):
Blinkered Bat – 25m E2 5c. T. Rankin, C. Adam. 17th October, 1998.
This eliminate route takes a direct line up the arête between Bats Belfry and
Cloisters and contains some good delicate climbing. The best start is to climb pitch
1 of Bats Belfry; otherwise climb the original start of Cloisters to the same point
or abseil to the ledge down Cloisters. From the belay, move out right into a short
corner. Climb this for a few metres, then its left edge to a sloping ledge below a roof

on the arête. Arrange protection, then cross the roof going rightwards and return left to the arête. Continue boldly up the right side of the arête to join and finish up Cloisters.

Red Band Cliff (p 98):

Breech Birth – 20m E5 6b. W. Moir. 27th August, 1998.
Start just right of the huge southerly cave. Climb up to place strenuously a high runner in a horizontal break. Move back down and make a sensational heel-hooking traverse leftwards along the lip of the cave (good protection after the initial moves). Climb the pink wall (crux) to gain the big corner which leads to the top.

Yosemite Sam – 25m E4 6b. N. Wharton (on sight), J. Wilson, N. Morrison. March, 1998.
Start as for Shawangunks Wall, then climb more directly up the wall to a rest below the obvious hanging corner in the red band. Climb this imaginatively, then move right and finish up the walls above.

Downies Stack (p 108):

Black Saki – 20m E3 6a. W. Moir. 13th August, 1998.
Climb the overhanging crackline left of Howler Monkey, then go left to finish up the left edge of the wall.

Yorkshire Whipper – 10m E5 6b. T. Rankin (unsec.). August, 1998.
Climbs the very steep crack left of Downside Upwindies. Very powerful climbing leads to the top past a crucial Fr#+ at two-thirds height.

Vanilla Slice – 10m E2 5b. T. Rankin, A. Crofton. July, 1998.
An eliminate up the right edge of the Black Napkins corner. Start as for Cream Doughnut. Move left on the break to climb the right side of the edge. Finish straight up. Very strenuous but with adequate protection in the breaks.

Craig Stirling (p 123):

Tuskeneer – 15m HVS 5a/5b. T. Rankin, J. Ormond. 6th July, 1998.
Climbs the roof and wall left of Walrus. Start as for Walrus. Climb up left to below the roof. Surmount the roof direct. Continue up the centre of the wall to cross the overlap 2m left of Walrus. Climb the black-streaked wall trending left to finish just left of the highest part of the wall. Escapable at half height.

Newtonhill (south of it, p 134):

Park as for Harbour Wall and Dyke's Cliff. Head south for 200m and descend as for The Enemy Within. Scramble lower and head further south to a 5m cave. The following routes surround this cave on adventurous rock.
Snap, Crackle and Drop – 20m HVS 4c**. C. Adam, G. Lennox. 2nd May, 1998.
Climb steeply up the cave's left arête, trending slightly leftwards. Move left below a small roof. Head right climbing a small corner to finish. Bold.

Ramp On – 15m V. Diff. G. Lennox. 2nd May, 1998.
Climb the obvious ramp right of the cave on to easy ground. Repeated and thought Diff.

Blow Out – 15m E1 5b*. G. Lennox, C. Adam. 2nd May, 1998.
The right-hand wall of the cave extends to an overhanging arête. Climb the

horizontal breaks below the ramp, breaking out right below steep roofs to finish easily. Pumpy.

Bloodthirsty – 9m E4 6c***. G. Lennox. 2nd May (one rest); 7th June (free), 1998.
This test-piece lies before the above area. On the same path descend seawards towards a concrete sewer vent. Above black-streaked slabs north of this, a fine crack splits a roof. Safe but desperate.

Brown Crag (p 17):
New Frontier – 15m E2 5c. W. Moir, P. Allen. 23rd May, 1998.
Start right of I.G.Y. Climb a small corner to an overhang. Pull over this to gain a niche above on the right and finish easily.

Smuggler's Cliff (p 141):
The Smuggler's Waltz – 50m VS 4b***. G. Robertson, I. Fischer, J. Currie. 26th April, 1998.
A rising right to left girdle, starting at the bottom right end of the cliff (non-tidal) and finishing above the huge roofs. Great climbing, immaculate rock and very exposed in its latter half.

The Graip (p 142):
Collieston Calling – 10m E1 5a. G. Robertson, I. Fischer, J. Currie. 26th April, 1998.
The hanging arête left of Slain's Corner (starting up that route). Bold.

Perdonlie Inlet (p 183):
The long east wall of Perdonlie has only a small amount of good rock and only two routes. The south wall, however, only had the traverse route Zwango, which found an easy way along the foot of the face and on to Walrus Ridge. From the Zwango ledges the face rises up in a series of grooves and cracks to a diagonal fault line which splits the cliff from bottom left to top right and in summer would appear to be a nesting site for various birds (as usual). Above the fault, another steep little buttress has several lines. The right side of the crag is dominated by an arête and a large groove just to its left which is the line of the first new route here.
Access is easiest by abbing in from the boulders above the crag, good thread belays, which take you down steep grass and then down the line of Crazy Water / Blue Moves. For routes left of Grey Seal an abb down into the belay alcove, and down to Zwango would allow the rope to be used to back up the belay. Routes described from the arête leftwards:
Lady Samantha - 30m E4 6a. M.Reed, T.Rankin. 10th October, 1998.
Start at the east end of Zwango, below the middle of three grooves with a green streak running down it. Climb the green groove to a break (possible escape), stand up and reach good holds shared with Crazy Water, move right and climb up steep rock to easier ground just by the start of the arête proper. Climb the arête's right wall staying as close to the edge as possible, then directly to the top via an obvious small spike. The arête is an eliminate and escapable up to the spike. Previously top roped.

Crazy Water – 30m E4 6a**. M. Reed, I. Fisher. 20th March, 1998.
Start on the small raised ledge below the big groove and arête, under a small diagonal chimney. Enter the chimney, reach up and out for good holds and climb to the base of the groove. Enter the groove (crux) continue up to a weird downward pointing spike, swing left into another groove and up to the fault line, belay here

or continue up easy ground and grass to the boulders above. The green groove of Lady Samantha could be used as an alternative start. Previously top roped.

Blue Moves – 30m E5 6b**. M. Reed, T. Rankin. 20th August, 1998.
This hard route climbs directly from the Zwango ledge, to the small right-facing hanging groove, just left of Crazy Water. Start between Timidity Splits and Crazy Water, at the obvious cracks in the bulging wall below the groove. Climb boldly up to a niche just right of Timidity Splits, then make hard moves up and slightly right to holds on the arête, pinch the arête and then move left to enter the small groove. Continue up the groove merging with Crazy Waters upper cracks. On sight, apart from the top groove brushed.

Timidity Splits – 30m E1/2 5c. I. Fisher, M. Reed. 20th March, 1998.
This takes the next big groove line left of Crazy Water. Climb delicately up the wall below the groove, bearing right , then move back left into the groove, follow this to the fault and belay or go on to the top via Empty Sky or Madman.

Grey Seal - 30m E3 5c. M. Reed, N. Anderson. 17th August, 1998.
The deep groove immediately left of Timidity Splits. Climb the short wall below the groove rightwards aiming for a good hold on the right arête (gear). Pull left into the groove and continue to easier ground. Belay on the fault line, or better, climb the big crack of Shoulder Holster. This should become the preferred line and would be worth two stars.

Shoulder Holster – 25m E2 5c*. M. Reed, N. Anderson. 15th September, 1998.
This route tackles the obvious big left-slanting crack on the upper buttress. Start up the groove left of Grey Seal for a few feet to a crack in white-streaked rock on the right. Climb this to the break, then go up the crack line to the grassy alcove at the top. Fine, sustained climbing; the rock is not 100% but will improve with traffic. If climbed via Grey Seal first, it would be solid E3 5c and two stars.

Chameleon – 25m E4 6a*. M. Reed, N. Anderson. 10th September, 1998.
Climb the groove left of Grey Seal to the break, layback up the hanging flake and crack above to the roof, go right , and up, past a white bulge and up the crack and shallow groove above. Belay in the grassy alcove on the right. Climbed on sight. Again, the rock may be less than perfect in places, and gets worse as the routes go farther left.

Come Down in Time – 25m E3 6a. M. Reed, N. Anderson. 15th September, 1998.
Climb the slabby groove left of Chameleon to ledges at the left end of the break (possible belay.), then attack the sloping roof directly (crux), aiming up into the steep curving crack above and another small roof left of Chameleon. Go over this from the right and climb a crumbly crack to a mantel finish. Move right along poor rock to the alcove and belay.

Razor Face – 25m E2 5b. M. Reed, N. Anderson. 2nd October, 1998.
This takes the big hanging crack near the left end of the crag. The rock is still a bit crumbly. Start up a black-streaked groove near the left end of the Zwango ledge to wet but easy ground below a steep triangular slab. Climb the finger crack to the overlap, pull into the tight groove to stand on the flake, then enter the crack and layback up it to a good hold above. Move gingerly but easily right, passing a reasonable in situ thread, to the alcove belay.

Bite Your Lip – 20m E4 6a. M. Reed, T. Rankin. 10th October, 1998.
Essentially a variation on Razor Face. From the overlap, continue left to the white spike and go over the overlap into a small smooth groove (left of the big crack) climbed with much difficulty and exposure to easy but grassy ground above. Finish as for Razor Face. Previously top roped.
Note: The big bay above the left hand routes contains a lot of loose rock and vegetation, tread very carefully. A possible exit goes up the left-slanting crack at the back of the bay at Scottish VS.

UPPER BUTTRESS:
Empty Sky –15m VS 5a. M. Reed. T. Rankin. 20th August, 1998.
This fine little pitch is the first to climb the gold-coloured upper buttress and can be used as a top pitch to all of the previous routes instead of going up Perdonlie Edge again..Climb the slim groove/corner on the right edge of the upper buttress, following the crack all the way until forced out right onto the slab left of Perdonlie Edge and the easy ground above.

Madman Across the Water – 15m E4 6a. W. Moir, N. Morrison. 30th August, 1998.
The left-slanting crackline, starting just left of Empty Sky. Climb the crack until forced round left off a layaway (crux). Step back right to finish via an undercut (near the top crack of Shoulder Holster).

The next routes are described from the arête rightwards.
Kyles Groove – 10m HVS 5b. M. Reed, N. Anderson. 10th September, 1998.
Climb the third groove right of Crazy Water, (close to the green crack of Lady Samantha) up perfect pink granite, bearing right up the crack to a jug, then up the groove left to easy ground and belay. Either go up the Severe crack of Rocket Man on the right or continue easily up to a steepening. Climb up and left towards the arête aiming for the small spike of Lady Samantha, in a very exposed position, then make an awkward move up the arête and continue to belay above Blue Moves at E1 5b (eliminate). A third option is to traverse right along the big ledge above the pink rock, and descend Perdonlie Edge (Diff.) to climb one of the following routes.
On the south east nose of the crag is a small pink buttress of perfect granite easily reached by reversing Zwango to easy ground below the routes.

Mona Lisas – 12m VS 4c**. M. Reed, N. Anderson. 8th October, 1998.
A lovely wee pitch, started below Perdonlie crack. Climb a line of left-trending jugs to a prominent small spike on the edge of the pink rock (the groove round to the left is the top of Kyle's Groove) Climb the small groove directly above the spike on the left edge of the buttress to the ledge, belay. Above the belay is the groove/crack of Rocket Man (Severe), which goes up to the top of the crag. This is probably the variation to Perdonlie crack mentioned in the guide as climbed in 1968.

Mad Hatters – 14m E2 5b**. M. Reed, N. Anderson. 8th October, 1998.
A very delicate pitch. Climb Mona Lisa's jugs to the crack at the start of the obvious overlap, traverse right along the overlap to its widest point then go straight up the small cracks to the ledge. Previously top roped.
The main crack is the line of Perdonlie Crack, a fantastic three-star Severe on impeccable rock.

Amoreena – 12m VS 4c*. T. Rankin, M. Reed. 10th October, 1998.
Climb the wall and crack right of Perdonlie Crack to the ledge.

Mr Frantic – 12m VS 4b*. M. Reed N. Anderson. 2nd October, 1998. This takes the left-trending ramp right of Amoreena then up into the groove on the right edge of the pink buttress.

The big corner of Perdonlie Edge is next right and right of this is a vast area of virgin rock awaiting someone's attention!
Over on Walrus Ridge, the small square slab of pink granite on the east face gave:
Angel Delight – 20m Severe. N. Anderson, M. Reed. 15th September, 1998.
Climb the crack up the centre of the slab, over an overlap and up to the gendarme, turned on the left. Belay on the ridge or, better, carry on over Walrus Ridge to the headland.

Rob's Butt (p 186);
Butt-Kicker – 18m E3 5c. W. Moir, P. Allen. 15th August, 1998.
The thin crackline right of Whisky Galore, climbing right of the crack in the middle section.

White Lightning (with extended finish) – 18m E2 6a. W. Moir, G. Elrick, M. Reed. 15th August, 1998.
Climb the crack as per guidebook, thought to be 6a, then continue up the hairline crack through the overhang up on the left.

Longhaven Quarries, Lochan Buttress, South Face (p 203):
Stuka, Mesherschmit Finish – E3 5c. M. Reed, P. Wormold. 22nd October, 1998.
Climb Stuka (5a on poor rock, with a loose jug at one-third height) to the ledge at the top. Traverse the crumbly break left to pull up into the crack in the arête, then climb the crack to the top. The rock above the break is good, perhaps 6a?. Previously top roped.

Go Humble – 8m E6 6b/c. M. Reed (unsec.). 22th October, 1998.
The slim groove between Stuka and Levitator, capped by a block and crack. Start at an undercut in the black rock. Go up into the groove using a tiny hold in the base, and up the groove (rock#3) to the roof, then climb the hand crack to the top with continued interest. 6c for the short. Very sustained and technical, fairly bold, and is a touch crumbly lower down. Previously top roped (often).

Red Tower (p 210):
Baloo – 20m E4 6b. J. Lines (solo). Summer, 1998.
The thin crack and arête left of Shere Khan.

Red Bull – 12m HVS 5a. J. Lines (solo). Summer, 1998.
The SE Arête of the Red Tower itself.

Meakie Point (p 222):
Methadonia – 20m E4 6b. W. Moir (on sight), J. Wilson. June, 1998.
A more direct version of The Method. From the runners on the shelf, go diagonally left to grab the obvious flake.

Playstation Crag (new crag just south of Herring Cove; map p 223):
Banjo Kazooie – 15m E2 5c. W. Moir, G. Elrick. 22nd August, 1998.
The right arête of the crag, climbed direct.

Herring Cove (p 228):
Shellfish Finish – 10m VS 5a. T. Rankin, M. Reed. June, 1998.
Climb the jam crack and arête above where Herring Chimney moves left.

Souter's Hole:
Feelin' Groovy – 10m E3 6b. W. Moir (on sight), N. Ritchie. 14th June, 1998.
The short overhanging groove at the seaward end of the crag.

Cummingston, Prophet Walls (p 237):
The Prophet Walls have been equipped with new stake belay anchors in 1998.
Atcha –10m E3 6a*. C. Hornsby. 1998.
An extended boulder problem starting up The Gripper and then moving left on to
the hanging wall (small wires possible). Finish up or down climb The Gripper.

Surf Nazis Must Die – 15m E5 6b***. L. Johnson, C. Hornsby. 1998.
A superb route taking the hanging wall to the right of The Gripper. Boulder up
directly to a small overhang. Make a powerful move off an undercling to a small
hold on the left of a short slab. Move precariously up and right (Friend#0 in a small
horizontal slot) using a crucial vertical edge. Climb the fingery wall (peg) to a break
(Friend#3). Finish on slopers to the right.

Bat Attack – 15m E4 6a**. C. Hornsby. 1998.
A poorly-protected excursion with a decidedly bad landing. Climb the edge of the
roofed recess between Aesthetic Ape and Orange Ape. Use a horizontal spike
(potentially loose!) to gain small edges above and pull awkwardly into the finishing
crackline. Easy to the top.

Statutory Ape – 15m E6 6c**. D. Woodward. 1998.
A technically desperate climb with reasonable protection on the crux. Boulder up
the right edge of The Shield – 3m to the left of Bat's Wall. Gain a ledge and clip
two pegs under a shallow inverted V. Reach up to a poor pinch on the right edge
of the rib above. Make an 'impossible' move (dyno?) to a poor sloping hold high
and left. Continue awkwardly via a series of slopers (PR).

Monkey Mafia – 15m E4 6b**. L. Johnston. 1998.
A strenuous and technical outing taking the hanging crack leading leftwards out of
the deep cave on the right of Bat's Wall. Gain a sloping ramp from either left or
right. Place medium size wires in a vertical crack and move boldly up and left to
a small spike under the roof. Enter an arena of lactic acid accumulation and
undercut leftwards (well protected) with some technical moves. Gain the freedom
of a groove and finish with difficulty.

Mayne Line – 15m E3 6a*. C. Hornsby. 1998.
A variation start to Noddy Machine, climbing the gently overhanging finger crack
to the left. Gain the top of the crack, place Friend#3 and reach right into Noddy
Machine (crux). Finish up the latter.

Jaded Arête – 15m E2 5c*. A. Nicholson, J. Scott. 1998.
Climb the obvious hanging arête on the right of Noddy Machine. Arrange good
protection in the roof crack. Pull over the left side and finish above.

Bay Watch – 80m 6b***. C.Hornsby. 1998.
A complete left-to-right boulder traverse of the Prophet Walls providing a fine and technically demanding stamina exercise. Start at the far left side of the bay by some boulders and follow the chalk! The crux areas are beneath Surf Nazis, crossing The Shield (below Statutory Ape) and crossing the wall beneath Mayne Line. The climbing is sustained with few rests and ends at the start of the grass bank on the far right.

The Doubt Wall (p 241):
Bob Line – 12m E4 6a. C. Hornsby. 1998.
The hanging arête on the right wall of The Lum gives a committing and poorly protected climb on crimps and layaways. Exit as for The Lum.

The Arch Wall (p 243):
Welcome to the Beach – 12m E5 6b***. C. Hornsby. 1998.
A fine and bold climb taking a direct line up Arch Wall. A difficult start leads to fingery climbing on pockets. Reach up to small ledges in the centre of the face and clip the solitary peg. Make a difficult move to a small flat hold high and right. Finish directly.

Variation –12m E5 6a*. N. Green, C. Hornsby. 1997.
After the initial starting sequence, traverse left to gain layaways leading up to a Friend#3 placement in a vertical slot in a right-facing corner. Move right, clipping the peg and finish directly.

Pass of Ballater:
Juniper Crush (p282) – 12m E5 6b. I. Fischer, G. Robertson. 10th May, 1998.
The very faint groove line straight through the roofs right of Ton Ton Macoute. A scary route, previously toproped. Climb the wall just right of Ton Ton to the first roof where dodgy gear can be arranged, then pull strenuously up and slightly right to a good hold at the end of a sloping ramp (peg runner). A hard step left, then up (crux).

HIGHLAND OUTCROPS

ARISAIG, Rhu (MR 613 838):
D. Collier notes: Out on the point of Rhu there are small outcrops with rock of generally poor (loose) quality though there is some potential for short routes and bouldering. D. Collier soloed the obvious chimney with a large chockstone at the top in a west-facing crag which may also provide some harder climbing. Named Crac 'an Eigg Chimney, 12m, Diff., 31st May 1997.

DUNTELCHAIG, Dracula Buttress:
Neck Nippers fae Tammytool – 30m E4 6a. I. Taylor, P. Thorburn. March, 1998.
Climbs the exposed hanging wall left of Vampire.
1. 20m 4c. Climb the first pitch of Dracula, then traverse right to the right end of the roof.
2. 10m 6a. Climb up to a peg runner, then move up and left to reach the start of a thin crack. Follow this to the top.

Seventy Foot Wall:
False Friend – 15m E3 6a. R. Webb (unsec.). September, 1997.
Climb Sweeney's Crack to where it traverses left. Instead, traverse right and pull

through the roof (fairly long reach for a jug on the lip) into a hanging corner and finish up this.

TYNRICH SLABS:
Trumpet of the Dead, Direct Start was soloed on sight with wire brushing by J. Lines on 25th August, 1998 and graded E4 5c. The start of Slippery Jack is graded higher but may be about the same standard, not saying which grade is right – Ed.

ASHIE FORT (Guide p.159):
The crag is surprisingly solid. All routes were cleaned on abseil (except Raeburn's Original Route).
Points of Departure – 10m E2 5b. I. Innes, R. Webb. August, 1998.
The crack left of Throw Lichen to the Wind.

Raeburn's Original Route – 10m Scottish VS. I. Innes, R. Webb. September, 1998.
The dank wet and vegetated chimney right of Throw Lichen.

X File – 10m VS 5a. I.Innes, D.Balfour. October, 1997.
The X-shaped cracks climbed from bottom left to top right.

Sick Whipper – 10m E3+ 5b. R. Webb, I. Innes. August, 1998.
Right of X Files is a scoop with a prominent guano-covered hold. Climb to the guano hold, exit left and continue to the top. Serious.

Whipper Snapper – 10m E4 6a. R. Webb, I. Innes. August, 1998.
Climb to the guano-covered hold. Ascend the corner above, exit right to a ledge and finish by the obvious crack. Serious.

Bodysnatchers – 10m E1 5b. R. Webb, G. McKnight. September, 1998.
Right of Whipper Snapper are two left to right diagonal cracks that become more defined with height. Climb the left-hand one (named after the decomposing sheep removed from the bottom).

Harpic's Crack – 10m E1 5b. M. Hynd, G. Lowe. August, 1998.
The right-hand crack.

Welcome Pebble – 10m E1 5b. R. Webb, I. Innes. September, 1998.
Right of Harpic's Crack is an overhang at mid height. Climb through the overhang at its right-hand end to rach the welcome pebble, tie it off and continue to the top.

Woolly Jumper – 10m E1 5b. R. Webb, I. Innes. September, 1998.
The left to right crack right of Welcome Pebble. Named with reference to Bodysnatchers.

Kenny's Revenge – 10m Severe. I. Innes.
Right of Woolly Jumper is a fine prow that has so far defeated all comers. Right again is this chimney.

32 Feet per Second – 10m H. Severe. I. Innes, R. Webb. September, 1998.
The right-bounding rib of Kenny's Revenge. The first runner is at 9m.

Quark Strangers and Charm – 10m HVS 5a. I. Innes, R. Webb. September, 1998.
Right again is a right-facing corner leading to an overlap. Ascend the corner and take the overlap direct.

Pickpocket – 10m Severe. I. Innes, D. Balfour. August, 1997.
Right again is a shallow left-facing corner. Climb this, moving to the left wall at two-thirds height.

Fat Bird – 10m VS 4c. R. Webb, I. Innes. August, 1998.
The obvious crack that leads to a small tree right of Pickpocket.

One Move Wonder – 5m Severe. I. Innes. August, 1997.
Go right again to an obvious cleaned crack and climb it.

BINNEIN SHUAS, The Fortress:
Greatness and Perfection – 40m E7 6c. P. Thorburn, R. Campbell. June, 1998.
Start under the runnel right of Storming the Bastille. Pull over the bulge into a scoop on the left, then gain the runnel and follow it to the roof. Traverse right to a diagonal crack and climb it to a slab and heather.

Eastern Sector:
Windy Wall – 40m E1 5a*. G. Latter, J. Rabey. 3rd September, 1998.
A fairly bold pitch up the grey wall right of the top pitch of Flypaper. Start on the narrow grass terrace, 10m right of that route. Climb a slightly right trending line to a Friend #2 placement in a horizontal break at 15m. Move left, then head diagonally leftwards to finish rightwards up a vague crack-line (2m right of the more prominent crack-line of Flypaper). There is a single nut placement on the slab for a belay - a thread in a block farther back can be reached on a 55m rope.

DIRC MHOR:
Ripping Yarns – 40m E2. T. Whitaker, S. Richardson. 30th August, 1998.
Approximately midway between Ship Rock and the projecting buttress of Carry on up the Khyber, is an attractive smooth wall set above a shallow grassy bay. This route takes the right side of the wall following a line just left of the two-tiered arête. Climbed on sight.
1. 25m 5b. Start up a short right-facing groove just left of the right edge, and continue up the wall above (bold) to an awkward exit into a ramp. Move along this to belay on the right.
2. 15m 5b. Return back left to the obvious break which cuts through the steep wall above the ramp. Pull past some precarious blocks to reach the upper arête which leads easily to the top.

Windrush – 40m E2 5b. S. Richardson, T. Whitaker. 14th June, 1998.
The impending arête 15m up and right from Carry on up the Khyber. Start just left of the edge bounding the mouth of the descent gully. Climb a crack to reach hanging grooves in the arête. Climb these to a steep exit onto a slab. Climb this to the top (easier on the left). Climbed on sight.

KINDROGAN CRAG (Sheet 43; MR 049 627):
This crag lies in dense forest just south of the A924 between Pitlochry and Kirkmichael. From Enochdhu follow signs towards Kindrogan Field Centre. After crossing the river the road swings right. Carry on to a junction at a house on the right. Fork left here and park round a bend at a gate. Do not go through the gate but take a small track up into the forest. After 400m the track crosses a forestry road, turn right along this (the crag can now be seen ahead) and at its end continue into the trees. It is best to head for the top of the crag (there is a faint path, hard to find) as

the bottom is dank and gloomy. Descend to the routes by abseil or by going down at either side of the cliff. The climbs are described from left to right.

Forest Enterprise – 30m E3 5c**. G. Nicoll, M. Nicoll, G. Muhlemann. 2nd August, 1998.
The tall pillar at the left end of the crag. Start at the toe of the pillar and climb up and left before pulling right, above a bulge, to gain a small ledge. Move delicately and boldly right to the arête (crux) and climb up to a good runner. Move back left and up to an overhang. Turn this on the right with difficulty and continue to the top.

Kindrogan Corner – 30m E2 5b*. G. Nicoll, W. Wright. 28th June, 1998.
This is the impressive deep corner towards the left side of the cliff. Start up an unpleasant gully, then boldly pull left through a bulge into the corner. Follow this to the overhang, pull round and continue up the superb upper corner to a grassy terrace. Finish up the right edge of the slab above.

Ash to Ash – 25m E2 5b. G. Nicoll, K. Howett. 9th August, 1998.
Start at a big rowan tree below the right side of the crag. Climb the tree and a dirty slab leftwards to gain the top of a grassy buttress. Climb the obvious but loose fault line rightwards to the big roof. Pull round at the right end and climb up leftwards in an exposed position to finish at a small rowan.

GLEN LEDNOCK, Creag na h-Iolaire, Low Wall:
Private Chancer – 20m HVS 5a. C. Pettigrew, T. Burley. 2nd July, 1998.
Start as for Sultans of Swing. Once established in the crack, climb directly up the slab face and follow the detached block on its right-hand side to the top.

Sultans of Swing, Proper Direct Start – 5c. M. Robson. 19th April, 1998.
Climb straight up to the niche of Sultans of Swing (hard to imagine it has not been done before).

Left Branch Eliminate – 12m E1 5b. M. Robson, T. Ward. 19th April, 1998.
Start at the chockstone above the start of Sultans of Swing Direct Start (Route 11a in Guide). Climb straight up into a steep finger crack, move right at the top of this and continue to the top.

Balnacoul Castle, Hanging Buttress:
Pump up the Groove led free and on sight by A. D. Robertson, R. Campbell and N. Craig on 10th May, 1998 at E5 6a**.

GLEN OGLE, Sunnyside, Beinn Leabhainn:
The crag below the TV mast at the head of the glen (p 330 in the guide). The crag comprises three distinct sections. The left-hand section is characterised by a striking crackline on the right of the front face. The central section contains a prominent arête on the left and is detached from the hillside behind. It is separated from the left-hand section by a gully. The right-hand section is slabby and mossier in appearance. It contains the route described in the guide, Ex Officio. The routes were pre-cleaned by abseil.
The first two routes described are located on the left-hand section. The last route is on the steep left wall of the central section.
Hedwig –15m Severe. S. Kennedy, C. Grindley. July, 1998.
A wide crack runs up the left side of the leftmost crag. Steep moves lead directly into the crack which is followed to the top.

Voldemort – 15m E1 5b. S. Kennedy, C. Grindley. July, 1998.
The striking crackline on the front face a short distance to the right of Hedwig. Start just inside the gully at the right edge. Climb steeply up left into the base of the crack. Follow the crack to a wide sloping ledge. Move right and finish easily up the edge.

Polyjuice – 10m E3 5c. S. Kennedy, C. Grindley. 10th October, 1998.
The central section has a gently overhanging left wall containing a prominent crackline. Follow the crack to where it fades at a horizontal break (Rock#7, Friend $^1/_2$). From the break pull out rightwards to reach a flat-topped bulge. Pull over the bulge to finish. Short but sustained.

Creag nan Cuileann:
The following routes lie at the right side of Creag nan Cuileann, at the far right end of the main wall and around the far right-hand edge where there is a recessed section. The Bournville Wall lies about a minute's walk, a little up to the right. Although there is a layby directly beneath Creag nan Cuileann the best approach is from the last layby on the right (beside a bridge) before the road bends right at the top of the glen. Cross the fence to reach a pylon and follow the path to the second pylon, then rise gently up the hillside following a path across a stream, around the hillside and on to a rowan tree visible on the skyline. A short ascent past large boulders gains the right end of the crag. Routes are described from left to right. The first, route lies on the steep little wall at the left-hand end of the crag, just right of a short, roofed chimney.
Idiot Wind – 10m 7b**. R. Anderson. 11th October, 1998.
Five bolts to lower-off.

There are then the six 'traditional' routes covered in the guidebook, before the eight sport routes at the right-hand side of the main wall.
Fight or Flight – 15m 6c+/7a. G. Ridge. 19th September, 1998.
Over the roof and up the wall just right of Poison Ivy and left of a shallow, blocky chimney.

Slaphead – 15m 6b+. G. Ridge. 11th October, 1998.
The roof and bulge immediately right of the blocky chimney.

Fat Chance – 15m 6c*. G. Ridge. 24th September, 1998.
The short, thin crack in the roof/bulge just right of the shallow, blocky chimney.

Fight the Flab – 15m 6c+*. R. Anderson. 24th September, 1998.
Climb the roof left of Let it All Hang Out, then the short, blunt slabby nose. Approach from the right as for Let it All Hang Out and take great care with the block under the line – do not stand on the left-hand/lower block.

Let it All Hang Out – 15m 6c+*. R. Anderson. 30th August, 1998.
Thug the roof close to its widest point, then continue up the slab to a lower-off in the trees.
Hang On! – 15m 6c**. J. Horrocks. 19th September, 1998.
Climb the small roof just right of Let it All Hang Out, then continue up the featured wall and slab.

Step on It – 15m 6a+. G. Ridge. 1998.
Start right of Hang On! and move up left into it for a finish.

Life in the Fat Lane – 15m 6b+*. R. and C. Anderson. 29th August, 1998.
The short, steep crack right of George's Route, just before the crag turns the edge.
Lower-off on the heather ledge, beyond the rowan tree.

Just around the edge, facing down the glen, is a short arête with a leaning side wall,
where there are three routes.
Chasing the Bandwagon – 15m 6a+*. C. Milne. 1998.
The left-hand line left of the arête.

Reaching the Limit – 15m 6c*. R. Anderson. 4th July, 1998.
The line on and just left of the arête, sharing the lower-off and the first two bolts
of Chasing the Bandwagon.

Clutching at Straws – 15m 7a/7a+*. R. Anderson. 20th June, 1998.
The leaning side wall and arête at the left side of the recess, aptly named!

Up the slope to the right, the wall faces directly towards the road, the main, left-hand
part of the wall is slightly recessed. There is a small tree-lined ledge cutting across
the wall at mid-height.
Dazed and Confused – 20m 6a. J. Horrocks. 29th August, 1998.
The leftmost route on the recessed section uses the tree to gain the mid height ledge.

Having a Little Flutter –15m 6c**. G. Ridge. 29th August, 1998.
The wall to the left of the thin crack in the headwall.

Ceuse Jimmy – 15m 6c**. G. Ridge. 30th August, 1998.
A line to, then up the obvious thin crack in the headwall.

Kinmont Times – 10m 6a+ (6c)*. G. Ridge. 30th August, 1998.
The right to left-slanting diagonal crack cutting across the other routes on the
recessed section of wall to finish on the left edge as for Dazed & Confused. Direct
to the lower off is 6c.

Lichen Virgin – 15m 6a+*. J. Horrocks. 30th August, 1998.
Hollow flake, wall and groove bounding recessed section of wall.

The following two routes share a lower-off.
Loose Living – 15m 6a*. R. and C. Anderson. 14th June, 1998.
The obvious groove.

Ghost Trail – 15m 6c**. R. and C. Anderson. 14th June, 1998.
The white streak at the extreme right-hand end of the crag, a little gem.

The Bournville:
The Dirty Dozen – 6a. I. Watson, C. Milne. 1998.
Leftmost route.

ABERFELDY, Weem, Weem Rock:
Blinded by the Night – 18m 5+. G. Ridge. 4th October, 1998.
The central corner on the vertical wall.

Staring at the Sun – 18m 5. G. Ridge. 10th October, 1998.
The arête just to the right of the corner.

Lap Dancing –18m 6b+*. R. Anderson. 13th September, 1998.
The wall between The Trial of Brother Number1 and The Llama Parlour. Surmount
the roof at the top.

Crowing at the Enemy – 10m 6b+*. R. Anderson. 10th October, 1998.
The shallow groove at the far right end of the crag.

BEN NEVIS, AONACHS, CREAG MEAGHAIDH

BEN NEVIS, Observatory Buttress:
Never-Never Land – 170m VI,6. S. Richardson, P. Takeda. 9th March, 1999.
A good icy mixed climb between Rubicon Wall and Observatory Buttress, Original
Route. The route takes the line of least resistance up the lower buttress before
tackling the unlikely-looking headwall above. Start just right of the initial snow
runnel of Original Route.
1. 50m. Climb mixed ground right of the runnel, then move left to reach the shallow
depression of Original Route.
2. 45m. From the top of the depression climb up then left to gain the line of snow
ledges which cuts from right to left across the buttress. Follow this to the end and
belay below a short steep wall. Junction with Observatory Buttress Direct.
3. 40m. Climb the wall as for Observatory Buttress Direct, then instead of trending
right, climb straight up towards the headwall. Surmount another short steep wall,
then move right to belay below the prominent right to left groove system which cuts
through the headwall.
4. 35m. Enter the groove from the right , and climb it pulling over a small roof at
the top (crux). An excellent pitch in a superb position. From here easy ground leads
to the Girdle Traverse Ledge. Finish as for Original Route.

Secondary Tower Ridge:
Butterfingers – 220m V,6. S. Richardson, R. Clothier. 13th February, 1999.
An interesting mixed route up grooves in the right flank of Pinnacle Buttress of the
Tower. Start 5m right of a small snow bay, below the icefall of Pinnacle Buttress
Direct.
1. 50m. Move up for 10m to below a small inverted triangular wall. Step left
(Pinnacle Buttress Direct goes right from here), and continue up mixed ground left
of the icefall of Pinnacle Buttress Direct to reach the terrace.
2. 30m. Climb the gully just right of a steep corner to gain a left-trending ramp
which leads to the cave stance at the end of pitch 2 of Stringfellow.
3. 35m. Exit the cave on its right side and follow easy-angled grooves which cut into
the right flank of the buttress, until a short slot leads up and left to a large flat stance
on top of a huge block.
4. 30m. Trend up and right along an awkward ramp until a steep chimney leads up
to the large platform on the crest of the buttress (junction with Stringfellow).
5. 25m. Avoid the steep headwall above, by climbing the narrow ramp on the right
side of the buttress (as for Stringfellow Original Finish). Take the left of two
grooves to reach the crest.
6. 50m. Follow the easy angled crest to the foot of the Great Tower on Tower Ridge.

Comb Gully Buttress:
Big Bad Ben – 190m VII,7. S. Richardson, R. Clothier. 19th April, 1998.
A direct line up the right edge of Comb Gully Buttress. The lower section, which
approximates to the summer line of Comb Gully Buttress, banks out in heavy snow
conditions. The crux upper section takes the impending headwall right of Roaring
Forties. Start to the right of the lowest rocks below a prominent 25m V-chimney in
the right flank of the lower buttress.
1. 40m. Climb the V-chimney (or the arête just to its left) to easier ground. Move
up to belay below a steep tower (The Tooth).

2. 30m. Climb a steep corner on the left side of The Tooth and continue over the top of the tower and down into a col.

3. 40m. Ascend snow slopes to the headwall. Belay 15m right of the chimney of Original Route below a steep shallow gully.

4. 20m. Climb the gully (as for Roaring Forties) to a ledge on the right.

5. 30m. Move back left, continue up the gully and the impending right-facing corner above (crux). Continue up the line of the corner to a belay on the arête overlooking Comb Gully.

6. 30m. Continue up the line of the corner to where it disappears, move down and right along a ledge into the funnel of Comb Gully, and finish up this.

The Comb:

Naïve Euphoria – 180m V,5. S. Yates, P. McVey. February, 1988.

The icy groove between Mercury and Pigott's Route. Climb the chimney-flake of Pigott's Route and move up and left into the groove. Continue up the groove for two pitches to a snowfield. Climb this, cross the barrier wall and continue up the left side of the summit tower as for Pigott's Route.

Naïve Euphoria, Direct Start – 30m V,6. S. Richardson, J. Bickerdike. 14th February, 1999.

An independent start to the right of the chimney-flake of Pigott's Route. Start just left of Mercury and climb a steep mixed wall to the right end of the terrace of Pigott's Route. Continue up the smooth open corner above exiting left at its top to reach the top of the chimney-flake of Pigott's Route.

Bigot's Route – 180m VI,6. N. Gregory, K. Pyke. 9th January, 1999.

A difficult mixed climb between Naïve Euphoria and Mercury, finishing up the front face of the summit tower.

1. 45m. Climb the chimney-flake of Pigott's Route, and continue straight up to below a steep corner just right of the icy groove of Naive Euphoria.

2. 40m. Climb the corner, pull left around a bulge (crux) and continue up easier ground to a steep awkward wall. Climb this to a belay.

3. 45m. Go straight up and cross the snow field to a large off-width corner-crack in the barrier wall. Climb this and continue up the snow bay to belay at left side of front face of the summit tower.

4. 30m. To the right of an easier gully is a steep groove. Climb this via a narrow V-slot, and continue up a thin icy runnel until it is possible to pull left over a short wall into a small gully. This leads to a massive block belay on the summit ridge.

5. 20m. Cross the ridge to the summit plateau.

Number Three Gully Buttress:

The Banshee – 120m V,5. C. Cartwright, S. Richardson. 1st January, 1999.

An approximate winter version of the summer route. Start at the toe of the buttress as for Sioux Wall.

1. 40m. Climb a right-slanting line of grooves and chimneys past a huge and prominent poised flake to a steep wall. Climb this via a crack on the left to a stance.

2. 10m. Avoid the blank wall above by stepping right into Thompson's Route and following it to a good belay on the right.

3. 40m. Move left into the right-angle corner of The Banshee, and climb it to the platform of Number Three Gully Buttress.

4. 30m. Continue up Number Three Gully Buttress to the top.

Hobgoblin – 110m VI,7. S. Richardson, C. Cartwright. 5th December, 1998.
An excellent mixed climb taking a direct line through Gargoyle Wall. Start at the foot of the flake as for Gargoyle Wall Summer.
1. 30m. Climb the flake and continue up and right for 15m via a steep crack system to a short right-angle corner. Climb this to a good platform level with the base, and to the right of The Gargoyle.
2. 30m. Move up and right up a wall and crack to reach stepped edge. Climb this to the 'corner' of Gargoyle Wall below the steep cracked wall.
3. 10m. Climb the steep cracked wall to a ledge (as for Gargoyle Wall).
4. 30m. Move left along the ledge and climb the chimney-crack of Gargoyle Wall to where it goes left. Continue up the steep offwidth above to a ledge.
5. 10m. Finish easily up and right.

Creag Coire na Ciste:
Blockhead – 70m V,6. C. Cartwright, S. Richardson. 4th April, 1998.
The prominent ramp and corner on the right wall of Number Three Gully. Start 10m up and left of Cornucopia in a small alcove.
1. 30m. Take the leftmost fault leading out of the alcove up a short steep corner to reach easier mixed ground at the start of the ramp. Follow the ramp below a steep wall on the right.
2. 20m. Continue up the ramp to its end below a steep corner.
3. 20m. Climb the corner to the top.

Tick Tock Croc – 90m IV,5. J. Ashbridge, S. Richardson, R. Clothier. 21st March, 1999.
A short mixed route between Wendigo and Place Your Bets. Some sections climbed before. Start below the icefall of Place Your Bets below a left-trending gully-ramp which is hidden from below.
1. 30m. Climb a steep step and follow the ramp to the platform of Wendigo.
2. 40m. Traverse right for 5m and pull over a bulge just left of a prominent fin of rock. Climb the groove above to an easing (Wendigo crosses here from the left) and continue up the continuation groove above.
3. 10m. Climb the crest of the rib to the cornice.

Carn Dearg:
Staircase Climb Direct – 190m VI,7. S. Richardson, C. Cartwright. 24th January, 1999.
A direct version of Staircase Climb starting up Kellett's Straight Chimney and avoiding the deviation into Waterfall Gully higher up.
1. 15m. Follow the initial ramp of Staircase Climb to near its right end below the deep cut chimney. Move up to its base.
2. 15m. Climb the chimney past a chockstone to a ledge on the right. A desperate exercise in body jamming.
3. 40m. Continue up the chimney past a couple of difficult sections to where it eases.
4 and 5. 80m. Climb more easily up the left side of the buttress to belay beneath the prominent pinnacle.
6. 40m. Instead of descending into Waterfall Gully to turn the pinnacle, climb a turfy ramp on the right side of the pinnacle to the col. Regain the original line, and finish up the broad chimney above to reach easier ground.

Moonlight Gully Buttress:
Note: C. Jones and C. Ravey made a winter ascent of Moonlight Arête (IV,5).

South Castle Gully Area:
Plum Line – 250m V,6. C. Bailey, P. Downthwaite. 6th March, 1999.
Approx. 30m right of the corner of Compression Crack and where South Castle Gully narrows for the last time, an icefall cascades down the arête immediately bordering the left of the gully (this forms the rightmost of three icefalls on this wall). Climb a steep groove in the ice with a crux bulge at 30m and continue steeply above, exiting on to snow slopes and moving up to another icefall (60m). Step left on to the ice and climb this direct, trending right at the top to the slopes above (60m). Easier ground and snow slopes lead to the top.

MULLACH NAN COIREAN, Black Buttress (MR 123 668):
Ramp Route – 100m II. J. Ashbridge, C. Cartwright, S. Richardson. 6th December, 1998.
Start on the right side of the buttress and follow the right to left ramp to the crest. Climb a steep step via a jammed block, step right and continue up a short gully. Easier ground leads to the top.

AONACH MOR, Coire an Lochain:
Stirling Moss – 75m VI,7. M. Pescod, P. Winterbottom, D. Sykes. 15th April, 1998.
This route climbs the obvious triangular niche on the right of the front face of the buttress immediately right of The Prow (i.e. closer to Easy Gully than Stirling Bridge by approx. 50m). Start at the lowest point of the buttress.
1. 45m. Climb cracked slabs trending rightwards to a large ledge (15m, possible belay). Continue trending right and gain the base of the triangular niche. Climb this and step left (crux) at its top. Continue up the obvious groove.
2. 30m. Continue in the same groove to easy ground and the plateau.

Gowan Hill – 60m VI,7. M. Robson, D. Jarvis, T. Ward. 25th January, 1998.
The obvious hanging off-width crack high on the front of the barrel-shaped buttress between Homo Robusticus and Homo Sapiens. Start at the toe of the buttress and work up leftwards to a good ledge to the left of the crack. Gain the crack and pull steeply round the overhang (good rest). Continue upwards using the wall right of the crack, as well as the crack itself, to ledges. Move leftwards to finish.

Muck n' Brass – 100m VI,6. A. Powell, J. Aylward. 14th March, 1999.
Takes the appealing buttress between Molar Canal and Broken Promise.
1. 40m. Climb an icy bay up the front of the buttress, then a steep wall and slabs on the left before stepping right into a turfy groove which leads to the crest.
2. 30m. Follow the crest in a fine position, then traverse under a steep wall to join Golden Promise in the bay on the left.
3. 30m. Cross the upper gully of Molar Canal and outflank the cornice on the right.

Foosyerneeps – 50m IV,5. A. Clark, J. Davis. 13th April, 1998.
Two pitches up the clean pillar at the far right of the corrie. The route climbs the pillar via cracks and corners slightly right of the prow to finish directly through a V notch at the top (crux). Excellent protection and clean cracks throughout.

AONACH Mor, West Face:
Solitaire, Combination Start – 110m IV,4. J. Lyall, B. Newton, R. Wills, P. Wright. 22nd January, 1999.
An icy start up the wall about 15m left of the normal line. Left of a large roof, ice leads up left to a steepening groove which is followed to a final bulge which is

passed by the left rib and slabs. An easier snow and ice fault leads up right to the crest of the normal route.

AONACH BEAG, West Face:
Prominent Chimney – 100m III,6. R. G. Webb, N. Wilson. November, 1998.
The prominent chimney between North Buttress and Crevassed Rib (guide p.252).

Raw Egg Buttress:
Top Gun – 160m V,6. S. Richardson, A. Mullin. 23rd February, 1999.
A good mixed route between Aonach Wall and Raw Egg Buttress, Original Route. Start 30m right of Original Route below a left-slanting chimney-ramp which starts 5m up and right of the toe of the buttress.
1. 40m. Climb the chimney-ramp to its top, and move up to the barrier wall of Original Route.
2. 40m. Climb the wall by a short icefall, continue up then right up chimneys to a good platform. (Salmonella pitch 1 finishes here).
3. 50m. The upper buttress is cut by three parallel right-slanting grooves. Climb the central one (between Original Route and Salmonella) to a good ledge below the right side of the headwall. Step left and belay below a steep corner with a prominent series of vertical flakes on its left wall.
4. 20m. Climb the corner to a good platform. An excellent pitch.
5. 10m. Continue up the corner to the top.

CREAG MEAGHAIDH, Raeburn's Gully Buttress:
Barry White – 160m IV,6. A. Clarke, A. Perkins, I. Taylor, P. Thorburn. January, 1999.
On the left-hand side of the buttress, just right of the start of Eastern corner, a curving fault runs rightwards- the start. This fine climb offers well protected mixed climbing, a good early season venue, or when the big ice routes are buried under snow. Follow the curving fault to a ledge below an icy crack (55m). Climb the well protected crack (good hooks) to easy ground (30m). Go easily to the base of the final tower split by a chimney (55m). Steep rock leads into the chimney and the top of the buttress. The finish is the groove climbed optionally by Do What Thou Wilt (*SMCJ* 1995, p680).

Benny Hill – 110m V,5. A. Clarke, D. McGimpsey. February, 1999.
A parallel line of turfy grooves lies up and left of Barry White. Steep turf leads to a short awkward corner and turf ledge, then move right to a slanting corner crack (30m). Go up the corner to an open ledge, then move into a hidden chimney on the left (40m). An awkward wall leads to a system of turfy grooves and the top of the tower.

Loch Roy Corrie, Carn Dearg Buttress:
Roy of the Rovers – 160m II. D. McGimpsey, A. Mullin, A. Nisbet. 27th January, 1999.
Climbs a central line up the buttress right of The Spin, with a right-slanting squeeze chimney at half height and an easy finish.

Royal Buttress – 170m III,4. D. McGimpsey, A. Mullin, A. Nisbet. 27th January, 1999.

The well defined buttress left of The Spin. Start just right of the base and take a zig-zag line on steep turf followed by a traverse left to the crest. Follow the crest more easily to the top. A long left traverse was required to pass the cornice, somewhere near the finish of Big Red Van (which looked about Grade II in these very snowy conditions).

MONADHLIATH, Geal Charn:
The buttress between Valentines Gully and the snow gully reported in *SMCJ* 1998 was climbed at Grade I using a left traverse in above steep slabby ground by D. Morrison and R. Simpson on 20th Decenber, 1998.

GLEN COE

BUACHAILLE ETIVE MOR, Slime Wall:
Grogblossom: On a recent ascent by G. Robertson and I. Fischer, a large flake broke off from the bottom of the groove at the start of pitch 2. Since this is below the first gear, the route would appear to be both harder and more serious.

Stob Coire Altruim:
The Howling – 110m VI,6. M. Bass, S. Yearsley (alt.). 9th January, 1999.
This varied route climbs the steep front face of the main buttress between Dalmatian Couloir and Central Couloir before joining the easier angled hanging gully which runs parallel to the upper section of Dalmatian Couloir. Start 15m left of Dalmatian Couloir at a line of weakness falling from beneath the very obvious large free hanging icicle.
1. 10m. Climb steeply up ice and mixed ground to a thread belay in a small cave behind the free hanging icicle. A strenuous pitch.
2. 15m. Move out right behind the icicle on to ice on the front face of the buttress, and continue upwards over a steep wall to enter the hanging gully line.
3 and 4. 80m. Follow the enjoyable shallow gully to the summit.

BEINN FHADA:
On the lower tongue of slabs forming the east side of the large gully splitting the north face of Beinn Fhada is a shallow groove. This may have been climbed before as an old peg was found.
Groovy – 60m HVS 4c/5a. F. Coleman, T. Sykes. May, 1996.
Climb the groove and slab to a belay. Finish up slabs above. An attractive looking line.

Lost Valley Buttress:
Velocyraptor – 160m V/VI, 7. R. Anderson, R. Milne. 6th March, 1999.
The crackline between Tyrannosaur and Cold Feetus. Just up from the toe of the buttress is a leftfacing comer leading into the crack of Tyrannosaur which starts up the very short shallow chimney just to the right, where a slender buttress projects from the wall. Next to this is a straight crackline which runs up the middle of the projecting buttress and opens out into an off-width.
1. 60m. Immediately right of the shallow chimney is a thin crackline which is climbed, initially up a shallow groove, then across an casing (possible belay) and on through a niche and up an offwidth to a huge block-like feature.
2. 50m.Continue, as for Directosaur, rightwards up short corners, then up snow grooves.
3. 50m. Easy to the top.

Prehysteria –190m VI,7*. R. Anderson, R. Milne. 1st November, 1998.
Climbs the system of corners just left of Directosaur, starting from the ledge beside
that route at the foot of a short corner. This is just left of the buttress edge, down
and right of the big corner of Delusion.
1. 15m. Climb the corner and ensuing short wall to a ledge.
2. 20m. Step up left and awkwardly climb above the belay, then go up left via two
short corners to belay at the foot of the main corner.
3. 20m. Climb the left-leaning corner and continue to a good ledge.
4. 55m. Step down and around right to climb a blocky corner and follow the obvious
shallow fault line/gully to a ledge.
5. 60m. Move left and follow another shallow fault line to where the angle eases.
6. 20m. Easy ground leads to the ridge.

Lost Valley Minor Buttress:
The following two routes vary in grade according to the amount of ice:
Chimini Minor – 75m IV/V,6*. R. Anderson, R. Milne. 15th November, 1998.
The thin, chockstoned chimney-crack just up the wide gully from Minor Adjustment.
1. 25m. Climb the chimney to a small ledge.
2. 50m. Follow the groove to the top.

Over the Influence – 90m IV,4*. R. Anderson, C. Anderson. 10th January, 1999.
The long corner/grooveline immediately left of Chimini Minor. Easier in good
conditions. Start from a belay just to the right of the chimney.
1. 50m. Move left into the cornerline and climb to just below where it kinks right.
2. 40m. Continue in the corner to easy ground, then snow slopes leading to the top.

STOB COIRE NAN LOCHAIN:
The Dual – 130m IX,9***. D. Cuthbertson, R. Anderson. 24th February, 1999.
A modern test-piece which provides a sustained and intimidating prospect with
absorbing climbing and superb situations.
1. 30m. Start to the right of Scabbard Chimney and climb up, then across this
leftwards to gain a ramp which leads to a block belay, thread below.
2. 40m. Clip the *in situ* gear up on the left (poor), then move back down to the base
of the wall and climb this trending fight to the break in the overhangs. Climb the
corner and move right (ignore the peg/krab a move or so away) to the edge, then
go up and around this to gain a small ramp at the foot of the upper ramp.
3. 35m. Climb the ramp and the wide crack *(in situ* thread and large gear, Friend#6
useful) into a chimney which leads to a terrace just above.
4. 25m. The left-hand of three comer lines leads to easy ground.
Easily for 50m to the crest, then another 180m to the top.
Note: Climbed on fifth attempt. 'The Wall' pitch approached on sight and climbed
ground up on fourth attempt in 1997. The 'chimney-crack' pitch climbed with
summer knowledge.

Death or Glory – 50m VII,7. S. Paget, A. Mullin. 4th March, 1999.
This route climbs the open corner 5m left of Innuendo. Start in the obvious snow
bay.
1. 20m. Climb up the corner on poor rock until a small roof is reached and good
runners can be placed on the right. Turn the roof on the left to reach a small groove
leading to ledges.

2. 20m. Continue up the easy looking open groove and then a smaller continuation groove to the left side of a huge pinnacle.
3. 10m. Climb the short wall and corner immediately left to reach easy ground. Abseil from a block below or continue up Scabbard Chimney.

GLEN COE CRAGS, The Bendy (p 280):
Simmering Psycho – 25m E2 5c. D. Gunn, C. Ducker. June, 1998.
Climb either the obvious deep groove that seperates the crag right of In Seine or better the vertical crack leading to the big tree with the dead branch. Behind the tree is a shallow corner. Climb this to the top. Sparse protection on the crux.

Jim'll Fix It – 25m E2 5b. D. Gunn, M. Waugh. June, 1998.
At the left edge of the crags and left of Roaring Silence at the edge of the trees is a brown wall with a flat ledge. Climb the wall to a large hold then go up the cracks on spaced jugs until a long reach (crux, RP protection) and good holds. Finish up the crack to a ledge and the short crack above.

Creag Doire-Bheith:
The Happy Whistler – 40m HVS 5a*. G. Latter, J. Rabey. 3rd September, 1998.
200m up and left of Creag Doire-Bheith (the crag containing Aian's Arête) is an obvious crack up a blunt arête. Start on a ledge at the base of a right-slanting heather rake.
1. 30m. Climb the wall just above the rake to gain the base of the crack. Follow this, then the fine easy rough slab to a grass terrace and flake belay on the wall above.
2. 10m. Walk right 7m, then ascend the wall leftwards, leading to easier ground. Belay from a large boulder 25m farther back. The smooth pale wall in the centre provides a fine boulder problem (good grassy landing) on small sharp holds at 6b.

NOTE: G. Latter has repeated several of the recent additions hereabouts. Both Alan's Arête and Jim'll Fix It were thought to be barely worth a star!

Dry Gorge Leaning Wall:
Crimp – 18m E2 5c. D. Gunn (unsec.). June, 1998.
The thin crack at the right edge of the crag, right of the obvious wide crack of Sin Nombre.

GLEN ETIVE, Trilleachan Slabs:
Angel – 215m E7***. D. Cuthbertson, J. George. 3rd July, 1998.
A superb route with difficulties found on steeper rock than you might think! Take a good selection of very small to medium cams. Start at the foot of The Long Reach slab.
1. 30m 5c. Climb up and right via a pocket to the right side of a thin overlap at 6m. Gain and follow a quartz vein above, eventually gaining The Reach. Belay as for Spartan Slab/Long Reach.
2. 45m 5c. Follow The Long Reach as far as the left end of the horizontal quartz band. Now move up and right to climb an intermittent groove/flange to join the crux traverse of Pause beneath the first big overlap. Traverse left to belay at the small tree on Swastika. This pitch is also known as Band of Hope Direct.
3. 15m 6b. Traverse right for 5m until beneath a vague crack-cum-groove close to the widest part of the overlap. Make a difficult move to gain the obvious small ledge on the lip (shallow placement for a Metolius cam #00 or smallest Alien at the back of the ledge). Mantelshelf on to the ledge and if successful, Continue for 5m to

scoop ledges. Above and to the left, a thin grassy break provides excellent belays using small nuts and cams.

4. 55m 5c. The rippled slab between The Long Reach and Long Wait. Climb up and slightly right to a pocket. Trend right again to a small pocket (Roller#3 if you own one), then back left to another pocket (Roller#5) and continue to a scoopy ledge tapering up to the right, above which another pocket provides an assemblence of cam protection. Go up and left to an overlap and via a vague ripple, pad up and slightly right to another pocket (Quadcam#4 or similar). Continue up the ripples to a right-facing flake and so to the left-hand end of The Long Reach intermediate overlap. Take the slab directly above and go over a small bulge on good, but slightly mossy, rock to a belay at the top of the grass column of The Long Walk, 10ft beneath the second big overlap and 8m right of the diamond-shaped overlap of The Long Wait.

5. 50m 5c. Trend up and right to a pocket on the slab beneath a short undercut wall (in the main overlap). Pull directly on to this using an obvious small flange and gain the easy-angled slab above. Climb a left-facing flake and near its top, step right past a pocket to reach a left-trending band of quartz leading to the tree-lined ledge beneath the final wall. After the flake, this section is more or less unprotected. Either belay at the left end of the tree-lined ledge at the foot of a vegetated corner (later descend 5m for a belay for the last pitch) or traverse horizontally left before reaching the ledge and belay in the corner beneath the undercut left arête of the terminal wall.

6. 20m 6b. To the right of the undercut arête there is a dark streak in the sidewall above an overlap. Pull into the short crack above the overlap and awkwardly attain a standing position (Friend#0 or similar cam backed up with a nut. Above this is a placement for an RP#1 and above that, an HB offset#1 on its side was used.) Step up and make a long reach left to a thin break issuing from a stepped ramp (Friend#0 or + useful). Follow this break down towards the left arête and make thin moves up to gain the next break. (There is a 'reasonable hold' towards the left side of the shoulder from which a position can be attained to place a small Alien or Metolius cam#00. This placement is crucial as the crux is above.) Gain the next break (nut and Friend#0) and continue up the arête to an exciting finish. For the belay, a Friend#0 located 3m to the left and a Friend#+ or 1 in crack 3m-4m above.

ARDNAMURCHAN POINT:
Park at the new visitor's centre. Approach Keeper's Cottage, then down and right along grass to cliffs. Vertical walls can be seen forming an impressive corner with an obvious overhang on the left-hand side. This is the Left Wall area. When the tide is out, around the right edge of these cliffs is a barnacle-encrusted wave-cut platform. This is the Main Wall area, bounded on the left edge by a rightward-slanting chimney. The tide come in quickly once it reaches the wave-cut platform. The rock is gabbro, varying from excellent to poor.

Left Wall:
Muck Climb – 10m Severe. D. Virdee, A. Briggs. 7th June, 1998.
To the left of the overhang is a curving crack running up to the top. Climb the crack (wet and slimy) and the flakes. The direct (harder, 4a) start can be avoided by climbing the flakes and ledges to the left, then easily traversing right to meet the crack.

Right of the overhang is a large steeper wall, the main section of the Left Wall area.

The rock here is much more compact and harder to protect. It is also very loose in places near the top.

E-numbers – 15m E1 5b. E. Hudson, D. Virdee. 20th July, 1991.
Starts 5m right of the left-hand corner. Go straight up the middle of the wall, after an initial start near the bottom left. Poor protection.

Incoming Tide – 15m VS 4c/5a. D. Virdee, E. Hudson. 20th July, 1991.
Twin cracks in the centre of the wall to a loose finish.

Loose Rock – 15m VS 4b. E. Hudson, D. Virdee. 20th July, 1991.
Five metres right of Incoming Tide is an undercut which allows access to the crack above. Not recommended.

Main Wall:
The Chimney – 15m Diff.
The obvious right-slanting chimney guarding the left edge of the Main Wall.

Home for Tea – 15m Severe*. D. Virdee, A. Briggs. 4th June, 1998.
In the middle of the wall 10m right of The Chimney is a leaf of rock forming a crack between it and the wall behind. It forms a slight roof at the bottom. Follow this to the top.

Westering Home – 15m V. Diff. L. Curtis, E. Vokurka. 10th May, 1998.
A squat block protrudes from the main cliff 10m right of Home for Tea. Climb the corner between the block and the main cliff to reach the top of the block. Step off the block on to the main cliff and pull through a bulge to reach the top.

Eigg Scramble – 15m Diff.
Starting 5m right of Westering Home, climb up the right-hand corner between the block and the wall.

Patch – 15m V. Diff. D. Virdee, A. Briggs. 7th June, 1998.
Climb overhanging arête to the right of Eigg Scramble, then move left on to the wall.

Whelk Route – 20m VS 4c**. D. Virdee, L. Curtis. 10th May, 1998.
Go around the corner and arête which forms the start of Patch to reach a steep open-book corner with a thin crack. Climb the crack and the capping bulge. A superb route.

Regeneration – 15m VS 4b. A. Briggs, D. Virdee. 7th June, 1998.
Climb the middle of the wall to the right of Whelk Route.

THE ARDNAMURCHAN RING CRAGS
An attempt to delegate for a second year has failed and the Journal has been left without coverage of the many routes climbed here recently. The new guide is scheduled for summer 2000.
Note: The Apron Slabs on Meall Mheadoin are extremely close to a very important nest site and should not be climbed on between March and the end of July.

Meall Sanna (MR NM 453 686):
C. Stead notes that the routes on this crag in *SMCJ* 1998 are not new. They were climbed some 30 years ago and thought too trivial to record.
Note: C. Stead's note illustrates a common problem, as the acceptable height of routes has decreased over the years. There is a similar problem with the acceptable separation of routes. The cliffs at Reiff were also climbed on before any routes were written up.

SOUTHERN HIGHLANDS

MULL OF KINTYRE, Creag Na Lice:
The Bowling Alley – 20m H. Severe 4b. S. Burns, D. Crawford. 24th May, 1998.
Climb the prominent deep cut chimney between the left-hand and central sections of the buttress.

Picnic Rock (Sheet 68, MR 769 155):
The small crag on the left side of the beach. Short routes, but a pleasant setting.
Loaded – 7m E2 6a. M. Robson, T. Ward. 4th May, 1998.
Tackles the hanging crack and arête. Start at the graffiti 'LMI 1992', pull up and use a hidden hold to reach across right to the crack which is climbed to a ledge. Continue up the arête.

The Adjuster – 7m VS 4c. M. Robson, T. Ward 4th May, 1998.
Right of the arête is a hanging chimney-crack with a tree in it. Climb the centre of the wall right of the chimney-crack.

Midships Crag:
Kissing the Gunner – 30m E4 5c. M. Gartwaite, C. Smith. 17th May, 1998.
More dangerous than Kissing the Gunner's Daughter. Start 8m left of that route. Climb a short wall to a ledge, then the clean crack in the shallow corner on the left. Move up to below the steep wall and follow the very thin seam to an alcove below the upper wall. Move up and left, then back right to the top.

CREAG THARSUINN, Upper Buttress:
Rite of Spring – 30m E3**. C. J. Watt, N. J. Smith. 24th May, 1998.
To the right of Deception is an open book corner with a smooth right wall containing a vertical crack right of centre. The right wall of the open corner gives a sustained technical wall climb with the crux high up. Protection is good but fiddly to arrange; take plenty of small wires, micros and small cams. Top-roped prior to lead.
1. 20m 6a. Climb the wall by the crack, with occasional deviations, to a horizontal break at half height (not seen from below but near a quartz band). Arrange a cluster of protection in the crack above and move up and left to gain a small V-shaped pocket (crucial Friend 1). Above, a slanting crack trends left to a black moss streak. A hard move gains a good hold in this crack and further good holds in the original crackline which lead to an awkward finish on to heather.
2. 10m 4a. The short wall above is climbed to the top (as for Firebird).

Firebird – 35m HVS 5a*. N. J. Smith, C. J. Watt. 19th May, 1998.
To the right of Rite of Spring is a fine arête and right of this a narrow slab with a crack in its right side, the start of V-Groove Direct. Good climbing but a little dirty. Climb the cracked slab to a small roof (leave the vegetation intact for the turf heads). On the left wall is a small hollow flake which is not seen from below. Standing on this, reach up for good holds and layback up left into a recess. Bridge up the short groove above to a small bilberry ledge. Traverse hard left on good footholds across a fine slabby wall to an arête and climb the left side of the wall to a welcome finger crack. Pass a small overhang on its right and exit left to another small ledge

(possible belay). Easier climbing up the mossy and heathery buttress ahead leads in 10m to easier ground.

Counting Down – 30m VS 4c. D. Kirk, C. McNee. 20th June, 1998.
Start at the foot of an open book corner 3m left of Deception. Climb the corner either directly or by starting up its left wall, then directly up the cleanish slab above, left of the upper part of Deception.

BEN VORLICH:
Logical Progression – 25m M9 or XI,10 for on sight. M. Garthwaite (red point). 23rd February, 1999.
The route climbs an overhanging crackline on a crag just below the summit of Ben Vorlich, facing Loch Sloy. It is best approached by cycling to the Loch Sloy dam, then walking up and slightly left to the summit. The crackline is largely hidden from below, but is on the highest band of crags and becomes more obvious as you approach. The route was top-roped over several days, then led on gear pre-placed on abseil. The gauntlet is down.

BEN VORLICH CRAGS:
These crags are just below the summit ridge, face west, get the evening sun and are relatively midge free. Approach from the tourist path that leaves the road about half-a-mile before the dam. Walk straight up the hillside until just below the summit ridge. Cranium Crag is the obvious dome-shaped crag on the left.

Cranium Crag (MR 300 110):
Method Own Madness – 30m E4 6a***. M. Garthwaite, A. Murray, C. Smith. 10th May, 1998.
Move out right along easy blocks to below a short thin crack. Climb this, then the crack on the left to a shake below a steepening. Climb straight up the smoother wall into the scoop above. Exit the right side of the scoop and climb to the top in a wild position.

Whizz Kids – 30m E5 6a**. M. Garthwaite, T. Harrison. 25th June, 1998.
Start as for the previous route. Climb the initial crack for 3m, then move right to below obvious small overlaps. Move up (hard), step right, then up to good holds at the very base of the slab. Follow the very thin left-trending seam (bold), then straight up to the top.

Chasing the Dragon – 25m E4 5c. M. Garthwaite, C. Smith. 12th May, 1998.
Climbs the shallow groove right of the previous route to finish up the top slab. Move out right along the broken blocks to belay below the groove. Move up, then left into the base of the groove. Climb the groove boldly to step right at the top, then back left to a ledge below the top slab. Step left on to the slab, then climb straight up without any gear to the top.

Bottom Crag:
This is the obvious crag immediately down and in front of Cranium Crag.
G-String – 20m E2 5c**. M. Garthwaite, C. Smith. 2nd June, 1998.
Climbs the shallow corner on the front face. Climb the wall below the corner, stepping right at the top to belay. Easy scramble off.

V.P.L. – 20m E4 6b***. M. Garthwaite, C. Smith. 2nd June, 1998.
A fantastic route climbing the double corners on the right-hand face. Climb the first corner to its top and make hard moves right to the base of the second corner. Follow this to the top.

Right of Bottom Buttress is another wall.
Colon Stress – E3 5c*. C. Smith, M. Garthwaite. 30th June, 1998.
Start just right of a small cave at the base of the crag. Follow the crack up and left, then back right to the arête. Climb the arête and finish up the scoop at the top of the crag.

THE COBBLER, South Peak, North-East Face:
T. Halliwell and M. Morton note the following route on the left margin of the face at 50m, III,5. It would seem to count as a variation start to SE Ridge. From the toe of the SE Ridge, ascend a ramp diagonally right towards the NE Face but after about 5m climb steeply on to the left end of a rising ledge. Follow the ledge right into a deep corner/niche with a crack running directly up from this. Climb the crack (crux) to the left end of another rising ledge and a cave/niche (25m). Step down and traverse right on ledges to a wide groove, climbed to the crest of the SE ridge (25m).

Centre Peak Buttress:
Turftastic – 75m VII,7. M. Garthwaite, C. Smith. 17th January, 1999.
A diagonal route crossing Chimney Route providing very good but escapable climbing. Start in the big overhung bay down and left from Chimney Route.
1. 25m. Climb an easy groove leading to the right arête of the bay and swing round on to the front face. Traverse right and slightly down to the obvious turf ledge, then move along this a few feet before moving up the wall and back left to below the crux of Chimney Route.
2. 25m. Move right up the easy ramp to the left-hand of two cracks and climb this (crux) to a small bay. Move left and up a small corner to below a roof, traverse right beneath this and pull up to below an obvious chimney.
3. 25m. Climb the chimney and the continuation line to the top.

MEALL BUIDHE, Lower Buttress:
AC Joint Test – 95m IV,5. G. E. Little, C. Schaschke (alt.). 6th December, 1998.
Start just to the left of an obvious low block roof at the foot of the relatively clean buttress to the right of the starts of Rampling and Spirit Level.
1. 45m. Move up and left to a corner. Ascend it, move right, then climb to a slight groove in a wall of clean rock. Ascend the groove with increasing difficulty to step right at its top. Cross a tricky slab above, then continue to belay in a shallow bay. A nippy pitch!
2. 50m. Move left from the bay, then climb straight up to reach easier ground leading to the top of the buttress.

BEN CRUACHAN, Drochaid Ghlas:
Tiger, Tiger – 130m VII,7. C. Cartwright, S. Richardson. 7th March, 1999.
The 'compelling unclimbed corner' to the left of Into the Fire mentioned in the *Arran, Arrochar and Southern Highlands Guide*. A superb mixed route climbed on thin ice and frozen turf. The base of the groove is guarded by blank bulging slabs, so the corner was gained by a left-trending ramp which starts 10m farther right.

1. 20m. Climb turf for 5m then move left across a bulging wall to gain the ramp. Follow this to a good stance at the base of the corner.

2. 40m. Climb the corner to a good platform where the angle eases.

3 and 4. 70m. Climb the wall directly behind the belay then move up and right to gain easier ground. Continue up the chimney and easy gully above as for Into the Fire to the top.

MEALL NAN TARMACHAN, Cam Chreag, Fan Buttress:

The Cider House Rules – 80m III. J. Irving, G. Allan. 21st December 1998.

Left of all previously described routes is a wide face of mixed ground At the left hand side is a rock tower with a chimney running up the right-hand side. This is the most obvious line on this part of the crag and corresponds to no previously described features. Easy ground leads to the chimney. A 40m pitch ascends to a large spike belay on the left, then easy ground leads to the ridge.

Creag an Lochain, Arrow Buttress:

Flight of Fancy – 105m III. S. Muir, G. E. Little (alt.). 7th February, 1999.

This route takes a left-trending line up the centre of the vegetated face to the left of Arrow Chimney. Start about 50m up and left of the foot of Arrow Chimney below a cluster of scraggy saplings.

1. 55m. Climb up to below a short wall, turn it on the right, then break back left. Climb straight up to a niche on the right below a slanting roof.

2. 30m. Move left to enter the obvious groove. Climb it to a ledge, then move left to the foot of a short corner. Climb the corner and exit left above to a thread at a turf mound. A characterful pitch at the upper limit of the grade.

3. 20m. Continue straight up on easier ground.

BEN LAWERS, Coire nan Cat, Creag an Fhithich:

Stray Cats – 115m III*. C. Bonington, G. E. Little, S. Muir (alt.). 1st February, 1998.

1. 35m. Climb the first pitch of Felinity to the small pinnacle on the right.

2. 30m. Move back left and climb a short ice step to steepening ground. Move slightly right, then step up left. Surmount a short wall (crux), then trend up and right to a turf ramp.

3. 50m. Continue up the ramp and broken ground above to the top of the crag.

Alley Cat Gully – 100m II*. G. E. Little. 9th March, 1998.

The east flank of Creag an Fhithich (which terminates in the short East Gully – Grade I), presents a distinctive vertical featureless wall. Start below this wall at a shallow diagonal gully. Follow it, with one little chimney pitch, to reach its termination at a small col overlooking East Gully. Drop down into this and finish via easy snow.

Bealach Crag (MR 636 423):

This short turfy north-facing crag lies 250m due south of the main bealach between Ben Lawers and An Stuc. Its only real merit is that it lies above 1000m and is in condition for most of the year!

Wild Frontera – 65m II. G. E. Little, C. Bonington (alt.). 24th January, 1998.

Starting just right of an indistinct gully, climb a fairly central line in two pitches.

ARRAN

BEINN TARSUINN, Meadow Face:

Snakes And Ladders – 50m E2 5b***. C. Moody, W. Hood. 16th May, 1998.
A slab of perfect rock between The Curver and Meadow Grooves which is good for a second route of the day. Easily seen from the slopes on the right, it has a vertical heather crack on the right-hand side. Start up a bulge on the left side and follow the crack to a downward-pointing flake. Traverse right for 5m, then climb straight up on seams and pocks to the left of the heather crack. A Friend#2 protects the top section, a Rock#6 can be threaded just below it. The route was gained by abseil off chockstones at the top; traditionalists can reach the start by two pitches of grassy grooves.

CIR MHOR, Lower East Face:

Papinootme – 40m HVS 5a*. W. Hood, C. Moody. 1st August, 1998.
The crack between South Ridge Original and The Crack. Start just right of S.R.O. Climb up then move right to gain the right side of the flake (it might be better to start further right and climb direct to here). Climb the flake, step left and climb the crackline; towards the top avoid twin grassy cracks by pockets just left. Easy for the grade.

LOWLAND OUTCROPS

GLASGOW SOUTH AND AYRSHIRE, Neilston Quarry, The Right Buttress:

Hyperreality – 15m VS 4b. D. Crawford, S. Burns. 19th September, 1998.
Immediately to the right of Fornication is an undercut slabby wall. The route follows a direct line to the top. A scoop leads to an overlap at 3m, climb this and the wall above to a bulge (crux) which is taken direct.

Whitehorse Rib – 15m Severe 4b. D. Crawford. September, 1998.
Right of Jig-Saw Jive is an undercut blunt rib. Start directly below it. Pull on to the slabby rib where unprotected moves gain easier ground (but no protection). Finish left up the upper groove of Jig-Saw Jive.

THE GALLOWAY HILLS, Craigencaille, Main Wall:

To the right of the Main Wall is a huge roof with a smooth corner (Old Mortality) on its right side.
The Whirling Dervishes – 50m E3 6a**. A. Fraser, A. Murdoch. 19th August, 1998.
A sustained but very well protected climb with some excellent moves. Easy for the grade.
1. 15m 6a. Start as for Old Mortality and climb this for 5m. Traverse left across a steep and difficult wall for 3m to holds on the edge, above the big roof. Move up then left across a slab to a prominent flake under the roof. Layback up right into a niche, then move up right to belay.
2. 35m 4b. Traverse left for 3m, then climb an easier but mossy wall to a ledge. Continue up the left edge above then follow the trail of bones up to, into and out of an impressively large nest (the crux in the nesting season) to the slope above (35m-4b)

NOTE: Old Mortality (*SMCJ* 1995 p. 688) and The Heretic (*SMCJ* 1996 p.113) are the same.

THE DUMFRIES OUTCROPS, Clifton Crag, Jigsaw Buttress:
Liptrip – 10m VS 5a. S. J. H. Reid, D. Bodecott. 24th April, 1998.
The obvious groove between Lipstick and Hotlips had previously been ignored due to a large bramble bush in situ. This has now been removed. The main groove, 1m right of Lipstick, is gained by strenuous jamming over the roof (thread in lip). Finish more easily up the newly gardened chimney/groove.

THE SOUTH-WEST SEA CLIFFS, Portobello, Shark Fin Bay:
At the top right end of the bay, reached up a grass slope, is a buttress with a large roof at mid height.
Walking the Plank – 20m HVS 5a**. A. Fraser, A. Murdoch, A. Taylor, I. McGill. August, 1998.
A sustained and interesting route with a sensational crux. Start at the left toe of the buttress and climb a right-curving crack just right of the left edge of the buttress and leading to the A-shaped recess at the top. Step right into the recess, then swing down and out onto the lip of the overhang. Climb the headwall to the top.

Larbrax (MR 966 608):
These cliffs are situated on the coast about four miles south of Kiln O' the Fuffock, reached along the idyllic beach at Larbrax. The climbing to date is on a series of greywacke slabs above the beach. The rock is perfect, the climbing is very fine and the situation superb. Also of note is the excellent bouldering on the beach underneath the cliff, one of the few good bouldering areas in Galloway.
From Glasgow follow the A77 to Stranraer, then go west on the A718 to Leswalt. Turn left in the village (signposted to Portpatrick) and take this for two miles to a junction. Follow the main road left for one-and-half miles to Larbrax. Take the track immediately opposite on the right, signposted to Bay House, then follow this down to the beach. Walk north (along the beach) for 10-15 minutes to a series of pinnacles on the beach. The slabs are just beyond above a grass shelf. Routes are described left to right, with the seaward slab first.

Seaward Slab:
O'er The Dyke – 15m HVS 5a*. G. Brookes, L. Walker, J. Nelson, M. Dale. 1st July, 1995.
The crack at the left edge of the slab, reached directly from below.

Haste Ye Back – 17m E6 6b/c***. M. Dale, G. Brookes. 1st July, 1995.
The classic of the crag, taking the slab at its blankest. The climbing is excellent and thin and the gear is just thin. In the centre of the crag, where the left overlap meets the ground, is a thin crack. Climb the crack for 7m to the first overlap/ripple where a line of reasonable footholds lead leftwards towards the edge of the overlap. Move left along these for 1m or so until small finger pockets and very thin edges lead to the second overlap (RPs in the crack to the right). Move left and up (crucial RP#2 on the left) until a stretch back right can be made to a good flat V-shaped hold. More extending moves lead to the top on improving holds.

Ceud Mille a Failte – 17m E4 6a***. R. McAllister, A. Fraser. May, 1998.
Another superb route, taking the most obvious weakness in the centre of the slab. Gear improves with height. Start as for Haste Ye Back and climb the initial crack of that route for 7m. to the first overlap/ ripple. Move 2m. right(crux) to a rest at

a large pocket. Continue directly to start of leftward slanting fault, then move right with difficulty to reach and finish up crack at top right of crag.

Ace is Low – 15m E2 5c*. G. Brookes, M. Dale. 19th November, 1994.
At the right side of the slab is a crack leading to a spike/ pinnacle. Climb the crack and stand on the spike. Tricky although reasonably well protected moves lead into the thinner upper cracks and the top.

The Central Slab:
Soor Ploom – 16m E3 5c**. M. Dale, G. Brookes. 3rd July, 1995.
Start from about the middle of the slab. Make a bouldery pull leftwards to start, then move up and left to below a very thin crack which splits the overlap (good wires). Climb the thin crack to reach an obvious pocket from where moves left gain a pod/ crack just right of the left edge of the slab. Climb this via some odd moves and the last protection, then run it out up the arête and the slab to the top. The centre of the slab remains dirty (not for long!).

Mealy Pudding – E1 5b**. G. Brookes, M. Dale. 3rd July, 1995.
The right-hand line on the slab, up obvious finger cracks via some nice finger jamming with good protection, moving slightly right near the top.
The Right-hand Slab:
A last great challenge, blankety blank. Boldissimo.

Cranberry Jam – 18m Severe. M. Dale. 3rd July, 1995.
The left-bounding slab and wide crack.

Laggantalluch:
Peregrine Corner – 25m HVS 5a*. J. Fisher, A. Brockington. June, 1998.
Between Small Bay and Main Cliff is a mossy raised wall split by a clean corner. Sustained and well protected.

GLASGOW SOUTH AND AYRSHIRE, Loudon Hill, Central Wall:
The Cat – 15m E1 5b. C. Pettigrew, T. Burley, H. Bruce. 10th May, 1998.
Climbs the 5m steep corner-crack 6m left and up of the old drystane dyke. Climb the crack with difficulty to the loose block at the top, pull over this and continue easily to a belay at the bottom of Young's Stairway.

Le Chat – 20m VS 5a*. C. Pettigrew, H. Bruce, T. Burley. 10th May, 1998.
A direct Start to Young's Stairway. Climb the front face of the buttress on the left. Instead of the traverse right on Young's Stairway, continue direct to an obvious thin crack (with seep marks) and climb this crack direct on small holds.

FIFE OUTCROPS, The Hawcraig:
Hip Replacement – 15m HVS 5a. J. Dyble, J. Shanks. 5th August, 1998.
Start in the recess to the right of the normal start to Toerag's Wall. Pull through the overlap without using holds to the left (on the right side of Toerag's Wall) following rounded holds on the right and a thin crack to the left. Good climbing but a bit contrived; poorly protected.

Rib and Groove – 15m Severe. J. Dyble, J. Shanks. 5th August, 1998.
Between Hallelujah Wall and The Whang. Aim for a blunt dark rib 4m up and with a thin crack in its lower half. Follow it directly to the top via a thin groove line. Climbed before but not recorded.

MISCELLANEOUS NOTES

The W. H. Murray Literary Prize.

As a tribute to the late Bill Murray, whose mountain and environment writings have been an inspiration to many a budding mountaineer, the SMC have set up a modest writing prize, to be run through the pages of the Journal. The basic rules are set out below, and will be re-printed each year. The prize is run with a deadline, as is normal, of the end of January each year. So assuming you are reading this in early July, you have, for the next issue, six months in which to set the pencil, pen or word processor on fire.

The Rules:

1. There shall be a competition for the best entry on Scottish Mountaineering published in the *Scottish Mountaineering Club Journal.* The competition shall be called the 'W. H. Murray Literary Prize', hereafter called the 'Prize.'

2. The judging panel shall consist of, in the first instance, the following: The current Editor of the *SMC Journal;* The current President of the SMC; and two or three lay members, who may be drawn from the membership of the SMC. The lay members of the panel will sit for three years after which they will be replaced.

3. If, in the view of the panel, there is in any year no entries suitable for the Prize, then there shall be no award that year.

4. Entries shall be writing on the general theme of 'Scottish Mountaineering', and may be prose articles of up to approximately 5000 words in length, or shorter verse. Entries may be fictional.

5. Panel members may not enter for the competition during the period of their membership.

6. Entries must be of original, previously unpublished material. Entries should be submitted to the Editor of the *SMC Journal* before the end of January for consideration that year. Lengthy contributions are preferably word-processed and submitted either on 3.5" PC disk or sent via e-mail. (See Office Bearers page at end of this Journal for address etc.) Any contributor to the SMC Journal is entitled to exclude their material from consideration of the Prize and should so notify the Editor of this wish in advance.

7. The prize will be a cheque for the amount £250.

8. Contributors may make different submissions in different years.

9. The decision of the panel is final.

10. Any winning entry will be announced in the *SMC Journal* and will be published in the *SMC Journal* and on the SMC Web site. Thereafter, authors retain copyright.

The W. H. Murray Literary Prize (1999).

FOR THE second time, several jurors had their reading of the Journal spoiled somewhat by the requirement to read its articles pre-publication! So Bryan Fleming – Hon. President; Ken Crocket – Hon. Editor; Simon Richardson – SMC member, and Dave Hewitt – columnist and editor of the *Angry Corrie,* made their delibera-tions, whether in an armchair, on a hard route or long walk, or by parallel processing while engaged in some other duty. This year was deemed to be more difficult, due to several articles being close to each other in quality. In the final analysis and totting up of points, *Welcome to the Club* by a Leeds schoolteacher, David Hughes, is the 1999 winner.

The article is, of course, published in this issue, and will also be found on the SMC web site in full. It is a story of a solo hillwalk with an ending which should make the hairs on the back of your neck tingle. Some comments from the jurors are given below. As I have mentioned the closeness this year, it is worth mentioning some worthy runners-up. Also judged highly were *Risk and Mountaineering; The Classic Scottish Ice Routes,* and *On Seeing the Cuillin from the Cairngorms – Again.*

'*Welcome to the Club* is my number one choice. It was a good story, the descriptions of winter hill-walking were evocative, accurate and vivid. Further-more the *hero* of the tale was such an arrogant so-and-so, one felt it was about time he met his maker.'

'A spooky story, with a solid, if indirect, message of mountain safety implica-tions behind it. It must be synchronicity at work again, as I have come across several ghostly or spiritual stories this year and indeed am struggling to finish one myself.'

FAMILY PHOTOGRAPH – a cautionary tale from Douglas Anderson

NORDRE IKERASAQ is not the sort of place where you take things for granted. I knew its menace in the past. From its placid southern entrance it looks like a pretty ordinary fjord. However, deep in the fjord, beneath its towering rock walls, currents run stronger than Lofotens' famous Maelstrom.

In winter the coast freezes to provide good sledging but here the currents weaken the ice and the traveller is in constant danger. Perversely, in summer these currents trap the passing floes, cramming them between islands and promontories, the ice often broken into fragments polishing the rock as it goes by. Though our 15ft boat was small enough to dodge between the swift moving ice, its survival often seemed in the balance.

This day the family's ambitions were tempered by close-packed ice floes jostling and rafting onto each other in the swirling current. After a struggle and no small excitement we extricated ourselves and steered into a welcoming inlet. We set up camp and sat down to consider lesser adventures that might keep us busy until more favourable ice conditions would permit us to continue.

After a day's reconnaissance a plan was laid for a sledge journey inland. A depot was left and the minimum of materials for a four-day sojourn divided up. Unfortunately for me this division was made pro-rata on body weight (something of which I have ample supply). It was with gloomy resignation that I surveyed the deadly load and the 2000ft of rocky hillside leading up to the glacier. By the time I had struggled to the top it was 10pm.

Wilderness travel with a young family is synonymous with late starts – good to have such an excuse – but by 2pm everyone was ready and enthusiastic to be in harness. No great challenge – just happily plodding across the pristine landscape. The day wore on and the frequency of chocolate stops increased. I cast around looking for a suitable camp site. In this part of the world the air is so clear that anything that looks close is far away, and anything that looks a bit farther I knew would take days to reach . The kids were beginning to get tired and even riding on the sledge was not enough to keep them entertained. A site for Camp 2 had to be found soon but there was nothing obvious in sight.

I tramped off towards an unlikely looking summit on the west bank of the glacier to see if from its pinnacle I could spot something. Steepening snow led to a rocky scramble and then a large slab perched just below a tiny rock summit. The slab was at least 50ft across. The actual summit was not more than 15ft higher. The approach was benign but to the north the ground plunged 1000ft vertically to an ice field far below. The sudden exposure was as frightening as it was unexpected. Beyond the summit was a remarkable grassy ledge just the right size for our tent. Sheltered by a low wall of rock but on two sides dramatically open to both the view and the drop to the glacier, a real mountain eyrie. An hour later Camp 2 was pitched there and made safe for the kids with a rope fence. Snow was melted, tea brewed and food prepared, and we were well set for a night on top of this remote mountain in Greenland.

If ever a family photograph was called for this was one such time. Fearing the drop I took excessive care in moving everyone back to the summit. Flushed with success they spontaneously adopted poses appropriate to brave mountaineers. The place to take the picture from was the middle of the 50ft slab. Keeping most of the slab between me and the abyss to the north I established myself near its middle, and taking up my camera I composed the frame. Taking the first picture I thought a second would benefit from more background, so I sidled backwards; camera to eye. My foot caught and rocked on an unevenness in the smooth expanse of granite. It caused me to stop. I took the second picture. It captured a great moment in a great day. Nearly my last.

I looked down to see what my foot was rocking on. I could not understand the white, five-foot circle by my heel. I paused, trying to make sense of the illusion. The instant realisation dawned I leapt away, propelled by a surge of adrenaline. Staring back, I stood shaken by terrible thoughts.

The sun's light had spread the rock's colouring evenly to hide a hideous trap. After standing transfixed for a few moments I got down on my stomach and inched back to the very lip where my heel had rested, and looked in. The hole was almost circular, about five feet across, its walls some 20ft deep and of exactly the same lichen covered colouring as the top surface of the slab. The sun lit its sides and top equally, flattening them into a single plane.

Viewed just two feet from its edge, this hole was invisible. At the bottom where shadow ought to have formed there was none; there was no bottom, only air. The slab was completely undercut, and light, reflected upwards from the glacier far below, lit the sides of the hole with the same evenness and intensity as the slab above, creating a devilish illusion. Only when the observer stood on its very edge was the hole visible. Peering down I could make out a mysterious granular texture before recognising huge blocks of ice lying on the glacier below, the remnants of a massive avalanche. I remembered my family sitting a few feet away, now mystified by my antics and the stream of expletives assaulting their ears. I contemplated again the disaster so narrowly averted, another inch – overbalancing, the sides so smooth, flashing past – and then the free fall 1000ft to the glacier below! I'd have felt so silly in that free fall, like a man walking reading a newspaper stepping into a manhole – one minute content with life – the next...

The following day we sledged onward, still comforting myself with the occasional expletive. I had cause to remember Edward Whymper's words: 'Go into the mountains if you must but think well to every step...' – Timeless advice!

Scottish International Winter Climbing Meet 1999

OUR MAN in High Places, Simon Richardson, reports:– In early March, 60 climbers from 24 countries met up with 50 British hosts at Glenmore Lodge for five days of winter climbing. The weather was superb, and the Scottish mountains were in their best snow and ice climbing condition for several years.

Guests and hosts alike were quick to appreciate their good fortune, and a feast of superb climbs was done from Glen Coe to Torridon, and Nevis to the Dubh Loch. Naturally, many climbers were eager to sample the great Scottish classics, and numerous ascents were made of Zero, Point Five, and Hadrian's on the Ben and Smith's and North Post on Meaghaidh.

Many visitors focused on mixed routes, and in the Northern Corries, Fallout Corner, Savage Slit and The Message had many ascents as did Sticil Face and Scorpion in the Loch Avon Basin. Superb ice conditions on Liathach meant several teams enjoyed Poachers Fall and Salmon Leap, and the renowned Test Department was hammered with at least four ascents.

The appetite for hard climbing by some of the more accomplished visitors was awe-inspiring. Marko Prezjelj from Slovenia, for example, notched up ascents of Red Guard, Sticil Face Direct, Citadel, Shield Direct, Test Department, Salmon Leap, Deep Throat and Fallout Corner – a lifetime's worth of hard Scottish classics in a mere five days! Alex Huber from Germany concentrated on technical snowed-up rock climbing in the Northern Corries and came away with a repeat of Big Daddy, a new direct finish to White Magic, and the first ascent of the desperate Great Escape on Fiacaill Buttress. America's Pete Takeda climbed Men In Black in the Northern Corries and on the Ben made an early repeat of The Shroud and ventured onto the headwall of Observatory Buttress to make the first ascent of Never-Never Land.

For those with energy to spare, the evenings were kept full with seminars on ethics, the environment, and a review of mixed climbing standards throughout the world, which left little time for networking at the bar – perhaps the most important aspect of an International Meet!

All in all, this was a superb five days and congratulations must go to the MCofS and the BMC for hosting the Meet, and Glenmore Lodge for their warm hospitality. Sincere thanks are also due to the UK Sports Council, the Scottish Sports Council, and Marmot, for making the Meet possible. And whoever chose the dates deserves a medal – this was the best possible advertisement for Scottish climbing one could ever imagine.

The Mariner's Horizon

ALAN HUNT reports: Reading Derek Fabian's notes on his trip to New Zealand in the 1997 Journal prompted me to recall my own ascent of Mount Aspiring.

In September 1994 I left Inverness with my wife, Fiona, and our two children, Ross and Rachel on our yacht, *Blue Biscay,* and transited the Caledonian Canal bound on a west about circumnavigation. We had planned on two years away. In the event it turned into three.

After a few minor excursions in Madeira and Gran Canaria it wasn't until we reached the Pacific, where the cooling waters of the Humboldt current eased the effect of the tropical heat, that the urge to climb a high point on the islands we visited was again translated into some form of definitive action. It began in the Galapagos where the hills are reminiscent of the Paps of Jura and nearly ended there in the ensuing battle with the evil thorn scrub that protects the middle and lower slopes. French Polynesia wasn't much better with fights in almost vertical rain forest that finally finished off my family outings. Here the local 'guides' had hacked a way up the main peaks of the island and even fixed the Aonach Eagach-like awkward sections with bits of extra fat binder twine. Fiji's Mount Victoria, the same height as Ben Nevis, although a long way inland, was a snip. At its base, we stayed in the home of the local village chief, a traditional offering to visitors that is both hospitable and generous. They don't eat people any more but you are expected to join in the ceremonial drinking of a potion made from dried Kava plant root, mildly narcotic and rather like over-dosing on Fisherman's Friends.

New Zealand's high points are many and some still active. In North Island several volcanoes were climbed complete with soaks in the hot springs on the descent and perfect weather in South Island saw family trekking at last become a popular activity in the Fiordland and Mount Aspiring Parks.

In 1984, Fiona and I had retreated from French Ridge hut on Mount Aspiring in typical 'Norwester', stair-rod rain. Here I was again, this time with perfect weather but no gear. Trainers are fine for bush walks and even gravely volcanoes. Aspiring needed proper boots, crampons, ice axe, rope, harness, prussik loops and a companion to pull you out of the 'slots' and generally be around in moments of anxiety.

My yachty's proper mountaineering kit comprised of a pair of rock boots and a harness, (you never know when you may need them) and a day sack. The rest was make do, including very non-breathable waterproofs. Fiona dropped me off at the road head, Cameron Flat in the Matukituki in the late afternoon and I was soon at Aspiring Hut. I had hired boots, crampons and an ice axe from Geoff Wyatt, a Wanaka guide. He had also given me a copy of a route description for the ascent of Aspiring via the Colin Todd Hut and a photocopy of the appropriate map section. I didn't have a rope or anybody to tie it to. Shortly after I arrived at the hut a descending UK forces team of six or more turned up. They had climbed Aspiring by the North-west Ridge two days previously, returned to the Colin Todd Hut on the descent and carried on down the following day. I quizzed one of the less knackered members of the team as to the difficulties of the route and was reassured by his response. Not technically difficult if you hit the right way but sufficiently awkward to slow you down when moving together roped up. It had taken them 12 hours for the round trip from the Colin Todd Hut. Moving together wasn't going to be a problem. Let's hope I would find the right route.

I only made one error the next day, when I followed the wrong track in the bush and wasted an our or so climbing toward the Liverpool Hut. Should have had a proper map. After that I hit the right river crossing, an easy way passed Scott's Bivvy, an exciting scramble to the right of the headwall stream that promised an even more gripping eventual descent and finally arrived at the Bevan Col. Only the Bonar Glacier to cross and I would be at the hut, but what about the slots? More luck, a helicopter arrived right on cue and dropped a Kiwi Guide and clients off. They were going to camp on the glacier and climb the South-west Ridge the next day. Yes, they would keep an eye open for me as I followed the UK team's track across the glacier to the hut. It was fine, just a few big strides here and there and lots of light walking. The tiny beat-up old hut was due for replacement later that season with a smart new model but this would suit me fine for one night. Gear on two of the bunks suggested company and sure enough high up on Aspiring's summit cone I could see two figures. I reckoned they wouldn't be back until late and it was well dark when the door burst open and two young stuffed but pleased Aussies came in.

I left the hut an hour before dawn and reached the main ridge at first light. The toppo from Geoff Wyatt was spot on and made route finding not too difficult, or perhaps I was lucky. The route was rather like an elongated Clach Glas to Blaven traverse, until the final snow slopes and summit crest and made for relatively risk free and speedy solo travel and I was on the summit just before midday in perfect weather. What a buzz! What a great climb. What views. What a day. Gobsmacking beyond belief. Then check in with the park authority. The Aussies asked me if I had enjoyed my 'walk' and where had I been. I have to admit a deal of smug self satisfaction when I told them. Then across the softening glacier, schussing the névé slopes, down the lethal headwall scramble and more down, past Scott's Bivvy and on to the Aspiring Hut, 36 hours after I left it. Impelled by momentum, high on adrenaline and full of being alone, the prospect of a night in the busy hut didn't appeal but my rendezvous with Fiona at the road head wasn't until the following day, so I pressed on and spent the night in the tiny bothy of Cascade Hut, about an hour from the road head with nothing but the mice for company.

After that the Glasshouse mountains, north of Brisbane, with the children, seemed a snip but the company was welcome. Odd high points were climbed as we voyaged up the Queensland coast but the inviting Lochaber like peaks of Hinchinbrook Island proved to be well protected by estuarine crocodiles and impenetrable bush. We should have got up something in Indonesia but our cruising permit didn't allow the time and the next high ground visit was Penang Hill in Malaysia's humid atmosphere. That really made us sweat. Above the tea plantations of Sri Lanka, we once again enjoyed the cool mountain air and the vision of 'blue remembered hills' stretching into the distance, even if most of the journey had been by public transport. An attempt on the Great Pyramid was thwarted by the whistle blowing Egyptian guards but we did manage a walk around the pine forested Mt. Troudos on Cyprus. You can drive to the summit and walking around offered a more pleasant alternative. A gorge walk in Crete and a great day out on the second highest peak on Majorca and that was it. Now it's back to ticking off those Munros. Twenty something to go at the last count.

THE SLUGAIN HOWFF STORY

By Ian Mitchell

MY FAVOURITE chapter in Tom Patey's *One Man's Mountains,* is without doubt *Cairngorm Commentary,* which describes the sub-culture of the mountaineering world there in the later 40s and through the 50s. For, apart from the intrinsic charm and humour of the writing, it describes the Cairngorm scene much as I stumbled upon it a generation later in the 60s. The Gorms were still relatively quiet – at least on the Braemar side – utilised largely by Aberdonians, though of a newer breed, and it was interesting to find that the almost universal nick-naming we practised had a pedigree in Patey. While our group sported names like Fishgut Mac, Stumpy, and Mealie Pudding – and a later one adopted the collective epithet of Winers and Diners – Patey's associates ran about with names like Sticker, Esposito and the Hash Kings.

The bothies were the same; Corrour, and Luibeg (with old Bob Scott) being a favourite. Another aspect of the Cairngorm mountain culture Patey describes is the howffs, especially those of Beinn a' Bhuird, still widely used in the 60s. According to Patey howffing was given a popularity boost by the appearance of Jock Nimlin's article in the 1949 issue of the *SMCJ,* and the piece's initial effect was to lead to the construction of the Smith-Winram howff, or Mac's Howff in one of the corries of the mountain. However, there is a bit of Cairngorm Confusion in Patey's account of a couple of the other howffs lower down the mountain, and I have been an unwitting conveyor belt for this confusion, in the book *Mountain Days and Bothy Nights.* I would like to correct the account given on pp.78-9 of *One Man's Mountains,* regarding this 'village of howffs' as Patey describes them, and which I retailed. I am able to do this because of the simultaneous and entirely serendipitous contacts recently established with two of the persons involved in the construction of what were the pair of major howffs in that village.

As is common with oral history, the details in Patey's article are largely correct, but mis-transposed, conforming to the good old Aberdonian principle: 'Nivver spyle a story, wanderin gin it's true.' Leaving aside Mac's howff, already mentioned, and the Raymond Ellis howff, which had no attempt at concealment and whose ruins are visible from the walk in to Beinn a' Bhuird, there were two main howffs, both heavily concealed rivals for the title of the Secret Howff. One was Freddy and Stickers howff, constructed by the Kincorth Club, the other was, in Patey's book, called Charlie's Howff; the latter is the present, extant – though still secret – still used Slugain howff.

Patey gives 1954 as the date of the construction of Freddy and Sticker's Howff; this is an error. That howff was built *before* its rival, Charlie's Howff, whose construction can be dated, by accurate hangover methodology, to exactly 1953, and Freddy Malcolm (telephone conversation with myself, 25.11.98) recalls his and Sticker's howff was built about 1951 or 1952, as a base for Freddy and his companions' explorations and new routes in Coire na Ciche.

Among the new routes Freddy was involved in were : Trident, the Carpet, and Hourglass Buttress, characterised in the 1965 SMC guide as 'the best and hardest route in Coire na Ciche and one of the best in the massif'.

Patey describes the howff's building as taking place in the much-quoted passage:

'The building materials were brought from Aberdeen to the assembly line by the Herculean labours of countless torchlit safaris which trod stealthily past the Laird's very door, shouldering mighty beams of timber, sections of stove piping and sheets of corrugated iron.' *(One Man's Mountains,* p.78).

Again this is an error, or rather, a transposition. Freddy informed me that the bulk of the building materials for the Kincorth Club howff came from the ruins of Slugain Lodge down below in the glen. This howff lasted, Freddy recalls, till the early 60s when it fell into disuse; on my first visit to Beinn a Bhuird in 1965 the Kincorth Club howff was ruinous, but Charlie's Howff was in good repair – and still is, approaching its half-century. Freddy did say however, that his hut was *not* the dive Ashie claims it was in the attached account of the construction of the still-existing Charlie's Howff; though it was clad in peat for camouflage, Freddy suggested the inside of his howff was as comfortable as, indeed initially more cosy than, its rival. Perhaps the pair should get together for a few drams to resolve the question. There was certainly an element of friendly rivalry in the construction of the howffs. Ashie recalls being miffed that Freddy and Co. had snaffled the debris of Slugain Lodge, and envious that they had been beaten in the construction race, and he challenged his rivals thus: 'Oh aye, it's a richt using second-hand material tae save a six-mile cairry, bit fit aboot weet rot and wid worm? Will it stand the test o' time?'

It is clear from the attached, wonderfully fresh account by Ashie Brebner, that the howff which involved the smuggling of materials past the laird's door, was the still extant one, not its Kincorth rival. Among those who constructed the howff, Ashie is himself cited by Patey as 'Ashy'; 'Charlie' was probably the Charlie Smith, the Harbour Board diver in Ashie's account, mentioned by Patey as whistling some obscure aria on the Strachan's bus, and the stone mason in charge of construction, Jim Robertson is described in *Cairngorm Commentary* as being always 'engrossed in Marx', on trips from Aberdeen to Braemar. Clearly an interesting group of working-class heroes, whose tale remains to be more fully told.

With all due respect to Nimlin, other West Coasters and to the caves of Arrochar, the howffing tradition in the Cairngorms goes back much farther than any other. There is the Shelter Stone, used by bandits in the 14th century, there is the Black Bothy in Glen Geldie, a construction marked on Farquarson's map of 1724, still used by hill-goers in the 60s, and now a listed archeological monument. The Beinn a Bhuird howffs are certainly the most numerous, and hopefully the wee gem approaching its half-century, described in awe and astonishment by my 10-year-old son as 'the best place in the world', will continue to provide the service it does to mountaineers until at least its centenary. In times to come it might even attain the archeological status of the Black Bothy. In the meantime, it should certainly, in the interests of historical and nomenclatural accuracy, regain its title of "Charlie's Howff."

Ashie's letter missed the re-type setting *of Mountain Days...*by a few nights. It will probably be another decade before I can make amends for that, but hopefully this note goes part of the way to rectifying my repeat of an old mistake.

Letter

THOUGHT I would drop you a line to clear up a few points about the Slugain Howff.

My nephew sent me a copy of your excellent book recently and drew my attention to the chapter on the Howff. I was one of the original builders in 1952-3.

Let me explain how it came about. I can be specific about the dates because of a few things which will become clear in the story.

Between 1949 and 1952, a group of us climbed a lot on Beinn a' Bhuird camping as usual in the Fairy Glen. We got fed up coming back soaked to a wet tent and so the idea of a bit more permanent residence came up.

Freddy Malcolm and StickerThom had built a dark hole out of peat with a tin roof on the other side of the gully from the present howff. (They were the Kincorth Club). But it was dark and dingy and we wanted a more up-market residence.

Six of us were involved. Jim Robertson a stone mason; Charlie Smith a diver with the Harbour Board (in the days of diving suits with steel helmets); Doug Mollison who worked in the Town House; Jack Doverty, a steel erector; Jack Innes a dental mechanic, and myself, Ashie Brebner.

It was quite clear that though we were being harried by the keepers all the time, they never came into that gully so it was a logical place to build. The back wall of the rocky outcrop seemed the ideal place because it would save us building a fourth wall.

We spent the whole autumn of 1952 building the walls choosing the right stones from the nearby scree. We came across a few hibernating adders I remember. This was all easy stuff because all the materials were at hand. We now had the problem of carrying in the other parts past the keepers.

At that time, most of us had to work on a Saturday morning. Charlie was the only one who could get up the Slugain on the Friday night and he managed to smuggle some of the basic materials past the keepers' houses late at night.

We usually took the 3.15pm Strachan's bus on the Saturday and it must have been February or March 1953 that we were ready for the heavy materials to come in. I say this because there had been the Great Gale in January that year which took down most of the trees around Invercauld and would play a part in the story.

We all arrived at Bon Accord Square with all the roof parts. Mostly timbers and a tarpaulin which would be a temporary cover until the corrugated iron could be smuggled in. The problem was we were going to arrive at the Invercauld gates while it was still light so the plan was for us to come off the bus at Inver spend some time in the pub and catch the next bus up under cover of darkness.

One of the big brewers had taken out a special 'Coronation Ale' which was great potent stuff. (It was Coronation year) and by the time the next bus arrived we could hardly stand up. I well remember that I had the tarpaulin which was laid across the frame rucksack and was both gigantic and heavy. The conductress was almost rolling on the floor at our antics in trying to get all the bits and pieces through the narrow bus door.

As you know, it's no distance to the gates and we staggered off the bus into total darkness. So total that we immediately lost touch with each other. We stumbled through the gates completely forgetting that all the trees from the gale had never been cleared. We clambered over fallen trunks and branches and within a few yards each of us was completely disoriented. I found myself with Jim Robertson and we decided that as soon as we found a clear space we would set up his Arctic tent. You may remember these had a sock as an entrance and the tent poles went up through a seam on each side of the sock. In our befuddled state we couldn't find the seam so just stuck a pole up and draped the tent over us.

We woke at first light to discover we were in full view of the big house and got up in a panic, gathered all our scattered materials and set off in search of the others. The first one we found was Doug Mollison. He was lying upside down, rucksack still on fast asleep with his legs draped over a trunk. He had fallen over it the previous night and fell fast asleep in his present position. We roused him and located the others. It was still very early so we decided that we would take a chance and get past all the houses as quickly as possible. Once in the Slugain we were able to slow down.

When we got to the building site, we discovered that Charlie was quite annoyed that we hadn't turned up the previous night. We had an arrangement that he being there ahead of us, would walk to an outcrop at about the time we were leaving the trees and into the open glen. We would flash a light, he would flash back and he would go back to the howff and put the tea on ready for our arrival. He was even more annoyed when he discovered we were in the pub.

The building work went very well. The only one with any building experience was Jim Robertson. He had taken all his stone mason tools and acted as foreman giving each of us a job to do.

He told me I would help him put in the dwangs. I hadn't the faintest idea what he was talking about but soon discovered that they were pieces of timber driven into cracks in the cliff wall to which the roof timbers were nailed. By the Sunday night we had all the roof timbers in position, the tarpaulin in place and another course of stonework on top to hold it down regardless of wind.

Over the course of the next few weeks, we kept a tighter control of the 'Coronation Ale' and managed to get in all the corrugated iron so that by the spring it was complete.

We were all mad about Italian Opera and before the days of transistors Charlie would have miles of aerial trailing everywhere, twiddle the knobs in a tiny radio and with earphones in a billy-can we could all hear opera broadcast directly from Milan. That was a great experience at that time.

We used the howff regularly over the next few years but by 1957 life was taking each of us in different directions. That was the year of Asian Flu and I am afraid Jim Robertson died during the epidemic. We scattered his ashes on top of Beinn a' Bhuird.

When Bob Scott retired to Alanaquoich, Charlie started knocking about with his daughter. I met him again once when I was with Bob. It was only recently that I was up the Quoich and looking at a favourite camp site of ours on an island in the middle of the river. I saw a small stone and when I put binoculars on it discovered it was a memorial to Charlie who had died in 1984. I assume Bob's daughter had put it there.

You may be interested to know that the same group erected the memorial to Bill Stewart at Foxes Wells on Lochnagar. Jim Robertson carved the stone and we carried up the materials.

If you decide to reprint your book sometime and require any information about that period I would be happy to assist.

P.S. I came up to Strathpeffer in 1963 to start a business running natural history holidays, walking and climbing, from which I am just about to retire, so happily was able to continue with a love of the hills professionally. But the hills of Braemar are still home to me. Went back with my son to the Slugain and decided to show him where the howff had been. Was absolutely delighted to find it still in use and some refurbishing had been done.

Ashie Brebner.

THE SCOTTISH MOUNTAINEERING TRUST – 1998-99

TRUSTEES met on June 4, October 1, 1998 and February 11, 1999 (the meeting on February 12, 1998 was covered in last year's Journal).

During the course of these meetings support was given to the 1998 Scottish Savoia Kangri Expedition; the Jonathan Conville Winter Course 1998-99; the purchase of a PC for the New Routes Editor, and replacement of gas installation at the JMCS Coruisk hut. Support was also given to a number of footpath projects – Clachnaben Footpath Trust, The Footpath Trust (formerly known as The Ross and Cromarty Footpath Trust) for Stac Pollaidh and Beinn Damph. Further support was given to the National Trust for Scotland for footpath works in Glencoe.

Standing grants are made over to the MCofS toward administration costs, including the Access Officer, and of course the SMC benefits through annual royalty payments for the use of the Club's name in publications and a substantial portion of the production costs of small-print Journal pages is met by the Publications Company.

Footpath projects consume most of the Trust's available income. Although advice is sometimes sought on the technical aspects of a footpath project, any feedback from Club members regarding any SMT-funded path work would be appreciated.

The Munro CD Rom project is achieving reasonable sales. If sales continue steadily more copies may have to be produced early next year.

The Directors of the Publications Company during the period are T. B. Fleming (Chairman), D. J. Bennet, K. V. Crocket, D. F. Lang, N. M. Suess, A. Kassyk and D. C. Page.

The present Trustees are R. T. Richardson (Chairman), T. B. Fleming, D. C. Anderson, D. C. Page, C. D. Grant, A. Kassyk, S. Murdoch, P. W. F. Gribbon, S. M. Richardson and B. R. Shackleton. A. Kassyk and D. C. Page are Trustee Directors and provide liaison between the Publications Company and the Trust.

Bryan Fleming has recently stepped down as Treasurer and we should all record our heart-felt thanks for his long service. J. Morton Shaw, 7 Kirkbrae Terrace, New Deer, Turriff, is the new Treasurer.

The following grants have been committed by the Trustees.

General Grant Fund

1998 Scottish Savoia Kangri Expedition	£500
Jonathan Conville Winter Courses 98/99	£1000
SMC PC for New Routes Editor	£510
JMCS Coruisk Hut Gas Installation	£1000

Footpath Fund

Clachnaben Trust	£2000
Footpath Trust – Stac Pollaidh	£8000
Footpath Trust – Ben Damph	£3000
National Trust for Scotland, Glencoe	£20,000

James D. Hotchkis.

THE SPOON
Part 2

By Malcolm Slesser

For the first part of this modern tale of archaeology, if that's not too Irish, see the 1998 SMCJ. And the truth, as we all know, is still out there...Hon. Ed.)

HAVE YOU ever thought what life would be like without a spoon? A fork, a knife, a plate, a mug, but no spoon. Well, of course you could manage, no doubt adapting to dog-like licking or slurping noisily from your mug. Nonetheless, the lack of a spoon definitely undermines the quality of one's life. This would be further aggravated if all those around you had their spoon. A certain paranoia would be inevitable. But imagine the frustration if someone else claimed and captured your spoon, even if the loathsome fellow lent 'his' to you after he had tucked into his own supper.

It was knowing the unique value of a spoon that led me on a certain Greenland expedition some 40 years ago to bore a hole in the handle, thread a string through it, and, when not in use, keep it at all times around my neck. You would think this policy was fail-safe. Not only would the spoon look different (by virtue of hole and string) from those possessed by others, but it would be impossible to counterfeit.

To the mountaineer accustomed to the luxuries of mountain huts, these precautions may seem to be bordering on the manic, but I can assure you I have seen spoonless expeditioners, and it is not a pretty sight. They are like dogs waiting at the master's tables. They cannot eat as fast as the rest, and so go hungry.

I did not adopt the hole-and-string approach in my early expedition days. I was then naive, believing in the essential goodness of Man, especially mountaineers, and the *esprit de corps* that must surely envelop expedition life. It took me but weeks to come to terms with the *homus economicus* of Arctic expeditions, where it requires a ruthless streak simply to stay alive.

And so, as we embarked from our plane at Mestersvig, NE Greenland in July 1958, I had my spoon dangling around my neck, yielding a comfortable pressure between my chest and my outer clothes. I had no worries and the prospect of an exhilarating two months with eight good comrades and true. Little did I know that even then one of them was already coveting my spoon.

My first surprise was to find someone else was also up to this expeditionary trick. I saw at once that an additional secret mark was necessary. So with the pointed end of my trusty knife I etched a elegant 'S' on the handle.

Well, all went well, and for seven happy weeks I had a spoon and ate well, if frugally. One day, carelessly laying it down after washing it to attend to some other task it was no longer there on my return. Searching, beseeching my stony-faced companions, combing the screes and moraines all yielded nothing. At the next communal meal I asked Dr. S if I might have a look at the spoon dangling from his neck. Begad and begorrah if it was not mine! I can tell you, when one has lived as close to a spoon as I had for those seven weeks I knew every stain on the string, every blemish on its faded silver, every dent in its scratched surface. MY spoon was around Dr. S's neck! Naturally, I assumed that this was just an amusing practical joke. But the aforesaid doctor assumed an altogether proprietorial attitude. He had the gall to pretend it was his spoon. You would have thought that caught red-handed, with the evidence of an 'S' on the handle he would have humbly handed it back, perhaps even with a word of apology. Not a bit of it. The scoundrel maintained that he also had etched an 'S'. I pointed to the fact that my 'S' was a craftsman's 'S'. He countered with some stuff about how he was accustomed to wielding a delicate scalpel, and that this was his 'S'. I was unwilling to enter into the unseemly procedure of dragging it off his neck by force, and anyway he is bigger than me.

So the last week of the expedition was spent sharing my spoon, which when not in use found its way back round Dr S's neck! I do not claim that Dr S's bugs, viruses etc. are any more virulent than my own, but I can bring forward seven witnesses to testify that washing, either himself or his spoon, was not a common sight. I survived, however. And there the matter would have rested had it not been for the following quote given in an article by Charlie Orr in Vol. XXXVI, No 189 (1998) of our Journal. 'Given the nature and constitution of your party take very good care of your spoon'. I am reliably informed that this remark came from the aforementioned Dr S. Some people will go incredible lengths to cover their traces.

In 1960 I happened to return to the site of the camp at which my spoon had changed necks. Like many sites in the Arctic, nothing had changed over the intervening two years. The same boot marks stood out clearly on the shingle, the ground where tents had stood still showed a depression, and there was the ring of boulders where we had sat around the cooking tent. And there, adjacent to one, was Dr. S's spoon – string, hallmark and a'.

I have often wondered at what was the sequence of events back in 1958 and what had gone through Dr. S's mind. Bearing in mind the essential goodness of the man I come up with the following theory. Dr. S finds his spoon missing, sees mine upon the water's edge and claims it – shall we say innocently, though that says little for his powers of observation, if much for his survival instincts. He then (later) finds his own spoon.

It is now too late to retract without loss of face. So as one of the last to leave that camp, he carefully deposits the spoon partially hidden under a boulder. He is not to know I shall be the first person to re-inhabit this camp two years later. He could, of course, have thrown the evidence into the fjord, but as a good Arctic man he couldn't bring himself to waste anything.

What is really amazing is that, Para Handy like, he has convinced his own inner consciousness of his version of the story. If ever there was a case for psychological analysis, this is a classic.

Dr. S is still expeditioning. My advice to anyone travelling with him is, if I may quote his own words, 'take very good care of your spoon'.

MUNRO MATTERS

By C. M. Huntley (Clerk of the List)

This year there are 153 names to add to the List of Munroists and the numerous amendments follow. The columns used are Munroist's number, name, year of Munros, Tops and Furths. * SMC member. ** LSCC member.

No.	Name	Munros	Tops	Furths
1914	Janet M. Parkin	1998		
1915	John S. Dickson	1997		1989
1916	Ian Hunter	1998		
1917	James L. Snedden	1998		
1918	Peter Simpson	1998		
1919	Brian Jarman	1998		
1920	Ernie Potter	1998		
1921	Chris Chadwick	1996		
1922	Gerry Moore	1998		
1923	Leslie Fraser	1998		
1924	C. W. V. Harris	1998		
1925	Patrick Hamilton	1998		
1926	Yvonne Holland	1998		
1927	Christine Carter	1998		
1928	Norman Carter	1998		
1929	Jon Metcalf	1998		
1930	Martin Scoular	1998	1998	1998
1931	Julie A. Stone	1998		
1932	Joyce Durham	1998		
1933	Dave Irons	1998		
1934	Colin Maclachlan	1998		
1935	Simon Pledger	1998		
1936	Malcolm R. Booker	1998		
1937	Richard Blake	1998		
1938	R. N. Day	1998		
1939	James Leslie	1998		
1940	Andrew L. Smith	1998		
1941	Andrew Armstrong	1997		
1942	Gordon J. McInally	1998		
1943	Michael J. Hurst	1998		
1944	Cathie Collins	1998		
1945	Harry Poole	1998		
1946	David Brown	1998		
1947	Sandy Edward	1998		
1948	David G. Barnes	1998		
1949	G. R. Lund	1998		
1950	William F. MacTaggart	1998		
1951	Margaret Prentice	1998		
1952	Douglas Prentice	1998		
1953	Trevor Bridges	1998		
1954	Robert Davidson	1998	1998	
1955	David Moulding	1996		
1956	Gordon Gauld	1998		
1957	James Ferguson	1998		
1958	Samuel R. Logan	1998		
1959	Grant D. Sneddon	1998		
1960	**Janet R. King	1998		
1961	Dave Jones	1998		
1962	Dick Sim	1998		
1963	Michael Hoult	1998		
1964	Kenneth Christie	1998		
1965	Andrew A. Isles	1998		
1966	David Brotherton	1998	1998	
1967	Christine Murison	1998		
1968	David Murray	1997		
1969	Alexander May	1997		
1970	Andrew Jeffreys	1998		
1971	Tim Clancey	1998		
1972	Rona Connolly	1998		
1973	Marion McFarlane	1998		
1974	Gillian Steele	1998		
1975	Kate James	1998		
1976	Helen E. Ross	1998		
1977	J. Plume	1998		
1978	William G. J. Joss	1993		
1979	William Robb	1998		
1980	Iris Coghill	1998		
1981	Bill M. Edgar	1998	1998	
1982	Ken G. Forman	1998		
1983	D. F. Easton	1998		
1984	Keir W. Gordon	1998		
1985	Donald Gow	1998		
1986	Walter Russell	1998		
1987	Howard Barlow	1998		
1988	Joanna Bradshaw	1998		
1989	Keith Bradshaw	1998		
1990	Alan Fraser	1998		
1991	Pat Hay	1998		
1992	Alan Crichton	1998		
1993	John Nisbet	1998		
1994	Campbell Singer	1998		
1995	Neil Hutton	1998		
1996	C. Keith Theobald	1998		
1997	Michael Curtis	1998		
1998	Malcolm S. Webster	1998		
1999	Clare Chiba	1998		
2000	Rati Chiba	1998		
2001	Gordon Morrison	1998		
2002	Charles Kennedy	1998		
2003	Bob MacDonald	1998		
2004	Chris Wright	1998		
2005	Varlien R. Vyner-Brooks	1998		
2006	David Price	1998		
2007	David Oldham	1998		
2008	Ian R. Williamson	1998		
2009	Alan Dawson	1998	1998	1987
2010	Mary Cox	1998	1998	
2011	Keith Adams	1985	1991	
		1991	1995	
		1995		
2012	Dave Tyson	1998	1998	1987
2013	Stephen B. Gaughan	1998		1998

2014	*David Kirk	1998	
2015	J. Gordon Grant	1998	
2016	Allan G. Carr	1998	
2017	J. M. P. Steven	1998	
2018	Jim McCaig	1998	
2019	Norman Veitch	1998	
2020	Ernie J. Wilkins	1998	
2021	W. R. Strachan	1998	
2022	Graeme Gatherer	1998	
2023	Phil Broughton	1998	
2024	William Rankine	1998	
2025	Edward T. Meek	1998	
2026	Colin D. G. Pennycoo	1998	
2027	Chris Danson	1998	
2028	Paul Cook	1998	
2029	Gregory M. Cox	1998	
2030	Campbell C. Watson	1998	
2031	Robert J Cattanach	1998	
2032	Anthony Shellard	1998	
2033	Malcolm J. Mackenzie	1998	
2034	Kenneth J. Mason	1998	
2035	Eleanore Hunter	1998	
2036	David G. Niven	1998	
2037	Michael Blackwell	1998	
2038	Jonathan Barclay	1998	
2039	Geoff Mattock	1998	1998
2040	Arthur Whittaker	1989	
2041	John Donohoe	1989	
2042	Brian McDaid	1990	
2043	Dave Reynolds	1992	
2044	Douglas Philp	1998	
2045	Ron Bryson	1997	
2046	Joan Sherry	1998	
2047	Peter Birbeck	1998	
2048	Linda Lane Thornton	1998	1998
2049	Andrew Thornton	1998	1998
2050	Gordon Laverie	1998	
2051	Robert J. Keery	1998	
2052	Ronald R. Tutty	1998	
2053	Bruce Brown	1993	
2054	Eddie Gillespie	1994	
2055	Steven J. Marsh	1998	
2056	Elaine Gray	1998	
2057	Alan J. Murray	1998	
2058	Alan Stewart	1998	
2059	Stephen Ward	1998	
2060	Keith Foster	1996	
2061	*Ronnie Robb	1998	1998
2062	Dave Robb	1998	1998
2063	Howard Roper	1998	1998
2064	Robert Garrett	1998	
2065	Dave Little	1998	
2066	James G. Anderson	1998	

AMENDMENTS AND CORRECTIONS

The multiple rounds continue to rise and I understand that I should be expecting even more from Stewart Logan (327) now into his 10th round as he has recently retired and expects to devote more time to the hills! Also I had news from Miles Hutchison (23) who is believed to be the earliest Munroist still amending, with a third round and a first for the Furths. The following Munroists have added to their record in the List. To save space only the year of the most recent round is given with the second line referring to the number of rounds. In some cases the entry is to correct an error from the List published in the 1997 edition of the Tables, although the amendment may have already appeared in an earlier *SMCJ* i.e. the Griffins had their second round omitted. Also Stewart Logan was reported as having added a ninth round in 1997 although I have since confirmed that this was premature and the entry below is correct. The columns given are Munros, Tops and Furths.

		Munros	Tops	Furths				Munros	Tops	Furths
23	*M. Hutchinson	1998	1955	1998		636	John Allen	1998		1996
		x3		x2				x2		
82	W. Shand	1968	1968	1969		670	Willis Marker	1989		1998
83	G. G. Shand	1968	1968	1971		692	Chris Peart	1989		1990
108	Brian Edridge	1994				700	Terry McDonagh	1998	1990	
		x4						x2		
189	David Lane	1979	1980			955	Joyce C. Stephens	1991	1991	
327	R. Stewart Logan	1998	1998	1981		1040	James Gordon	1998	1994	
		x9	x9					x3		
391	Brenda D. Griffin	1994	1989			1256	Keith Yates	1998	1997	
		x2						x2		
392	Mervyn Griffin	1994	1989			1258	Michael Hanlin	1993	1998	
		x2				1397	Douglas R. MacLeod	1995	1997	1998
346	John L. Brown	1998	1990			1526	John Farrow	1995	1995	1998
		x5				1559	Graham G. Hemsley	1996		1997
634	Bill Miller	1987	1998	1991		1612	Steve Mann	1996		1998

1630	James M. Thomson	1996	1996	1998	1711	Stewart Newman	1997	1998	1998
1640	Geoff Scott	1994		1997	1809	Roger Smithies	1995		1997
1660	John Kirkham	1996	1998		1879	*Peter Stewart	1997	1997	

As extrapolated a few years ago the 2000th Munroist is now listed only a few months ahead of the other Millennium. By a quirk of the transition through the 1000th Munroist, we had the names Robertson and Munro reappearing. This time, the second millennium of Munroists finishes with Rati Chiba (2000); not a name previously seen in the List although, perhaps, from a strong mountaineering pedigree as his family originally came from Bombay, the home of the Himalayan Mountaineering Club and the *Himalayan Journal*. The alternative 2000th Munroist can be considered as Charles Kennedy (2002) if the blank numbers of 284 and 666 are not counted.

The third millennium of names has already included a member of the church – the Rev. Gordon Grant (2015) thus continuing the link started with the first two Munroists. However, the subsequent Clerks of the List have not maintained the early fashion of affording Munroists of the church their rightful titles and so while the Revs Robertson (1) and Burn (2) keep theirs, (2015) stays as plain Gordon. When Jonathan Barclay (2038) rang me to ask about the procedure for registering a compleation he casually mentioned that he had done the round in 99 climbing days within eight months based in what I thought he said was Grantown (on-Spey). However, the fast round became even more impressive when I received his letter from Grantham and he described his tour as including 17,000 miles of driving in order to tick all the Munros and most of the Tops. Lengthier rounds have been registered by William Rankine (2024) 37 years, Alan Stewart (2058) 44 years and Bill Edgar (1981) 60 years. In addition, there have been rounds taking slightly shorter times but concluded at fine ages. For example, Harry Poole (1945) 70 years and Robert Keery (2051) 72 years. At the opposite end of the age scale is the final Munro party of Alan Fraser (1990), in which Alan was proud to introduce his five-year-old son to the delights of the hills in a joint First and Last celebration.

Slightly more decrepit company joined Helen Ross (1976) at her Last Munro evening celebrations, in the form of the effigy of none other than Sir Hugh, who was last out and about at the Munroist's Centenary Dinner in 1991. It seems that if you invite Robin Campbell to a Munro DO, 'Sir Hugh' won't be far away! Varlien Vyner-Brooks's (2005) illustrious company for his last Munro included Bear Grllys apparently fairly fresh from his ascent of Everest last May. Less sociable was Norman Veitch's (2019) last tick in which he found himself ascending Stob na Broige solo, as his companion for the day cried off at the last minute. David Kirk (2014) also had a low turnout for his celebrations on the top, as his colleagues had ensured that the serious celebration happened the night before the ascent. As a result, few mobilised themselves the next day, although when he finally came to walk out from Coruisk, he had the pleasure of finding his car adorned with shaving foam, care of his lethargic friends. I'm surprised the Skye rain had held off long enough to leave the foam in place. Perhaps the embarrassment restrained David from recording his compleation for five years.

Another very delayed report came from Keith Adams (2011), who then countered the delay by declaring a triple compleation. Selecting your final Munro is never easy and Stephen Ward (2059) chose Ben Lomond since it was the nearest hill as the crow flies, although in reality a 200-mile drive since he has to circumvent the Lochs Long and Lomond from south of Dunoon. Another resident of Scotland with a long journey time to the 3000+ hills is Dick Sim (1962) now living in Arran. However, few would complain at being so close to such a select group of Corbetts, of which Dick says he has climbed Goat Fell at least 100 times.

The vast majority of Munroists record that the accumulation of ticks was more a slow erosion of the list over many years of walking, rather than a clear start date, and Robert Keery (2051) describes well the transition from casual interest to serious intent to addiction to finally total obsession. Most Munroists are well qualified to express an opinion on the finest hills of Scotland although Campbell Singer (1994) goes one farther and expresses opinion on the best bar meals (i.e. Loch Leven Hotel gets a good rating). Alan Murray (2057) found that the worst experiences always involve a bad dose of midges.

A number of errors get corrected every year spread throughout the List. Of these Fred Siddaway (1511) was the hardest done by. He duly registered compleation in 1997, and in 1998 was listed again as having added the Furths. Unfortunately, he was completely (compleately?) omitted from the List that went into the Tables. He discovered the error while browsing the book in a shop in Ullapool and was dismayed to find no Siddaway at number 1511 and no Siddaway anywhere else. Needless to say no purchase was made other than a stamp to fire off a letter to me. Similarly, John Greener (1728) found that at least his first name was in, although the surname was missing. Some errors originate in the actual letters that I receive. For example, when George Page (1398) and Ron Johnston (1399) wrote a joint letter of compleation George misspelled Johnston. As a result it appears that Ron has felt George is in permanent debt to him, usually taken in the form of a pint. However, when they were requesting certificates, George decided to get the List corrected and his debt cleared. During the year Dave Hewitt (of *Angry Corrie* fame) contacted me concerning the many duplicate names on the list and questioned whether there really are so many Robertsons, Smiths, Banticks etc., who climb the hills (see Dave's article elsewhere in the Journal). As much as I can confirm from the letters in the archives, none are duplicates, although if anyone suspects differently I would be pleased to know.

Finally, over the years I have received a number of inquiries on whether Sir Fred Hoyle should be on the List as he devotes an early chapter in his book *Home is Where The Wind Blows* to a round that was compleated on Blaven in 1980. Therefore I did manage to contact him to find that he was more than happy to remain within the ranks of 284 (formerly 277). Talking of the Unknown Munroist slot, the Munroist right next to (277) is Gerry Knight (276) who commented, when he wrote to order a tie, that he had at one time considered that he had the next best number to Munroist No. 1. Unfortunately, he has found that 276 is really a 'moveable feast' and his privilege is now a distant memory.

Those wishing to add their names to the List of Compleat Munroist should write to the Clerk at the address below. I am always pleased to hear of your experiences, time take on the round, age, etc., etc., and I much prefer to hear direct from the Munroist. Once registered, Munroists can claim a tie and/or Brooch. A colour A4 certificate is available to mark the Compleation so please enclose an A4 sae. All notification should be sent to Dr. C. M. Huntley, Old Medwyn, Spittal, Carnwath, Lanarkshire. ML11 8LY.

E-MAIL TO THE EDITOR
What's a Munro?

MARGARET SMITH, with husband Keith (both Australians and both closer to 60 than 50) spent seven weeks in May and June, 1998, sampling some of the walking and climbing trails in England, Wales and Scotland. We started with sections of the South-West Coast Path in Cornwall, then we hiked up Pen Y Fan, Corn Du and Cribyn in the Brecon Beacons National Park. In superb weather, we climbed Snowdon, which was similar to the climb up Victoria's highest mountain, Mt. Bogong (just over 6500ft) and then we climbed some of the higher peaks looking over Wastwater, in the Lake District National Park. Next stop – Scotland.

Driving north towards Roybridge, browsing in a guidebooks, I saw a reference to 'The Munros' and 'Munro bagging'. 'What's a Munro and what on earth is a Munro bagger?' 'Sounds like a carpetbagger in a kilt,' said the driver. 'Wonder if we'll meet any?' Well, we did meet a Munro-bagger or two, or maybe 102. In fact, everywhere we went we met people with packs and maps and books, all earnestly studying the routes up the next Munros on their lists. We also found that these enthusiastic people, without exception, were friendly and cheerful, and happy to tell us all we wanted to know about Sir Hugh Munro, the Rev. Robertson, their own achievements, the lists of Munroists and all about the 280 (give or take a few) Munros.

Ben Nevis was initially our first choice, but as our days at Roybridge went by, the weather got progressively worse and our opportunities washed away with the rain. Eventually, we continued, without a Munro, but confident that things would improve as we travelled west. We had four days at Cluanie Inn, during which time the deteriorating weather gradually undermined our optimism. We read a lot, spent a rainy day in Skye, and another rainy day travelling to Plockton and Torridon. There were many Munros, but we couldn't see them through the rain.

Finally, with time running out, and by now desperate to conquer just one Munro, we informed the staff at the Inn ('Are you sure? In this weather?') that we were going to climb Creag a' Mhaim (3107ft), which we assumed was where our OS map said it would be. We certainly couldn't see it. So we set off, following the old road for about 6km, then finding the track up the ridge leading to the summit. The views would undoubtedly have been spectacular, but unfortunately, we didn't see much of them through the swirling cloud and mist which got progressively thicker as we ascended. At least the track was well defined!

Not much farther...or so we kept telling ourselves as the weather got wetter and colder and the wind ever stronger. Not much farther... Suddenly, looming out of the mist, there were two young men, faces concealed by balaclavas, looking as if they'd just arrived from Antarctica. 'Not much farther,' they said, 'but don't try and go beyond the summit, terrible weather up there, and the track is difficult to follow'.

We assured them we just wanted to reach the summit and had no intention of proceeding farther – did they think we were mad? Well, perhaps we were, anyway we pushed on and eventually reached the cairn, where we took the obligatory photographs – exciting studies of a pile of rocks against a white background. We retraced our steps as rapidly as possible, sleet blowing in our faces and the rain penetrating every seam and gap it could find, finally arriving back at Cluanie – wet, cold and bedraggled, but triumphant! We had bagged a Munro. One Munro...only 283 to go. The next morning, the sky was clear, and all the mountains surrounding Cluanie Inn were covered in snow. Was this summer? Why hasn't everyone in Scotland migrated to Australia? – *Margaret and Keith Smith.*

A Bird, four Bells, a Fish, no Tree: some thoughts on 2000 Munroists.

By Dave Hewitt

IT WOULD have been neat had the 2000th Munroist arrived during the millennial year, but it didn't work out that way. People, as they say, got ahead of themselves. Only a decade ago, the thought of so many folk having climbed so many Munros by the late 1990s would have seemed absurd, yet number 2000 approached as relentlessly as dusk on an autumn day. There was ultimately never any real question of when, merely of whom.

That, though, remains unclear, even now. Turn elsewhere in this Journal and you'll see that the 2000th Munroist slot was allocated, late in 1998, to the splendidly named Rati Chiba. But a rival claimant lurks just two notches farther on, at Munroist 2002: Charles Kennedy. Why? Because the SMC listing has for years included a couple of statistical Thearlaich-Dubh Gaps within its number line. First came the so-called Unknown Munroist, introduced in 1983 as a supposed stand-in for all non-registering refusniks. This I've never really understood (just as I don't understand the archaic use of 'compleat' for complete, as though the Club had swallowed Izaak Walton book, line and sinker). With each subsequent revision to the actual Tables, the Unknown Munroist has shuffled forward, from 276 to 277 and now to 284, in awkward and unfortunate fashion. The Unknown Munroist doesn't quite spin in the grave, but certainly shifts uneasily from time to time.

So no matter the number of the beast (oops – more of that in a moment), there has long been a silent, awkward gap on the parade-ground roll-call. Which would appear to shift Munroist 2001, Gordon Morrison, into the prime spot for claiming the kudos. Not so fast. There's need to consider the SMC's odd disinclination to allocate 666 as an official number, as though Eileen Drewery had been taken on as a Munro's Tables consultant. This is simply bizarre, not least because nothing similar has happened to other evil-eye numbers such as 13, or 87 (the Australian bogey), or 111. Banning 666 on spurious religious grounds is irrational; the Club might as well have refused the 178th registration, from D. A. Shanks, on golfing grounds, or demanded that Fergus Macbeth, the 819th Munroist, only be allowed in under the guise of The Scottish Munroist.

So the first 2000 Munroist numbers represent only 1998 people. So Charles Kennedy is really the 2000th person due to receive a tie and a crest or whatever it is they get. Or is he? It is possible that several folk have managed to slip into the list twice. I'm assured by official sources that there's been no repetition of the Brian Gardiner cloning incident, when the 971st and 990th Munroists were deemed one and the same person. (The 971 slot was 'reclaimed', in a way that no-one quite understands, by a person named H. H. Mills who had been dead for some time.) Strange goings-on, these, but who's to say what other sleepers lurk in the list? There are, for instance, two Allan Banticks, at 1006 and 1598. There can't be many Allan Banticks in Western Europe, let alone in the Munroist list, so is there duplication here? Similarly Sue Jardine, who turns up at 214 and again at 1597. And Kenneth Brown (657 and 1202). And Ian Dickson (1136 and 1556). And Graeme Morrison (485 and 1533). And W. A. Simpson (631 and 989). And that's without even starting to consider near misses such as James S. Bell (479) and James G. Bell (676), or maiden-name sneak-ins, or simple mis-spellings. (You want to see a good typo? Look in *Munro's Tables* at Munroist 1112, allegedly Denis A. Oidgeon – the kind of misprint to make you coo.) Then there are the sex-changes: the self-same *Munro's Tables* awards the 1511 berth to Mary Copping, yet only a few months later, in the 1998 Journal, 1511 belongs to Fred Siddaway. Maybe Mary/Fred should call in a film crew and make a before/after documentary on hormonally-challenged hillgoing.

And what about completely false claimants? Who can say what merry pranks have been inflicted on the list over the years, from both within and without the Club? The name A. Kinghorn (619) looks suspiciously like Hamish Brown in disguise, especially given the Fifer's predilection for 'outing' fellow Munroists whether they like it or not. The appearance of a Burt Burntisland would clinch the verdict.

Then there's the Braveheart Tendency. Five Wallaces and three Bruces is reasonable enough, but the Claymore and the two Swords look like extras in a flag-waving wind-up. There's also something uncannily apt in the Munros having been ascended by Erik Bigland (1464) and, R. Hillcoat (219). And then there's the debate over whether 'Derek Bearhop' really exists. I've received several letters from him over the years, but we've never actually met. Is he the Max Headroom of the Munro world?

In truth, no-one will ever know the ID of the 2000th Munroist. It has taken over from Fermat's Last Theorem as the greatest unsolved numerical mystery, and before I die I must ensure my papers include a note reading 'Discovered a truly marvellous proof of the 2000th Munroist's identity, which this margin is too narrow to contain.'

But enough of Mr or Ms 2000. What of the body of the kirk, the bulk of the legwork, the great egalitarian mass of the Munro-climbing lumpen proletariat? 2000 is a lot of people, a crowd with which most lower division football teams would be entirely pleased, and not far short of the average summer Saturday attendance on Ben Nevis.

2000 names, all having kicked at least 276 cairns. This means a minimum of 552,000 Munros climbed, up nearer 600,000 after adjustment for list-revisions. And that's without starting to include subsidiary Tops, or repeat rounds, or indeed those such as myself who have happily trudged up hundreds of Munros without approaching a full round. Nor does it include 'spare' Munros climbed by actual Munroists; when I met Richard Wood in May 1998, he had only one full round (number 88), but more than 6000 spare Munros in his bag. Overall, several million Munro ascents must have been made by now. In stark foot-pounding terms, the Norwegian football commentator can be aptly paraphrased: 'We gave your hills one hell of a beating.'

Various themes and theories can be teased from the list. In examining the first 2002 slots (the first 2000 named Munroists), the male/female split is around 85%/15%. Yet this isn't immediately obvious, due to many Munroists hiding behind semi-anonymous initials. Close on 300 folk display this old-fashioned and pre-dominantly male trait (is there a sociologist in the house?); certainly far more people now give – or are allowed to give – a full name. Of the first100, 95 are 'initialised'. Hamish Brown (62) was the first man with a first name, Barbara Tulloch (85) the first woman. By contrast, Munroists 401-500 include only three initialled folk (although no subsequent 100 has dipped any lower).

The name-breakdown is thesis-worthy in itself. Unsurprisingly, the most common surname is Smith (26 in the first 2002), before a big gap to Brown and

Robertson (16 each). It's good to see the first Munroist and the most famous both having encouraged their kin to follow their footsteps. Next come Taylor (15), Grant and Stewart (both 13), Wilson (12), Gray, Murray, and Simpson (all 11), then Clark (10, plus seven Clarkes), Fraser and Scott (10 each). Wylie and Wyllie combined give 10, as do Thompson and Thomson. The most common initial letter is M (277 including 119 Macs/Mcs); there are 209 Bs, 205 Ss, 164 Cs. Only one Q, though (Quine, 757), and no Xs or Zs.

119 out of 2002, or 5.9%, seems a relatively low proportion of Mac/Mc names given that this is a Highland-context list. Is there an Edinburgh bias over and against Glasgow? Perhaps: that vastly more Macs inhabit the Glasgow phone book merely highlights how the Highland diaspora drifted into Govan rather than Gorgie. This skewing also crops up in the nation's sports teams. The Scottish football eleven, deep-rootedly urban and with a West-of-Scotland slant, routinely includes several Macs. Conversely, the rugby fifteen, drawn largely from the Borders and the genteel parts of Edinburgh, frequently has no Macs at all. Is there a similar trend among Munroists? Possibly.

The gentility argument receives backing when forenames are studied: there's a whiff of Billy Connolly's old routine on how certain strata of Scottish society give their sons surnames as forenames. Hence Munroists christened Bryce and Campbell, Findlay and Fraser, Gilmour and Murray. Just how many different forenames appear is hard to assess, even ignoring initials-only folk. But lumping standard diminutives in with their longer forms (Jim with James, Val with Valerie) leaves 163 male forenames, and 118 female. This relatively greater spread of female names is interesting but not unique: genuine theses have been written on male/female naming patterns. Nor is it any surprise that whereas 57 male forenames reappear as surnames, only one – May – doubles up on the female side.

The most common male forename is John. I counted 125, and this, remember, excludes initials-only John Rooke Corbett, John Dow etc. David/Dave/Davie appears 105 times, Ian/Iain 68, James/Jim/Jamie 63, William/Willie/Bill 49, Peter 45 (including just one Pete), Alan/Allan/Alun 44, Andrew/Andy 43, and so on. The Ian:Iain ratio, 43:25, is instructive, suggesting a high overall proportion of Scots.

For the women, Margaret/Maggie leads out with 16, closely followed by Ann/Anne at 15, then 12 of Elizabeth and her diminutives. Various male names are unexpectedly rare: only three instances of Philip/Phil, two of Joseph/Joe, and just one lonely Grant (Sneddon, 1959). Female forenames don't yet include Kylie or Ginger, but the past few years have seen an Edna, an Ethel, and a Flora. Who says hill-climbing is a young person's game? Note however, that sexing names is a minefield: what of the various Pats, or the Chrises? And returning to the Copping/Siddaway dilemma, who's to say that some Melinda or Morag isn't betesticled, some Donald or Malcolm befrocked?

The most common full name comes with the four David Smiths: 522, 659, 1275, 1336. Robert Robertson occurs three times: 999, 1147, 1895 (although the last is listed as Bob), and David/Dave Jones also features thrice: 809, 1835, 1961. The shortest surname will stick at three letters until Ng follows Tsai as an Asiatic Munroist, while the shortest full names are Pat Hay and Tom Rix. Longest surname? Linklater-Shirras, but that's cheating, as is Hill-Cottingham. Hollingsworth (1847) has a more legitimate claim, followed by the 12-letter trio of Brocklehurst, Hetherington and MacGillivray.

There are no overall palindromes, merely a Hannah, nor any self-anagrams of the

Eric Rice variety, but some odd patterns do occur. The first Munroist, Archibald Eneas Robertson, famously appears as A. E. Robertson, yet less well known is his covey of copycats: A. E. Robinson at number 48, A. E. Lawson (126), and A. E. Law (143). No wonder there's a village near Dumfries named Ae: they all went there for their holidays. And who would expect the first100 names to include three folk answering to G. G. – Elliot (7), Macphee (20, grandfather to Matthew Shaw, 661), and Shand (83)?

Then there's Proud and Humble, Bird and Fish, Wolf and Lamb, Mason and Lodge, Gold, Rich, and Fortune. But while there's Emmerson and Palmer, there's no Lake (and quite right too – it would have had to have been Loch). There's Price and Purchase, Lincoln and Durham, France and Holland, Butcher and Baker (but no Candlestick-Maker). There's Morning and Town, but no Ride.

At risk of sounding like the New Years Honours announcer, the world of entertainment is represented by Peter Sellers, James Brown, James Taylor, and John Peel, while David Niven just misses out (he's Munroist 2036). Sportsmen include David Steele (remember him?) and two George Grahams – but then he did play in a double-winning side. There are two Crams but no Coe, which seems wrong, somehow.

And since this survey started with a politician, Charles Kennedy, it should end with his peers. There are 12 Wilsons, two Heaths, a Callaghan, a Thatcher, and two Blairs, but no Major. Chris Smith (719) is touted as the only MP to have completed the Munros, but what of Gordon Brown (1800), George Galloway (1390), and Bruce Malcolm (1634 and a DemLib)? Then there's Cyril Smith, number 579. Crikey, imagine dear old Cyril on the In Pinn; they'd need a crane.

TOPPING TIMES

By Peter Warburton

AMATEUR historians, particularly perhaps those of mature years but with minds, in their own view, still more or less intact enjoy having their attention diverted to agreeably time-consuming research projects. Such a line of inquiry was prompted by the realisation that three of the nine tops added in the 1997 edition of the Tables had been listed for periods in the past and that of the 15 newly-deleted tops, five had joined the company as recently as 1981. The nagging need to know focused on the question of how many different locations have been classified as tops over the period 1891-1997. Pushing back the frontiers of knowledge in a useless direction? Of course, and why not.

A preliminary requirement is a definition of what constitutes a separate location. Those examples where improved mapping has produced a different grid reference for the spot the selectors always had in mind are excluded from the count. On the other hand, the category of resited summit qualifies for inclusion. Typically, these changes are described in compass point terms, e.g. the N Top is found to be higher than the S Top. The old and the new can be quite far apart; it is a mile-and-a-half walk from An Socach (Glen Ey) E to W Top.

Every Munro summit is by definition also a top. For practical reasons of presentation, chiefly to keep tables to manageable proportions, it is convenient to consider the two categories separately, taking first the Munro summits. In 1891 there were 283 and in 1997 284 listed Munros, but the closeness of the totals conceals a significant turnover in numbers. In addition to those currently accepted, there have, adopting the criteria suggested above, been 32 temporary Munros, giving a total of 316 Munro sites. Table 1 analyses the current crop by historical seniority and Table 2 lists the 32 that were, but are no more. It will be seen that all but five of the casualties remain in the 1997 edition as tops. The thorough-going Munroist is likely to have visited three of them *en route* to something tickable and may well also have crossed Meall a' Chaorainn, the original Munro on the moorland plateau to the east of the Pass of Drumochter that few revisit. The fifth, Beinn an Lochain, is now a Corbett.

The purpose of the inquiry was not to reason why, a direction that quickly leads to contentious ground. However, Tables 1 and 2 do suggest that the majority of the changes have been dictated or strongly influenced by map corrections or clarifications, leaving less scope for the exercise of whimsical judgment than hostile critics would have us believe. Of the 30 net post-1891 Munros, five (Refs 275, 276, 280, 282, 284) owe their inclusion to map changes giving new heights of 3000ft+, three were probably only omitted from the original list because the inadequate mapping of Skye in those days left their height in some doubt and a further 10 can reasonably be attributed to minor OS changes having enhanced their status relative to neighbouring hills.

Similar comments apply to the former Munros. Although only Beinn an Lochain has lost its place on absolute height grounds, 10 more are direct counterparts of those referred to above, one was a clerical error (An Garbhanach, included by mistake for An Gearanach in 1921 and corrected in 1933) and two – Creag Toll a' Choin and Sgor an Iubhair – have been subject to third thoughts, as Munros, of the out:in: out variety. Another case of third thoughts – Sgor an Lochan Uaine (Cairn Toul) is the sole in:out:in example and so is not itemised in either Table, since it was listed in both 1891 and 1997.

'What constitutes a Top?' inquired Mr Inglis in 1933. Subsequent editors have not taken up his suggestions on the subject so that the only answer remains: 'That is a Top if the editor of the day so determines.' So far as this paper is concerned, tops are simply the listed points that are not Munro summits. There were 255 in the first list, rising to a maximum of 268 in 1953 and thereafter declining to the present figure of 227. The first net reduction came in 1974 but the main years of execution have been 1981 and 1997. In the context of the stated aim of this study – to arrive at a net total of distinct top locations – the most teasing complication proved to be the need to eliminate double counting. At times when cross-checking revealed mysterious discrepancies or when some unconsidered permutation came to light among the demoted Munros, promoted tops, the vagaries of the in and out brigade, the drastic name changes etc; at such times Mr Ling's peroration to the *Introduction* to his *Northern Highlands Guide* (1932) has come to mind – 'On with the Work'.

The nature and quality of that work are well illustrated by the case history of Slioch where the original Munro was located some 300yds ESE of the present site and given a height of 3260ft. The supporting evidence was an OS 3250ft contour and a note in the Kinlochewe Hotel visitors' book by a Captain Kirkwood RE suggesting 3260ft. The Captain was immortalised in footnotes to editions of the Tables for more than 60 years, long after the disappearance of the visitors' book. From the early days SMC members expressed doubt; the nearby OS spot height of

3217ft seeming to many to be the higher point. The contour interval at heights over 1000ft was then 250ft, so that maps were less helpful than now in establishing altitudes. Members' aneroids were accordingly much to the fore.

At Easter 1934-5(?) Mr Parker's painstaking survey concluded that the true summit was indeed the 3217ft point (NNW in Parker's report, known now as the North Top) which he estimated to be up to 5ft higher than the recognised SSE point. The OS admitted error and deleted the false 3250ft contour in time for the 1947 One-Inch map. Early metric sheets gave the two points equal heights of 980m and ratification of the North Top's solo summit status (981m) only came in the 1997 edition, fully vindicating Parker's findings at last.

Table 3, like Table 1 something of a by-product, illustrates the extent of the turnover in tops and the degree of mobility between categories. Only 169 of the original 255 tops remained, as tops, in the 1997 list. The balance of 86 comprises 21 Munros (marked in Table 1) two others (Sgor an Iubhair and An Garbhanach) that also became Munros but reverted to the status quo ante and, having been original 1891 tops are included in Table 2 not 4, which leaves 63 unlisted (see Table 4). Of 58 surviving post-1891 tops 25 were once Munros. Amid all this change there are inevitably a small number of surprise judgments. It is easy to imagine the adjudicators caught in the cloud on one of those days when:

> Molehills seem mountains and the ant
> Appears a monstrous elephant

as perhaps in Glen Tilt where Carn a' Chlamain N established some sort of record by unexpectedly appearing in the 1981 edition, only to be buried, without a word of obituary, three years later. The admission to the list of a stretched image of Knight's Peak is a notable recent flight of fancy.

Table 4, a list of former tops, is the nub of the matter. It chronicles the gradual weeding out of the less likely of the original choice, including some found lacking in feet. This process may not be complete. On the other hand one of the 1997 comeback tops – Stuc a' Choire Dhuibh Bhig (Liathach) – is a founder member, deleted in 1974 for want of inches but restored as a consequence of further map revision. This Table also shows the attention given by past editors to the elimination of perceived anomalies such as the over-representation of particular hills or ranges. Reforming editors of the future will perhaps be tempted farther along this road.

The Compleat Fanatick will already have done the arithmetic. For others the answer, E & OE, is that there have been 593 separate listed locations, as Munro summit or Top, over the period 1891-1997.

Gross		**Net**	
Munros (1997)	284	Munros (1997)	284
		Former Munros not in	
Former Munros	32	1997 listed as tops.	5
Tops (1997)	227	Tops (1997).	227
		Former tops not in 1997	
Former Tops	97	listed as Munros.	77
	640		**593**

TABLE 1

CURRENT MUNROS BY YEAR OF FIRST LISTING

1997 Tables nomenclature and references. Former Tops:

1891		**254**		
1921	*Meall Glas		2-3	199
	*Sgiath Chuil		2-5	270
	*Na Gruagaichean		4-11	74
	*A'Bhuidheanach Bheag		5-5	240
	*Carn Bhac		6-14	221
	*Stob Poite Coire Ardair		9-10	76
	*Meall na Teanga		10-1	275
	Mullach na Dheiragain		11-32	167
	Sgurr Mhic Choinnich		17-8	217
	Sgurr a' Mhaddaidh		17-15	277
	*Am Basteir	**11**	17-18	242
1974	*An Socach (Glen Ey)		6-16	227
	Beinn a' Chaorainn (Laggan)		9-2	80
	Ruadh Stac Mhor (Fisherfield)		14-4	276
	Beinn Tarsuinn (earlier unnumbered)		14-5	238
	Beinn a' Chlaidheimh	**5**	14-10	280
1981	*Creise		3-22	50
	*Garbh Chioch Mhor		10-8	116
	Sgurr nan Ceannaichean		12-17	284
	*Mullach an Rathain (Liathach)		13-6	108
	*Sgurr Fiona (An Teallach)		14-25	73
1984	Beinn Teallach	**5**	19-1	282
1997	*An Stuc	**1**	2-29	34
	*Stob Coire Sgreamhach		3-36	65
	*Stob Coire Raineach		3-40	263
	*Stob na Broige		3-41	207
	*Sgurr na Carnach		11-3	134
	*Tom na Gruagaich		13-4	268
	*Spidean Coire nan Clach (Beinn Eighe)		13-13	150
	*Slioch North Top	**8**	14-1	170

284

TABLE 2

FORMER MUNROS

1997 Tables references. Direct replacements in parentheses

1891-1921	Beinn Cheathaich (Meall Glas)		2-4	413
	Meall a' Churain (Sgiath Chuil)		2-6	486
	Beann a' Chuirn		2-18	466
	Sgor Choinnich		4-50	437
	Glas Mheall Mor		5-6	443
	Beinn Iutharn Bheag		6-13	362
	Carn Bhac SW (Carn Bhac)		6-15	478
	Carn Binnein		6-19	497
	Creag an Leth-choin		8-24	121
	Carn Eas		8-48	84
	Creag an Dail Mhor		8-49	304
	Mullach Sithidh (Mullach nan Dheiragain)		1-34	301
	Sgurr na Lapaich		11-40	153
	Creag Dubh		12-8	386
	Bidean an Eoin Deirg		12-14	136
	Stob Poite Coire Ardair E (Stob PCA)			
	Meall a' Chaorainn (A'Bhuidheanach Bheag)	17		
1891-1974	An Socach E (An Socach)		6-17	409
	Beinn a' Chaorainn S (Beinn a' Chaorainn)	2	9-3	128
1891-1981	Clach Learhad (Creise)		3-23	77
	Meall Dubhag		8-3	230
	Carn Ban Mor		8-4	123
	Geal Charn		8-7	481
	Carn Cloich-mhuillin		8-9	395
	A'Choinneach		8-35	184
	Carn Ban		9-18	394
	Carn Ballach		9-19	477
	Beinn an Lochain	9		
191-1997	Slioch Trig Point (Slioch North Top)	1		
1921-1933	An Garbhanach (An Gearanach)	1	4-10	292
1921-1981	Creag Toll a' Choin (Maoile Lunndaidh)	1		
1981-1997	Sgor an Iubhair	1	4-5	218
		32		

TABLE 3

CURRENT NON-MUNRO TOPS BY YEAR OF FIRST LISTING

1997 Tables nomenclature and references. Former Munros.*

Year	No.	Name	No.	Name	No.
1891	**169**				
1921		Stob Coire Dhomhnuill	38	Beinn Fhada	367
		*Carn Eas	84	*Creag Dubh	386
		*Creag an Leth-choin	121	Sgurr na Banachdich C	397
		Eagle's Rock	125	*Beinn Cheathaich	413
		*Bidean an Eoin Deirg	136	Sgurr a' Fionn Choire	421
		*Sgurr na Lapaich	153	*Sgor Choinnich	437
		Stacan Dubha	186	*Glas Mheall Mor	443
		Sgurr an Lochan Uaine	266	Sgurr Thormaid	459
		*Mullach Sithidh	301	*Beinn a Chuirn	466
		*Creag an Dail Mhor	304	*Carn Bhac SW	478
		Sgurr a' Ghreadaidh S	306	*Meall a' Churain	486
		Sail Liath	360	*Carn Bhinnein	497
1974	**26**	*Beinn Iutharn Bheag	362	Bhasteir Tooth	503
	3	Beinn a' Chaorainn S	128	*An Socach E	409
1981				Sgurr nan Saighead	438
		*Clach Leathad	77	Carn na Con Dhu	314
		An Riabhachan SW	86	Creag Leacach SW	393
		*Carn Ban Mor	123	*Carn Ban	394
		*A'Choinneach	184	*Carn Cloich-mhuillin	395
		Beinn na Socaich	200	Meail Buidhe SE	396
		Sron a Choire	220	Sgurr na Sgine NW	398
		*Meall Dubhag	230	Luinne Bheinn E	416
		Stob Choire a' Mhaill	252	Tom a' Choinich	422
		Stob a' Choire Liath Mhor	267	*Carn Ballach	477
		Mullach Choire Mhic		*Geal-Charn	481
		Fhearchair E	272	Sgurr Dubh	491
1997	**23**	Byack Beg	305	Creag na Caillich	504
		Druim Shionnach W	411	Stuc Faoch Choire	493
		Meall nan Tarmachan SE	468	Stob Coire na Cloiche	509
	6	Stob an Duine Ruaidh	492	Knight's Peak	511
	227				

FORMER NON-MUNRO TOPS

The 77 deleted Tops not later reinstated or elevated to Munro

1891-1921 (13)
An Socach (Wyvis)
Sron dha Murchdi (Lawers)
Creag a' Bhragit (Stob Binnein)
Leachd Riach (Monadh Liath)
Carn Ballach SW (Monadh Liath)
Big Brae (Ben Avon)
Beinn na Socaich (Stob Coire Easain)
Druim nan Bo (Mullach Clach a' Bhlair)
Creag Meagaidh E
Sron a' Ghaothair (Meagaidh)
Cruach Ardrain NE (3376ft, 6" map)
Cruach Ardrain (NN413217)
Beinn a' Chreachain (NN377448)

1891-1974 (4)
Faochag (Sgurr na Sgine)
Sgurr na Creige (The Saddle)
Am Bathaidh (Sgurr a' Mhaoraich)
Glas Leathad Beg W (Wyvis)

1891-1981 (37)
Meall Luaidhe (Carn Mairg)
Meall Buidhe SE (Glen Lyon)
Stob a Fhir Bhoga (Heasgarnich)
Mam Coire Easain (Clach Leathad)
Carn Beag Dearg (Carn Mor Dearg)
Stob Coire an Fhir Dhuibh (Aonach Mor)
Sron Garbh (Geal-Charn Ericht)
A'Bhuidheanach (Carn Liath)
Snechdach Slinnean (Carn Liath)
Sail Chaoruinn (NH141148)
Creag nan Clachan Geala (Ceathreamhnan)
Ben Avon SW
Mullach Fraoch-choire NE
Stob Coire Coulavie (Sodhail)
Ciste Dubh (Sodhail)
Braigh a' Choire Bhig (Mullardoch)
Creag a' Choire Aird E (Affric)
Rudha na Spreidhe (Mullardoch)
Creag a' Chaorainn (Mullardoch)
Creag Dhubh (Beinn Eighe)
Fiachlach (Wyvis)
Stob Bac an Fhurain (Ben Avon)
Mullach Lochan nan Gobhar (Ben Avon)
Stuc Garbh Mhor (Ben Avon)

1891-1981 (continued)
Stob Dubh an Eas Bhig (Ben Avon)
Sron a' Cha-no (Cairngorm)
Creag an Leth-choin N (Cairngorm)
Fiacaill a' Choire Chais (Cairngorm)
Fiacaill Coire an t-Sneachda (Cairngorm)
Stob Coire Sputan Dearg (Macdui)
Stob Coire an Lochan (Braeriach)
Diollaid Coire Eidart (Feshie)
Druim Sgarsoch (An Sgarsoch)
Beinn Garbh (Atholl)
Carn nan Sac (Carn a' Gheoidh)
Creag Leachdach (Cairn Bannoch)
Creag Mhor (Meagaidh)

1891-1997 (9)
Sron nan Giubhais (Stob Ghabhar)
Aonach Eagach (Stob Ghabhar)
Cac Carn Mor (Lochnagar)
Ben Macdui N
Beinn Mheadhoin SW
Stob Poite Coire Affric E
Stob Coire nan Dearcag (Ceathreamhnan)
The Saddle W
Sgurr Dearg (Cuillin)

1921-1974 (1)
Sgurr nan Ceathreamhnan E

1921-1981 (5)
Beinn an Eachan E (Tarmachans)
Stob Choire Claurigh N
Fiacaill na Leth-choin (Cairngorm)
A'Chioch (Beinn a' Bhuird)
Little Cairngorm (Derry Cairngorm)

1921-1997 (1)
Cotrag Bhuidhe Buttress (Teallach)

1953-1974 (1)
Carn a' Bhutha (Carn Bhac)

1981-1984 (1)
Carn a' Chlamain N (Tilt)

1981-1997 (5)
Ben Lui NW
The Saddle E
The Saddle Trig Point
An Riabhachan NE
Slioch Trig Point

SCOTTISH MOUNTAIN ACCIDENTS 1998
REGIONAL DISTRIBUTION

(Geographical Divisions are those used in SMC District Guidebooks)

| REGION | CASUALTIES (of which fatalities are bracketed) | | | | INCIDENTS | | | | | | | | Animal Rescues | Non-Mountaineering Incidents |
| | | | | | Actual Rescues | | Other Callouts | | | | | | | |
	Injuries	Exhaustion/Exposure Hypothermia. Hyperthermia	Illness	Total Casualties	Incidents with Casualties	Cragfast or weatherbound	Separated	Lost	Overdue or Benighted	False Alarms	Total Incidents			
Northern Highlands	13 (3)	– –	– –	13 (3)	13	1	3	1	9	1	28		–	–
Western Highlands	11 (3)	1 –	3 (2)	15 (5)	15	–	1	–	2	–	18		–	–
Ben Nevis	15 (4)	1 –	4 –	20 (4)	19	4	–	1	2	–	26		–	–
Glen Coe (Inc Buachaille)	15 (2)	1 –	2 –	18 (2)	18	6	–	–	3	2	29		–	–
Other Central Highlands	17 (6)	3 –	2 –	22 (6)	16	3	4	–	2	2	27		–	1
Cairngorms	25 (2)	8 –	5 (2)	38 (4)	34	6	3	6	17	4	70		–	3
Southern Highlands	25 (2)	3 –	1 (1)	29 (3)	27	3	2	1	11	2	46		3	18
Skye	13 –	– –	– –	13 –	13	4	–	3	3	3	26		–	–
Islands (other than Skye	6 –	1 –	1 –	8 –	8	–	2	–	6	–	16		–	–
Southern Uplands	1 –	1 –	– –	2 –	2	2	–	2	3	–	9		–	13
All Regions 1998	141 (22)	19 –	18 (5)	178 (27)	165	29	15	14	58	14	295		3	35
Previous year 1997	189 (17)	24 (1)	25 (11)	238 (29)	212	11	11	12	44	13	305 + 2n/k		3	36

MOUNTAIN RESCUE COMMITTEE OF SCOTLAND

SCOTTISH MOUNTAIN ACCIDENTS 1998

Compiled by John Hinde

Police have not been mentioned in every incident as they are involved in all.

NORTHERN HIGHLANDS

JANUARY 11 – Girl (5) ran off into woods at Rearaig, Ardaneaskan, Lochcarron. HMCG helicopter. Found safe. 8.

JANUARY 17-18 – Slip caused recurring knee injury for soldier (40) on military exercise in Fannichs. One of four went for help while other three sheltered in ponchos and bivvy bags in snow on hill path. Recovered by Dundonnell MRT using Argocat. Reference given was only 1.5km from shelter in Lochivraon Bothy. 54.

JANUARY 27 – Two men (46, 30) used a quad vehicle to get 8km north from A838 to Whiten Head for whelk collecting. Quad bike broke down on return so they had to walk. Wearing wellies and lacking navigation gear they got benighted at Cnoc nan Gobhar, Loch Eriboll. Coastguard Auxiliary, Police and HMCG helicopter searched. They were found by a light seen by searchers checking a route out to Freisgill Bothy. 88.

MARCH 1 – Two male climbers (34, 27) overdue from first ascent of Spindryer Buttress on West Face, Cona Mheall, Coire Ghra of Beinn Dearg, walked out safe, unaided, prior to search. They had been delayed by deep snow and extreme weather. Dundonnell MRT had been notified.

MARCH 21-22 – Descending Sgurr nan Each, Fannichs, (m41) got separated from his three friends. After a search they went off to get help. He got down to Amhainn Cuilleig (river) but was lost without map or compass at night so he bedded down. Found by Dundonnell MRT searching likely routes and walked out with them. 69.

APRIL 13-14 – Two male hillwalkers (28, 22) overdue from An Teallach in snowy conditions walked out at Dundonnell after midnight. Dundonnell MRT. 4.

APRIL 13 – Man (36) slipped on snow on west bank of Coire Mhic Nobuil, Torridon, when only 80m north of road. He fell 18m into river. Alarm raised by one of his companions. Taken from river by Torridon MRT and treated for minor cuts and bruises. 4.

APRIL 21-22 – Walking at east end of Loch Garbhaig, Letterewe, man (28) damaged his knee. Spent night in boathouse at west end of loch, but still unable to continue so companion went for help. Stretchered out by Torridon MRT. 45.

APRIL 24 – Having walked pass from Achnashellach to Torridon, four walkers attempted return route. Three went ahead leaving a novice (42) behind. She could not be found by one of the others who back-tracked to look for her. Torridon MRT callout was initiated. Novice had walked back to Torridon hitched to Dingwall, phoning youth hostel at 22.50. 16.

MAY 3 – Whistles heard from south side Spidean Coire nan Clach , Beinn Eighe at about 400m. Walker (49) had been hit by rock dislodged by a member of the party of eight, suffering leg and suspected spinal damage with mild hypothermia. Rescuers guided to him by torch flashes. Airlift By RAF Sea King. Leuchars and Torridon MRTs. 53.

MAY 14-15 – Solo walking in Fannichs, man (40) failed to rendezvous with friend at 17.00. Searches by Assynt, Dundonnell, Kinloss and Torridon MRTs, SARDA and RAF Sea King. His body was found 1km NNW of Sgur Mor by sweep search next afternoon and was stretchered off the hill. He had apparently fallen about 150m. 641.

MAY 16 – Party (f37,34, m26,26) attempting Cioch Nose of Sgurr a'Chaorachain was delayed by two novices. Reported overdue from youth hostel they were found uninjured at foot of climb by two SARDA dogs before midnight. 4.

MAY 17 – On path, 1.4km east of Flowerdale Mains, Gairloch, teacher with his party of six heard six whistle blasts from NE. He got no acknowledgement after twice replying with three blasts. Dundonnell MRT member checked it all out and climbed An Groban. Nothing found. 2.

MAY 24-26 – Walking between Kinlochewe and Shenavall Bothy, man (48) twisted his knee on 24th. Could not walk out on 26th and showed some cold symptoms, so companion went on to Dundonnell. Search by Dundonnell MRT. Airlift by Inverness Air Ambulance. 22.

MAY 31 – Descending wet, rough south slopes of Ben Klibreck, just above Loch a'Bhealaich, man (39) fell awkwardly, dislocating ankle and fracturing lower leg. Companion went for help. Winched by RAF Sea King. 12.

JUNE 8 – Walking on wet hillside above Lochan Coire Mhic Fhearchair, Beinn Eighe a woman (63) slipped, breaking two bones of a leg. Two of the party of seven ran off the hill for aid. Casualty airlifted by HMCG helicopter to Broadford Hospital. Later transferred to Raigmore. 30.

JUNE 17 – Woman (70) walking with her husband to see a monument at 210m above Berriedale, about 4km inland from the east coast of Caithness. She slipped on heather and fractured an ankle. Evacuated by gamekeeper in Argocat and local rescuers. 18.

JULY 22 – Woman (26) injured her ankle near Shenavall Bothy. Aided by Dundonnell MRT to end of track. 10.

JULY 25 – In a party of four descending SE Slopes of Stac Pollaidh in rain and mist, a woman (53) was killed by a fall of 75m. She had slipped from a mossy, rock ledge. Dundonnell MRT in HMCG helicopter. 27.

AUGUST 23-24 – Lost on the path to the high waterfall, Eas a Chual Aluinn, woman (67) and man (63) tried to walk out westwards along Loch Glencoul. They were benighted at a uncrossable river (probably Unapool Burn). Daylight revealed bridge and road within easy walking distance. Assynt MRT assembled. HMCG helicopter standby. 9.

SEPTEMBER 2-3 – Trainee gamekeeper (17) taking quad bike to a shot stag got lost in mist and rain on Knockfin Heights (438m) on Caithness boundary 5km east of A897 at Kinbrace. He had only a few weeks' experience. He lost his jacket and just had a T-shirt. Next day he was searched for by Assynt and Kinloss MRTs, RAF and HMCG helicopters. He was found at 16.30, 8km farther east by a stalker on his way to check Gobernuisgeach Bothy. He walked out. 324.

SEPTEMBER 19-20 – Overdue, but having left a route plan, experienced solo woman walker (63) was with dog on rugged west slopes of South Ridge of Ben More Assynt, NE of head of Dubh Loch More. Her body was found by RAF Sea King. She had fallen 10m in good weather from rocks to stream/rocks. There have been several accidents in this area over the last few years. Assynt and Kinloss MRTs. 318.

SEPTEMBER 20-21 – Underestimating time needed for ascent of Cioch Nose, Sgurr a' Chaorachain, two men (40), (26) got benighted near top. They flashed torches to raise alarm. Reached by Torridon and Kintail MRTs at first light Transferred to HMCG helicopter. 85.

SEPTEMBER 30-NOVEMBER 1 – Four guest spectators (m26, f26, f25, f23) viewing a deer stalk on Creag Ruadh in Kildermorie Forest, 23km NW of Evanton, got lost in mist and spent the night on the hill at 650m. Next day they followed a stream to their vehicles. Rescue helicopters alerted.

OCTOBER 10-11 – Two men (m35, f28) got lost in bad weather and dark on Sgurr Fiona. They bivvied and were found descending Corrie Hallie path by Dundonnell MRT and SARDA who had also bivvied due to weather. RAF Sea King search called off due to weather. 122.

OCTOBER 24-25 – Four cavers trapped in Clayonite Cave, Inchnadamph by rising storm water. Found safe and fed by divers assembled for SCRO annual dinner in village. Walked out when water level dropped. Assynt MRT helped communications. 40.

NOVEMBER 6-7 – Group of four separated descending Stac Pollaidh. Two women (39, 26) got lost and benighted in heavy rain and gusty wind. Found OK by Dundonnell MRT and SARDA and aided off. 104.

DECEMBER 5-6 – Casualty (32) walked off Liathach after splitting up with friend. Descending south between two eastern tops he stepped into a small hole twisting his knee. When his head torch battery failed he used camera flash to raise alarm. Torridon MRT dropped by HMCG helicopter carried him back to top of ridge, where he was airlifted. 55.

WESTERN HIGHLANDS

APRIL 25-26 – Woman (49) and man (39) got separated from a group of six on Bidein a'Choire Sheasgaich. Poor navigation caused benightment. Found and airlifted from near head of Loch Monar on SE Ridge Beinn Tharsuinn by HMCG helicopter. Kinloss and Torridon MRTs. 76.

MAY 9 – Male hillwalker (37) died of heart attack on Forcan Ridge, the Saddle, Glen Shiel. RAF Sea King. 22.

MAY 16-21 – On May 21 the body of a walker (78) was found on craggy north slopes of Sguman Coinntich, Killilan. Solo, he had probably slipped and fallen on May 16. He was reported missing on May 19. His car was found in Killilan. Searches were carried out by Glenelg, Kinloss and Kintail MRTs with up to 12 SARDA dogs. No route plan had been left but fresh information lead to concentration on Beinn Killilan and Sguman Coinntich. Casualty was spotted by HMCG helicopter when going to refuel after dropping teams. 890.

MAY 17 – Student (23) in good weather slipped on steep, wet, rock slab on summit of Beinn Tharsuinn sustaining head and leg injuries. His two companions got him down to Bhearnais Bothy whence he was lifted by RN Sea King. 13.

JULY 4 – On July 18 body of a walker (23) was found by a fisherman downstream from Loch Eiragoraidh and 3.7km ESE from Mallaig Pierhead. He seemed to have climbed 9m on rock and fallen, sustaining fatal head injuries. HMCG helicopter transported witness, Police, CID etc. Recovery on stretcher to A830 by Lochaber MRT. It is likely that the accident occured on July 4, 1998 as casualty travelled from Ayr to Mallaig on July 3. 67.

JULY 4 – Descending An Riabhachan by Coire a'Mhaim to Loch Mullardoch, a solo walker (49) slipped on wet grass, going over on his ankle and fracturing a fibula. Whistle blasts alerted four Leuchars MRT on exercise. Airlift by RAF Sea King. 20.

JULY 8-9 – Schoolboy (15) on an outdoor course suffered asthma when hillwalking at the head of the track up Glen Mallie (Loch Arkaig). Two from group of 10 went for help. Lochaber MRT attended with an estate worker on a quad bike. Casualty taken to Belford Hospital. 14.

JULY 18 – Taking a short cut off South Cluanie Ridge by Sgurr a'Chuilinn, then descending NE Ridge, man (43) slipped on wet rock and grass and was killed by a fall of 30m. Companion raised alarm. Kintail MRT, RAF Sea King. 53m

JULY 21 – Lochaber MRT and helicopter alerted when two boys (13,12), wearing trainers, unequipped and without a plan, went walking in rain and mist on to rugged An t-Sleubhaich south of A830, Glenfinnan. A half-hour jaunt stretched to four hours but they turned up OK. 14.

JULY 26 – Student (17) suffered only bruising after a spectacular small hours fall of 15m into River Moriston, just below A82 bridge. After being swept downstream he managed to swim to the foot of the bankside crag, grab something and eventually pull himself on to a ledge at water level. More than four hours later he was stretcher hoisted on ropes despite overhanging rock and vegetation. Dundonnell MRT, Police, Ambulance Service. 113.

AUGUST 1-2 – With damaged ankle ligaments, caused by jumping over a peat hag descending vegetation on North Ridge Ciste Dhubh, a schoolgirl (17) was helped to tent by seven companions. The aggravated old injury had not improved by next morning when she was evacuated by Kintail MRT, on stretcher supported on quad bike over easier bits. 46.

AUGUST 7 – At a campfire at Plockton Monument in the small hours a barefoot female (25) stood up, slipped on wet grass skidding down a slight incline, over a sea cliff. She fell 10m, stopping on a ledge sustaining cuts to her head and a knee injury. Kintail MRT needed for stretcher evacuation. 26.

AUGUST 22 – One of 12 TA recruits descending Sgurr Fhuaran by NE Ridge into Gleann Lichd, a man (25) suffered exhaustion with collapse and disorientation. Party put him in survival shelter and raised alarm. Kintail MRT supervised stretcher carry. 7.

AUGUST 27 – With a companion descending north slopes of Sgurr na Sgine above Bealach Coire Mhalagain, a walker (32) slipped on rock, fell 10m gashing his knee. Used mobile phone. Winched by RAF Sea King to Raigmore. 21.

SEPTEMBER 7-8 – Birdwatcher on Carn Bad a'Chreamha (634m) 4.5km ENE of Eilean Donnan Castle, lost track of time. When it got dark he stayed put then walked off in daylight. Kintail MRT. 17.

SEPTEMBER 20 – Man (45) stumbled near Bearnais Bothy, Achnashellach, injuring his back. Companion raised alarm. Evacuated by Raigmore Air Ambulance. 12.

SEPTEMBER 28 – Woman (69) fractured ankle by going over on a grass tuft Smirisary, Glenuig. Stretchered By Lochaber MRT. 15.

NOVEMBER 6 – Man (46) suffered fatal heart attack after descent to glen from summit of Sgurr Choinnich of Sgurr a'Chaorachain, Achnashellach. Stretchered by Torridon MRT. 45.

BEN NEVIS

JANUARY 14 – Two men (24, 22) flashed torches International Distress. After ascent of No. 2 Gully they lost 282° bearing for West Flank and got cragfast in Five Finger Gully. Airlift at 22.00 by RAF Sea King. 22.

JANUARY 17-18 – Three men (29, 23, 23) benighted on Tower Ridge Eastern Traverse due to poor snow. Lochaber MRT lowered to them, escorted them up to plateau and down to Halfway Lochan for RN Sea King airlift. Lomond and RAF MRTs. 399.

JANUARY 25-29 – On January 23, Fort William Police received a Fax with a plan for a fell runner (60) to complete all 4000ft peaks and finish on Ben Nevis on January 25. On January 25 he phoned from Dalwhinnie that he had gone slightly off course, was running late and would arrive in Fort William on 26th. It was known he was well equipped and experienced with good local knowledge. On 29th Kinloss and Lochaber started search, also nine SARDA dogs and two RAF Sea Kings. About noon his body was found in Five Finger Gully by R137 helicopter. A single set of footprints in snow could clearly be seen leading to the edge of a 12m ice cliff down which he had fallen, then slid 60m before stopping on a small level snow patch. He had sustained head injuries, cuts and bruises. Wearing fell running trainers he carried crampons but no helmet. 345.

FEBRUARY 2 – Two men (both 19) soloing Tower Gully were a metre from the top when the cornice collapsed. The avalanche went over the head of one, uninjured, who went up to plateau then walked off. The other suffered abrasions when he was swept 200m to 15m below the foot of Tower Scoop landing in soft snow. He went to CIC Hut and was escorted down. Lochaber MRT. 17.

MARCH 7-8 – On Eastern Traverse, Tower Ridge, student (21) slipped and fell 15m to near a cave, suffering slight head cuts and bruised ribs. His uninjured female companion abseiled to join him. Casualty shouted to climber ahead to raise alarm. He was stretchered and airlifted by RAF to Belford for overnight observation. Companion also lifted. Lochaber MRT. 194.

MARCH 21-22 – Losing time climbing Tower Ridge, two men (41, 25) got benighted at Eastern Traverse then failed to progress next day. Passers-by alerted by whistles. Mobile phones also used. Lochaber MRT assisted them to climb to the top, then walked them uninjured to RAF Sea King airlift. 100.

APRIL 4-5 – Last seen at 11.00 on 4th, climbing Slingsby's Chimney roped, two men (28, 27) were found by Lochaber MRT dead, still roped together on NE Buttress. One body was recovered on 5th but poor weather delayed second recovery till April 6. RAF Sea King 15 flying hours. It is not known what the primary cause was. 549.

APRIL 29 – Descending Nevis Track, (f50) slipped just above Red Burn breaking her wrist. Mobile phone used. Airlift by RAF Sea King. Lochaber MRT. 30.

MAY 2 – At the first zig-zag above Red Burn (m45) collapsed with kidney pains of which he had a history. His companion used mobile phone for help. Airlift by RAF. Lochaber MRT. 12.

MAY 24-25 – Female (24) descending Upper Coire Eoghainn, Ben Nevis slipped and twisted her knee at 15.00. She decided to rest overnight then continue descent next day. She failed to rest due to injury and used mobile phone to call help next day. Evacuated by Lochaber MRT and RAF Sea King. 45.

MAY 29 – Female (21) in party of nine involved in Three Peaks Challenge had repeated asthma attacks on plateau 1km from Nevis summit. Evacuated by RN helicopter. 10.

MAY 30 – Male (34) fell on loose rock on Nevis summit with slight injuries to head

Jacksonville, Glen Coe. (see page 53.) Photo: Jimmy Marshall.
Lesley Pyper outside the Slugain Howff. (See page 165). Photo: Derek Pyper.

and hip. Passer-by used mobile phone. Rescued by RAF Sea King. Lochaber MRT. 23.

JUNE 12 – No ropes were carried for a midday climb up Castle Ridge by four men during excellent weather. 75m up the climb the deceased (47) who was last in line of ascent, slipped and fatally somersaulted several times to the bottom. He had worn adequate boots but rock was wet in places. His helmet was damaged in the fall. Companion called for help on mobile phone. Stretchered by Lochaber MRT. All winched by RAF Sea King. 62.

JUNE 13 – Involved in Three Peaks Challenge, (f37) suffered exhaustion descending Nevis Track in a party of four. She was just below the Red Burn crossing. Flown to Belford by RN Sea King. 17.

JUNE 13 – Descending Nevis Track in Three Peaks Challenge, (m29) got sore knees when he got down to the lowest aluminium bridge. Companions contacted Police from youth hostel. Airlift by RN Sea King in the area. 9.

JULY 4 – Attempting to climb Tower Ridge four men (33, 22, 20, 20) got as far as Little Tower and decided to descend. Mist came down and they got cragfast. Used mobile phone to alert Lochaber MRT. Four of the team helped to lower them off. RN helicopter involved. 52.

JULY 8 – Man (74) who took 8.5 hours to climb Ben Track was reported overdue. Leader of Lochaber MRT went up alone, met him at Red Burn where he was found to be OK, and escorted him down to Achintee. 9.

JULY 18 – Leader (28) of a rope of four on Long Climb fell when 90m up climb in good weather. Fall caused by loose rock. Fall arrested by belay but he sustained a fractured skull and elbow. Mobile phone used for alert. Winched off face by Lochaber MRT and RAF Sea King to Belford Hospital. (later Glasgow Southern General). 87.

AUGUST 1 – Sufferer from muscular dystrophy (29) experienced an epileptic fit during an ascent of the Ben Track at the third zig-zag above Red Burn. Her companion also had a form of physical impairment. A passer-by alerted rescuers using a mobile phone. Both were taken to Belford Hospital by RN Sea King. 16.

AUGUST 26 – Female (40) repeatedly twisted ankle descending Nevis Track despite wearing adequate boots. At YH track junction she could walk no farther. She was splinted and entonoxed by Lochaber MRT and stretchered off. 22

SEPTEMBER 9 – Outdoor centre student (16) stumbled down scree for 6m, sustaining cuts and bruises when descending Number 4 Gully in a party of 13. He also suffered cold trauma. Mobile phone alerted Lochaber MRT and he was stretchered to below cloudbase, then airlifted by RAF Sea King. 103.

OCTOBER 10 – Descending Nevis Track in calm weather with mist and rain, four men (23,22,21,21) got benighted and lost at Halfway Lochan. They had inadequate clothing and no navigation gear. They made contact by mobile phone and were escorted down by Lochaber MRT. 8.

OCTOBER 30 – Solo walker (46) descending Nevis Track had knee cartilage problems. Aided down by Lochaber MRT. He declined medical help. 21.

OCTOBER 31 – Charity walker (29) with 200 others descending Nevis Track when she took an epileptic fit near Halfway Lochan. Airlifted to Belford Hospital by RN Sea King on training exercise. 5.

DECEMBER 5 – Carrying, but not wearing, crampons, (m46) slipped on icy path 500m below CIC Hut, breaking his ankle. Airlift by RAF Sea King. Lochaber MRT. 16.

DECEMBER 12-13 – Couple (f40, m37) climbing Nevis by Carn Mor Dearg Arête got trapped by weather and nightfall and spent night in summit shelter. Found when descending by RAF Sea King. Lochaber MRT. 40.

Keith Milne on Pitch 15 of the Lotus Flower headwall, Lotus Flower Tower, Cirque of the Unclimbables, N.W. Territories, Canada.

Keith Milne belaying on the South East Buttress of Mount St. James O'Brian. Photos: Steve Helmore.

GLENCOE

JANUARY 17-18 – Traversing Aonach Eagach E to W alone, (m52) slipped on snow at the Pinnacles at 13.30 and fell 120m down south side. Other climbers communicated and found he had injured his back, but alarm not raised till 22.15. Found by Glencoe and Leuchars MRTs at 04.00. Lifted by RAF Sea King at 09.00 to Belford Hospital. Detained for bruising to back and swollen knees. 268.

JANUARY 25 – Nearing the top of Summit Gully, Stob Coire nam Beith, unroped male (26) fell 25m fracturing wrist and opposite ankle. He was stopped when he fell into a snow bank. Companion went for help. Airlift by RAF Sea King to Belford. Later transferred to Raigmore Hospital. Glencoe MRT. 56.

JANUARY 31 – Two men (27, 27) got cragfast trying to descend Clachaig Gully West after traverse of Aonach Eagach E to W. Distress signals by torches brought rescuers who escorted them down uninjured. Glencoe MRT. 29.

JANUARY 31-FEBRUARY 1 – Pair (m27, f25) completed E to W traverse of Aonach Eagach but benighted on Sgorr nam Fiannaidh. Descended into Coire an Lochan where they overnighted, then walked off next morning. Glencoe MRT. 17.

FEBRUARY 1 – Returning overdue from climbing on Stob Coire nan Lochan two men (28, 24) benighted in Coire nam Beith with failed head torches and failed spare batteries. RAF Sea King spotted a very dim light. They were joined by two members of Glencoe MRT with new torches who aided them down. 29.

FEBRUARY 22-23 – Wet and slippery rock delayed three men (34, 33, 32) climbing Agag's Groove, Buachaille Etive Mor, so they were benighted at the top of the climb. Darkness prevented their intended descent of Curved Ridge so they waited till morning. Glencoe MRT found them abseiling Agag's Groove. No further assistance required. 14.

MARCH 21 – Cragfast in good weather on a ledge above scree on Gleann Fhaolain slopes of Bidean nam Bian, two men were aided down by passing climbers and not traced. Glencoe MRT and RAF Sea King stood down. 6.

MARCH 22 – False alarm. Cries reported heard on Beinn Fhada slightly above Lost Valley path. Glencoe MRT. RAF Sea King in area. Nothing found. 26.

MAY 30 – On E to W traverse of Aonach Eagach in good weather, walker (45) climbed 2m rock at the Pinnacles to pass elderly walkers going east. He fell 3m with face lacerations and bruising, stopping at the lip of another drop. Glencoe MRT and RAF Sea King in the area. 13.

MAY 31 – When second and third were still at the foot of the climb, lead climber's belay slipped on Bunny's Route, Gearr Aonach , causing him to fall on top of second man (44) dislocating his shoulder. Leader and third raised alarm. Glencoe MRT member in area aided second off the hill. Good weather and dry rock. 2.

JUNE 11 – Female (55) slipped from path, rolled 6m with cuts and abrasions to her body. With companion she was descending south side of Sgorr nam Fiannaidh. Passer-by alerted Glencoe MRT and RN Sea King. 33.

JUNE 17 – Male (33) traversing Aonach Eagach from east, reached Stob Coire Leith then slipped, fell 3m and injured his ankle. Passers-by alerted Glencoe MRT and he was winched by RN Sea King. 22.

JUNE 20 – At 03.30 (m37) and companion were at 300m climbing Sgor nam Fiannaidh to view sunrise when he fell 9m causing head injury and bruises. Stretchered by Glencoe MRT. 19.

JUNE 20 – (See July 4 similar incident nearby) Ascending main ridge of Bidean nam Bian from Lost Valley with a companion, woman (53) was struck by a falling rock which caused a fractured collar bone. She self-rescued. Glencoe MRT attended alerted by passer-by. 21.

JUNE 20 – (f25) descending Coire nan Lochan path in good weather was within 0.5km of Pipers' Layby when she slipped sustaining spiral fractures of tibia and fibula. Stretchered to A82 by Glencoe MRT. 13.

JULY 4 – (See June 20 similar incident nearby) Three were descending scree from Bidean Ridge NE into Lost Valley when rockfall occured. Female (57) was struck on calf by a stone, causing serious tissue damage. She was given entonox by Glencoe MRT and stretchered down to suitable RN Sea King winch point. 59.

JULY 10 – Three ascending Sgorr nam Fiannaidh reached 600m and found they were not on correct Clachaig Gully path. Leader, a police officer (32), paused to get his bearings. Another route-finder went up and beckoned the others to come on. Policeman slipped on broken slab and gravel, and fell 3m on to his head. Fatal. Winch by RN Sea King. GMRT. 26.

JULY 19 – Solo climber (42) climbing Curved Ridge, Buachaille Etive Mor slipped on wet rock and fell 23m sustaining head, pelvic and kidney trauma. Treated with oxygen, stretchered by Glencoe MRT to below cloudbase then winched by RAF Sea King. 73.

JULY 21 – Woman (38) descending Lost Valley path with companion slipped on rock falling 6m, suffering skull fracture and cuts. Glencoe MRT did manual transfer to RN Sea King. 18.

AUGUST 20 – Heart attack sufferer (m45) airlifted from Lost Valley to Belford Hospital by RN Sea King. Glencoe MRT. 56.

AUGUST 22 – Walkers reported three climbers in difficulty on East Face of Aonach Dubh. Glencoe MRT ascertained by shouts that they were OK. 14.

SEPTEMBER 5 – Pair completed Shackle Route on North Buttress, Buachaille Etive Mor. Boyfriend left to retrieve rucksack, returning to find girl (27) missing. She had no torch. She was found and guided down by Glencoe MRT. 19.

SEPTEMBER 13-14 – After traversing Aonach Eagach, walker (35) went down east of Clachaig Gully in failing light, instead of usual route down west of gully. He got cragfast and alerted rescuers with torch flashes. Glencoe MRT assisted him through a gully system. 48.

OCTOBER 3 – Having climbed Curved Ridge and suffered migraine and epilepsy, walker (50) tried to get off Buachaille Etive Mor by Coire na Tulaich but he could go no farther. Airlift by RAF Sea King. Glencoe MRT. 16.

OCTOBER 8 – Having completed most of Aonach Eagach, walker (m23) collapsed from exhaustion on Stob Coire Leith. Friend went for help. RAF Sea King spotted casualty flashing a cigarette lighter. Glencoe MRT. 53.

OCTOBER 10 – In good weather, instead of taking easier ground to west, a walker (26) went up Summit Gully of Stob Coire nam Beith where he got cragfast. His friend went for help. Glencoe MRT lowered him into coire whence he was lifted by RAF Sea King. 82.

NOVEMBER 5 – Central Gully, Bidean nam Bian. Unroped climber (49) within 30m of completing route when loose windslab gave way. He fell 45m fracturing ankle. Stretchered by Glencoe MRT to below cloudbase then airlifted by HMS Gannet RN Sea King. 77.

NOVEMBER 29-30 – Three men (45, 37, 32) took more than 24 hours to traverse Aonach Eagach in mist and later darkness, reporting progress on mobile phone till battery died. They had belayed and abseiled the entire length of the ridge. Met by Glencoe MRT when descending Sgor nam Fiannaidh. RN Sea King. 22.

DECEMBER 13-16 – Thought to have walked Aonach Eagach on December 13, searches took place for a man (34) on December 15 and 16. His body was found by RN Sea King at the foot of a vertical cliff on south side of Stob Coire Leith. Glencoe and Kinloss MRTs, SARDA, RAF Sea King. 411.

OTHER CENTRAL HIGHLANDS

JANUARY 8 – Client (51) in a guided party became ill, losing balance and vomiting, on east slopes of Aonach an Nidd going to climbs on Coire an Lochain of Aonach Mor. Recovered to Belford by Nevis Range tracked vehicle as Lochaber MRT en route. 39.

JANUARY 25 – Man abseiling West Gully, Beinn Udlaidh suffered back and leg injuries when his belay failed. Airlift to Southern General by RN Sea King. Strathclyde Police and Arrochar MRTs. 15.

JANUARY 25 – Strathclyde Police and Arrochar MRTs went on to Beinn Udlaidh to escort the companion of the above casualty. 24.

JANUARY 30 – Descending An Gearanach, man (43) got separated from three friends who thought he had gone a different way due to tiredness. Lost on path he got to top of Steall Falls then retraced. Benighted without a torch he was descending slowly when found by Leuchars and Lochaber MRTs and RAF Sea King. 28.

FEBRUARY – Man (33) suffered broken fibula and facial lacerations. He slipped climbing Centre Post, Creag Meagaidh due to a crampon balling up with snow. He then fell 35m colliding with a colleague belayed below. Their combined fall was then broken by the first ice screw of the pitch. His two uninjured companions lowered him off. Winched by RAF Sea King. Leuchars and Lochaber MRTs. 141.

MARCH 1-2 – After finding white-out on The Guardian, Aonach Mor, two men (both 21) overnighted in a ski-run storage hut and walked down next morning. Spotted by Nevis Range staff. Lochaber MRT and RAF Sea King. 55.

MARCH 9 - Man (29) stumbled in snow-covered heather at Bealach Cumhann, Ben Alder and strained knee ligaments. One of two companions went for help. Airlift by RAF Sea King. 10.

APRIL 14 - Walkers above Steall Bothy reported cries for help during snowstorm. Nothing found. Lochaber MRT. 33.

APRIL 25 - Sponsored walker (27) lost faint track after separation from group of 100. She walked out to Kinlochleven from Luibeilt. Glencoe MRT. 20.

APRIL 25 Ascending Sgurr a'Mhaim man (31) told two friends he would take more difficult route up a rocky outcrop and meet them above it, but he headed down towards Steall Hut. They searched for him then alerted Lochaber MRT and RAF Sea King. Meantime, he went to Stob Coire a'Chairn hoping to meet them as the original plan was anti-clockwise Ring of Steall. Self recovery. 35.

MAY 16 – Morning descent of west slopes of Sgurr a'Mhaim by a party of four was complicated by mist. They strayed off the path on to steep ground. Man (22) fell 4m with head injury. One went for help thinking injury serious, but casualty came round. He was helped down by the others. Discharged from Belford after treatment for bruises, abrasions and seven-stitch scalp laceration. Lochaber MRT and RN Sea King. 28.

MAY 29 - Guide on Carn Mor Dearg heard dog barks and whimpering from West Face Aonach Mor. Searches by Lochaber MRT and RN Sea King found nothing. 19.

MAY 30 – Walker (71) slipped and sprained his ankle at Allt a'Chaorainn, Newtonmore. Airlift by RN Sea King. No medical treatment required. Cairngorm MRT. 10.

JUNE 6 – Woman (23) got separated from her party of seven on Geal Charn, Drumochter. Reported lost she was found by passers-by and escorted off. Cairngorm MRT on standby. 15.

JUNE 13 – With three companions at Loch na Lap, Corrour, woman (50) stumbled, fell a few feet and badly fractured her shin. Friend went for help. Airlift by RN Sea King, in the area for rescues on Ben Nevis, to Belford. Later transferred to Raigmore. 7.

JULY 20 – (See August 30) Swinging on a rope swing near Steall Cottage, Glen Nevis, woman (20) fell and hurt her back. Stretchered to Belford by Lochaber MRT on a full body vacuum mat. 46.

JULY 21– Walking Ring of Steall from Glen Nevis, two men (26, 26) got lost on west slopes of Sgor an Iubhair and spent the night out. Self recovery before Lochaber MRT and RN Sea King search got underway in wind and rain. 34.

JULY 30 – Member of outdoor education group (19) slipped when crossing river (Amhainn Rath) at Luibeilt Bothy, Loch Treig, injuring her ankle. Airlift by RAF Sea King. Glencoe MRT. 29.

AUGUST 28 - Man (61) ascending Devil's Staircase from A82 above Glencoe suffered minor stroke. He recovered sufficiently to walk back to road with help. Later discharged from hospital. Glencoe MRT. 13.

AUGUST 30 – (See July 20) Swinging on a rope swing near Steall Cottage, Glen Nevis, boy (14) lost grip and fell on his hands, breaking both wrists. Father alerted passer-by. Stretchered out by Lochaber MRT. 14.

SEPTEMBER 20 - Roped pair of males had completed Swastika on Trilleachan Slabs in sunny weather. Second (37) moved 30m above leader on final belay up less steep ground without placing runners. He slipped on wet rock or gravel, falling back over cliff, landing on slab 30m below. Died instantly from head injuries (not wearing helmet). Lowered by Glencoe MRT to base of slabs and lifted by RN Sea King. 63.

SEPTEMBER 26 - Descending from Carn Mor Dearg along aréte towards Ben Nevis, walker (50) slipped on dry rock and pulled his knee. Alarm raised by passers by with mobile phone. Lochaber MRT lifted to area by RAF Sea King then stretchered casualty off hill. 89.

SEPTEMBER 29 – Glencoe MRT traced walker (67) where he had gone to sleep after benightment on Glas Bheinn Mhor. 35.

OCTOBER 20-21 – Spotted climbing Sgurr Eilde Mor from Coire an Lochain, a lone walker (68) got lost on summit, went down wrong side and failed to cross spate rivers. He was forced north during snowfall and darkness and was found south of Luibeilt. Taken to road by Kinloss team. Glencoe and Lochaber MRTs, RAF Sea King. 135.

DECEMBER 28-29 – On Aonach an Nid Face of Aonach Mor, mountain guide demonstrating ice-axe arrest to six students triggered avalanche. After being buried for 14 hours three survivors (m45, f25, m24) were found and rescued by Lochaber MRT. They suffered minor injuries and hypothermia. Four others buried nearby and evacuated (m30, f29, m28, m28) died from asphyxia. Leuchars, Lochaber and Tweed Valley MRTs, SARDA, RAF Sea King. 472.

DECEMBER 31 – Party of four at col east of Sgorr Dhearg, Beinn a'Bheithir. One glissaded and knocked off a man (26) who fell down north slopes into Coire Guibhsachain, sustaining bruises. Mobile phone alarm. Glencoe MRT prepared him for evacuation by RAF Sea King. 72.

DECEMBER 3 -JANUARY 1 – After walking from Stob Ban to Sgurr a'Mhaim summit, descending a ridge of rock, snow and ice towards Glen Nevis with two companions, a man (38) had crampon problems. He removed them and continued along the ridge on all fours. He slipped and failed to self arrest with his ice-axe, falling 450m into the main gully of the north face of Sgurr a'Mhaim. Fatal. Found by Lochaber MRT. RAF Sea King. 161.

CAIRNGORMS

1997 late reports: JULY 12-15 – After camping on Tom Dubh summit, carrying a heavy rucksack, student (20) descending into Glen Geusachan over boulders and heather slipped and broke her ankle. Two companions carried all rucksacks 4km to Corrour Bothy then went back for her. She had crawled some way downhill. They all bivvied and she was helped to Corrour next day for a third overnight. It was not known the injury was so serious. She was the most experienced and the effective leader. Next day swelling and discolouration increased and one went for help. Evacuated by all terrain vehicles. Braemar MRT. 15.

JULY 28 – Descending from Lochnagar by Glas Allt, (f49) was 150m from track at Loch Muick, when she slipped on tree roots on a steep part of the path breaking a tibia and fibula. Braemar MRT. 19.

SEPTEMBER – 9-11 Grampian Police MRT and RAF Sea King searched rim of An Garbh Choire, west of Angel's Peak when a rucksack was found and reported. A camper had left it there and gone off to another top. When he could not find the sack he went home. He phoned in when his wife heard of the incident on the radio. 92.

SEPTEMBER 25 – Almost a year after a successful hip replacement, and after seven months of progressive walking, a man (64) contoured Loch Muick and went up Glas Allt to above the waterfall. Descending Land-Rover track to Allt na Giubhsaich his hip socket fractured. Aid by Air Ambulance and airlift by RAF Sea King to hospital for eight weeks of traction hopefully without further surgery. 4.

SEPTEMBER 26 – Two drunken men climbed Craig Coinnich (538m) a rocky height at Braemar. One fell off and suffered bruised ribs. The other went for help but could not describe casualty location. Braemar MRT found and stretchered him out. 38.

NOVEMBER 30-December 1 Two men (both 54) were overdue returning to their car at Linn o' Dee from Beinn a'Chaorainn having been disorientated in Yellow Moss area. Self recovery but Braemar and Aberdeen MRTs and RAF Sea King called out. 318.

DECEMBER 30-31 – With no definite plans, three men (24, 23, 23) got lost in rain and mist SW of Loch Muick. At 10.30 next day they found the ponyman's hut at Broad Cairn/Sandy Hillock bealach. One suffered mild hypothermia so he was left at the hut while the others headed for Glen Muick. Passers-by found the cold one and attracted an RAF Sea King on search. All three airlifted. Aberdeen and Braemar MRTs. 222.

1998: JANUARY 1 – Descending icy path from Lochnagar near Meikle Pap col walker (31) slipped and pulled hip ligaments she had previously torn. Helped by companions to shelter and warmth at Allt-na-Giubhsaich. One of party tried to break lock of gate to drive up to house. Police rescued her and reported damage to Balmoral Estates. 2 .

JANUARY 1-2 – A party of seven (males 52, 37, 23, 18 and females 27, 21, 5) did a local walk from Tomintoul expecting to reach Lynachork, Glen Avon 156189. Lost at dusk without a map they sheltered at Creag Loisgte Bothy, Glen Brown 124167. Rescuers found them at 03.00. Aberdeen and Braemar MRTs. 119.

JANUARY 2 – Male and female student pair overdue from climbing Milky Way, Coire an Lochain. Turned up at 20.40 as Cairngorm MRT began search. 4.

JANUARY 6-7 – Walker (26) strayed 50m from seven companions on Macdui Plateau and got lost without a compass. Survived 19 hours in shallow snowhole and group shelter unharmed till found 100m NW of Macdui summit by rescuers who walked him to Hutchison Hut. Braemar, Cairngorm and Kinloss MRTs, SARDA. Airlift by RAF Sea King. 312.

JANUARY 10 – Tayside MRTs were just starting search for two local men (25, 23) with limited equipment (no map and compass) when they got down to Clova Hotel before midnight. They had been lost in mist for some time around Loch Brandy and Loch Wharral. 34.

JANUARY 13 – Party of five on headwall of Coire Cas. (f26) without crampons/ice axe fell 100m on ice. Reached by Kasborer, but airlifted with double clavicle fracture and abrasions to face, back and hip areas by RAF Sea King. 20.

JANUARY 16 – In a party of five climbing Hidden Chimney, Coire an-t'Sneachda, casualty (25) was belaying for others when he was struck on the back by a falling boulder. Glenmore Lodge MRT assisted him to the road suffering arm and facial injuries. 9.

JANUARY 18 – Two snowboarders (m34, m33) last seen at foot of Coire na Ciste main tow turned up at 17.45, two hours late. Cairngorm MRT took no action.

JANUARY 20-21 – After a climb in Coire an-t'Sneachda, male (32) walking in front of companion trying to find their way off the plateau in gale and snowfall, went through a cornice near Aladdin's Buttress. He fell 220m, landing in 2m deep soft snow sustaining severe bruising. Passer-by went for help. Stretchered out by 05.30 by Cairngorm MRT. Meantime, companion helped off plateau by passer-by as she had been left without a map. 360.

JANUARY 28-29 – False alarm. Lights reported from Hell's Lum. Nothing found. Cairngorm MRT. 18.

JANUARY 29 – Party of 12 learning winter skills on Glas Maol and Creag Leacach were overdue because of late start, spending too long on skills and one twisted knee. GPol MRT. 2.

JANUARY 31 – Female (20) twisted her ankle in Parallel Gully A, Lochnagar. She fell 2m but her crampon caught. Helped down to tent by three companions then stretchered to Gelder Shiel by Aberdeen and Braemar MRTs. 180.

JANUARY 31-FEBRUARY 1 – Male (21) leading top pitch of The Corridor, Creagan a'Choire Etchachan, fell 5m, injuring an ankle. He allowed his partner to complete the route then he got up with assistance from the rope. After a night at Hutchison Hut he was helped to Derry Burn footbridge. Aberdeen MRT stretchered him out. 56.

FEBRUARY 1 – Two male climbers (34, 32) finishing The Escalator, Hell's Lum Crag reached easy slopes above the main climb and moved together still roped. Slope avalanched and they were swept 200m to the bottom. One had damage to L1 and 2 lumbar processes and fracture to top of hip. Other had L3 process fracture. Both had severe bruising but fortunately they had stayed on the surface of the avalanche debris. Cairngorm, Glenmore Lodge and Kinloss MRTs. Airlift by RAF Sea King.

FEBRUARY 1 – Initial reports said that four people had been avalanched out of The Escalator. What really happened was that two climbers on Kiwi Gully fell out of the gully at the same time as the avalanche (12.45) and landed in the same locality as the avalanche casualties. Not badly injured they stayed around till 16.50 then quietly disappeared and remain unidentified.

FEBRUARY 28 – Pair, climbing Route Major, Carn Etchachan, in thin conditions, were overdue but turned up at 23.35. Cairngorm MRT.

MARCH 6-7 – Together climbing Aladdin route of Coire an-t'Sneachda, three men (51, 46, 35) got separated by weather and benightment on the plateau. As a pair and a single they dug in for the night and walked off next morning, Cairngorm, Kinloss and Leuchars MRTs and SARDA. 140.

MARCH 6-7 – Climbing Savage Slit, Coire an Lochain, two men (29, 24) got benighted in the area in atrocious weather, dug in for the night and walked off next morning. Cairngorm, Kinloss and Leuchars MRTs and SARDA. 140.

MARCH 8-9 - Two students (m25) attempted Broad Cairn, Lochnagar circuit in deep, soft snow, underestimated timing. At 15.00 one turned back, but other (no torch) did not get back to Clova till midnight. Both Tayside teams, SARDA, RAF Sea King. 56.

MARCH 24-25 – Experienced walker (67) separated from his two companions and was overdue at Kilbo Path rendezvous. Slowed by old knee injury and loss of contact lens from one good eye. Found by RAF Sea King by torch signal from top of Craig Maud, Glen Doll. Both Tayside teams involved. 110.

MARCH 28 - Descending rough part of Jock's Road near Creag Lungard, Glen Doll, schoolboy (14) in party of five tripped and damaged knee ligaments. Stretchered by Tayside MRT. 18.

APRIL 14 – Trio (m 56, 25, f55) crossing Lairig Ghru from Linn o' Dee got delayed by heavy snowfall north of the top of the pass. Walked out unaided. Cairngorm MRT. 14.

APRIL 23 – Housewife (35) walked into hills suffering depression. Found sitting on open ground by RAF Sea King near Craigs of Succoth, Glass, Huntly. Braemar and Kinloss MRTs. 33.

May 1 – Leader of party of nine used mobile phone to alert Police Land-Rover which evacuated expedition member (18) from 4km north of Derry Lodge. He was detained for a day in hospital suffering abdominal pains. 5.

MAY 2-4 – Male (55) overdue at Coylumbridge doing Munros in area of Lairig Ghru. Searches by Cairngorm and Kinloss MRTs and SARDA. Found by RAF Sea King on third morning suffering mild hypothermia near Coylumbridge. Leuchars stood down en route. 532.

MAY 17 – Man (36) separated from party and got cragfast on sea cliffs to escape tide at Cullykhan Bay, Pennan, Banffshire. Lowered by HM Coastguard for airlift by RAF Sea King.

MAY 24 - A poor belay contributed to a fall on Craig a' Barns, Dunkeld. Roped climber (m29) sustained chest and arm injuries. Stretchered by Taypol SRU. 4.

MAY 24-25 – A rope of 2 students (m26, f26) went off route on Mousetrap, Creag an Dubh Loch, got benighted, then extricated themselves unharmed. Braemar MRT and RAF Sea King. 71.

JUNE 7 – RAF Sea King airlifted cragfast woman (17) from sea cliffs at Tarlair, Macduff. RNLI inshore lifeboat also involved.

JUNE 16 – Walker (64) overdue from Lochnagar despite being in regular contact with a ranger by mobile phone. He took unintended track to Glas Allt Falls, then retraced to Allt-na-Giubhsaich track. Search by Grampian Police vehicle. 3.

JUNE 20 – Fording Derry Burn at Derry Lodge, (f33) slipped on a stone tearing groin muscles in both legs. She continued a little way (sponsored Lairig Ghru walk) but was airlifted by RAF Sea King to Raigmore. 5.

JUNE 21 – Student (21) twisted her ankle at 750m descending Sron Riach Ridge from Ben Macdui, but managed to continue to Luibeg track. Grampian Police 4WD. 2.

JUNE 23 – Male (23) injured his spine abseiling late at night at Craig a' Barns, Dunkeld. Poor belay. Cliff lower and stretcher carry by Taypol SRU. 10.

JUNE 27 – Family group of four males (73, 53, 16, 11) exhausted at Derry Lodge after walking Lairig Ghru from Coylumbridge. Another incident at Linn o' Dee caused confused messages, so Braemar MRT was called out. 8.

JULY 2 – Roped climber (26) in party of four on Warfarin, Craig a' Barns, Dunkeld, injured his leg. stretcher carry by Taypol SRU and Ambulance Service.

JULY 6-7 – On an award hike, pupil (17) slipped at Pools of Dee causing sprained ankle aggravating a previous injury. She was able to walk to camp near Corrour Bothy and was evacuated by Braemar MRT next day. 12.

JULY 6-7 – Another pupil (17) in the same award hike group (see previous incident) also slipped at Pools of Dee very shortly afterwards. She also got to camp near Corrour and was evacuated by Braemar MRT with an ankle sprain. 12.

JULY 6-7 – Exhausted man (76) rescued from near The Saddle (Loch Avon) by RAF Sea King. Cairngorm MRT. Callout at 09.00. 9.

JULY 9 – HM Coastguard auxiliary teams helped in recovery of cragfast boy (9) from sea cliffs at Newtonhill, south of Aberdeen.

JULY 13 – Doctor (38) reported more than three hours overdue from round of four Cairngorm 4000ft peaks turned up having taken almost 16 hours, a reasonable time. Cngm. MRT.

JULY 17 – Walker (28) sprained or fractured ankle crossing River Feshie. Cairngorm MRT found him with companion on road near Achlean. RAF Sea King had been called because of wrong MF. placing casualty on hill. 10.

JULY 25-26 – Having crossed Ben Avon and Beinn a' Bhuird in cloud, two females (47, 46) got lost descending South Top and were benighted in Glen Quoich. Found uninjured by RAF Sea King before 06.00. Braemar MRT. 33.

JULY 30 – All members of a group of 30 walking Jock's Road from Clova to Callater were allowed to walk at their own pace, checking in at RVs. A man (45) with no navigation gear was missing at Crow Craigies, but he managed to find his own way back to Braedownie, Glen Clova. Braemar MRT. 15.

JULY 31 – Doing a round of Derry Lodge and White Bridge from Inverey, (m46) fell. This caused an ankle twist but he carried on. A second fall near Luibeg Bridge fractured the ankle. Both he and his wife stayed there and got very cold, although helped by a passer-by who gave both of them bivvy bags and food. Braemar MRT reached them seven hours after the fracture. Stretchered out. 22.

AUGUST 4 – RAF Sea King airlifted man (53) cragfast at Tronach Head, between Findochty and Portknockie. HM Coastguard units and Buckie RNLI lifeboat.

AUGUST 18 – HM Coastguard units rescued cragfast male (16) from cliffs at Lunan Bay, Montrose.

AUGUST 19 – Schoolboy (15) had been on campsite for three weeks, borrowed waterproofs, map, compass and whistle, then set off for Macdui at 10.30. Reported missing by gear lender. Cairngorm MRT and SARDA assembled, but despite mist he turned up at 22.45. 13.

AUGUST 22 – Man (43) killed by fall from gravel path 25cm wide with sheer sea cliffs of 45m either side at Bullers of Buchan, Aberdeenshire. He had heard there was a stranded sheep. His wife stopped when path got narrow. He carried on till he could go no farther and was returning at his wife's call when he slipped. HM coastguard, Peterhead lifeboat.

AUGUST 28-29 – Cairngorm MRT alerted for party of three overdue at Cairngorm Carpark from Carn a' Mhaim. Turned up just after midnight.

SEPTEMBER 6 – Man (68) died of a stroke when with a party of 20 on Glas Tulaichean. Stretcher carry by Tayside teams. 252.

SEPTEMBER 10-11 – Two overdue from Lairig Ghru arrived safe next morning. Cairngorm MRT. 2.

SEPTEMBER 12 – Descending Lochnagar path in snow and mist a woman (30) stumbled near Foxes Wells below Meikle Pap, twisting a hip. Companion used mobile phone. Directed by Grampian Police to walk to Land-Rover track unaided, then lifted to car. 2.

SEPTEMBER 13-14 – After a suicide note was found in a car at forest walks near Banchory, searches were made by Aberdeen and Braemar MRTs, SARDA and RAF Sea King. Man (55) was found on Hill of Tillylair, 1.5 km into woods, by search dog and taken to hospital suffering suspected overdose. 392.

SEPTEMBER 20 – After climbing all day helmeted and roped, student (18) scrambled, unroped with no helmet, up slopes of Red Craig, Glen Clova, to watch others of his party of 30 rock climbing. He slipped and fell. Evacuation by Tayside teams and RAF Sea King but he died in hospital. 54.

SEPTEMBER 20 – Ascending Coire Raibeirt after a night at Loch Avon, father and son (9) took up the rear of a party of eight. Person at front dislodged a rock which struck the son on the back of his head, cutting it. Members of party climbed to plateau to obtain good communications using a mobile phone. Airlift by RAF Sea King. 8.

OCTOBER 18 – Patient (34) suffering depression went missing in dense woodland near Crathie. She was found by a SARDA dog half submerged in a drainage ditch suffering disorientation and hypothermia. Airlift by RAF Sea King. Braemar MRT. 45.

OCTOBER 19 – Walking with his wife in wind and sleet up the path to Loch Callater, Braemar, man (74) died instantly. Well equipped for the weather they had walked 1km up a gentle incline. He had a heart by-pass 10 years ago. Grampian Police. 2.

OCTOBER 25-26 – Three young men were in trouble in bad weather near Shelter Stone, Loch Avon. The youngest (17) was soaking and hypothermic. He was succoured by two hillwalkers, with hot food, dry clothing, sleeping bag and tent space. He was left with his two companions in the hillwalkers' tent. They then undertook a night walk via Strath Nethy to Glenmore Lodge to alert rescuers. RAF Sea King airlifted him, dropping casualty and three Cairngorm MRT at Glenmore Lodge by 03.30 hours. 24.

OCTOBER 26-27 – Using only a guidebook diagram, father (42) and son (12) with three dogs got lost on north side of Lairig Ghru. Although intending to stay on Glenmore side of range they walked through to Carn a' Mhaim shoulder and were found in bad weather by SARDA and Braemar MRT, Cairngorm MRT. 387.

NOVEMBER 1 – With no torches and poor clothing, woman (64) and man (59) attempted a waymarked low-level walk of 12km from Mar Lodge to Invercauld Bridge, Braemar. Overdue, eight hours later, they were found by Grampian Police MRT still 4.5km west of their objective. Although they had a photocopied map and good weather, the delay was caused by inability to navigate. 3.

NOVEMBER 8-9 – Near Clachnaben, Glen Dye, Banchory, a couple (36, 35) were lost between Charr Bothy and Creaganducy Hill throughout a windy night. RAF Sea King, Braemar MRT.

NOVEMBER 8-9 – Party of two reported at 09.00 on 9th in trouble in Fiacaill Couloir of Cairn Lochan. Cragfast on route from previous day. Cairngorm MRT.

NOVEMBER 18 – Three men, not all equipped with torches, were benighted returning to Linn o' Dee carpark from Macdui area, not having planned for short daylight. Got themselves down before midnight. Grampian Police MRT. 4.

NOVEMBER 18-19 – Delayed by others ahead of them, a roped pair (m34, f30) ice climbing Jacob's Ladder, Coire an t-Sneachda were cragfast overnight. Too weakened by cold to climb next day, alarm was raised by another climber. Winched by RAF Sea King during a weather window. Cairngorm MRT. 31.

NOVEMBER 24-27 – A man (23) equipped with tent, sleeping bag, spare clothing, ice axe, rope, harness etc. camped near Shelter Stone one night, then north of Macdui next night. On third day, trying to get to Macdui summit his map blew away. He had a compass and GPS but without a map did not know which direction to go off the mountain in cloud. He dialled 999 twice on his mobile phone and was connected with Grampian Police, then Tayside Police. However, he could not be contacted with directions because he turned off the phone to conserve battery. His phone was pay-as-you-talk which had not been paid. Phone company gave him two-day credit but there was still no reply. After being buffeted in his bivvy bag by strong winds for four hours he went down to Loch Etchachan but he slipped on rocks and fell in the loch. He got out, went to north of loch, changed into some dry clothes, pitched his tent and camped a third night. On 27th he walked north towards Loch Avon and was found by RAF Sea King. Overnight there had been a full-scale search involving helicopter and SARDA, Aberdeen, Braemar, Cairngorm and Grampian Police MRTs. 987.

DECEMBER 5 – Walker damaged knee tendons but carried on for two hours till unable. Evacuated from Glen Einich by Cairngorm MRT using fwd vehicle. 10.

DECEMBER 5 – Solo walker (22) avalanched in Coire Raibeirt, Cairngorm, fell 125m with facial cuts and limb bruises. Three passers-by heard his shouts and tented him. One went for help. Cairngorm MRT and RAF Sea King. 76.

DECEMBER 20-21 – Three men (53, 20, 19) overdue on Macdhui got down to police vehicle at Derry Lodge at 01.10 hours but did not know which route they had descended from summit. 10.

DECEMBER 26-27 – Tayside MRT deployed after car reported in Glen Clova in atrocious weather. Couple had intended to do two Munros but had trouble with car and found bed in closed youth hostel. False alarm. 35.

DECEMBER 28 – 'Abandoned' tent reported on plateau between Cairn Lochan and Lurchers. Checked out by local climbers/rescuers. Owner claimed it next day.

DECEMBER 29 – At 18.15 hours a pair of inexperienced walkers reported two people in distress on Cairngorm Plateau. They turned up OK an hour later. Cairngorm MRT.

SOUTHERN HIGHLANDS

JANUARY 10 – Rescuer (29) on exercise was descending into a burn 1.4km north of Ben More summit, Crianlarich when a rock gave way. He fell 1.5m striking his head on rocky opposite side of burn bed. He sustained six-stitch scalp wound, slight compression to C spine and bruised knee. Winched by RN Sea King. Leuchars MRT (on scene). 14.

JANUARY 15 – False alarm. HM Coastguard searched Beinn Ghuilean, Kintyre, on report of white light flashing on summit. Nothing found. 39.

JANUARY 16-17 – Solo walker (50) with limited mountain experience and suffering a heart defect changed his plans. Teams searched Ben Oss, but distress whistles and shouts were reported on Ben Lui where he was found cold, but uninjured, cragfast on ENE Ridge. Lowered down crag then escorted down to airlift by HMS Gannet helicopter. Killin, Leuchars, SARDA. Rewarming aids used. 660.

JANUARY 17-18 – Three men (47, 47, 41) left Inverarnan at 11.30 to climb Beinn Chabhair. Due to wet weather turned back before summit, but were very slow and got benighted. Attempting river crossing in dark one got swept downstream but gained bank. Reached hotel 22.30 but informed no-one till 09.30. Police searched hill and main roads after the three were reported missing at 05.45. Killin MRT on standby.

JANUARY 21-22 – In a party of one man and three dogs, Spikey a Jack Russell terrier bitch (12) occupation – ratter, failed to jump across a rock fissure on A'Chrois, and was lost by her shepherd-owner during gathering. Arrochar MRT descended 39m vainly because fissure continued too small for men. Shepherd returned and heard barking so second team mobilised and eventually retrieved Spikey, alive but in shock having fallen 42m.

JANUARY 25 – Woman (32) in party of 11 on SE Ridge, Creag Mhor, Glen Lochay slipped on ice and snow and fractured her left ankle. Airlift by RAF Sea King. Killin MRT. 8.

JANUARY 25 – Two climbers attempting West Gully, Beinn Udlaidh in calm freezing conditions retreated from 6m up it at 14.15. Abseil piton held for first descender, but failed for the second who got probable spinal injuries. Airlifted about 17.00 by RN Sea King. Arrochar MRT. 44.

JANUARY 25 – Male (26) in party of three descending gully between Beinn an Dothaid and Beinn Achaladair at night (20.53 hours) slipped and got leg injury. Winched by RAF Sea King. Strathclyde Police MRT.

FEBRUARY 15 – Woman (62) in a party of at least six, slipped on the Law, Ochil Hills fracturing tibia and fibula in three places. Stretcher carry by Ochils MRT. 29.

FEBRUARY 20 – Walker (28) with three others searching wet forest at night to find Glen Loin caves, slipped and damaged his knee. Stretchered out by Arrochar MRT. 30.

MARCH 7 – Two men (56, 55) separated from six others walking on Ben Oss, Beinn Dubhchraig. When others returned to tents, pair were missing. They turned up later, overdue from poor navigation. Killin MRT. 3.

MARCH 15 – Killin and Leuchars teams were on night exercise using searchlight at Loch Dochart. Hoaxer went up Ben More and flashed a light to try to get rescuers to go up to find him. MRTs did not respond. 9.

MARCH 24 – Descending S. Ridge, Cobbler, walker (56) slipped injuring her leg. Helped down part way by partner who then went for help. Stretchered by Arrochar MRT. 42.

APRIL 10 – Man (25) descending NW Ridge, Beinn Dubhchraig, using walking poles, stumbled and fell to ground fracturing his lower leg. With two companions during snow and strong wind. Killin MRT, RN Sea King. 18.

APRIL 21 – SARDA searched dense woods at Todholes Farm for two boys (11, 10) who had run off, tired, wet and hungry, after climbing Meikle Bin (570m), Carron Valley Reservoir, Fintry. They walked out OK. 20.

APRIL 26 – Man, in party of two, fell from S. Peak, Cobbler. Alarm raised by mobile phone. RAF Sea King on exercise with Glencoe MRT aboard diverted and airlifted casualty who sustained head, pelvic and abdominal injuries. Arrochar and Strathclyde Pol MRTs. 8.

MAY 4 – Walker (57) descending south side An Caisteal fell sustaining open femur fracture and serious head injury. Airlift by RAF Sea King and Killin MRT but he died shortly after admission to hospital. 104.

MAY 16 – Paraglider (38) on tuition holiday lost control taking off from Ochil Hills, near Myreton Hill. He injured a leg and was stretchered to a 4WD vehicle by Ochils MRT. 34.

MAY 17 – Unroped climber (46) fell from The Gendarme on the Whangie, Kilpatrick Hills, when setting up a top rope for his partner. Severe injuries were saved from being worse because he was wearing a helmet. Ochils MRT (on site) 6.

MAY 19 – Man (66) collapsed near summit of Beinn Dorain. Airlift by RN Sea King to Vale of Leven Hospital, but he had died from a heart attack. Strathclyde Police MRT. 17.

JUNE 3 – Two cragfast persons rescued from sea cliff at Elie, Fife. HM Coastguard.

JUNE 7 – Taypol SRU stretchered fallen walker (f32) from Schiehallion in bad weather, suffering leg injuries. Carried to winching point by RN Sea King. 28.

JUNE 13 – RAF Sea King winched fallen walker (54) from NE Ridge, An Stuc, Ben Lawers. He had head, chest leg injuries. 8.

JUNE 14 – Female in Duke of Edinburgh group slipped on path in good weather in Glen Donich, fracturing her ankle. Stretchered out by staff of Scout Activity Centre.

JUNE 21 – Four scouts on challenge hike in Ochils area missing after last checkpoint. Found on road by Ochils MRT about seven hours overdue. 13.

JUNE 29 – Lost looking for alpine flowers in Coire Heasgairnich of Beinn Heasgairnich, man (68) followed burn down into Glen Lochay, then track back to his start point. Killin MRT. 2.

JUNE 30 – Six girls (c18) on award hike, last seen at Glashoile, Loch Katrine, went too high above Bealach nam Bo, struggling round steep slopes on Ben Venue. Walked into camp at 23.00. Killin MRT. 11.

JULY 8-9 – Killin MRT stretchered pupil (12) down from remote scout camp west of Tarmachan Range, Glen Lochay. He had suspected cold trauma but was discharged after hospital check. 46.

JULY 18 – Mountain biker (52) injured his head and chest on a track near the head of Loch Turret Reservoir, Crieff. Airlift by RAF Sea King. 8.

AUGUST 6-7 – Search by Arrochar MRT for dog, Fudge, lost during wet weather in thick forest and crags of Glen Goil. Dog was passed but had not barked. Found by owner on crag next day. 15.

AUGUST 9 – Minnie, a Jack Russell terrier, walking with her owner, slipped down a slope to the river in Dollar Glen. Lifted out in a rucksack by Ochils MRT. 6.

August 11-12 – Killin MRT, five SARDA dogs and RN Sea King searched NE slopes of Ben More, Crianlarich for four inexperienced men (35, 34, 33, 16) lost overnight in mist and rain. The men spotted a dog upwind of them above the treeline. They followed him and alerted his handler. Airlifted, cold, wet but uninjured. 98.

AUGUST 22-23 – Separated from two companions, woman (51) hurt ankle descending An Caisteal and got benighted. Found next morning by Killin MRT search on north slopes Stob Glas and airlifted by RN Sea King, No hospital treatment required. Lomond MRT and SARDA stood by. 236.

AUGUST 23 – Attempting to reach Cruach Ardrain by a very muddy forest path from Crianlarich, man (24) tripped and fell, breaking a wrist. Killin MRT did first aid and friends escorted him to hospital. 1.

SEPTEMBER 17-18 – Biker (57) attempting circuit of Loch Katrine was unequipped for cliffs at water's edge. At dark he stopped for the night. Killin MRT got him out by boat at 01.00. 8.

SEPTEMBER 26-27 – Having lost a compass, pair (m73, f48) were delayed in mist on the plateau of Meall Glas, Glen Dochart, and were reported adrift by a companion who had turned back. They turned up OK at 05.10. Overnight searches by 21 of Killin MRT. 158.

SEPTEMBER 26-27 – Lost in rain, wind, mist and darkness on Beinn Dorain, a couple (m61, f27) were found by Strathclyde Police MRT and escorted to Bridge of Orchy overnight. 68.

OCTOBER 1 – Cragfast person rescued from sea cliff at Kirkcaldy, Fife. HM Coastguard.

OCTOBER 10-11 – A car parked below Ben Ledi caused police inquiries which could not rule out an accident. Killin MRT and SARDA searched in sleet, rain and strong wind finding a couple (f30, m27) who said they planned to stay out overnight but left no route card. 44.

OCTOBER 13 – Ochils MRT searched for two schoolboys (16, 13) camping overnight in rain and gale in Alva Glen. They turned up OK but it was thought they had been at Balquharn Dam, 2km distant. 5.

October 16 – Male shepherd returning from tending his sheep was crossing a small bridge which was carried away due to heavy rain. Wind was ESE near gale and visibility poor. Doctor pronounced him dead on bank of burn 5km inland from Southend, Kintyre as Southend Coastguards arrived. Airlift to Machrihanish. 15.

OCTOBER 21 – Three men (31, 24, 17) canyoning down a fast river through Devil's Pulpit (Carnock Burn at Finnich Glen) were impeded by a fallen tree. Stuck down the steep 20m gorge they were rescued by Lomond MRT abseilers who attached harnesses and hoisted them. Suffering abrasions they were cleared by ambulance men. RN Sea King stood by in case of hypothermia. Central Police Underwater Team. 40.

OCTOBER 26-27 – Solo walker (55) with inadequate torch and waterproofs got benighted in deteriorating weather on forested hills to north of Inversnaid . He had not allowed for clocks going back previous night. He got down to West Highland Way at Loch Lomond and stayed put. Found by teams in small hours. Killin and Lomond. 35.

NOVEMBER 16-17 – Wife carried on walking and got lost when husband stopped to put on knee brace to descend from Ben Venue summit. She wandered down north side and got stuck on steep ground with no equipment. Husband returned down Ledard path, the route they had ascended. Unsuccessful night search in freezing but good weather by Killin and Lomond MRTs and SARDA. RN and RAF Sea Kings. She would have been found if she had a torch. Found uninjured next day by crag search. MRT spotted her red hat using binoculars. 290.

NOVEMBER 16-17 – Starting from Callander, man (59) underestimated time to walk up Ben Vorlich (L. Earn). He found shelter till daylight then was found very cold by helicopter. The aircraft was able to search above cloud due to a temperature inversion. Killin and Tayside MRTs, SARDA. 29.

NOVEMBER 17 – Walker (52) descending Ben Ledi path alone slipped on icy rocks breaking her ankle. RN Sea King dropped first-aiders but could not evacuate casualty. Stretchered by Killin MRT. 30.

DECEMBER 28-29 – After traversing Ben Oss and Beinn Dhubhchraig, man without crampons (34) and dog, were both slipping on ice descending. Several routes were attempted vainly, then they sheltered and set off down at first light. Spotted by Killin MRT and RN Sea King. Man and dog walked off. RAF Leuchars MRT. 160.

DECEMBER 29 – Descending the North Ridge path of Ben Vorlich (L. Earn) in snow and ice, a man (51) without crampons slipped and lost his axe as he fell 150m. Sustaining head and chest injuries, he was stretchered by Killin MRT then winched by RAF Sea King. Both Tayside teams involved. 214.

SKYE

APRIL 4-5 – Party of seven descended Inaccessible Pinnacle then took a wrong bearing. Two went down leaving five cragfast overnight on icy rock on Coruisk side of the pinnacle. Winched by RAF Sea King. Skye MRT. 295.

APRIL 2 – Men (34, 32) and a woman (32) underestimated time required and severity of a roped rock climb (VD) in Harta Corrie. No route plan was left, resulting in an extensive search by Skye MRT. Airlift HMCG helicopter. 159.

MAY 15 – Experienced member (43) left his party on Dubhs Ridge to find alternative route, but could not find way back to other seven. They descended, reported him missing, but he got down OK. Skye MRT. 1.

MAY 29 – Walker (57) slipped on sand and gravel path, falling awkwardly and breaking her leg. Found by passer-by near the Old Man of Storr. Skye MRT and Ambulance Service. Winched by HMCG helicopter. 11.

JUNE 1-2 – One of a pair (f39, m38) got cragfast and was freed by the other, probably in the upper part of Eastern Gully, Sron na Ciche. Then physically and mentally fatigued they were unable to complete route, using whistle and orange bag to raise alarm. Skye MRT and airlift by RAF Sea King. 29.

JUNE 1-2 – Two pairs climbed Fiaclan Dearg on west of Marsco. Unroped pair took route on south side and were delayed. Pair who had climbed farther north route and descended thought the others were cragfast and raised alarm. RAF Rescue 137 Sea King found them benighted on Marso summit and winched them off. 23.

JUNE 2-3 – One of seven in Eastern Gully, Sron na Ciche, on Left Edge Route upper Cioch Buttress, roped male (25) fell 10m on to feet when 70m up route, injuring both legs. HMCG helicopter and Skye MRT. Winched by RAF Sea King. 159.

JUNE 4 – Doing the Ridge and traversing An Stac with three companions, a man (41) was struck by a rock dislodged by another. He fell 6m which caused broken wrist and ribs. Stretcher lowered by Skye MRT to airlift by HMCG. 68.

JUNE 16 – Man (33) climbed gully thinking it would get him to the Quiraing Table. He got cragfast. Passer-by contacted Police on mobile phone. He was talked down by Skye MRT. 19.

JUNE 20 – Man (50) left behind by 13 companions on Am Basteir in good weather. Seen OK well off route on steep loose ground. Found by passer-by with head, chest and arm injuries, abrasions and bruising. Flown by RN Sea King to Glasgow Southern General Hospital. Skye MRT. 18.

JUNE 26 – Walking in party of four near col of Sgurr nan Each/Clach Glas. Rocks gave way under man (32) who fell 18m with facial lacerations and ankle fracture. Winched by RAF Sea King. Kintail and Skye teams assembled. 32

JULY 1 – Descending through forestry below the Storr, woman (33) slipped, landed heavily and broke her ankle. Winched by HMCG helicopter for treatment at Broadford. Skye MRT. 16.

JULY 7 – Descending in good weather through forestry below the Storr, woman slipped and broke her ankle on rocky path. Airlifted by HMCG helicopter to Broadford. 11.

JULY 28 – Using tourist guide as a map five lads (all 17) thought they had climbed Inaccessible Pinnacle, but mistakenly descended from the Main Ridge on the Coruisk side in mist, rain and wind. Three stronger ones walked round. Other two winched from Coruisk area by HMCG helicopter. Skye MRT. 67.

AUGUST 8 – Woman (55) in a party of 24 descending path from Old Man of Storr, went over her ankle, breaking it. Skye MRT and HMCG helicopter. 25.

AUGUST 12 – False alarm. Climber reported whistle blasts from Sgurr a'Bhasteir. Skye MRT thought it would be single piping of a golden plover, but search was made to ensure no person in trouble. 21.

AUGUST 20 – Housewife (58) slipped on wet grass on Quiraing Tourist Path injuring an ankle. Helped by passers-by then taken to hospital by husband. Skye MRT. 11.

AUGUST 30 – Poor navigation in good weather led to five novices finding themselves in very difficult ground between Sgurr Alasdair and Sgurr Sgumain. Man (28) fell 25m with head, back, arm and punctured lung injuries. Winched by RAF Sea King. Skye MRT. 56.

AUGUST 30 – Woman (23) got cragfast on Sron Mhor, Talisker Bay. Companion went for help. Two coastguards walked her to the summit after nightfall and she was airlifted by HMCG helicopter. 42.

SEPTEMBER 24-25 – Extensive search by Skye MRT and RAF Sea King when distress shouts from a male person were reported from Meall Odhar of Sgurr a'Bhasteir. Nothing found and no-one overdue. 80.

OCTOBER 4 – Walker (26) in riding boots, inadequately clad and unequipped, underestimated time and difficulty of walk from Loch na Dal to Kylerhea. In rain and wind she had river-crossing problems and got lost and exhausted trying to descend woodland in darkness. Used mobile phone repeatedly. She was eventually found by Skye MRT less than 2km from start point at Kinloch Lodge. 34.

OCTOBER 7-8 – Crofters answered a flashing light signal from near the Prison, Quiraing. They got a response to their reply and searched. Their later shouts were not answered so Skye MRT were involved. A US national was found bivouacking in a cave. He was left there because he did not wish to be rescued. 66.

OCTOBER 8 – Wife (45) slipped on loose ground on Quiraing Tourist Path and fell 9m into a gorge sustaining head injuries. HMCG helicopter airlift. 8.

OCTOBER 8 – Husband (45) went to the rescue of his wife after the previous incident He slid down the slope but also fell into the gorge with minor injuries. Passer-by called Police and Ambulance Service. Winched by HMCG helicopter. 8.

OCTOBER 27 – Walker (39) slid on Old Man of Storr path, breaking her ankle in freezing hail and rain during a gale. Aided by others she descended till pain became excessive. Then she was stretchered by Skye MRT. 16.

ISLANDS OTHER THAN SKYE

FEBRUARY 9 – Missing female at Back, Lewis. HMCG helicopter.

APRIL 10 – Missing person on South Harris. HMCG helicopter.

APRIL 16 – Schoolboy (16) cragfast and suffering hypothermia on A'Chir Ridge, Arran in conditions of icy rock. Arran MRT. Winched by RN Sea King. 28.

APRIL 29 – HM Coastguard searched for angler (68) overdue from Loch Gorm, Islay. He got back late but OK. 4.

APRIL 26 – Climbers returning from Cir Mhor, Arran, jumped into Rosa Burn to cool off. Student (20) did not realise shallowness and broke his ankle. Stretchered by Arran MRT. 13.

MAY 5 – While wife visited Cathedral Cave, Eigg, spouse (53) climbed rocks near it. Foothold gave way and he fell 4m shattering teeth and fracturing pelvis. Mobile phone used for HMCG helicopter airlift to Belford Hospital. 13.

MAY 29 – Missing person at Ness, Lewis. HMCG helicopter.

JUNE 8 Hermaness Nature Reserve, Unst, Shetland. Walker broke ankle 3km from nearest road. HMCG helicopter.

JUNE 20-21 – Walker (f33) on Ronas Hill, Shetland was reported overdue by another walker worried about mist, but the west side of the hill where she had been was mist free and she wanted to see midsummer sunset. Walked out unhurt. Northern Constabulary, HMCG Auxiliaries. 54.

JUNE 26 – Angler with broken leg at Loch Langahat, Lewis. HMCG helicopter.

JULY 26 – Missing person at Scaliscro Estate, North Harris. HMCG helicopter.

Lofoten: View from below the ridge from the Budalstinden to summit of Vagakallen. Photo: Derek Fabian.

(Left): Canadian ice fall climbing. Alan Kerr on 'Kemosabe' (Canadian Grade III,4), Naiparous Creek in the Ghost Valley area north of Calgary. Photo: Peter Stewart.

Whiteman Falls (Canadian Grade IV,6), Opal Creek, Kananaskis, Canmore.. Photo: David Ritchie.

TREVOR RANSLEY

SANDY COUSI

JIM DONALDSON

ROSS HIGGIN

AUGUST 7 – Reported missing after separation from companion in mist on Stacach Ridge, Goat Fell, (m57) was found at ferry terminal. Arran MRT. 12.

AUGUST 12 – Injured angler airlifted by HMCG at Loch Langavat, Lewis.

AUGUST 15 – Person over cliffs airlifted by HMCG at Aird Uig, Lewis.

SEPTEMBER 13 – HM Coastguard assembled in Jura to search for two hillwalkers overdue. They were spotted descending. 13.

SEPTEMBER 14 – Male (43) and female (42) waymarking and painting a new tourist route from Bosta to Tobson, Great Bernera, Lewis were overdue. They walked out uninjured. HMCG helicopter.

SOUTHERN UPLANDS

MARCH 28-29 – All four S. Uplands MRTs and SARDA searched forests of Ewesdown Fell, Megget Water for lost deerstalker (29). He was found exhausted next day and evacuated by RAF helicopter. No compass, spare clothing or food. 272.

MAY 31 – Borders SARU, Tweed Valley MRT and SARDA searched Pentland Hills for five lost children from a group of 10 on Duke of Edinburgh gold award hike. They had waited in tents for rescue. Found by RAF Sea King. 25.

JUNE 20 – Walker (52) descending Craiglee, Glen Trool, found the going too difficult. Her husband went for help. Meantime, passers-by strapped up knee and ankle and helped her to their car. Galloway MRT. 6.

JULY 1 – Two men (25, 23) ahead of schedule on 234km boundary charity walk in Galloway Hills heard on local radio that they were missing – so they phoned in. Galloway MRT on standby.

AUGUST 15 – Cragfast person rescued from sea cliff at Peace Bay, Berwickshire. HM Coastguard.

AUGUST 17 – Cragfast person rescued from sea cliff at Eyemouth, Berwickshire. HM Coastguard.

AUGUST 22-23 – Competitor (45) in 32km Rings of Fire event in Galloway Hills got tired. He failed to check in at the Sluice of Loch Enoch and was found in Newton Stewart. Galloway MRT and SARDA. 63.

SEPTEMBER 26 – Fell runner found well off route, cold but uninjured by Moffat MRT providing safety cover for hill race. 40.

OCTOBER 20-21 – Walking Southern Upland Way alone in storm conditions a man (75) was unable to ford a spate burn in the dark. He survived the night in a bivvy bag in a wood at Loch of the Lowes (near Tibbie Shiels Inn) and walked out next day. His luggage (containing heart medication) had gone ahead by bus so he only carried a day bag. Tweed Valley and Borders MRTs, Moffat MRU and SARDA, RAF Sea King. 347.

NON MOUNTAINEERING

Late report: JULY 18-21, 1997 – Grampian Police, Braemar and Aberdeen MRTs searched Bedford/Powis area of Aberdeen for body of a murdered child (9). A man was arrested and the body of the child was recovered by police after the arrest. 973.

Late report: (1997 incident). JANUARY 4-5, 1998 – Searches of Aberfoyle woods by four SARDA dogs, Strathclyde, Central Scotland police and police helicopter for couple (both 38) missing since December 18, 1997. Subsequent find in a grave in Ayrshire led to murder inquiry. 67.

JANUARY 7-September 4, 1998 – Searches by Ochils MRT and SARDA on January 8-9 for prison officer (38) missing near Alloa. He had been receiving treatment for depression. His body was found hanging in overgrown woods near Stirling Castle on September 4, 1998.

JANUARY 16 – Search of woodlands on edge of Sheriff Muir, Dunblane, for woman (69) missing from retirement home. She was found OK but cold. Police and RN helicopter and SARDA. Rewarming aids used. 56

JANUARY 20 – Positive find by SARDA. Two dogs were used in search for two men (90, 74) missing from nursing home in Croftamie. Police helicopter. Lomond MRT. Both men had been stuck in a gully; one having slipped and fallen, the other having slithered to help him. 22.

JANUARY 21-22 – Arrochar and Strathclyde Police MRTs, SARDA and RN Sea King searched North Kintyre for rescue beacon picked up by satellite. It moved at each satellite pass. Teams stood down when told beacon could be anywhere in 25km radius. Eventually, a detector traced beacon to a yacht in Tarbert Harbour. 241.

FEBRUARY 2 – Search by Tweed Valley MRT and SARDA of hospital grounds for two people (m80, f78) suffering dementia, ill-clad for weather. Found in locked-off part of building more than four hours after last seen. Staff heard noises and they were seen on security video. Checks by staff and doctor. 45.

FEBRUARY 16 – Tweed Valley MRT searched woodland, river and housing for depressed woman (29) with tablets. She returned OK, but wet and cold. 33.

FEBRUARY 19 – Successful SARDA two-dog search for diabetic youth (18) who had drunk alcohol. He was found semi-conscious and hypothermic by dog in dense woodland in Falkirk. 17.

FEBRUARY 24 – SARDA *en route* to search woods for girl (13) missing near Bannockburn when she was found safe. 6.

FEBRUARY 25-26 – Braemar and Grampian Police MRTs searched near Ballater Golf Course and found man (66) face down in River Dee, who had apparently committed suicide. 13.

MARCH 16 – SARDA searched river banks for man (31) missing from home at Dumgoyne. Police dogs searched West Highland Way. He returned home well. Lomond MRT. 37.

MARCH 28-29 – Two boys (17, 16) in borrowed boat capsized in Loch Lomond. One managed to swim 1km to shore using Inversnaid Hotel lights. RN helicopter and Luss rescue boat found upturned boat. Lomond MRT searched W and E shores. Divers have continued search but no body has been found yet. 150.

APRIL 25-28 – RAF Leuchars MRT helped Fife Police search open ground and banks of River Leven, Methil, for man last seen April 25 who failed to reach home on far side of river. Nothing found. 93.

APRIL 30 – Strathclyde Police MRT called out to remove body of suicide victim (m74) from sea cliffs at Culzean Castle, Ayrshire. 4.

MAY 9 – SARDA searched Gartmorn Dam, Alloa for man (23). Later traced by Police. 8.

MAY 23-24 – SARDA, Tweed Valley MRT , Borders SRU and Underwater Search Team searched woods and heavy undergrowth for man (51) missing from hospital. He suffered depression. Futher search next day found his body hanging from a tree. 187.

JUNE 11 – Extensive search of banks of swollen River Esk by Moffat MRT for missing fisherman. Body later found in Solway Firth. 184.

JUNE 13 – SARDA searched Dollarbeg for occupants of a crashed car, who may have been injured and wandered off. One woman (16) found with arm and leg injuries. 1.

JULY 4 – Body of a male suicide victim recovered from Loch Tulla by Strathclyde Police MRT. He had been located by police helicopter. 38.

JULY 7 - SARDA searched woods of Callendar Estate, Falkirk for missing woman who returned home safe and well after an emergency visit to Glasgow.

AUGUST 1-2 – Two ground teams, boat team, two helicopter passes, two dog searches, failed to find body of a man (67) trapped in debris in River Tweed at Waterburn. After drinking he walked his dog at 23.30 but dog went home alone. Found by Tweed Valley MRT search at 14.00 as river level dropped. Find was dependent on clarity and level of water. RAF Sea King, SARDA. 146.

AUGUST 4-5 – Tweed Valley MRT on standby to search at Jedburgh for missing woman who was found safe at home.

AUGUST 22 – Moffat MRT request SARDA search for person fallen in a river at Selkirk.

AUGUST 24 – Abandoned vehicle reported at edge of woods near Larbert. Police searched woods and quarry. Body (m51) found hanging from tree by police dog. Ochils MRT recovered body from deep undergrowth. 23.

SEPTEMBER 8 – Tweed Valley MRT and SARDA found man (63) suffering depression, hiding in woodland on Selkirk Common. He had to be removed by police.

SEPTEMBER 16 Two SARDA dogs en route to search for boy (10) missing in woods at Bannockburn, when he was found safe by police. 2.

SEPTEMBER 19 – SARDA requested but stood down. Depressed woman involved in minor road accident and made off. Car found at Logie Kirk at foot of Ochil Hills. Traced in a distraught state by police sweep search.

OCTOBER 6 – SARDA (S) declined police request to search woods at Balfron for a prolific criminal who had gone to ground.

OCTOBER 8-13 – Body of missing man (41) found on 13th hanging near his home in Tullibody by SARDA dog. Three SARDA dogs used. Evacuation by Ochils MRT. 94.

OCTOBER 15-16 – Walking 8km from Bucksburn to Clinterty, drunk student (16) got separated from group helping a friend who had fallen into a culvert. Due to poor weather and intoxication, Braemar and Grampian Police MRTs assembled to search, but he turned up, still drunk, after sleeping in a field. 78.

OCTOBER 22 – Braemar and Grampian Police MRTs, search dogs and volunteer estate workers searched the grounds of Drum Castle, near Peterculter, Aberdeenshire. Body of missing male (68) suspected suicide victim found by forestry worker in heavy woodland. 22.

NOVEMBER 1-2 – Moffat MRT, six SARDA dogs and police helicopter searched overnight in mist and sub-zero temperatures for missing elderly lady with dementia. Found at Kelloholm suffering mild hypothermia. 220.

DECEMBER 2-3 – Retired woman (65) shopping in village new to her (Greenlaw) slipped on grassy path after getting lost. She hugged her dog all night for heat. Found mildly hypothermic by SARDA dog on second day of search. Borders SAR and Tweed Valley MRT with five SARDA dogs. 21.

DECEMBER 16 – Moffat MRT assembled at Thornhill to search for missing elderly lady, whose body was found in River Nith by HMS Gannet helicopter. 28.

DECEMBER 17-18 – Tweed Valley MRT searched hospital grounds for woman (27) thought to be suicidal. Police located her OK elsewhere. 52.

DECEMBER 26-27 – Woman (18) in lightweight clothing probably took wrong turning 6km west of Perth when walking home from a party, dying from hypothermia. Found by RAF Sea King. Both Tayside teams, SARDA, divers and Strathclyde helicopter involved. 2000.

IN MEMORIAM

JAMES C. DONALDSON j. 1950

JIM DONALDSON was a lad o' pairts who during his long life served his fellow human beings and his Country to a remarkable degree. Born on January 18, 1913 in Falkland where his father was a bank manager who was killed while serving as an officer in the Black Watch in France in 1917. The family moved to Dundee, and subsequently, to Edinburgh in 1930. He was educated at Sedbergh School and Edinburgh University at which both establishments he excelled as a cross-country runner.

On leaving school he joined the Bank of Scotland where he spent his entire working life. Always a meticulous record keeper, the log of his mountain expeditions starts in April 1933 with the lone ascent of Sgurr Alaisdair and Thearlach. His last rock climb was also in Skye, Eastern Buttress Direct, which he climbed at the age of 73 with Bill Wallace. In the interval, and for a few years thereafter, he enjoyed expeditions, often alone, of considerable length which were prodigious by any standard, as well as making many rock and snow-ice climbs.

There is a gap from 1939 to 1946 in his log with the exception of Mount Hermon, in Jordan, in October 1942. In 1939 he joined the Black Watch along with his brother, George, and as 1940 closed they set off for Crete to join the 2nd Battalion. The invasion of Crete was the first major engagement against the German Army since Dunkirk and details of the enemy plan to land an Airborne Division at the airfield at Heraklion were known because the German code system Enigma had by this time been cracked.

To mask this knowledge for future operations the defences were laid out in an orthodox manner with the Black Watch at Heraklion. By accident or design the Battalion had been issued with Bren machine gun tripods which enabled the weapon to fire skywards effectively and very heavy casualties were inflicted on the descending paratroops before they reached the ground. Even so, bitter fighting continued for 10 days with great ferocity. During a battle on the airfield Jim drove a motor cycle across the field under fire to aid the crews of two British planes and was injured crashing into a bomb crater and was recommended for the Military Cross. Things did not go so well at the other end of the island and the British and New Zealand Garrison was evacuated by the Royal Navy in the teeth of terrific enemy bombing with heavy loss of ships and life. More than 200 of the Black Watch were killed on the voyage to Egypt.

In October 1941 the Battalion members were taken by destroyers at night into Tobruk to relieve the 9th Australian Division and on November 21 were ordered to break out to join the Eight Army advancing from Sollum. Within an hour it lost 25 officers and 300 men killed and wounded, among whom were Jim and George. Jim was wounded in the knee and waited patiently in a shell hole for 28 hours reading Tennyson waiting to be picked up. In hospital the brothers found that their cousin, Maisie, was one of their nurses and they had a high old time of it escorting her and her friends round the sights of Cairo, on the Nile and to the Pyramids.

After Tobruk the Battalion went to Syria, and in February 1942 embarked for

Rangoon. The Japanese had entered the war in December 1941 and so swift was their advance through Malaya and Burma that the convoy was diverted to Bombay and the unit was soon engaged in training in jungle warfare. In 1942 in West Bengal Jim was awarded his MBE, an almost unique honour for an infantry subaltern, for his attempt to extricate a ration party which had been cut off during a severe cyclone and tidal inundation in which 14 of his Platoon were drowned. An extract from the citation reads: 'Lieutenant Donaldson's gallantry and devotion to his Platoon's welfare, and his complete disregard of his own safety, saved many lives, and will remain an inspiring example of leadership and endurance.'

On his return home in early 1945, having reached the rank of Major, he was appointed Commandant of a Prisoner of War Camp at Monymusk, surely one of the most kind and gentle men ever to hold such a command. On demobilisation he returned to the bank, first in Edinburgh and then in Glasgow. On a climbing holiday in Skye he met Sheila and they were married in May 1949.

Among his climbing companions in the Glasgow JMCS and SMC, which he joined in 1950, were some weel kent members, including George Roger, Trevor Ransley, Hamish Hamilton, Ross Higgins, Russell Marshall and Bertie MacFarlane.

Jim was Treasurer of the Club from 1961 to 1976 during which period the Club's finances increased beyond recognition and he became President in 1976 and Honorary President in 1981. He was Editor of Munro's Tables for many years.

The Donaldsons moved to Braemar in 1958 and their daughter, Fiona, was born in 1961. Fiona, now Mrs Barry Watt, gave birth to a daughter, Catriona, a few days after Jim's passing.

Jim, typically, threw himself into the life of Braemar. He inherited from a long line of bank managers the Weather Recording Station which had been founded in the 1850s by the Prince Consort. He was a founder member and President of the Braemar Mountain Rescue Team and was Treasurer, and later Secretary and Honorary Vice-President of the Braemar Royal Highland Society and played a leading part in organising the Annual Games. For many years he was Session Clerk and Treasurer of Braemar Parish Kirk as well as being Treasurer of the Community Council and the Golf Club. Indeed there seemed to be little in the whole area of which Jim was not Treasurer or Secretary.

The Donaldson's house had a large attic and a caravan in their garden and these became a home from home for many a weary wanderer who enjoyed the marvellous hospitality which they lavished on their countless guests. Among his lovable eccentricities were swimming in summer in his favourite pools and gathering and sawing logs – many tons of which found their way into the homes of elderly folk. He took up cross-country ski-ing and acquired a mountain bike at an age when most men have put their feet up.

After Sheila's death he bought a bungalow at the Inchmarlo Complex at Banchory before moving into the nursing home there for the last two years of his life. From there he made short expeditions with his zimmer, for which the contraption had never been designed, to various spots from which he could sit, smilingly looking up at the hills. A visit to him, even when he became very frail, was an inspiration. To the end he was totally unselfish, modest and contented.

W. M. S. Myles.

SANDY COUSINS j. 1964

MY FIRST encounter with Sandy was in the late 1960s, when he gave me and a friend a lift to a Glasgow JMCS meet on Nevis. Still breaking in my own first proud pair of proper steel-shanked climbing boots, I was appalled to hear him describe with relish how he had recently dismembered and re-assembled a pair of expensive French boots (at that time renowned equally for elegance and for discomfort) to improve their fit and water-resistance. With hindsight, I recognise that that was typical of Sandy's whole-hearted, practical, 'can-do' approach: to life, work, climbing, and mountain conservation.

Another example was the famous Cousins Heatin (SMCJ, 1986 xxxiii, 354). Sandy was an inveterate engineer, tinkerer, modifier, creator. He had unlimited enthusiasm for emblems of affiliation: badges, logos, letterheads, and ties. When none existed, he would design them himself. Even without knowing its registration number, Sandy's estate car could be picked out in any Highland lay-by by the tidy row of official and unofficial badges across the rear windscreen. The Presidential gavel of the Mountaineering Council of Scotland, neatly shaped from an antler and with Sandy's own design for the Council logo lacquered into the butt, is one of his tangible legacies to the climbing community.

Sandy's mountaineering was marked by the same sense of conviction and whole-heartedness: he enjoyed the hills with a huge and comprehensive gusto. His solo walk from Cape Wrath to Glasgow in 1971 (SMCJ, 1972 xxx, 37-47) was a classic excursion. In its impeccable topographical logic, relaxed style, and sense of intense quiet enjoyment, it cast a stark light on the dour hard-driven ego-promoting expeditions of some other Big Walkers.

But above all, Sandy was foremost among those few who translate the SMC's sometimes rather abstract concern for the mountain environment into sustained practical action. He was one of the founding fathers of the Mountaineering Council of Scotland, and its first Honorary Secretary from 1970 to 1978. He was fired into action by the appalling fiasco of the building of the Coruisk track and bridges in 1968, ostensibly for mountain rescue (the fullest account of that saga, based on a report compiled by Sandy, can be found in the Journal, (xxix, 1969, 111-120). Sandy threw himself into the fray, badgering every relevant agency and organisation in strenuous efforts to prevent the work being done, and then to discourage attempts to make it good. The failure of mountaineering and conservation interests, including the ineffective Association of Scottish Climbing Clubs and the nascent Countryside Commission for Scotland, to defend that wild land sanctuary against intrusion drove Sandy and others first into direct action against the bridge at Scavaig ('The fairies at Coruisk' was how Sandy described it) and then into setting up the MCS in 1969-70. It also led him to propose that mountaineers should buy the Black Cuillin. At the time many scoffed, but with hindsight and the experience of the success of the John Muir Trust, we can see that in this, as in other matters, Sandy had more vision than most of us.

With characteristic acuity, Sandy saw at once that MCS would need an executive secretary of drive and energy, and accepted that he would have to supply those qualities himself if the organisation was to achieve the objectives for which he had helped create it. As Secretary he was hugely industrious and efficient. In those pre-word processing days he did much of the necessary writing in his own instantly recognisable sprawling longhand. His approach may at times have been character-ised more by dash than by finesse, but it got results. He wheedled a succession of the Grand Old Men of the SMC into serving as Chairmen of MCS to give it credibility, not least with the doubters of the Club. He belaboured the Scottish Sports Council into accepting – and grant-aiding – MCS as the governing body of mountaineering in Scotland, a feat that involved beating the recalcitrantly square peg of mountaineering values into the adamantine round hole of the SSC's wondrously bureaucratic criteria. The SSC could not comprehend (and for long would not recognise) a body that was not interested in actively enlarging partici-pation in its 'sport'.

He stretched the tolerance of his employers to breaking point by taking time off to attend a host of meetings: on access to the hills, outdoor education, mountain rescue, skills training for club members, mountain conservation, and much else. More or less single-handedly and in the face of the anarchist scepticism of many fellow climbers, he laid the foundations of the modern MCS, which now consumes all the effort and dedication of a small team of paid staff and a series of hard-working executive Presidents. Once he had demitted office, Sandy did not conceal his view that he had done as much work and achieved as much impact as his professionalised successors; but ironically it was his own industry and wide-ranging initiative that forged MCS's credibility and led to its workload expanding exponentially.

While he could be a terrier in defence of climbing interests, Sandy always believed that friendly discussion on site could resolve many problems of access or amenity, without recourse to formal procedures or public controversy. He may well have been right in his own terms, but few of us could match his apparently unsinkable self-confidence and social ease – or his extraordinary network of contacts: Sandy seemed to know everyone concerned with the Scottish hills, and certainly everyone seemed to know Sandy. As well as MCS itself, at different times he was also active, either through the Council or independently, on the Scottish Mountain Leadership Training Board, the Mountain Rescue Committee of Scot-land, the Mountain Bothies Association, the Friends of Loch Lomond, and the Scottish Countryside Activities Council – among other groups. And for Sandy, 'active' meant actively engaged; he never attended a meeting just to show his face or to make up the numbers.

In particular, Sandy was a forceful champion of wild land at a time when only a handful of people fully appreciated that quality of our Scottish upland landscape, or recognised the threats that faced it. An active member of the informal ginger group that evolved into the Scottish Wild Land Group in 1982, he served on the SWLG Steering Team for its first three years. In 1982 he promoted in the Journal (xxxii, 1982, 270-2) a set of guidelines for wild land management which anticipates many of the principles now applied by the JMT and by the National Trust for Scotland at Mar Lodge. He even encouraged his daughter, Eilid, as part of her geography degree, to undertake a useful small-scale research project into percep-tions of wilderness in Knoydart.

Organisations like the former Countryside Commission for Scotland quickly learned to take the MCS seriously when Sandy was its mouthpiece. W. B. Prior, Secretary of the Commission, used to talk (sometimes humorously, sometimes with exasperation) of 'the Hairy Knees Brigade' and its forceful assertion of the mountaineering interest. Sandy was the man he usually had in mind. As a quintessential 'man of independent mind', Sandy would probably not have thanked the Establishment had it seen fit to offer him one of its outdated imperialist baubles for the services he rendered to Scottish mountaineering, but I suspect he might have appreciated a token of acknowledgement from the MCS, or even from the SMC. Honorary memberships have been awarded for much lesser, and less altruistic, contributions.

The early AGMs of the MCS in the 1970s were held in the big common room at the Glencoe Ski Club's Lodge at Bridge of Orchy. It was not the least of Sandy's achievements that these meetings were imbued with a pervasive and positive sense of the community of Scottish mountaineering, which I have never felt so power-fully since. Club representatives, members, and guests gathered from across the country to squeeze up on the lodge's unyielding benches for an evening of debate and exchange of information. Many came fresh off the hill in patched breeks and darned sweaters, lending the atmosphere a fragrance now almost lost to us with the shift from organic materials in much hill clothing. The smell of food was in there too, for fine weather or stern rocks always delayed some parties, so that the meeting overlapped with the serious business of refreshing the inner man or woman. Some were still cooking or wolfing down their dinner. Big teapots circulated, as well as stronger refreshments. Outside the westering sun fired the wide gully-seamed slopes of Beinn Dorain (for memory says those were always some of the best days of May). Inside, discussion surged from plateaux of carefully-considered judgment to peaks of humour, insult, and authentic passion. The Creagh Dhu or the ubiquitous R. N. Campbell could be relied upon for a judicious injection of anarchy. Sandy, genial as host and ringmaster, fostered an informal, but powerful, collective purpose, and the intrinsic sense that the meetings were enjoyable as well as useful and educative.

It is at the centre of that scene that I remember Sandy best – usually in his kilt and home-made leather waistcoat, with his pipe, his goatee, and his grin. He was an engaging, energetic, invariably stimulating and occasionally maddening mixture of the practical man and the idealist, who put his heart and soul into conserving the wild mountain country that he loved. We all owe him a huge debt of gratitude.

R. Aitken.

Douglas Niven continues: DIFFICULT to forget the laird-like figure striding over the hill with Kilmarnock bunnet, cromach, home-made gear and gaiters and sometimes a home-made axe, and the awful pipe with its all-pervasive smoke. Sandy always had a dog with him; it was always a big dog, which filled a car with unrestrained enthusiasm – a beast which regularly went for your piece and not his on the hill. Then there was the embarrassment of coming down the hill, eyeing with some apprehension an aggrieved farmer or shepherd in the middle distance as the dog careered among sheep or cattle – under control he said – the locals clearly thought otherwise. Pointless arguments inevitably followed without resolution, as so often happens when Greek meets Greek. Our hill days together were mainly confined to day trips from Glasgow and always, it seemed, in indifferent weather. I suppose we argued about everything imaginable on those walks; I never convinced him on anything of any consequence!

Can any of us forget those pithy and sometimes bizarre comments on the doings of the Club at the AGM? Unkind members may have muttered audibly when he rose to his feet, but regardless of our views and in spite of ourselves, we all waited for Sandy's opinion just the same.

We should also remember his contribution to the expedition scene: his epic solo walk from Cape Wrath to Glasgow over countless Munros was both physically and mentally taxing and demanded good organisational and topographical skills. This imaginative ploy underlined his abilities as an all-round and competent mountain-eer on the Scottish hills.

Sandy's contribution to Scottish mountaineering and mountainous countryside in Scotland was and is both substantial and enduring: he was one of the founding members of the Mountaineering Council of Scotland, and became the first Honorary Secretary in 1970; he devoted considerable time and energy to establish-ing its credibility, not only with the Scottish Sports Council, but also with a largely sceptical mountaineering public. At one time or another, Sandy seemed to be involved in every possible aspect of mountaineering activity in Scotland. He was a member of the Mountain Rescue Committee – one of my recurring nightmares was the prospect of being rescued by a grinning Cousins on some dark Highland hillside. He gave time and skill to the Mountain Bothies Association and was, of course, Convenor of the Huts Sub-committee from 1967 to 1972, before handing over the dubious privilege to Bill Young. He was also involved with the Scottish Countryside Activities Council, Friends of Loch Lomond, and helped to form the Scottish Wild Land Group. A bewildering number of badges on the back window of his car testified to a wide range of interests in the hills.

Of his career outwith mountaineering, I knew surprisingly little; he served as a marine engineer at sea for many years and then as design engineer in the offices of Yarrows Shipbuilders. Latterly, he was with Denholm Shipping and finally Alfa-Laval until the long arm of redundancy finally caught up with him. Little deterred by this setback, he turned his hobby of model-making into a late and profitable career. He was a superb model-maker of ships and boats of all kinds; his sheer dexterity, application and attention to detail was exceptional, and was frequently noted in model journals.

Sandy and Moira had recently retired to North Connel to be closer to their daughter, Eilid, and her family. I always imagined him as a future Laird of Connel and possibly even as a recipient of a telegram from the Queen – but, unfortunately, this was not to be. In the spring of 1998 he was cruelly taken from his family and friends in an incredibly short space of time by a rapid and debilitating illness. I often pass Sandy's old house at Kirklee in Glasgow and somehow expect, quite illogically, to see him with a fistful of spanners and a car engine in bits in front of his close. I suppose I'll be doing that for a while yet, only more so now.

ROSS HIGGINS j. 1946

ROSS HIGGINS (Robert Ross Stewart Higgins) was born in 1914, and died peacefully after a stroke last December. As a leading Glasgow bookseller (with John Smith & Son) who ran Wylie's bookshop in Sauchiehall Street, the climber's then literary Mecca, he always had the books in stock or supplied them by return. Tall, dark-suited, he knew everyone – authors, publishers, customers – relevant to any subject you mentioned; and daily, with effortless understanding, he would usher fools, fogies or fanatics out of the door, their bookshelves and self-importance happily augmented. A true artist. In like manner, he ran the SMC for a decade.

He first appeared in the pre-war Journal as an active JMCS climber and versifier. Then war service took him abroad, later as Liaison Officer with the 2nd Polish Corps, a post which surely suited his imposing presence, unarguable efficiency and often overwhelming tact and flair. Such qualities made him – only three years after joining the Club – one of our really outstanding Honorary Secretaries. So great an efficiency, that we can offer you two obituaries of him by incorporating here the Obituary *(SMCJ* xxvii, 77, 1960) of his Secretaryship:

'So Ross has gone! That persuasive voice, that velvet glove, that discreet and innocent astonishment, that expert polishing of spectacles and Agenda – gone! Resigned and smiling from Vice-Presidential altitude. He was, as many have perceived, a far better Secretary than we deserved... Aloof from circling and ephemeral Committees, he became almost a Permanent Staff to lean upon. Any query from anyone, imperious, faltering or tetchety, and back by return came that postcard or that letter impeccably typed in red and blue beneath the Club's calm monogram, soothing and informative; incredible, but it happened, time after time. How anyone so unbearably efficient as Ross Higgins escaped early death by stonefall we do not know.

The selfless work he put in has been enormous. No-one else could have done this with so little fuss, have weathered so many storms so adroitly, have contended with and pacified so many thrawn and warring factions; and all without being driven to cynicism or the Arctic. The strain must have been great! But there he is, our new ex-Secretary, as courteously invaluable as ever, still dispensing impeccable infor-mation, and still as sincerely and practically dedicated to the Club's welfare as any man has ever been. Let, therefore, the Club's gratitude for Ross Higgins' most splendid services – so well voiced at the AGM – be recorded again here.'

These gifts also served him well later as the Club's representative to the NTS. That former faultless gliding, to everyone's approval, among displaced Polish gentry enabled him to propound there, without offence, the unfamiliarly Radical mountaineering viewpoint: he pushed to the limit whatever poise, charm and solicitude could achieve in those rarefied circles. So his maybe less gifted successors had to pursue a different, but equally effective, approach.

Ross, despite this social suavity, held firm opinions. When outraged, head far above the mob, his nose, jaw and lips set themselves exactly as in the portrait of his claimed ancestor Admiral Sir John Ross of the North West Passage, uncle of James Clerk Ross of the Magnetic North Pole and the Antarctic Ice Shelf – predecessors of stern resolve. He could pace his own quarter-deck: on our first acquaintance I was driving him to my house and happened to drop a remark he considered derogatory to Her Gracious Majesty (Elizabeth, not Victoria); he remained purply silent for some minutes until his powerful courtesy restored speech and complexion. I never noticed this, but: 'Do you know,' he said years later, 'I had half a mind to get out of the car...' Fortunately, he did not, for it was moving quite fast, and on a deserted hill road in Perthshire.

Until progressive lameness claimed him (he spent his last 15 years – lively as ever – in a wheelchair) he regularly climbed the hills, and remained devoted to mountains and the Club; he particularly welcomed to it characters as idiosyncratic and apparently antithetical as Robin Smith. For Ross loved style, in himself and others (after his cremation, all, by his decree were regaled with champagne and smoked salmon). Therefore, finally, as he has had two obituaries, let us – to the certain pleasure of his shade – quote, from his earlier departure 'Sage remarks, which many have desired to see in print' (*SMCJ* xxvii, 89, 1960): 'It would be wise to pause and consider whether we were tending to lose the Club atmosphere, so notably preserved during the past 70 years... There was a tendency to stick rigidly to high climbing standards, regardless of personal knowledge of the candidate. This was no proposal for lowering entry standards, but rather for a reversion to the older idea of considering character as well as climbing ability... We should not become just another Association which one joined for the advantages it offered, and cease to be a Club in the true sense of the word.'

With all of which Smith (yes, Smith) would have agreed.

G. J. F. Dutton.

TREVOR J. RANSLEY j. 1950

TREVOR qualified in civil engineering at Nottingham University and initially worked at the Royal Aircraft Establishment, Farnborough. Walking the Lakeland fells and classic Welsh rock climbing set him firmly on the mountain ladder. From 1947, he worked on the Loch Sloy project, based at Inverarnan – that cradle of Scottish mountaineering. Joining the JMCS, he climbed regularly around Arrochar, Glencoe and elsewhere. His companions and mentors were many, including Bill Murray, Tom Mackinnon, Jim Donaldson, Bill Mackenzie, Ross Higgins and Ian McNicol to name a few.

Trevor's next move in 1950 took him to Fort William to join British Aluminium, with its extensive hydro power resources. Here for my first job, surrounded by Lochaber's mountains and a new circle of climbing friends, I was the proverbial small boy let loose in the sweetie shop. Now it was Trevor's turn to pass on some of his accumulated mountain lore and perhaps temper some of my more impetuous intentions. I soon found him to be a meticulous organiser; every outing was planned in detail. Happy memories of these times include icy battles in the Nevis gullies, carefree Cuillin days and ski ascents of Beinn na Lap and Meall a' Bhuridh, before the advent of mechanical uplift.

He climbed in the Alps in 1949 with Alan Johnson JMCS centred on Saas Fee and again in 1951 with George Roger, George Freeman, Archie MacAlpine and Dan Mckellar. In 1950, he was with the British West Greenland expedition led by

Harold Drever, along with Norman Tennent and Malcolm Slesser. Trevor's report of the ascent of several virgin peaks on Upnervik Island appeared in the Journal.

While at Fort William, Trevor met Pat, his greatest love, and soon to be his lifelong companion. Together they completed the Munros in 1980 and 1984 respectively. Retirement gave the opportunity to continue walking the Scottish hills, enjoy active holidays in the Austrian Alps and expand his many interests. Valuable contributions followed to the Corbetts guidebook.

Trevor was an expert gardener with a wide knowledge of plants, alpines being special favourites. Hill expeditions were often planned to coincide with the flowering of a particular species.

Numbers and mathematics were always a fascination. Thus the granddaughters' homework problems and the *Scotsman* mind games were all grist to the mill. A practical application appeared in the 1971 Journal article *Naismith Reviewed.* His ability at chess and mastery of bridge and other games of memory were outstanding. A deep love of music from early childhood is shared by Pat. They both were founder members of the Wagner Society of Scotland.

Aged 74, Trevor died on July 27, 1997 in St. Colomba's Hospice after a courageous fight. The large gathering at his funeral reflected his wide interests. We are all the poorer for having lost him but enriched by his valued friendship. To Pat and their family we extend our deepest sympathy.

Miles Hutchinson.

This notice was sent in time for publication in last year's issue, but was somehow lost en route. We apologise for any distress this may have caused. (Hon. Ed.).

DAVID EASSON j. 1947

DAVID EASSON died in Stobhill Hospital on February 16, 1998 having been a member of the Club for more than half a century.

He was very much a technical climber being a member of one of the most active groups of his day comprising Humble, Nimblin and Murray. Indeed Humble endorsed his application by describing him as 'a very good leader on rock and snow'. Visits to Arrochar, Skye, Glen Coe and the Lake District were frequent in his early years and on his first meet of the Club at Easter 1948 he climbed Recess Route on the Cobbler on 'a very wet day'.

He clearly succumbed to the Arrochar disease of 'howffing' and it is recorded that on the 1949 New Year meet to Lagangarbh, he gave up the comforts of the hut for a howff in Coire Gabhail in the company of Humble and Nimlin.

Humble also credits him with having done much work on the first Arrochar climbing guide, having been out with all route-checking parties in the summer of 1946.

He was also a keen photographer and his family has been kind enough to offer his extensive slide collection to the Club.

J. R. R. Fowler.

ADAM STEWART j. 1960

ADAM STEWART left it late to join the Club not being elected to membership until the age of 50. However, his mountaineering career commenced some 10 years earlier, and while he never achieved high standards on rock or ice, he accumulated well over 100 Munros ascended at all times of year.

He was an active member of the Edinburgh Section of the JMCS, attending many of their meets and his frequent companions on these outings were James Russell and Robert MacLennan.

J. R. R. Fowler.

JOHN HUNT

THERE HAVE been, quite rightly, many eulogies to John Hunt, who died on November 7, 1998 at the age of 88. But little has been said of his involvement with the Scots and the SMC or of the 1963 Pamirs expedition. I know that he found us bewildering.

As a mountaineer he is chiefly remembered for his very effective leadership of the 1953 Everest Expedition, for which he was knighted. Both by temperament and military background he was the ideal man to direct a logistic exercise like the ascent of the world's highest mountain. I recall vividly listening to John and Ed Hillary being interviewed on the BBC short wave service while I was simultaneously driving my caterpillar track vehicle through a maze of crevasses off the east edge of the Greenland ice-cap. It was wonderful juxtaposition of emotion and situation.

He was president of the Alpine Club in 1957. His army career was a huge success, finishing up as Assistant Commissioner at the Military Staff College at Camberley. The Duke of Edinburgh then asked him to manage his Award scheme. In 1960 he conceived a youth leader expedition to the Staunings Alps in East Greenland. I received a letter asking for information from someone whose signature was illegible, so I cut out the signature and pasted it onto the reply envelope. He was enormously amused by this, and invited me, Tom Weir, Iain Smart and Roddy Cameron to join as group leaders.

We met again in 1962. Kenny Bryan and I had sought permission to climbed Peak Stalin (renamed Peak of Communism and no doubt something else now), the highest peak in the Soviet Union situated in the Pamirs. The Soviets put the cat among the pigeons by insisting the Alpine Club application and ours be melded into one team. Negotiations between us were protracted and the SMC ended up with four members and the AC with eight. During the expedition Wilfred Noyce and Robin Smith slipped to their deaths on Peak Garmo. John was the only one to witness the fall, and to his dying day he refused to say whose slip pulled the other off. Noyce was one of his dearest friends, and John felt unable to continue climbing and left the field to me and others to finish the expedition.

When he finally retired from the Award, he was elevated to the Lords, and became chairman of the parole board in England and Wales, a duty I am sure he carried out with scrupulous care and kindness. I am left with the memory of a complete gentleman, very firm, very quiet, and always generous in spirit, and one who deeply loved the hills.

Malcolm Slesser.

Notice has also reached us of the death of Charles Warren.

PROCEEDINGS OF THE CLUB

New members

The following were admitted and welcomed to the Club in 1998-1999.

Stuart D. Campbell, (30), Teacher, Dunfermline.

Douglas I. Cooper, (28), Mountaineering Instructor, Aviemore.

Quintin T. Crichton, (65), Chartered Accountant, Dundee.

David C. Gardner, (49), Architectural Draughtsman, Milngavie.

John Mitchell, (60), Artist, Lower Largo, Fife.

Colin A. Moody, (41), Fish Farmer, Aros, Mull.

Roger S. D. Smith, (52), Teacher, Malvern, Worcs.

The One-Hundreth-and-Eighth AGM, Reception and Dinner

Too small, too hot, too convenient. Lack of suitable alternatives to the Alexandra found us once again back in Fort William where the Dinner Secretary faced the usual problems of seats not equalling diners, last-minute seat-swapping, and some miserable wretches snaffling a Vice-President's wine. It was ever so, but first to the business.

The hall of the primary school was at its uncomfortable best as the President convened his final meeting and members were eager to hear about the revised plans for the hut on the hill. Some were to be disappointed. The proposal for toilet developments had been shelved but the wind turbine was to go ahead on the basis that it would provide a power source for servicing the building and reduce the dependence on gas. Many were not convinced that this was the way to go and felt that such a structure would reduce the credibility of the Club as an organisation committed to environmental protection. On the other hand, the hut men could legitimately claim that they had consulted through Press and the Internet on their proposals and adverse response had been minimal. This time the proposal was accepted by the Meeting, although with perhaps some unease as to public reaction.

The Journal, or rather the cost of producing the Journal, caused not a little excitement as the accountants had their say. It was clear even to the re-design enthusiasts that the losses were unsustainable and members solved the problem in the traditional way by forming a committee who will report this year.

And so back to the Hotel for the usual scrum around the wine table and a fair meal. The President congratulated the Club's Greenland members who had shown us their trannies in the afternoon and Curly Ross was in good form with Club song. Doug Lang had a go at the guests but was careful to spare Andrew Thin representing the John Muir Trust who had volunteered at pretty short notice to reply. Our other guests were the JMCS, the Cairngorm Club, the Fell & Rock, the Alpine Club and also Donald Orr as the first winner of the W. H. Murray Literary Award.

At the close of the evening Bryan Fleming was inaugurated as President, accepting Raeburn's axe and other junk as symbols of office, but sagely offered the war-wound excuse over participating in the outgoing President's walk to the CIC Hut where it was proposed to show those interested what all the fuss is about.

The Dinner continues as one of the great institutions of the Club but let's go somewhere different in 1999.

J. R. R. Fowler.

JMCS REPORT

Lochaber Section:– The membership remained healthy and active throughout 1998 with the number of paid-up members on the increase, a trend possibly due to the introduction of an Aberdonian Treasurer. The section meets informally in the Nevis Bank Hotel, Fort William, every Thursday evening and formally with outdoor meets throughout the year.

In April it was the turn of the Section to host the Whole Club AGM. The meeting was held in the Cairndow Inn, Loch Fyne, and was attended by just over a dozen members with all sections, bar the London section, being represented. The meeting was very informal and an enjoyable evening was had afterwards.

In May, a big gathering of members, past and present, and also friends, joined Harry Campbell on the summit of Ladhar Bheinn to help him celebrate the completion of his Munros. A great weekend was had with a lot of sore heads leaving Knoydart on the Sunday.

In June, two members, Donald Watt and George Bruce completed their round of the Corbetts, finishing with The Merrick in Dumfries and Galloway. Both have already completed the Munros.

Several members made trips to the Alps during the summer with the Chamonix area being the preferred base. Already this year, interest is being expressed by several members for a trip to Slovenia.

The Section's Annual Dinner was held in November at the Aultguish Inn, near Garve. More than 30 members and guests enjoyed an excellent meal and likewise the hospitality and the crack.

Also in November, Bert Bissell, an Honorary Member passed away. Bert had been associated with Lochaber for many years and up until recent years he regularly ascended Ben Nevis during his visits to Fort William. Several members attended the funeral service.

Officials elected were: *Hon. President,* W. Munro; *Hon. Member,* S. Scott. *President,* I. Walker; *Vice-President,* D. Ford; *Treasurer,* G. Bruce; *Secretary,* K. Foggo, 4 Parkan Dubh, Inverlochy, Fort William. *Hut Custodian,* J. Mathieson, 43 Drumfada Terrace, Corpach, Fort William, PH33 6NH, (01397 772599). *Meets Secretary,* B. Macpherson. *Committee,* J. Conlon, D. Leslie, and B. Campbell.

Perth, Glasgow, Edinburgh and London JMCS were asked for reports but failed to respond. (Hon. Ed.)

SMC AND JMCS ABROAD

Europe

JOHN STEELE reports:– Last September I visited the Austrian Alps with Barbara Gibbons.

Several weeks were spent touring in Austria. In the first week a traverse of the Zillertal was accomplished in the company of the Munich Mens' Drinking Club. The second week saw us in the Glockner region in the company of the Austrian Boys' Army.

Peaks and peaklets taken in along the way included, Kraxenberg, Silafhorn, Grosse Moseler, Johannisberg and a wintry retreat from the Gross Glockner. Refuge was found in the hamlet of Helingotblat, 2500m below Austria's highest peak, where thanks were given in the tiny Gothic church, which has acted as a staging post over the centuries for those contemplating crossing the Alps from the south.

ADAM KASSYK reports:– In June 1998, with Matthew Priestman from London we walked an 80km stretch of the GR5, from Landry to Modane across the Vanoise massif. At this time of the season we had the mountains (and the refuges) mostly to ourselves. While at the Col de la Vanoise we made an ascent of the Grand Gliere (3392m) by the SW Face (PD), descending by the East Ridge (F). We then moved on to Ailefroide, and made an ascent of the Barre des Ecrins (4101m) by the Couloir Nord and a traverse of the summit ridge (AD).

The weather here was more reminiscent of Scotland – mist, rain and very poor snow conditions with the freezing level nowhere near the summits – day or night. Finally, we traversed Mont Pelvoux (3943m) by the Coolidge Couloir and the Violetres Glacier (PD), again very testing due to bad snow conditions.

A few weeks later I had a day in the Aiguilles Rouges at Chamonix with my brother, Andy. Having no maps or guidebooks on this occasion, and lacking time to seek information, we walked up the path from Tre-le-champs and climbed a line on the first attractive-looking peak we found. This turned out to be the Aiguille de la Remua (2860m) and our 17-pitch direct line on the SE Face (TD with a pitch of 6/5b) appears to be a new route, subject to further confirmation from the CAF.

Norway

DAVID RITCHIE reports:– Last summer I joined Neil MacGougan in his trimaran yacht, *Sophie,* for a sailing and climbing trip to Norway. We sailed from Oban via Stornoway to the Faroe Islands where we spent several days sailing throughout the islands and climbing some of the local hills. The weather was no better than that which Scotland was receiving, although we did have one fine day walking on Vagar. From there we sailed to Lerwick where we met up with John Morrison who introduced us to some quality sea cliff climbing in the locality. Colwyn Jones joined us here an together we sailed to Bergen in Norway where we were joined by Anne MacDonald.

The four of us then travelled by ferry to the Johenheim mountains, where we climbed Galhopigen and traversed Store Urdadalstrinder. We then visited the Hardanger hills to the south and made a wintry ascent of the beautiful Stove Skagastrolstind. Returning to Bergen Neil and I then sailed south via Stavanger to Loristiansund, exploring crags at Store Island, Uskedal, and Mandal *en route* and enjoying quality rock when the weather allowed. Steve Kennedy and Mark Shaw joined us from Scotland and we visited the Setesdal Valley where we climbed several established routes on the most accessible valley crags well documented in recent guidebooks.

We then explored several fine granite mountain crags in the higher hinterland to the west. This area has seen a handful of new routes during the past two or three summers and the area has huge potential. Several new routes were climbed mostly in the lower grades due to the incessant wet weather experiences although one or two dry days produced some harder offerings. We then spent a couple of weeks waiting for favourable weather for our return sail and explored some marvellous crags on the south-west coast of Norway between Egersund and Jossingfjord. We eventually departed for Scotland but broke a hull halfway across the North Sea forcing an exciting return to Norway. Despite this unfortunate end to our sailing and a very wet summer we still had enjoyed some fine sailing and excellent varied mountaineering.

A Long Way by Sea to Climb a Mountain: The Talisker Islands

DEREK FABIAN reports: It could be the Skye ridge, I thought, But no, this is gneiss – not gabbro! Or is it granite? And the sea below (some 2000ft? – never could think in those newfangled metres)…a more intense blue than from the Dubh ridge last year on the yacht meet. Jagged saw-tooth ridges of granite and gneiss stretched endlessly into a blue haze of sea and sky, in almost every direction. Plus, here and there, the glistening streak of a peeping glacier. Only to the east was there an arc of empty blue ocean, though with another magnificent backdrop of mountains and glacier beyond.

If only, say, Noel was here! He would know granite from gneiss. But it's not gabbro; at least that I do know. And, with Noel we would just scamper along this ridge to the summit. I tore my eyes from the mesmerising view for a moment to watch Brian. But, then Noel doesn't enjoy boats at sea; and if it wasn't for Brian we wouldn't be here in this mountain wonderland! Yes, Palaeozoic rocks, someone had said; and a long time ago (some 500 million years or so) this coastline would have been joined to what is now the mountain escarpment of East Greenland. Perhaps somewhere near Scoresby Sound, I was thinking, just about due west from here, some 2000 miles? And the same rocks there presumably as those around here; must check that out when we get back.

I urged Brian below to try the final rock gully to the ridge. He was looking down, and clutching himself closely into the narrow recess, where it became more a tight chimney. Brian doesn't enjoy rock, and certainly not exposure; nor does he profess to. My eyes strayed again; some 20 miles NE stood the highest, the superb snow-capped Higravtinden. I took the camera from my pack to record the view. Then, with Brian protesting that I should make the close-by summit of the Budalstinden alone, I descended to join him and we continued down to the enchanting fresh water lake nestling in the high valley floor. Without Brian I would not have got as far as Cape Wrath let alone Orkney; and certainly not Shetland where we had added John to our crew.

We had been four at the start – in Loch Moidart. But inside two days we had lost half our crew; one in Moidart to a minor illness, and another at Kyle of Lochalsh to someone else's illness. Bemusedly, Brian and I had taken stock; noting among other things that the stowing of our two months' stores had been done by Ewa and Clem, the lost crew! For the next few weeks we had been second guessing where to find longed-for food items as our appetites trebled. We were not short of single malt at least; for by way of apt consolation during delays in our departure from Moidart, while the wind had blown unfavourably from the north, the United Distillers plc had presented us with a case of its Talisker (it being the 30-year anniversary of the Canadian Government's adoption of the name Mt. Talisker for one of the then unnamed BC/Alaska border peaks climbed by a distant SMC-JMCS expedition led by the *Mistress Malin* skipper in 1965). Brian had promptly christened Norway's Lofoten the Talisker Islands. And these, we had decided in Kyle of Lochalsh, would remain our expedition goal.

Nor were we short of oatcakes, for us an important staple. Indeed for some 48 hours out from Lerwick, a plentiful supply of oatcakes with sweet lemon tea and occasional hot soup, had been our diet, oil drilling-rigs and production platforms our blazoning friendly giants at night, and three to four metre waves our adversaries. John, who'd had little or no time to gain his sea legs, had stood his watches manfully; and by evening of that second day we'd had the Ytterøyane ('outerly') Light abeam as the mist rolled back from the softly-lit hills at the entrance to the small (by Norway's standard) Skorpfjord. For the night we had anchored in a delightful tiny fishing harbour facing the strangely cleft mountain, Kinnlekova, on the island of Kinn; famous also for its 11th century stone and wooden church. On the hillsides surrounding this church, we learned next morning, thousands of people would congregate in the following few days to watch performances of a religious/historical Viking pageant.

After a few days of rain (and starter motor malady) we had headed north as the clouds lifted to give a superb display of light and colour on the snow covered Jøstedalsbreen Mountains, inland to the east. Past Måløy and the Hornelen Rock, the mist rolling ever upwards to reveal the whole of this impressive cliff face rising 2870ft sheer from the sea. Then out to open sea from the narrow Ulvesund (Wolf Sound) to cross the invisible line where the North Sea becomes the Norwegian Sea; but more visibly to round the notorious Stattlandet Peninsula, the first of many areas of sea we had traversed along the coastline marked on the Admiralty charts with 'Dangerous Waves' and 'Strong Current' warnings. The 'Stad', as this mountain peninsula is known locally, has a perilous reputation from Saga times; and for centuries fishermen have preferred, in bad weather, to haul their boats across the one-mile isthmus joining it to the mainland rather than risk rounding the Stad in stormy seas.

For us it had been calm and blue. For the next week we had covered 70-80 miles a day, alternating between open sea and the Indreleia (Inside passage) among spectacular mountain and island scenery, past such towns as Ålesund and Kristiansund and through carefully charted sounds like Buholm Rasa (race) and Brønnøysund where one of the many stunning bridges under which we had sailed along this coast joins a sparsely populated island to the Helgen mountain range of Nordland. With a sense of occasion and raised glasses of Talisker we had crossed the Arctic Circle (2300h, June 29), toasting first the Polarsirkelmerke, a huge symbolic 'wire' globe mounted on a tiny island of rock, and then Hestmannen (the Horseman), a shapely island summit through which the notional Circle line runs.

For an hour in undisguised excitement we had sailed due north awaiting local midnight and the sun, right on the bow in a blazon of colour, to touch and just to kiss the sea horizon amid a crimson and gold silhouette of mountain and island shapes. Then, sailing some 20 miles eastwards into the Nordland mainland to reach the Holandsfjord, we had anchored at the foot of the Engabreen glacier, one arm of the huge Svartisen (Black ice) glacier; to where we had scrambled at 3am with the sun already throwing friendly tentacles of gold around the tops and along the immense rivers of glistening silver. The scenery and lighting there had been about the finest of the voyage, and only surpassed by those here in Lofoten. And out to the west, across thousands of skerries and islands, we had seen the largest group Traena, where archaeological evidence has been found for nearly 5000 years of human habitation, from the stone age and iron age through to the 14th century; such has been the effect of the Gulf Stream on Man's settlement of this Arctic coast. Then back aboard, pausing for only a few hours' sleep, we had been under way for Bodø, gateway to the Vestfjord and Lofoten; and so to Svolvær, capital of Lofoten, to where Ewa and John's wife, Barbara, had flown from Glasgow. We had found a remote berth below the Svolværgeita pinnacle (the Goat), a magnet to visiting rock climbers.

The climb to the higher horn of the Svolværgeita is around V. Diff. The airy jump from there to the lower horn is the challenge; perhaps it was the beckoning cemetery 900ft below that had daunted us? The scenery everywhere in and from Svolvær could be described in one word: Breathtaking! Knife-edge rock ridges and summits, gleaming glaciers and corries, surround the harbour; enormous cod-drying racks fill every spot flat enough for their erection. Cormorants perch everywhere; white-tailed sea eagles soar in the air. In Bodø we had met the elderly Norwegian who has helped introduce these supreme birds to our island of Rum! And to a chorus of kittiwakes we had set sail from there dreamily – for midday temperatures could be 28°C – to circumnavigate Austvågøya (Easterly island of bays); roughly the shape of Skye in mirror image and, although only half its size in land area, all of it as sharply mountainous as the Black Cuillin, mantled with significant glaciers. It had been midnight when – just as dreamily for the word 'night' is entirely symbolic at Lat. 68°N – we had sought out the hidden entrance to Henningsvær; one of Lofoten's largest fishing villages and its rock-climbing centre.

From below the jagged ridge to Vågakallen, where Brian and I stood now, we had an aerial view of Henningsvær. Known also as the Venice of Lofoten, its harbour is formed by a string of bridges and causeways between a horseshoe of islands. During the winter months, when the spawning Arctic cod return from the North Cape, the harbour is packed full of fishing vessels; in summer it is empty but for visiting boats, and the fishermen's shacks ashore become convenient mountain huts for climbers.

After a welcome bathe in the lake (warmer I noted than any in the Hebrides) we retraced the Geriatric gully, as Brian had named it, regaining the track back to Henningsvær's Climbing Club bar; where the three remaining crew, nursing four KPs (knee problems) between them, were studying – between half litres of cool dark Sköl – the three wall clocks; set respectively, to our surprise and for no immediately apparent reason, to the local times at Ben Nevis, Mt. Vågakallen, and Mt. Kahperusvära in Finland.

Time regrettably was pressing (although I'm not sure why we had a deadline) and to explore the Higravtinden at closer range, we set sail from below one of the harbour bridges, taking the narrow sound separating Austvagøya from Vestvagøya (Easterly island of bays) and below yet another elegant bridge joining the two, to an anchorage of questionable shelter on their north-facing Atlantic shores. From here we could penetrate the Sløverfjorden to where the 3800ft Higrav western face drops almost sheer to the sea; but the expedition highlight came in Trollfjord, whose astonishingly narrow entrance in the east we reached by taking the long narrow Raftsundet separating Lofoten from its neighbouring, and equally magnificent and mountainous, Vesterålen Islands.

The Higravtinden has two glaciers, one above the Higrav face; another flowing five miles east along the (frozen-in-winter) lake-filled valley, Trollfjordvatnet, from where it spills out onto an amazing rock shelf above the mystical Trollfjord! Entranced, we explored and pondered; a month we could spend here alone, I thought, with time, and a climbing partner, I'll return one day to explore more. So too, on his first visit to Lofoten, had thought Norman Collie (of Tower Ridge and Skye exploration fame in the 1890s). With H. Woolley, in 1901, Collie made the first recorded ascent of the Higravtinden. He was also, in himself, a mystical man; as we can tell from his poetry in *A Reverie,* SMCJ 1898, and his account of hidden secrets of ennobled mountains, *On the divine Mysteries of the Oromaniacal Quest,* based on his SMCJ writings.

Meanwhile, time pressed. We had some 600 miles of southing to make; three of the crew had a ferry to catch, 10 days from now in Bergen. Mostly the weather remained blissful. Though re-crossing the Arctic Circle, in an enchanting anchorage off the island of Renga, the engine starter motor committed suicide. Blessed with a favourable wind we made Brønnøysund and there, in this town of just 3000 population, we found a specialist who had an 'off the shelf' replacement! A week later we were two once more, Brian and myself, to make the crossing to Orkney. The weather broke! And aborting our first attempt, in a strong westerly, we sought shelter in Fedje, the most western island of Norway. Here, in 1994, Robin, Donald, Drew and myself had also holed up, after sailing some 140 miles east along the Sognefjord for a brief expedition into the Jøtenheim Mountains (the Ringstinden and the Dyrhaugstinden were bagged; and we had caught 60 herring in an hour on a mackerel line). Brian and I fished, without luck; but in the night the wind fell calm and we then enjoyed the finest 36-hour sail of the whole expedition – to Shetland where luck returned, for Allan (of SMC Western District fame) had his flight to Kirkwall diverted by fog to Lerwick, and was on the pier there to meet us as we made it to harbour, and reached for the Talisker!

Brian could now make up time by P&O ferry to Aberdeen and eventually to his home in Nova Scotia. While for Allan and myself the hills of Fair Isle, and of Hoy in Orkney, awaited; the former hid their tops shyly in mist, the latter defended themselves with gale-force winds from the west. In the shelter of Stromness we sat out the storm and then, biding time for a slack-water escape from the notorious Hoy Sound, we headed out on the last of the ebb into the awful tidal rost caused by the westerly swell piling up there. For nearly an hour then we corkscrewed horrendously, the bow of *Mistress Malin* digging itself deeply into each oncoming four-metre wave and emerging like a submarine to throw off the massive cascade of water in proud disdain. We cowered in the cockpit making sure with the helm that she took those waves head on. I'm not sure if we were frightened; she seemed reassuringly to have the measure of those seas. But never she told us firmly, try this other than at slack water! And 12 hours later she brought us safely, if drenched, round Cape Wrath, to shelter in Kinlochbervie.

In the blissful blue seas that then prevailed, Scotland's West Coast too – a rugged sandy and rocky foreshore with rounded saw tooth line of mountain munros beyond – is magnificent, in a different and contrasting way to Norway's. We explored leisurely, and eventually in perfect clear skies, returned to Loch Moidart; 10 weeks, 2510 nautical miles logged, and with the SMC pennant aloft throughout!

For *Mistress Malin* however, Moidart and its Castle Tioram, with Eigg and Rum as nearby mountain haunts, remains her favourite wanderland. Perhaps in time, her crew will write their account of the expedition, as did Iain Smart – retrospectively 'from the wilderness of time' – of his 1986 expedition to Petermann Peak of East Greenland. I quote Iain from a 'remote corner' of the SMCJ of 1995: 'Madeira wine improves in flavour when carried around in the hold of a ship. So is the memory of a good expedition if allowed to rock around for a few years in the bottom of your mind. The original experiences grow or diminish in relative importance and achieve a balance unsuspected at the time when they were being harvested from the ambient universe.' Which says it all! Mystical memories abound for ever when we ponder past moments in the mountains!

Greenland

STEPHEN REID and Colwyn Jones report:– The SMC Staunings Alps, East Greenland Expedition 1998. Colwyn Jones (Joint Leader), Stephen Reid (Joint Leader), John Bickerdike, Brian Shackleton, Jonathan Preston, Colin Read, John Peden and Chris Ravey.

On a Polar expedition begin with a clear idea of which Pole you are aiming at, and try to start facing the right way. Choose your companions carefully – you may have to eat them.

W. C. Sellar.

The expedition landed by ski-equipped Twin Otter on the Sefstroms Glacier (1210m) in the Western Staunings Alps on May 6, 1998. The landing was two days later than planned owing to bad weather.

Next day, Jones, Bickerdike, Reid and Preston attempted the most northerly of two unclimbed peaks, circa 2700m (mentioned on p83 of Donald Bennet's guide, *Staunings Alps,* West Col, 1972, and probably the highest unclimbed peak in the Staunings) situated between Attilaborgen and Trinity. The route took the left hand of two obvious couloirs on the East flank of the mountain. The couloir gave unrelenting Grade II snow for about 600m until the ridge joining this peak to Attilaborgen was gained. Here a short rock step led to steep snow below a steep rock wall, possibly four or five pitches high and still a long way from the summit. As an alternative to the rock wall, a steep basin to the south gleamed with hard, blue water ice. Jones and Bickerdike made an attempt on the wall which was found to be very loose and, after pulling off several large blocks, quickly followed Preston and Reid who were already descending.

During the day, exploration and observation was made of the glacier features giving access to this face. They named several of these features. The main glacier was called the Essemmceebrae while the northerly branch was called the McKenzie Glacier. A view was obtained into the intriguing Inner Sanctum, a glacier basin between Trinity and the Helmspids, flanked by rock pillars and guarded by vast crevasses that extended completely across the entrance. A possible route was observed up the northern flank of the most southerly peak, starting from a point near the entrance to the Inner Sanctum. This would be a long and complex climb, but seemed relatively free from objective danger once the face had been gained.

Meanwhile, Shackleton, Reid, Peden and Ravey attempted a fine unclimbed snow peak, one of two unclimbed mountains, the other a superb rock spire, lying in the area between Sussex, Magog and Cantabrigia on the Cantabrae. Access was via a couloir left of a hanging glacier on the NW Face. This led to a snow ridge where Shackleton and Reid, having exhausted themselves by kicking steps in soft snow for several hundred metres, turned back. Ravey and Peden following them carried on and, in the early hours of the morning, reached the summit via a short, but difficult, rock slab (V). This peak has been named Hecla (2400m) and graded PD. The team also named the spur glaciers flowing into the Cantabrae from the region of this peak the Great Cumbrae and the Little Cumbrae.

On the May 9, Reid, Preston, Bickerdike and Jones climbed the highest of four unclimbed peaks on the dividing ridge between the Upper Sefstroms and Grantabrae glaciers (the northerly of the two marked on Bennet's map). The ascent was by linking a series of couloirs and ice fields with occasional mixed climbing on the SW Face. Starting up a broad, left-slanting couloir, the first major rightward branch was taken, and a long rising traverse made into a ragged gully leading straight up under the summit tower. Shortly before the top this gully was abandoned on the left through a short section of steep mixed ground which gained a steep ice-field whereby the summit tower was outflanked on the left. This led to a short, easy rock section and a spectacular summit block – the latter could be easily seen from Base Camp. This peak was called Tillyrie (2415m) and the route graded AD. From the summit, it looked as though a considerably easier approach could be made of both this peak and its neighbours via a branch of the Lang Glacier which abutted the mountain on the east. The party descended by the same route.

Meanwhile, Peden, Ravey, Shackleton and Reid made the first ascent of the unclimbed rock spire south of Emmanuel (pictured in Bennet guide, illustration 5). This peak is particularly spectacular when viewed from the Upper Sefstroms where it is seen to have a large hole or 'window' directly through the summit. The spire was gained via a long couloir on the SW Face, between it and Emmanuel, and the seven pitches of rock (up to IV) led to the top. The peak was named Tupilaq (2450m) and the route graded TD.

This team summited at 1am and during the descent, Brian Shackleton sustained a facial injury when loose rock was dislodged by an abseil rope. As they had been away for more than 30 hours the others set off from Base Camp on the morning of May 10 and met the Tupilaq team skiing back to base. The facial lacerations were later treated by the team medic ,Colwyn Jones, on return to base camp.

Later, on the 10th, Bickerdike and Reid made the first ascent of a small, but prominent, unclimbed southerly outlier of Kapelle. This peak has an extraordinarily rotund and Christmas pudding like appearance and overlooked Base Camp. The route was via an easy couloir and snow fields to its east and the peak was called Rabsontinde (1640m – F).

On May 11, Preston, Reid, Bickerdike and Jones climbed the second highest of the four unclimbed peaks on the dividing ridge between the Upper Sefstroms and Grantabrae glaciers (the southerly of the two marked on Bennet's map). This has a double rock spire summit reminiscent of a lobster claw when viewed from the Sefstroms. It was climbed via a broad couloir (which they named the Coltart Couloir) lying between the mountain and the headwall of the Sefstroms Glacier which led to a snow ridge. A short rock pitch (V) led to the summit. The peak was named Coltart (2395m) and graded PD+. Descent was by reversing the route of ascent.

On May 12 it snowed heavily for 24 hours but on the 13th it dawned clearer and, while Bickerdike, Jones, Preston and Reid, rested and planned a renewed attempt on the first peak they had tried, Peden and Ravey tackled an unclimbed snow peak south-east of Coltart. This was climbed via the Coltart Couloir and a snow ridge. The slightly higher rickety rock spire to the west was not attempted. Descent was via the South Ridge and the Sefstroms Glacier Headwall. This peak of 2350m has been named Seanearbheinn. It was graded PD+.

At the same time, Reid and Shackleton attempted a group of three rock spires lying to the north-west of Tillyrie, via a couloir on the SW Face. Intense cold and ice-glazed rock forced a retreat just short of the summit.

Next day 36cm of snow put paid to further climbing and on May 15 they began the journey back to Mesters Vig via the Kirkbrae, Col de Pulkes, Lang Gletscher, Trumpington Col, Schuchert Gletscher, Skel Pass, Skeldal and then pack ice to Mesters Vig air strip which was reached at 1.30am on the morning of the 21st. A considerable number of unclimbed peaks were observed in the area of the Upper Lang Glacier. None of the passes crossed was especially difficult, though all involved carrying loads, and there was no more than the standard level of objective danger to be expected in such terrain.

During the journey, there were further falls of snow which made the towing of pulks very strenuous and tiring. On lower passes, such as the Skel, conditions were abysmal with the party wading through chest high snow. One member of the team fell into a bergschrund but was fortunately saved by his rucksack which wedged on the upper lip. He was quickly rescued.

The party were flown from Mesters Vig at midday on the 21st and were swimming in the Blue Lagoon later the same day – their first bath for three weeks!

The team would like to express their appreciation to the following bodies who supported the expedition with grants: The Mount Everest Foundation, The British Mountaineering Council and The Gino Watkins Trust.

Himalayas

GRAHAM LITTLE reports:– I spent seven weeks in Tibet as a member of the 1998 British Sepu Kangri Expedition led by Sir Chris Bonington. Our major sponsor was National Express, although many other companies and funding bodies gave us their support.

Sepu Kangri (White Sky God), an unclimbed 7000m peak, is by far the highest peak in the eastern sector of a great range of mountains called Nyainqentanghla Shan (lying to the north-east of the main Himalayan chain). This sacred mountain towers above a sacred lake fed by calving glaciers and is surrounded by many splendid unclimbed 6000m-plus peaks.

Our journey to Base Camp, at 4750m, was hampered by recent storms that had washed away many bridges and by the difficulties of hiring yaks at the height of the barley harvest. Transporting all our kit the 50 km to Base Camp had its fair share of drama including the crossing of single yak hide ropes strung across raging rivers and fending off the attentions of savage dogs.

Despite the good wishes of a hermit called Zamteng, who lives all year round at an altitude of 5000m below the mountain, poor weather and atrocious snow conditions frustrated two attempts on Sepu Kangri although Victor Saunders and Scott Muir got to within 200m of the summit on the second attempt. Graham Little and Scott Muir attempted Chomo Mangyal, 6236m, turning back 300m below the summit due to dangerous snow. The same pair made the first ascent of the relatively easy, but enjoyable, Thaga Ri, 5930m. Graham Little rounded off the trip with a solo ascent (of the final section) of Seamo Uylmitok, the Turquoise Flower, 6650m.

This expedition (and the one in 1997) will be the subject of a book (Bonington/ Clarke) and a television series (Channel 4) in the spring of 1999.

All in all, the expedition proved a wonderful blend of travel, exploration, culture, technology (laptops, satellite communications, WEB site, video etc.), religion, politics, tourism, mountaineering, bridge (to an altitude of 6530m) and pumpy ice cragging on the overhanging flanks of the glacier – a unique and unforgettable trip.

Two Short Trips to India

Geoff Cohen writes:– In July 1997 Hamish Irvine and I took a three-week holiday in Lahul, India. Returning to Manali after a 14-year absence I was unpleasantly surprised by the phenomenal growth in tourism. Scooter rickshaws and professional beggars have made their way up from the Indian plains, and the numbers of hotels must have increased four-fold. Compensations are a greater variety of good restaurants, especially Tibetan ones, and, if you are so inclined, opportunities to go rafting, parapenting, abseiling (!), motorbiking on the high mountain roads, and of course, trekking with every kind of support. Quite a change from the sleepy little village that I first visited 25 years ago, and even more so from the Manali of the 1950s when a Royal Air Force Mountaineering Association (RAFMA) team, including the young Donald Bennet, had a successful expedition here. It was only quite late in my researches for the trip that I realised that the Kulti glacier, which lies directly opposite the Rohtang Pass, had first been explored by Donald and his companions. Since that time there had been a few Indian and Japanese expeditions, but considering the ease of access it did not seem very popular. With so many higher and more spectacular peaks to choose from, in Kullu, Lahul and Spiti, perhaps this isn't so surprising, especially as many would prefer a more remote location over an easily accessible one – as we ourselves would have done had we had slightly more time.

For our first foray we went to Darcha and did a three-and-a-half-day trek back to Khoksar over the Tempo La (4930m). This is a little-used pass – the locals said it could be done in a day, but we saw very little sign of any passage, just a few shepherds lower down below 4000m. The approach to the north side of the pass is a long trudge up moraines enlivened by excellent views back towards the Koa Rong peaks. From the pass itself, a lonely spot adorned with a single small cairn, our gaze was drawn enticingly towards the central Lahul peaks. On the south side we had a very easy descent at first and then a slightly trickier negotiation of a dry glacier, that would have been quite straight-forward to ascend but presented a few route-finding problems and some worrying moments in descent, given our inadequate trekking footwear. Lower down the nala narrows and has big crags on the west side, before debouching into the main Chandra valley.

After restocking in Manali we took one porter and returned over the Rohtang for a six-hour walk up to a base camp in the Kulti nala. Climbing above this through a short rocky barrier we found ourselves in a large glacier basin, almost entirely moraines at this time of year. Compared with Donald Bennet's pictures the icefalls looked smaller and more difficult, and the glaciers less attractive (the RAFMA team's visit was earlier in the season, in June). Wet and grey weather, lack of fitness, lack of time, unpleasant moraines – all combined to put us off venturing towards the higher peaks surrounding the basin, although Akela Kila, first climbed by Bennet and Stewart looked a fine objective. The unclimbed north-east ridge of Ashagiri also looked accessible and would make a very attractive snow and ice climb. Lowering our sights we climbed instead a shapely rocky pyramid, marked as P. 17,291ft on the RAFMA map, which provided a very pleasant scramble on reasonably sound rock, with no necessity for rope, axes or crampons. From our summit we saw immediately to our south an easy glacier leading south-east with some moderately straight-forward peaks at its head.

After a descent to base camp and some prospecting up the hillsides opposite we decided to explore this 'East Kulti' glacier, as no record apparently exists of anyone visiting it. But before doing so we had an appointment to fulfil at the 'Muni Hotel' – Hamish's apt description of the boulder camp next to our tent where a couple of Gaddi shepherds were installed with their flocks. Under a splendid Himalayan night sky a bottle of 'raksi' (local spirits) was quickly despatched, followed by a fiery noodle dish and the inevitable rice and dall. Conversation was limited unfortunately, but without words there was a friendly atmosphere and Hamish entered the lean-to kitchen to record an impressive arrangement of pressure cookers that saw the shepherds through the summer.

Next morning after an icy paddle across the river we climbed steadily up to the East Kulti glacier, managing to avoid all difficulties, and the following day succeeded in reaching the highest peak at its head (about 19,500ft). The glacier was very easy, and as we climbed gave us increasingly fine views of the peaks of Central Lahul. About 800ft below the summit a fluted snow face led directly upwards, but owing to my tortoise-like progress earlier the sun was up and the snow already softening. Hamish bravely led up a narrow avalanche runnel, but after a few hundred feet we moved to the break between the snow and a rocky face to the right for some interesting pitches, and finally traversed right onto the rocks for an exciting final pitch. As I reached the crest I was rewarded with a wonderful Brocken Spectre and views to the Kullu peaks, including the fine Mukar Beh which Donald had made the first ascent of so many years ago. The ridge was now very Alpine and gave us a short, but tiring, traverse on bad snow to the summit. The daytime cloud was beginning to swirl in but we had time to glimpse the mysteries of peaks above the Kukti and Chhatru nalas to the east which do not appear to have been visited. The descent was also Alpine – i.e. I felt light-headed and sleepy, the rock was bad and the abseils required patience. But we got down quite early in good order and next day reached base in terrific rain, which proved that the monsoon does indeed sometimes reach into Lahul!

Having enjoyed this successful trip I decided to attempt a similar venture with Mungo Ross in 1998. This time we wanted to go rather earlier, in May/early June, and consequently, had to choose an area some hundreds of miles south-east of Kullu. I had always wanted to go to the Gori Ganga, which was partly traversed by the intrepid 1950 Scottish Himalayan Expedition of Murray, Scott, Weir and McKinnon. Earlier in the century it was used by Longstaff to explore the eastern approaches to Nanda Devi, and before that it was known to the surveyors of the British Raj as the home of the most famous 'pundits' who explored the farther reaches of the Himalaya in disguise. The valley has only recently been re-opened to foreigners and was the base for the successful Panch Chuli expedition a few years ago (see SMCJ 1993).

Having suffered severe pre-monsoon heat in Delhi and a hellish bus ride to Haldwani we were greatly relieved to reach the roadhead at Munsiari on May 18. Though known to tourists, both Indian and foreign, this village is at a very different stage of development from Manali. It is still a quiet place, with little of interest in the bazaar and no-one trying a hard sell. The position of the village is very fine, several thousand feet above the Gori Ganga with thick forest above and a spectacular view across the valley to the Panch Chuli range.

We engaged three young porters and set off up the valley. The old path by the river had been swept away in a landslide and is currently being rebuilt, so on the second day we had to climb 3000ft to a little col and descend again through wonderful chestnut forests. The Gori Ganga is an old trade route to Tibet and also used for annual movements of shepherds with huge flocks of sheep and goats. But we were a little earlier than the main animal migrations, so our company on the track was largely pony trains supplying the army posts that guard the upper reaches of the valley against the possibility of Chinese incursion. The scenery in the narrowest part of the gorge was stupendously beautiful – huge vegetated rock walls, a mighty torrent pounding enormous boulders and an ancient paved track, sometimes virtually in the river (and only preserved by gabions), and sometimes clinging to steps carved out of crags high above it.

Farther up the valley opened out and on the third day we reached the village of Martoli on a wonderful alp high above the junction of the Gori Ganga with the Lawan Gad which flows from Nanda Devi East. I had read so often about this village both in Tilman's book (he and Houston traversed out of the sanctuary this way after the successful 1936 ascent of Nanda Devi), and in Bill Murray's account of the 1950 Scottish expedition. Now we found, on a beautiful sunny afternoon with unbelievably bright grass shining in the fields, a silent deserted ruin. I was almost in tears as I wandered about the substantial village of several hundred houses nearly all completely ramshackle, with their gardens and interiors full of waist high nettles and weeds. It was as bad as any deserted Highland clachan, perhaps worse because more recent. The story is that after the Indo-Chinese war of 1962 the trade with Tibet was completely stopped and these higher villages, which had once been quite wealthy and had sent their men trading hundreds of miles into Tibet in the summer and down to the Indian plains for the great fairs in the autumn, lost their *raison d'etre*. To anyone who has seen a living Himalayan village, its alleyways full of grubby smiling children and animals, and the surrounding fields a hive of activity, it was painfully poignant to see this dead remnant.

Yet it wasn't totally dead. A voice called from one house and invited us in. Our host Natho Singh had arrived that day from down the valley. He had already set up his water pipe and little garden (including rare medicinal herbs taken from high on the glaciers). The rooms of his house were clean and well ordered, he had a good stock of food and the wisdom and skills of generations of hill men. It was a great pleasure and privilege to stay a few days with him.

Our first foray was up a nala on the east side of the Gori Ganga to look at the unexplored west face of Burphu Dhura. The path was poor, and as far as we got the prospects didn't look too good. The lower peaks were still smothered in soft snow and the way to the higher peaks would have required a long, hot and exhausting glacier trudge. Returning to Martoli we decided to go up the Shalang Gad, which runs south-west from there. It offered an easy approach and we were unlikely to be troubled by the company of other parties. The alternative was to take the Lwan Gad to Nanda Devi East base camp. This was a more interesting and difficult walk but it seemed that the base camp was quite popular with trekking parties. As it turned out we were so early in the season that no-one would have bothered us and it would perhaps have been a more rewarding place to go – the base camp of Narspan Patti must have a fabulous situation under the huge face of Nanda Devi East, and with open views to Nanda Kot, shown attractively in Longstaff's 1905 photo.

Next day, accompanied for the first few miles by Natho Singh, and Nitya, a plucky American solo traveller who had turned up the previous evening, our little party set off for the Shalang. The freshness and clarity of the air early in the morning, and early in the season, were incredible: from a shoulder before we turned into our valley we sat and gazed at the beautiful mixed south-east ridge of Nanda Devi East, with the true goddess only partially visible behind. Our Shalang Gad gave us lovely warm grass for a few hours, but higher up we got into soft snow, still covering most of the shepherds' summer campsites. We encouraged the porters on, but next morning they walked less than an hour before leaving us at the last place where fresh water was running, still some way from the glacier. We prospected up a pretty curving moraine ridge with the huge but rather loose and unattractive south-east face of Nanda Kot towering above us.

We had already realised that with only a week at our disposal and everything covered in deep soft snow we could only attempt the nearest peaks. Our choices were Shalang Dhura (5678m), a very easy snow peak on the south side of the glacier, and Nandakhani (6029m), a shapely little peak dwarfed by the bulk of Nanda Kot on its right. We chose Nandakhani and over the next few days gradually moved ourselves up its east ridge to a camp on a flat section at about 5300m. Pre-dawn we had very easy walking on the lower glacier, and lovely cramponing up the initial slopes of the ridge, but from 7am onwards the heat and the snow made upwards progress unappealing. The result was a good deal of festering, unhelped by terrible problems with our primus stove. After a couple of nights at this top camp we were lucky to get a slightly cloudier day, and on May 29 had an easy, but interesting, climb to the summit. Although we carried rope and gear we had no need of it as the snow was in quite good condition, though not well frozen. We got views of most of the surrounding peaks including back across the Gori Ganga to the excellent Kalabaland mountains. Nanda Kot loomed over us to the north, obscuring Nanda Devi and the other peaks of the sanctuary.

It was good to get down next day off the snow to grass and water, and then to return to Martoli and Natho Singh's 'home cooking'. It had been a little strange being up there before all the shepherds, and indeed before most of the spring flowers. Only a few weeks later all those upper alps would be alive with men and their flocks, but we had had the valley to ourselves.

We spent a day visiting Milam, the highest village in the Gori Ganga, formerly home to many famous pundits and climbers, and vividly described by Bill Murray in his book of the 1950 expedition. It was a thoroughly depressing experience. An ill-cared for army post staffed by bored recruits guarded entry to another largely ruined, roofless and insanitary village with only a few unhealthy looking families lurking here and there. Perhaps it was the fact that I myself was feeling unwell, but even sight of the splendid 7000m peaks Tirsuli and Hardeol at the head of the Milam glacier failed to lift the spirits. I felt a lot happier when we descended and sampled again the beauties of the lower gorge where more and more flocks jostled up the old trail, and on the untracked opposite bank troops of monkeys watched us curiously from the jungle. All in all, we felt happy to have seen another wonderful area of the Himalaya with, as ever, untold potential for further climbing of every level of difficulty.

RONNIE ROBB writes of his expedition last year to the Kanchenjunga region of East Nepal. The small team of three included Dave Robb (his brother) and Bruce Bricknell. They had permits to attempt the unclimbed Dhromo (6900m) and Tengkongma (6210m) which has had three previous ascents. They were part of a larger group 'Medical Expeditions', which had permits for the North ridge of Kanchenjunga (8586m) and Ramtang (6700m). Aside from the mountaineering,

Medex's' objectives were to carry out research into high altitude illnesses which they very successfully achieved after basing themselves at the common base camp for the area, Pangpengma for more than two months.

The first disappointing aspect of the trip came when Ronnie and his group met Doug Scott and Roger Mears during the 16-day walk-in where they proudly announced the first ascent of Dhromo! Along with this disappointing news came information about a difficult route with poor protection and one which required good weather, acclimatisation and hence a lot more time than was available.

The Kanchenchenjunga team had abandoned their attempt at the castle (7400m), 43 days after arriving at BC in the face of terrible weather and depleting resources. Ronnie and his team therefore turned their attention to Tengkongma after a brief acclimatisation period.

They left base camp on October 20, and established a high camp at 5500m. The following day the three climbed an initial ice cliff and crossed 2km of glacier to a high col. At this point the weather deteriorated and the visibility reduced to 30m. A broken rock buttress led onto an exposed ridge with huge cornices overhanging the Broken Glacier 1000m somewhere below. More worrying than the weather was the snow conditions. The team was moving up on wind slab slope interspersed with small seracs and crevasses and it was now 2pm.

Eventually, they decided that the risks were too great and descended approximately 150m from the summit. They returned to base camp the day after and commenced the return journey over the Mirgin La and back to Suketar, 12 days later via the Omje Kohla.

The area is very remote with superb views of Kambachen, Cross Peak, Wedge Peak and Jannu. During the trip they also attempted to follow in the footsteps of Dr. Sandy Kellas, a fellow Aberdonian explorer who came this way in 1912. They were beaten to this as well by Lindsay Griffin who made an ascent to the Longridge Pass in the pre-monsoon period of 1998.

Finally, after all the near misses on the hill, Ronnie come closest to death when he was stung by a flying insect and discovered that he suffers from Anaphyloxis, a severe and potentially fatal allergy to insect venom. If ever there was a time to be surrounded by doctors and sufficient supplies of adrenaline it was now and he made a complete recovery. Who needs to go climbing to be an adrenaline junkie?

Australasia

DAVE BROADHEAD reports:– One of my long-standing ambitions as a schoolteacher had been to do a year's job exchange in either Canada or New Zealand, close to some interesting hills, but as is oft the way with the best laid plans, it did not work out quite like that. Arriving in Brisbane, Australia in January 1997 I was as excited as the rest of the family at the prospect of sunshine, ocean and rainforest, but rather hazy about the climbing prospects in south-east Queensland, if any.

A few weeks before, at the Annual Dinner in Strathpeffer, Tom Weir had reminded me of A. L. Cram's extensive antipodean adventures, faithfully reported in various *SMCJs* which I hastily perused as I transferred my precious volumes to the loft, out of the way of the incoming Aussies who were to live in our house. Hamish Irvine agreed to look after Ling Hut and lent me a guidebook to Frog Buttress just outside Brisbane where he had climbed on his travels some years before. Willie Jeffrey supplied a list of names and addresses of possible climbing partners and Steve Chadwick knew Brisbane well enough to extol the virtues cragging at Kangaroo Point beside the river near the city centre where the City Council kindly floodlight the cliffs to allow climbing in the cool of the evening. Another convenience for the Brisbane-based climber is that most of the half-dozen gear shops are located next door to each other in Fortitude Valley, along with an indoor climbing wall and most of the city's Chinese businesses.

With so many other things to do my rock shoes and the Frog Buttress guide did not get as much use as hoped, but we did discover the pleasures of bushwalking. The *Bushpeoples Guide to Bushwalking in South-East Queensland* published by Bushpeople Publications provides an extensive introduction on skills (no surprises here), some superb colour photos and lots of useful sketch maps, suggested walks and route details. Peak-bagging has never really taken off in Queensland, presumably because many of the most notable peaks are featureless and covered in forest, including Mt. Superbus, at 1375m the highest peak in the area. However, there are enough interesting hills to provide a number of enjoyable outings.

A short drive to the north and close to the Bruce Highway, the Glasshouse Mountains rise abruptly from the fiat coastal plain. The remains of volcanic plugs, they were named by Captain Cook and present dramatic profiles, low enough that all or most of the eight peaks can be climbed in an energetic weekend. Second highest and most spectacular, Mt. Coonowrin (Crookneck (377m) has one exposed traverse (known as Salmon's Leap after an early pioneer bushwalker Bert Salmon) which keeps away all but the most intrepid. Mt. Beerwah (556m) and Mt. Tibrogargan (364 m) are popular slabby scrambles with extensive views across fields of pineapple and exotic conifer plantations out to the coast and there are legends to go with their beautiful Aboriginal names.

South of Brisbane, enormous volcanic activity about 22 million years ago centered on Mt. Warning (1157m) which is now a distinctive landmark and a fine viewpoint of the remains of the surrounding caldera. Leading into the northern New South Wales interior, the Cunningham Highway crosses the Scenic Rim through Cunningham's Gap – a handy starting point for half-days on Mt. Cordeaux (1135m) and Mt. Mitchell (1168m) despite the rumble of trucks spoiling the sounds of the rainforest. On nearby Mt. Barney (1351m) our views were limited by the haze of late winter (dry season) bushfires. One of the most popular local hills with a choice of routes to the top, the well trodden South (Peasants) Ridge is highly recommended. My wife, Moira, climbed the South East Ridge with a party from the Brisbane Bushwalking Club (led by an expat. Scot) which involved considerable bushwacking.

Farther afield, on the way to Canberra we spent a few days in the Warrumbungle National Park, where a half-day around the Grand High Tops (Pineham) Trail gives splendid views of an impressive jumble of spires, dykes and domes, the remains of another volcano, with some good rock climbing possibilities. Deep in outback Queensland, beyond Roma though still east of the Great Dividing Range, Carnarvon Gorge National Park has miles of spectacular sandstone cliffs cut with narrow side canyons. On the Queensland coast, Fraser Island, the world's largest sand island has no mountaineering interest whatever, but what a wonderful place to spend a few days wandering among magnificent forests and freshwater lakes. Moreton Island boasts the world's highest sand dune and the chance to try sand tobogganing. So if you ever get the chance to visit south-east Queensland, remember to take your boots (and a compass).

REVIEWS

A Dream of White Horses - Recollections of a Life on the Rocks:– Edwin Drummond, (Baton Wicks. 1997. £8.99, 224 pp, illustrations, paperback. ISBN 1-898573-220).

This is the second edition of a book which first appeared in 1987. It was reviewed in the 1988 Journal by Geoff Dutton, who should be consulted for a more analytical opinion. This is a justly famous book and many of you will already have the first edition.

For those who do not, I can say that this is probably the pinnacle of the solipsist school of mountaineering writing and will either fascinate or repel. Drummond is a poet, a writer, a political activist and a mountaineer. He is other things besides. This book is heady stuff – mainly Ed's head. The reader is taken on a detailed topographic tour of his emotional states with occasional bits of rock sticking through. In 1968 he wrote to Royal Robbins asking him to act as reporter for his, Drummond's, project to make a solo ascent of North American Wall. He is honest enough to quote from Royal's magisterial reply: 'It sounds more like hubris than love of the warm rock beneath your hand…I want nothing to do with it.' This book can be read as the history of the Gods' protracted and convoluted revenge.

It is a vividly written mixture of autobiography, accounts of highly-uncomfortable ascents of big walls and poetry. It also includes the famous essay on Jim Perrin's biography of Menlove Edwards. This stands apart from the rest of the book and reveals an analytical and intellectual individual (albeit over-keen to remind us that he too had a University education). This is worth the purchase price alone.

Some readers may be put off by the continuous emphasis on Drummond's thoughts and emotions and suspect that the mountain is treated more as a stage than as an object of desire; but few writers can convey such a sense of tension and uncertainty in perilous situations. His ascents range from Romsdal to Yosemite by way of St. John's Head. Epics are described here, or rather the emotions of experiencing epics. Anyone wishing to repeat his routes will have to look elsewhere for topographical guidance. In those days big wall climbing was not a weekend excursion, several weeks would be spent on a suitable piece of vertical rock proving Drummond's Law of Face Climbing. This states that the time taken for a route is an exponential function of the number of haul bags. His capacity for suffering in the cause of his art is thoroughly documented and at times one wonders if he is undergoing penance (a slowly ascending Simon Stylites) rather than fulfilling mountaineering ambitions.

His emotional experiences on the horizontal also take up much of the book. He appears to have crunched his way to the cliffs over a scree of women. Few mountaineering books are as honest about the conflicting demands of domesticity and real living.

In summary, this is a terrifically written piece of mountaineering autobiography with some good (if not always totally successful) poems and an interesting essay thrown in to spice the dish. Best taken in small doses, each preferably followed by a cooling chapter of *Hamish's Mountain Walk* or some such native product.

Bob Richardson.

The Munros CD-Rom:– Edited by Donald Bennet and Ken Crocket. (The Scottish Mountaineering Club, 1998, multi-media CD, £40, ISBN 0-907521-56-8).

With a 16-year-old son whose main hobbies are mountains and computers, what better present, I thought to myself last Christmas, could I buy than the new CD-ROM –*The Munros* produced by the SMC. What better way to study and learn about the hills and mountains of Scotland except by being out on the hill himself?

It has taken us (I now use it continually as well) several months of extensive use to examine everything this CD ROM has to offer – there is so much!

Once the CD is loaded, you are presented with the main menu of icons (small pictures) representing the different sections of the disc. The largest area is undoubtedly the Munros area itself. On choosing this you are presented with a map of Scotland split into 17 areas e.g. the Cairngorms, Glen Affric and Kintail, and Skye and Mull, to name but three. Clicking the mouse in an area takes you to a description of that area and a more detailed map showing each Munro along with major roads, rivers and lochs.

You can now click on a Munro and after being given a Gaelic pronunciation, you get a description of the ascent route which can be printed out if need be. You are also presented with more icons which allow you to record your ascent in a log book; view an animated route map, and receive a commentary on the route. You don't get someone talking to you from a book!

There is also a series of photographs of each mountain; some have virtual flights of the mountain and surrounding area.

At all times a help icon is available if you are unsure of what you are doing. You can search for particular mountains you want to appear next, and move backwards and forwards through those which you have viewed. Many of the mountains have a Harvey's map icon showing, indicating that such a map is available for that Munro.

The next section of the main menu is the Logbook, which not only brings together the individual logs found with each Munro, but allows you to add extra details of the ascent – who your companions were etc.

The Gallery section gives 280 stunning full-screen photographs of the Scottish mountains. The clarity and depth of the photography loses nothing from being presented in this digital form and these photographs truly show the mountains of Scotland in their full glory.

The Web icon gives a wide variety of e-mail addresses and internet sites which may be of interest to both hillwalkers and climbers. These range from weather information to manufacturers such as Berghaus to the Mountain Bothies Association. All these links are 'live' which means that if you have an internet connection open while you are viewing the CD-ROM, you can go to any of these sites to view the information provided there.

It is the next section – Backpack, which shows the real advantages of providing information in an electronic form. This section is divided into seven sub-sections:

History – first hill-walkers, Sir Hugh Munro, how Munros were defined, etc. *Flora and fauna* – the wildlife and vegetation of the Scottish hills. *Clothing and equipment, avalanche awareness* and *navigation* – the three sections which clearly show why this CD-ROM is so much better than a book. The information given is in many cases expanded on by the use of video clips on, e.g., new outdoor fabrics, use of general and winter equipment, how to test the snow for avalanche danger, how to use a map and compass and so on. There is a tourist information section which gives e-mail and internet addresses of Scottish tourist organisations and finally a *Glossary* explaining a whole range of terms from abseil to wind-chill.

The Trivia and Quiz section is an interesting little section which gives you really important information such as the record for Munro ascents was, until recently, 6278 while the highest number of completed rounds is 9! The quiz involves reaching the top of a mountain by answering correctly a series of easy/moderate/ severe questions on Munros. If you fail to reach the top and descend before nightfall you are gobbled up by a wolf.

Do I have any criticisms? Yes, but only one or two and they are minor. I would have liked to see a comprehensive list of summits with their tops and their heights. Also, the music played at intervals throughout the sections can get a bit irritating at times, but I suppose that's because I linger too long at certain places.

All in all I would thoroughly recommend this CD-ROM. It may be slightly overpriced at £40 , but considering the lists of contributors at the end, you are receiving only the very best information and advice. The whole package is highly informative, educational, easy to follow and most importantly, it is fun.

David Mackie.

The Ordinary Route:– Harold Drasdo (Ernest Press 1998, 258 pp., £12.50, ISBN 0-94815-346-6)

I have to admit that this book presented me with a dilemma. As a reader I wanted to go slowly, to savour passages, to reflect on what the author is saying. As a reviewer I needed to finish it quickly so I could put pen to paper (or rather fingers to keyboard). Drasdo, after a lifetime of experience, not just of climbing, but of teaching, travelling and observing, has something to say, and a reflective style to help him say it. So much climbing literature is either written by, or about, elite climbers and their achievements – something for the reader to admire but not to identify with. Drasdo sets out deliberately to follow the Ordinary Route, and to use it as a symbol for the more commonplace, yet often extraordinary personal experiences that climbing provides.

The format of the book is essentially a series of recollections and reflections on a lifetime of climbing. It starts (and ends) with a somewhat autobiographical tone, which somehow seemed a little out of place. Perhaps this material could have been worked into some of the other chapters to better effect. He considers some of the essential by-products of the climbing lifestyle – ethics, getting lost, nights out, falling ('it was only the cliff that flashed before me, never my life'), death – and he reflects on the value of these experiences, how we deal with them and what we learn from them. There are lengthy deliberations on access, conservation and climbing as an art form. An historical section on the development of the West Yorkshire climbing scene in the 1950s and the Wall End Barn era in Langdale provides some well-observed characters, and shows that despite changing times there is still much to connect experience then and now. Some climbs are described, but always in the context of place, companions, motivations and other incidentals that are often central to the plot.

In this book it is the scenes and experiences that go with the climbing, rather than the actual climbs themselves, that combine to give so much interest to the content. The moves, the difficulties, the details of the pitches, are rarely described fully, and you don't miss them. It is the world through which the climber moves, and which is observed so accurately and intelligently, that is the substance of this book. The climber's predilection for challenge, for looking round the next, unlikely corner, for coping with uncertainty and persevering against resistance, does not just find its expression on climbs, but in an outlook on life and a persistent curiosity. Interestingly, the author's 'finest hour', at least in terms of British rock climbing, was the first ascent of North Crag Eliminate; yet in the reading of the book it comes across merely as an averagely exciting day out. By comparison scenes and experiences described elsewhere – sometimes not even climbs – are described far more vividly and intensely, as true Ordinary Routes.

Drasdo's writing brings his observation to life. It is rich in analogy and metaphor – maps as poems without beginning or end, first ascents as scientific discoveries (the common thirst for knowledge, exploration and personal recognition); hitch-hiking as the original inspiration for Waiting for Godot. A quasi-biblical ascent of Mount Sinai, resonant with thousands of years of human experience of the wilderness; the lone echoing trumpeter at Montserrat; the limestone mountains surrounding Athens warmed by the Mediterranean light – these scenes are evoked with finely-crafted prose, often understated, to sometimes dazzling effect.

The metaphor of the Ordinary Route (as the most logical, elegant and simplest solution to a particular challenge) can be applied not just to rock faces, or mountain climbs, but to all manner of human endeavours, and even to one's passage along the journey of life itself. This is, to me, what Drasdo seems to be getting at. On the strength of this book, the Ordinary Route is certainly an ascent worth aspiring to.

Adam Kassyk.

Scotland's Mountains before the Mountaineers:– Ian Mitchell. (Luath Press, 1998. £9.99, ISBN 0-946-487-39-1).

Mountaineering activities in Scotland have been recorded in detail for little more than a century, but obviously, there was much mountain involvement by people for many different reasons and throughout a long period. This must extend back to prehistoric times when settlers first moved into the Highlands. This book is not about the mountains themselves and does not seek to describe them, nor does it try to deal with the movement through and among the mountains which must have existed since earliest times, except by occasional reference. As Ian Mitchell says in his introduction it is about the 'explorations, ascents, travels, social relations in the mountains before mountaineering became an organised sport from the middle of the last century'. He includes the 2000-year span since the hill forts were built although there is little specific material on which he can draw until about 1070 AD when King Malcolm Canmore awarded a prize to the victor of a hill race up Creag Choinnich at Braemar. The traditional Gaelic names which still exist for so many detailed features of the hills are evidence of abundant activity in the mountains from early times. However, it is not until the 16th century that ascents of particular mountains can be identified. Most of the material in this book inevitably relates to the next 400 years when there are written records.

Anyone who knows the substantial paper by D. B. Horn, *The Origins of Mountaineering in Scotland* from the 1966 Journal (Vol. 28) will recognise that this book contains much that is referred to in that article. Of course that in turn drew on a series of five shorter articles by different authors, *The Rise and Progress of Mountaineering in Scotland,* in the 1894 Journal (Vol. 3). Campbell Steven's *The Story of Scotland's Hills* (Robert Hale, 1975) is another of Mitchell's sources. However, much research has gone into the writing of this book and the useful bibliography lists no fewer than 163 references from 140 different sources. The text does not use footnotes; where direct quotations are used they are always clearly identified and a good many other direct references are bracketed. The bibliography must be consulted to track other sources. This departure from more conventional academic style is more fluid and easily read, while maintaining opportunities for pursuing further information.

Ian Mitchell divides the Highlands into four parts, relating to the familiar SMC divisions as follows: Central: Southern Highlands and Central Highlands excluding the Monadhliath. Cairngorms: Cairngorms District with the addition of the Monadhliath. West: Western and Northern Highlands combined. Islands: Islands including Skye. He takes each area in turn, giving the descriptions and recorded ascents of the principal mountains from the earliest travellers to the more interesting 19th century visitors. Inevitably, the reader will encounter the names of the more peripatetic several times but their full pictures will only be drawn once. If any confusion is felt it may be resolved by reference to a chronological list of events in the Appendix.

At times I felt that the attempts to identify the first recorded ascents of hills was overdone and pretty meaningless anyway, but it was interesting to read the evidence suggesting that the first Munro to have a recorded ascent was Beinn Fhionnlaidh in the 1580s (by Black Findlay of the Deer). I was surprised to find no reference to the first recorded avalanche accident (at Gaick in 1800), nor to the 1834 description by 'Frederick Fag' of Cairngorm as 'a dreary mountain where stones, gathered in the Andes and purchased in London for twopence a piece, are sold to the silly southern Sassenachs as real Cairngorms for five shillings each'. However, there was plenty of interesting information new to me. This is a user-friendly book and useful to have on the shelf as it is well endowed with the means to check on individuals or events by means of the index, the chronology or the bibliography. For me it also added character to some individuals who may have only been names vaguely remembered – why was Lugless Willie Lithgow (Goatfell, 1628) lugless? – why was Taylor who was on Mount Keen in 1618 called the Water Poet? – what did the confiscated estates Commissioner James Robertson (1771) actually climb when he was touring about the Highlands? – and the energetic minister George Skene Keith (1811)? – the remarkably indefatigable Thomas Colby and his team of the early Ordnance Surveyers (1819) – and J. D. Forbes the pioneer of glacial geology and first ascender of Sgurr nan Gillean (1836) – and so on.

Bill Brooker.

The Munroist's Companion:– Compiled and Edited by Robin N. Campbell, viii+328pp, published 1999 by the Scottish Mountaineering Trust, ISBN 0-907521-50-9, £16.

This is a retro Munro anthology. Its eight chapters divide loosely into three sections of roughly 100 pages each. The first examines *The Pioneers:* writings by and about Hugh Munro and the early completers of his list. Then comes the most innovative section, statistical Table talk by Bonsall, Purchase and others along with a complex *Variorum Table* of Munro changes that readers will either pore over or skip completely. Finally, a rag-bag of essays on *Technical Advice* (altimeter measurements, axe technique, navigation), followed by *Predicaments* (SMCers getting lost), and *The Modern Munroist.*

This review has neither space nor intention to analyse individual essays, most of which have appeared before. Suffice it to say there is much interesting (if often stodgy) material here, although the procession of well-heeled white males wears a little by the end. The early accounts are notable for their other-era feel, their exploration of unknown territories, their tales of crazy glissading and pipe-smoking, quaint talk of housemaids, trains to Callander and pony-trap 'machines'.

Anthologies such as this must be reviewed for overall approach, with attention focused on contents, introduction and footnotes rather than on the essays themselves. On this basis Campbell starts well, his short, but clear, preface promising much opinionated annotation ahead. But he then backs off, intervening far less than might be wished. Sure, he chips in with footnotes and cross-references plus occasional introductions to chapters, but he prefers to let unabridged texts speak for themselves rather than taking a hands-on approach. This has two consequences: the reader is denied Campbell's informed opinions on matters about which he is an acknowledged expert, and the book itself carries much ballast, essays appearing in full when some canny cut-and-paste editing might have seen less become more.

The image of Campbell as cautious editor should not, however, imply a lack of care. That this is a labour of love, born of much rummaging through archives, is seen most clearly in its marvellous photographs. These in themselves justify the book, and the publishers are to be congratulated for allocating full pages to superb portraits of Ronald Burn and Rooke Corbett. There is also an on-hill picture of James Gall Inglis where, with his van der Graaff frizz of hair, he looks like some Caucasian Don King. Textually, Campbell does well in rejecting 'compleat' and noting that 'Sir Hugh' is inappropriate in respect of the 1891 list since Munro was not knighted until 1913. He is very good on the background to the revisions, seeing off those who harp on about the infallible merit of the original version. There is detail on those quirk-Tops initially given precedence over main summits, and a perceptive observation that the first revision, in 1921, was far more substantial than any since.

Campbell's approach to footnotes does, however, seem oddly erratic, as with the absence of any translation of Munro's obituary notice from a French newspaper. Douglas and Raeburn then offer navigational advice based on 18° magnetic variation, when surely the modern figure should be appended lest some casual reader stow the old version for on-hill use. And there is mention of Colin Campbell of Glenure shortly after a (footnoted) account of the antics of Colin Campbell of Meggernie. This cries out for comment on whether these men were related, yet receives none – and this from a Campbell!

This is nibbling at the edges, however. The book's main disappointment is its failure to represent the great mass of Munroists, who rarely encroach beyond the endpapers. Post-Second World War is woefully under-represented (primarily by a mere 30 pages at the end including the book's best piece, by Sandy Cousins), while female Munroists are almost completely absent. With regard to the modern era, Campbell would presumably point to his preface, where he writes: 'Although there is a section containing accounts written by modern Munroists, I have excluded the writings of the swift, the multiply-completing [sic], the 277-in-one-gulpers, etc – for these are not typical Munroists.'

This is flawed thinking. It is unclear what Campbell regards as 'swift', since while he chastises Paddy Heron for 'bolting down the Munros in a few feverish years', he devotes considerable space to John Dow, who rattled round within six years. Dow technically started with Ben Lomond in May 1895, but completed a round, including Lomond again, between the Ardlui Vorlich on 9/8/27 and Beinn na Lap on 4/6/33. And gimmick completions surely started with Parker, who began with the southernmost on 19/7/1883 and ended with the northernmost on 19/7/27.

Perhaps 'swift' refers to single-expedition 'gulpers' like Brown, Murgatroyd, Keeping, Caldwell, Lincoln and Allum, but Campbell is unfair to also exclude their moderately swift colleagues. Although he claims (p288) to side with 'the Ordinary Munroist', he merely ends up looking prejudiced against the vast bulk of completions from unattached hillgoers or members of non-SMC clubs. Many ordinary Munroists will feel this book is no particular companion to them.

As to women, they are completely companionless. This is an overwhelmingly male book, with no articles by women nor indeed many women meriting mention. Campbell observes that Munroing is 'for Everyman (and, of course, Everywoman)', but so ignores his own point that it comes as a shock when Anne Macintyre pops up in David Broadhead's Monadh Liath piece near the end. Again the absence might be defended by the book having been built chiefly around Victorian and Edwardian journals of exclusively male clubs, but Campbell willingly draws in articles from elsewhere. Female narratives are available, and their absence is gaping, especially with the first two female 'Slammers' still alive. Anne Littlejohn and Lorna Anderson (née Ticehurst) deserve coverage in a book such as this, and their presence would have added greatly to its liveliness and credibility. Anderson particularly has had a remarkable, thrilling life, yet she doesn't merit even a footnote here.   Similarly, the first female Munroist remains 'Mrs J. Hirst'. John Hirst's wife might indeed have answered to this, but as Docharty names her Annie Wells there is evidence that she was considerably more free-spirited. Campbell has, ironically, done some good work in tidying the Munroists' list – removing the redundant numbering, introducing James Gall Inglis in 1938, commenting that Edred Corner should probably be in, and returning Alfred Slack to his correct 1950 position (although where is Chris Andrews, obituarised in the 1954 Journal as having completed the Munros?)

Campbell appears more interested in altimeters than in women. Aneroids feature heavily in the *Technical Advice* section, with accounts of hill-measuring by Collie, James Gall Inglis, Parker and Corbett. Campbell's zeal for subjective measurement is touching, but somewhat misguided. He comments that 'most of the heights "determined" by the pioneers using these methods turned out to be more correct than the mapped heights obtained by triangulation and levelling'. This, unqualified, is nonsense. Even 100 years ago the majority of map heights were reasonably reliable, and certainly to be trusted more than on-hill measurements made in uncertain conditions. The aneroid-carriers themselves undermine Campbell's statement, continually scurrying to known spot heights to check their hand-held readings. Not for nothing does Corbett speak of his 'pocket liar'.

Aneroids also feature in the book's most marked silence, its lack of comment on the promotion of Knight's Peak to Top status. Lacking any cartographic evidence, this was easily the most controversial element of the 1997 revision. The OS has published no 914m figure, while Harveys suggest 911.5m plus-or-minus a metre. There is suspicion that promotion arose through lobbying by Campbell himself (his article in the 1992 Journal, not reproduced here, says: 'If there is room to doubt the OS heights [...] Knight's Peak should be given the benefit of that doubt and included as a new Top'). Given this strength of opinion he is oddly quiet (apart from a picture caption) when Collie specifically discusses the Pinnacle Ridge. Then there is the entry in the *Variorum Table*. Campbell specifically codifies any 'approximate height measured by climbers', the implication being that all other heights are formal mappings. Hence the 1921 hand-held height of Carn a'Mhaim is marked, likewise for the now-deleted Faochag. But Knight's Peak receives a straight figure, with no mention of aneroid measurement. Is Campbell being coy? This reviewer found himself not quite trusting the *Variorum Table* because of this.

So, an interesting and worthwhile book, but a flawed one. Neither a flowing, hard-to-put-down history of Munro-climbing nor a truly entertaining dip into this vast and complex subject. The book lacks the lightness and variability in tone of miscellanies such as Chernev's *The Chess Companion,* or Ross's *The Cricketer's Companion.* Somehow, somewhere, it falls between a straight-forward celebration of its subject and a treatise arguing for a certain approach. Maybe Campbell is simply too deferential to the great hillgoers of the past, but more of his opinions would have made this a more relevant book for the modern generation.

This links with the question of the book's title, which feels slightly misjudged. An indefinite article would have helped, plus some time-frame context given the extent that Campbell majors on early Munroists. *The Munros – An Early History,* perhaps. Although *The Munroist's Companion* implies something for Munroists rather than about them, it is odd that Arran makes several appearances and that the cover paintings show people-free scenes from way before Munro, while many of Campbell's writers are not listed Munroists. Backhouse, Cohen, Collie, Dutton, Goggs, Lawson, Naismith, Raeburn, plus of course Munro and Campbell themselves; many humble but genuinely complete Munroists could be excused feeling a little cheated. And what of the 'First Munroist' himself, the Rev. Robertson? When Campbell quotes AER's notorious Wyvis statement ('near the top [...] I turned'), he doubts whether 'this matters greatly'. Such generosity is touching, but there does seem clear evidence that Robertson knowingly failed on Wyvis, didn't bother returning, and yet still claimed completion. Since Campbell has passed up his chance to be genuinely innovative here, this review ends by formally suggesting that Ronald Burn should be henceforth regarded as the first of the breed.

Dave Hewitt.

Valais Alps West, Selected Climbs:– Lindsay Griffin (Alpine Club Guidebooks 1998, 448 pp. plus 97 photo/diagrams, eight colour plates, £19.50, ISBN 0-900523-61-1).

The photograph of the Matterhorn on the cover of this new guide boldly announces that this is a rather different publication from the previous edition, the Robin Collomb *Pennine Alps West,* which was a slimmer volume covering a more limited area. The new AC series covers the Pennine Alps in two volumes; this guide extends from the Grand Combin massif in the west, to the Matterhorn and Dent Blanche in the east. The slightly arbitrary eastern boundary was presumably defined to create two volumes of equal size. In practice, it makes for a more interesting volume with a wider selection of different types of climbing than the earlier edition, including four of the increasingly popular 'vier-tausender'. The downside is that if you are intending to base your climbing trip in the Zermatt Valley you will probably have to buy both volumes.

This new edition is long overdue. Much has changed in this area, and plenty of new lines have been climbed. There are many references to the recession of glaciers and ice faces, and the consequent exposure of large areas of fractured rock. For this reason the guide often recommends climbs to be undertaken outside the peak summer season – not a bad idea if it popularises climbing at other times of the year.

The introductory notes are very comprehensive, and include sources for weather forecasts and information on valley rock climbs. Another useful feature is a list of climbs by valley base. More than 400 routes are on offer, including 17 different possibilities on the Matterhorn and a choice of 12 different lines on the north side of the Dent Blanche, for those so inclined. New rock climbs have been added to the lower peaks in recent years, and despite the reputation of Valais rock, they sound very fine. However, despite the famous north faces, this is still primarily an area for the lower to middle grade climber, bagging classic snow peaks and doing fine rock scrambles. There are still many routes where you would be unlikely to meet anyone else, and plenty of scope for long traverses and extended adventures.

I noticed that several of the established easier routes have been upgraded, and the text includes many usefully informative comments, particularly for that first alpine trip. The note that 'several parties have actually failed on the walk to the Col de Tsarmine – a strenuous and daunting undertaking for the unfit' evoked a wry smile. That was my first alpine day out – if only we'd known! A worthwhile investment, even at the (rather steep) price, whether just for your bookshelf or for that next trip.

Adam Kassyk.

Shouting Wind and Shining Cloud – The Bens of Jura:- Jonathan Macarthur Crow (The Celtic House, Bowmore, Islay, 1998, 52 pp., £4.95, paperback. No ISBN.)

This is the kind of slim book you might see displayed in a hotel foyer or on the counter of a coffee shop. The author has clearly been struck by the hills of southern Jura and has compiled a mixture of description, commentary, folk-lore (of even more dubiety than usual) and verse. There are illustrations and sketches. The book is true to its title and focuses entirely in its physical descriptions on the Paps and the hills to the south and ignores completely the bulk of this fascinating island.

This is not a book for the mountaineer or climber but it does have a certain charm while the author's diligence in bringing together historical references to Jura and the Paps is commendable.

Bob Richardson.

South Ridge of the Salbitschijen, Switzerland. Photo: Alastair Matthewson.
Family Holidays in the Arctic. Leif Anderson (8) is ' Just checkin' for them bears', Juno Sound, East Greenland. Photo: Douglas Anderson.

REVIEWS 247

Also received

Ticks, A Lay Guide to a Human Hazard:- George Hendry and Darrel Ho-Yen. (1998, Mercat Press, Edinburgh. 96pp, illus., £4.99. ISBN 1-873644-80-9.)

Flushed with the success of his earlier book on the dreaded midge, the author has bashed on to do this one on the slightly-less dreaded tick. I'm afraid though, that as a practical guide for walkers and tourists I regard the book as 95 pages of wasted paper. The only really useful bit is encapsulated in a text box on page 74, where it tells you, if you need to know, how to remove a tick (gently, with tweezers and no twisting.) There, I've given you the whole story in six words and saved you £4.99. I suppose I could gild the lily and advise sweaty gaiters in summer with strong DEET sprayed on. Biologically, given the statistically low incidence of Lyme disease, I'm more worried by *Giardia.*

The Kurt Diemberger Omnibus:- Spirits of The Air, Summits and Secrets, and The Endless Knot. (Bâton Wicks/The Mountaineers, 1999, £16.99, 235mm x 150mm h/back, 864 pages, 24pp of photo (8 in colour), ISBN-898573-26-3).

Yet again, Ken Wilson has done us a great service by making more accessible some mountain classics. I'm even going to give you his e-mail address, so that you can tell him how happy it makes you. kwilson@batonwicks.demon.co.uk

The Grahams and the New Donalds. Second Edition. Compiled by Alan Dawson and also including Grahamist and Donaldist data by Dave Hewitt. (TACit Tables, 1999. £2.80. ISBN 0 9534376 0 4).

As the *Introduction* to this second edition states, there have been no new hills and no deletions since the first edition. There are, however, revisions and additions to the notes, including revised drop figures for many hills and a set of line drawings.

Nanga Parbat Pilgrimage – The Lonely Challenge. Hermann Buhl. (Bâton Wicks/The Mountaineers, 1998, £10.99, p/back, illus. ISBN 1-898573-27-1).

Originally published in the UK in 1956 and later in the US as *The Lonely Challenge* (hence the subtitle above), this book was one of my seminal pieces as a young climber, as no doubt it was for an entire generation. It is still required reading for any climber with belly fire and bicep strength, and Wilson has continued his useful reprint series here with another classic.

Valais Alps East – Selected climbs. Les Swindin and Peter Fleming. (1999, Alpine Club, £18.50, ISBN-0-900523-62-x). The companion volume to Valais Alps West. (Reviewed by A. Kassyk elsewhere.)

Other books not sent in for review, but read by the Hon. Editor for enjoyment and continuing sanity as the *SMCJ* was being produced included: **The Essential Haiku – versions of Basho, Buson, and Issa.** (Edited by Robert Hass, The Ecco Press, 1994, $15, ISBN 0-88001-351-6). **Cold Mountain,** Charles Frazier (1997, Sceptre, £6.99, ISBN 0-340-68059-8). **The Blind Watchmaker,** Richard Dawkins (1991, Penguin Books, £8.99, ISBN 0-14-014481-1).

K. V. Crocket.

Clockwise from left: Nanda Khani (6029m) in the Kumaon Himalaya, India. Photo: Mungo Ross.
Wedge Peak (6750m) towering above Kangchenjunga base camp. Photo: Ronnie Robb.
Steve Kennedy on the first ascent of 'The Party's Over' (E2 5b), Setesdal, Norway. Photo: David Ritchie.
'Emmanuel' from Tupilag during first ascent. SMC Staunings Alps Expedition 1998. Photo: John Peden.

Journals of Kindred Clubs

The American Alpine Journal, Vol. 40, 1998. Editor Christian Beckwith.

As usual, this superb publication repays both those who are seeking out new corners of this world, (particularly in North America) and those who are interested in a thrilling read. Areas covered include the expected ones, although the Antarctic is clearly becoming more crowded.

For the second year in succession, the most gripping article is about a Slovene team – this time on Nuptse. As a member who gets most of his current information by flicking through magazines in New Heights (and by the way aren't these new plastic covers annoying to have to open?), how refreshing it is to get the original drama from the author of the climb. Tomaz Humar's account of his ascent with Janez Jeglic of the West Face of Nuptse takes the reader to climbing ground and recesses of the mind ventured by very few. Coping with the loss of his companion at the summit and descending a difficult face unroped and exhausted after five days on the climb, Tomaz's ordeal is one that most of us would happily forego.

There are other fine accounts of activities which are, frankly, nothing less than heroic. These occur both among small and large team efforts, (such as the Russian success on the West Face of Makalu and the Korean struggles on the West Face of Gasherbrum IV). While this reviewer is, like many, out of sympathy with the big team approach, the difficulty of these walls is such that these are none the less extremely brave efforts. As a member of one of the lighter teams, Fowler reminds us, light-heartedly as always, of the spectre that stalks close on every one of these long, high altitude routes. As he accelerates down the north face of Changabang, odds on a happy outcome similar to those of Scotland winning the World Cup, he despairingly recalls his last conversation with his wife.

'Be careful,' Nicki had said when left.

'I will,' I'd replied cheerfully.'

The remainder of the account is compelling with its description of tragedy, teamwork and fortitude.

North American interest differs only in lacking extreme altitude. The remoteness and seriousness of the routes climbed seems little different; certainly there is no shortage of new ground.

Away from attempts on mighty peaks, I thought one of the most fascinating articles was of two German explorers' lonely seven-week, 1000 kilometre crossing of the Tschang-Tang plateau in Tibet. The attempt was far from risk free, demonstrating that our world still offers remarkable dry land challenges for the explorer.

Environmental issues continue to take up more room in the pages of the journal. After 1500 nights of camping and bivouacking in Yosemite, John Middendorf decides to experience a hotel experience in the National Park and finds it lacking. A policy to increase Park revenues is driving an upgrade of hotel accommodation and a loss of camping and low-cost cabin space. Yosemite has a special place in the history of National Parks and developments here may be exported to other parts of the world. As well as being directly concerned, we in Scotland should monitor the situation in our own interests. Times change elsewhere. Photos of a 'porter training seminar' near Askole in Pakistan arouse curiosity and a little admiration in this reviewer's mind. However, mountaineers have created an environmental problem in the Indian sub-continent and attempts at solutions are to be applauded.

As one who (secretly) considers that he might just be approaching middle age, it is thought provoking to read of 58-year-old Galen Rowell's one day ascent of the Nose; Tom Frost at 60 making his second ascent of North America Wall (as well as three other routes on El Cap, and Fred Beckey in his 70s putting up a 5.6 in the Wind River Range. Rowell also rejoices in soloing a 2000ft new route on Mount Darwin in the Sierra which has sections of 5.8 (circa HVS). Such opportunities! Still, the SMC can hold its own in its home environment. Would these clean-cut gentlemen have fared as well as one of our own 87-year-old members who recently had to ford a raging river or two after a damp bothy weekend and who lived to tell the tale? I say not!

Des Rubens.

The Ladies' Scottish Climbing Club Journal 1998, No. 7. Edited by Anne B. Murray.

For a club which has been on the go for so long (since 1908), seven numbers in 90 years might not appear to be prolific. But we are talking of the female gender, who have a very different way of approaching things. Men enjoy collecting, women collectively enjoy perhaps. The editorial starts with a disclaimer, blaming the committee for any harassment as the editor did not volunteer for the task. In the end, the members were forced to overcome the normal female modesty and show that they do indeed travel and climb widely.

There is only one article looking back, with a visit to Black Rock Cottage in 1949. I would have expected a bit more in the historical vein, but activity in the current vein there is no shortage of. Expect to bump into LSCC members in China, Tibet, Alaska, the Karakorum, the top of the Old Man of Hoy and of course all over the Alps of Europe. Several poems and photographs to complement the articles round off another issue the members should be very pleased with.

Fell and Rock Journal XXVI (2) No. (76) 1998.

This now has two editors and is a bi-annual publication. The *SMCJ* Editor noted with grim amusement the 'profound deference' the current editors had for their predecessors '...particularly the lonely individuals producing annual volumes.' I can only guess that the workload and cost became too much to bear. The *FRCCJ* is also 'Typeset from the editors' disk by the Ernest Press' and 'Printed in China through Colorcraft Ltd.'

It is mean to compare two journals, though very tempting, so perhaps one or two salient points could be raised. Their cover is just as boring as ours. They have shiny paper inside and only a few more photographs. One article, on their club website, was interesting. If I read the figures correctly, the SMC website is getting about nine times the number of visitors, but then we are covering a country while the FRCC covers the Lakes in essence. I can vouch for the point that many visitors are from abroad, and that the Internet is very much the communication vehicle of the future, if not now.

K. V. Crocket.

OFFICE BEARERS 1998-99

Honorary President: W. D. Brooker

Honorary Vice-Presidents: Douglas Scott

President: T. Bryan Fleming

Vice-Presidents: D. Noel Williams, Roger Everett

Honorary Secretary: John R. R. Fowler, 4 Doune Terrace, Edinburgh, EH3 6DY **Honorary Treasurer:** Drew Sommerville, 11 Beechwood Court, Bearsden, Glasgow G61 2RY. **Honorary Editor:** K. V. Crocket, Glenisla, Long Row, Menstrie, Clackmannanshire FK11 7EA. **Assistant Editor:** I. H. M. Smart, Auchenleish, Bridge of Cally, by Blairgowrie, Perthshire. **Convener of the Publications Sub-Committee:** D. C. Anderson, Hillfoot House, Hillfoot, Dollar, FK14 7PL. **Honorary Librarian:** Ian Angell, The Old Manse, 3 New Street, Largs, Ayrshire KA30 9LL. **Honorary Custodian of Slides:** G. N. Hunter, Netheraird, Woodlands Road, Rosemount, Blairgowrie, Perthshire, PH10 6JX. **Convener of the Huts Sub-Committee:** W. H. Duncan, Kirktoun, East End, Lochwinnoch, Renfrewshire PA12 4ER. **Custodian of the CIC Hut:** Robin Clothier, 35 Broompark Drive, Newton Mearns, Glasgow, G77 5DZ. **Custodian of Lagangarbh Hut:** Bernard M. Swan, Top Flat, 8G Swallow Road, Faifley, Clydebank, Dunbartonshire, G81 5BW. **Custodian of the Ling Hut:** Hamish C. Irvine, Feoran, Craig na Gower Avenue, Aviemore, Inverness-shire, PH22 1RW. **Custodian of the Raeburn Hut:** William H. Duncan, Kirktoun, East End, Lochwinnoch, Renfrewshire, PA12 4ER. **Custodian of the Naismith Hut:** William S. McKerrow, Scotsburn House, Drummond Road, Inverness, IV2 4NA. **Committee:** Chris Cartwright; John S. Peden; Oliver Turnbull; Alex Keith; Brian R. Shackleton; Andrew Hume; Wilson Moir; R. Allan Smith. SMC Internet Address – http://www.smc.org.uk

Journal Information

Editor:	K. V. Crocket, Glenisla, Long Row, Menstrie, Clacks. FK11 7EA (e-mail: kvc@dial.pipex.com).
New Routes Editor:	A. D. Nisbet, 20 Craigie Ave., Boat of Garten, Inverness-shire PH24 3BL. (e-mail: anisbe@globalnet.co.uk).
Editor of Photographs:	Niall Ritchie, 37 Lawsondale Terrace, Westhill, Skene, Aberdeen AB32 6SE.
Advertisements:	D. G. Pyper, 3 Keir Circle, Westhill, Skene, Aberdeen AB32 6RE. (e-mail: d.pyper@leopardmag.co.uk).
Distribution:	D. F. Lang, Hillfoot Hey, 580 Perth Road, Dundee DD2 1PZ.

INSTRUCTIONS TO CONTRIBUTORS

Articles for the Journal should be submitted before the end of January for consideration for the following issue. Lengthy contributions are preferably typed, double-spaced, on one side only, and with ample margins (minimum 30mm). Articles may be accepted on floppy disk, IBM compatible (contact Editor beforehand), or by e-mail. The Editor welcomes material from both members and non-members, with priority being given to articles of Scottish Mountaineering content. Photographs are also welcome, and should be good quality colour slides. All textual material should be sent to the Editor, address and e-mail as above. Photographic material should be sent direct to the Editor of Photographs, address as above.

Copyright.Textual matter appearing in the Miscellaneous section of the Journal, including New Climbs, is copyright of the publishers. Copyright of articles in the main section of the Journal is retained by individual authors.

CREAGH DHU CLIMBER

THE LIFE & TIMES OF
JOHN CUNNINGHAM

JEFF CONNOR

xi

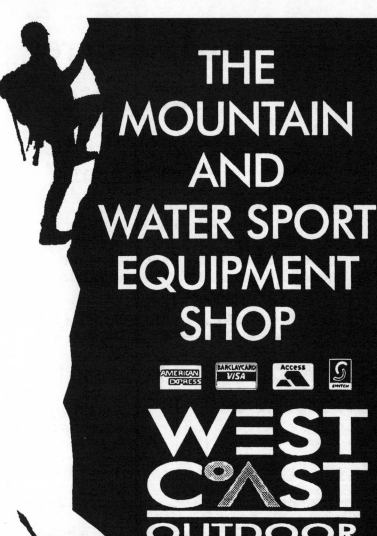

SCOTTISH MOUNTAINEERING CLUB JOURNAL BACK NUMBERS

166 – 1975 – £8
167 – 1976 – £8
168 – 1977 – £8
169 – 1978 – £8
171 – 1980 – £8
176 – 1985 – £10
177 – 1986 – £10
178 – 1987 – £6
180 – 1989 – £6
181 – 1990 – £6
182 – 1991 – £6
184 – 1993 – £6
185 – 1994 – £6
186 – 1995 – £6
187 – 1996 – £6
188 – 1997 – £7
189 – 1998 – £9

Indices for Volumes 28, 29, 30, 32, 33 are available at £1 each and the cumulated Index for Volumes 21-30 at £2. Postage is extra. They may be obtained from Derek Pyper, 3 Keir Circle, Westhill, Skene, Aberdeenshire, AB32 6RE.

xvii